BEYOND THE RUINS

BEYOND THE RUINS

The Meanings of Deindustrialization

EDITED BY

JEFFERSON COWIE

AND

JOSEPH HEATHCOTT

Foreword by BARRY BLUESTONE

ILR Press

An imprint of

Cornell University Press
Ithaca and London

First published 2003 by Cornell University Press
First printing, Cornell Paperbacks, 2003

Printed in the United States of America

Library of Congress Cataloging-in-Publication Data

Beyond the ruins : the meanings of deindustrialization / edited by
Jefferson Cowie and Joseph Heathcott ; foreword by Barry Bluestone.
    p. cm
Includes bibliographical references and index.
   ISBN 0-8014-3921-3 (cloth : alk. paper) — ISBN 0-8014-8871-0 (pbk. :
alk. paper)
   1. Deindustrialization—United States.   2. Plant shutdowns—United
States.   3. Industries—United States.   4. Industrial policy—United
States.   5. Working class—Economic conditions—United States.
6. United States—Economic conditions—2001–   7. United States—Social
conditions—20th century.   8. Globalization—Economic aspects—United
States.   I. Cowie, Jefferson R.   II. Heathcott, Joseph, 1968–
   HD5708.55.U6B49 2003
   338.6'042—dc21   2003007560

CONTENTS

Part III PLANS

Part IV LEGACY

Part V MEMORY

FOREWORD

BARRY BLUESTONE

The Deindustrialization of America: Plant Closings, Community Abandonment, and the Dismantling of Basic Industry first appeared in print in November 1982. It was an inauspicious time, as the nation's unemployment rate had just topped 10.8 percent, the highest monthly level since the Great Depression. Yet the soaring jobless rate served as no more than a final exclamation point to nearly a decade of lackluster growth, anemic corporate profits, shuttered plants, and mounting layoffs. Japanese and European imports were making significant inroads into the once dominant U.S. manufacturing sector. Sony, not RCA, was building the best color TV sets; Toyota and Nissan were eclipsing GM, Ford, and Chrysler in quality and automobile innovation. German engineering bested the finest in America while French and Italian design had captured the eye of the U.S. consumer.

With memories of the post–World War II glory days fading fast, many were asking whether the United States had lost its economic way. The nation's leading business journal, *Business Week*, had been sending up warning signs since 1980, editorializing that the country needed a comprehensive plan to revitalize its industry. In what Bennett Harrison and I called "a tone of uncharacteristic dismay," the journal's editors had already concluded that: "The U.S. economy must undergo a fundamental change if it is to retain a measure of economic viability let alone leadership in the remaining 20 years of this century. The goal must be nothing less than the reindustrialization of America. A conscious effort to rebuild America's productivity capacity is the only real alternative to the precipitous loss of competitiveness of the last 15 years, of which this year's wave of plant closings across the continent is only the most vivid manifestation."[1]

Indeed, the statistics on the economy had been dismal since the days of the first oil embargo in 1973. During the 1960s, real U.S. economic growth had averaged 4.1 percent, enough to push the unemployment rate below 4 percent for each of the last four years of the decade. Such buoyant growth permitted the average U.S. family to enjoy one-third more real spendable income at the end of the decade than at the beginning. The 1970s were altogether different. The nation's gross domestic product (GDP) grew by only 2.9 percent per year during the decade, permitting the typical family to increase its standard of living by a mere 7 percent (and all of that before 1974). As a result, by 1980, Switzerland, Sweden, Denmark, West Germany, Luxembourg, Iceland, France, the Netherlands, and Belgium had all surpassed the United States in per capita income.[2] By the early 1990s, the annual growth rate of the United States was down to just 2.3 percent.

At the root of the nation's economic plight was a near complete collapse in the rate of productivity growth. From 1949 through 1973, output per worker hour grew by better than 3 percent a year. This, combined with a better than 1 percent growth in the labor force, was responsible for the 4 percent annual growth rates we enjoyed during the postwar glory days. Beginning in 1973, productivity growth fell to no more than 1.3 percent per year and kept declining right through the first half of the 1990s.[3] Productivity improvement plummeted in the manufacturing sector from 4 percent to 2 percent per year. In retail trade and services, the breakdown in productivity growth was even more profound, falling to no better than half a percent per year after 1973. With such feeble gains in production efficiency making it difficult for U.S. companies to remain price competitive, plus a growing perception among many consumers that domestic goods were falling behind the foreign competition in quality and innovation, it was no wonder that imports flooded the country. As late as 1969, foreign-made goods and services comprised only 5.7 percent of U.S. GDP, just as they had all the way back in 1929, before the advent of modern communications and commercial jets. In the single decade of the 1970s, the import share nearly doubled to 10.9 percent. In the manufacturing sector, the import explosion was even more dramatic. Between 1969 and 1979, imported merchandise as a percentage of GDP originating in the U.S. manufacturing sector nearly tripled, from 13.9 to 37.8 percent.[4] For every hundred dollars spent on goods produced in the United States, families and businesses were now buying nearly thirty-eight dollars worth of imports.

In this context, it is not surprising that the message in *The Deindustrialization of America* rang true for many workers and their families as well as for many corporate leaders and a host of media pundits. U.S. producers seemed to have conceded defeat to imports and were in the process of closing many of their plants or moving them to new locations in a desperate attempt to regain profitability. By 1979, the average age of America's capital stock, from sprawling factories to intricate machine tools, was 7.1 years.[5] Hence, plants and equipment in operation predated the oil crisis, so they were more than likely energy inefficient and outmoded. To the extent that they were willing to build new energy-efficient plants at all, a large proportion of America's firms chose to relocate their production to places in the U.S. and abroad that promised lower wage costs and weak or nonexistent unions.

The impact on jobs was cataclysmic. Our analysis of Dun and Bradstreet corporate data reported in *The Deindustrialization of America* revealed a staggering number of lost jobs. Between thirty-two and thirty-eight *million* jobs disappeared during the 1970s as the direct result of private disinvestment or relocation of U.S. businesses. The chances of even a large, established manufacturing plant closing down during the 1970s exceeded 30 percent.[6] The life of smaller firms was more precarious. Only three-fifths of the smaller industrial establishments that existed in 1969 were still in business under the same owners in 1976. The old industrialized Northeast and Midwest were particularly hard hit by plant closings, but nearly half of the job losses occurred in the sunbelt states of the South and the West.

The personal and social costs of deindustrialization were immense. Automobile workers who lost their jobs were found two years later to have new jobs that paid on average 43 percent less than what they had been earning. Over the long run, auto workers recovered at best only about five-sixths of the pay that they would have earned if they had not been laid off. Similar long-term earnings losses were recorded for steelworkers, meat packers, aircraft employees, and those who refined petroleum, produced flat glass, and made men's clothing.[7]

The epidemic of plant closings and the downward pressure on wages reverberated throughout the economy for more than twenty years. Between 1973 and 1995, the average real (inflation-adjusted) wage of production and nonsupervisory employees in America *fell* by 10 percent. Real median family income rose by just 4 percent over the entire twenty-two-year period, despite the continued influx of women into the labor force, which added to family earning capacity. Household income, which had been growing more or less equally, on a percentage basis, for rich and poor alike for the first post–World War II generation, was now growing more and more unequal. Between 1973 and 1995, only the top 20 percent of the family income distribution saw any real gains in income. The bottom 40 percent, on average, experienced real declines.

Along with individual families struck by tragedy, entire cities and towns bore the brunt of deindustrialization. Detroit, Cleveland, and a host of smaller municipalities were brought to the brink of bankruptcy. The cumulative effect of plant closings and relocations took its toll on cities like

Camden and Youngstown. Inner-city populations were especially hard hit in places where traditional manufacturing remained the local economy's base. During the 1980s, the median income of black households in Detroit fell by 19 percent, while the city's population living in poverty neighborhoods jumped by 246 percent. The number of poor households in Chicago doubled during the 1970s, when the city's old manufacturing concerns closed down, and before new "information sector" firms took their place.[8] Right through the 1980s and even into the first half of the 1990s, the repercussions of deindustrialization were still felt in many parts of the country.

But just when many economists and journalists were telling us that we would have to get used to the new reality of slow growth and stagnating incomes, the economy began to undergo a grand renaissance.[9] America's real GDP growth rate snapped back to 3.4 percent in 1996 and then turned in spectacular back-to-back performances in 1997 and 1998. By 1999, growth was beginning to be reminiscent of the postwar glory days experience. From the beginning of 1996 through the middle of 2000, real GDP expanded by 4.2 percent annually. This was every bit as good as the record pace set in the 1950s and 1960s.[10] Such buoyant growth even surprised President Clinton's Council of Economic Advisers, which kept forecasting no better than 2.3 percent growth in each of its annual reports right through 1999. Only in 2001 did the economy stumble again, first as a result of the bursting of the stock market bubble and then because of the tragic events of September 11th. Still, the broad consensus is for long-term growth of better than 3 percent, much better than anything we experienced during the 1973–1995 era.

The renewed growth in GDP produced a new level of prosperity for workers and their families. By the end of the 1990s, a larger share of Americans were working than at any other time in the twentieth century. Officially measured unemployment fell to levels not seen since the late 1960s. For the first time in two decades, the median real wage rate stopped falling and actually rose slightly, even for those at the low-skilled end of the labor market queue. Real median family income was rising again. With all this good economic news, consumer confidence soared, hitting a thirty-two-year high in early 1999.[11] Nonetheless, there were winners and losers. Those with powerful technical skills won the largest share of the boom in earnings; those whose skills better suited old industries found themselves on the sidelines of the "new economy."

At the root of the economic renaissance in the United States was a strong recovery in productivity growth. The growing efficiency of the manufacturing sector led the way. Already by the 1980s, the rate of improvement in manufacturing productivity was back to 2.5 percent a year. By the early 1990s it hit 3 percent, and it soared to better than 4.5 percent a year between 1996 and 1998. The service sector of the economy followed, turning the corner in the late 1990s.

The revival in productivity can be traced to the information revolution that began nearly four decades ago.[12] Since it takes business a long time to move up the learning curve of new technologies and often longer still to diffuse new innovations throughout the economy, there has always been a long lag time between the initial introduction of a revolutionary technology and its payoff in the marketplace. After the introduction of the steam engine in the early nineteenth century, it took nearly two decades for the new-fangled machinery to yield a growth premium. Only after engineers had tinkered with its design for years, and only after a generation of mechanics had learned how to use it, did the steam engine provide for a sustained period of economic growth. The same pattern of invention, introduction, improvement, adoption, diffusion, and productivity improvement occurred with the electric motor at the beginning of the last century.

This same lag phenomenon has occurred in the revolution brought about by the integrated circuit, the computer, and sophisticated software.[13] It took more than two decades for the information age technology to become sufficiently user-friendly to revolutionize production in nearly every goods-producing industry and service sector. It has taken the same amount of time to educate a workforce to operate these marvels.

Unlike in the post-1973 era of weak investment and deindustrialization, U.S. business spent heavily on capital equipment in the 1980s and 1990s, especially on that which embodied new technology. During the mid-1990s alone, real nonresidential investment increased from $648 billion (1994) to $961 billion (1998).[14] An overwhelming share of the new investment was made in information processing equipment. As late as 1969, only 15 percent of new investment in durable equipment took this form. By 1995, such high-tech tools represented more than 45 percent of private sector capital investment.[15] At first, experimentation with the new technologies brought little or no productivity gain. But as the technology improved and business learned how to use it, the efficiency gains finally came.

There is reason to believe that many corporations also paid more attention to the quality of their products and to product innovation during the 1990s. *Business Week*'s 1980 invocation for "fundamental change" was apparently heeded by America's corporate leaders. As a result, the output and sales of U.S.-made goods were quite strong in the 1990s, making it possible for manufacturing to maintain its share of total real GDP and indeed increase it a bit. According to U.S. Department of Commerce figures, manufacturing was responsible for 16.9 percent of real GDP in 1989. By 2000, that figure had *increased* to 17.3 percent.[16]

While certain manufacturing industries continued to decline, others rapidly increased their sales and the value they added to final production. Consequently, there has been a profound shift in the U.S. from traditional manufacturing industries (e.g., instruments, apparel, paper products) to newer manufacturing industries in high-technology products (e.g., electronic equipment), industrial machinery, and sophisticated chemical and pharmaceutical products. Between 1989 and 2000, the real dollar value of apparel industry output fell by nearly 20 percent. Similarly, there was a decline of 28 percent in the instruments industry and of nearly 4 percent in the paper products sector. On the other hand, U.S. production of electronic equipment rose by nearly 400 percent, while production of industrial machinery increased by 155 percent. Even primary metal (e.g., steel), fabricated metal products, motor vehicles, and textile products have experienced an increase in real output since 1989.[17] Adopting new technology has helped each of these industries "succeed."

Yet, technologically driven productivity is a double-edged sword. While manufacturing is holding its own, manufacturing employment continues to shrink as efficiency gains make it possible to produce more output with fewer workers. Between 1959 and 1979, employment in manufacturing increased from 16.7 million workers to 21 million. In the subsequent decade (1979–1989), manufacturing employment declined by over 1.6 million— falling to 19.4 million—despite a nascent recovery in the national economy. In the next decade (1989–1999), manufacturing employment continued to shrink, to 18.6 million, even as full recovery materialized. With the 2001 recession and its aftermath, manufacturing employment fell to 16.5 million (December 2002).[18]

These numbers are by themselves unsettling. They take on even greater significance when compared to total U.S. employment. Going all the way back to 1959, we know that nearly a third of U.S. workers (outside of agriculture) were employed in the manufacturing sector (31.3 percent). By 1979, the proportion was down to 23.4 percent, and it has continued to decline steadily. By 1999, only 14.4 percent of the workforce was employed in this sector, and with the 2001 recession, the percentage was down to 12.6 percent—just a little over one-eighth of the workforce.

On balance, the totality of these statistics tells a good news/bad news story. The good news is that, contrary to the view that U.S. industry as a whole has lost its edge relative to foreign production, many U.S. manufacturers have learned how to produce more efficiently. The "bad" news is they have become so efficient (especially relative to service industries) that they require less and less labor to produce more and more output. Millions of workers are losing their jobs in industries in which productivity is growing faster than sales. This cannot be termed "deindustrialization," but for the workers affected it feels the same.

It is in this context of economic renaissance and restructuring that this edited volume is so helpful. It brings the deindustrialization debate up to date and examines the consequences of industrial change in a period of economic growth far different from the period when *The Deindustrialization of America* first appeared. It thus permits a better and more nuanced understanding of the culture, place, and timing of deindustrialization within the framework of capitalist evolution. It explores the ever-changing economic landscape in terms of industrial growth and decay, the shifting spatial distribution of production, and the impact all of this has on workers, their families, and their communities. It considers the issues of both economic development *and* economic justice in America's "new economy." Given the momentous changes in our economy's fortunes during the entire post–World War II period and the precariousness of any predictions about the future, this reassessment of deindustrialization is well timed and surely needed.

ACKNOWLEDGMENTS

We owe many debts to a broad range of scholars, activists, and family members who gave us reasons to undertake this project. The greatest of these debts we owe to workers, union leaders, journalists, and labor and social justice activists who have kept the issues of deindustrialization in the public eye over the years.

This volume grew out of a series of panels organized for the North American Labor History Conference, held in 1999 at Wayne State University. The vision and persistence of Tim Borden made these panels a success and provided a template for a greatly expanded collection of essays. Fran Benson at Cornell University Press has been instrumental in bringing this volume into the world; she recognized its importance early and has been a steadfast supporter throughout. Brigid Beachler at Cornell University's School of Industrial and Labor Relations helped organize and assemble this volume with patience, good humor, and intelligence. Finally, all of the authors in this volume owe deep gratitude to the anonymous reviewers, whose knowledgeable reports greatly strengthened our work.

Jefferson Cowie thanks Barry Bluestone, Lori Delale, Elizabeth Esch, Leon Fink, Larry Gross, Jack Metzgar, Ruth Milkman, Nick Salvatore, Tom Sugrue, the faculty and staff of the School of Industrial and Labor Relations, and all the contributors, who proved their patience in dealing with his lack of organizational skills. Janis Whitlock has been a true partner in both the life of the family and the life of the mind. Aliya and Aidan continue to affirm all that is real and important. Their grandfather helped to make precious time for this work—whether through stacking firewood or making room on his lap for his grandchildren.

Joseph Heathcott thanks the following people for their general support, specific editorial advice, and broader insights into the topic: Ashley Cruce, Casey Blake, John Bodnar, Michael Frisch, Andrew Hurley, Rosemary Feurer, Paula Lupkin, Matt Mancini, Maire Murphy, Jeffery O. G. Ogbar, Tiffanie Reed, Eric Sandweiss, Paul Schadewald, Ian Schmutte, Michael Smith, Thomas Sugrue, Todd Swanstrom, David Thelen, Sam White, and Cynthia Yaudes. Finally, and most importantly, he thanks his parents, grandparents, aunts, uncles, and cousins—an extended family of rare and wonderful comfort. He dedicates this book to his grandfather, Charles Heathcott Sr., who knows the real and painful substance of the book firsthand.

BEYOND THE RUINS

Introduction

The Meanings of Deindustrialization

JEFFERSON COWIE AND JOSEPH HEATHCOTT

The point of departure for any discussion of deindustrialization must be respect for the despair and betrayal felt by workers as their mines, factories, and mills were padlocked, abandoned, turned into artsy shopping spaces, or even dynamited. While economists and business leaders often speak in neutral, even hopeful, terms such as "restructuring," "downsizing" or "creative destruction," metaphors of defeat and subjugation are more appropriate for the workers who banked on good-paying industrial jobs for the livelihoods of their families and their communities. In fact, the first public use of the term "deindustrialization" identified the Allies' policy toward Germany just after World War II: an active process of victors stripping a vanquished nation of its industrial power. Indeed, to many workers who walked out of the factory gates for the last time in the sunset of America's golden age of industry, it must have felt exactly like an occupying force had destroyed their way of life, driving them not only from their workplaces but often their homes and communities as well. As "the great mills fell like broken promises" across the steelmaking region of Ohio and Pennsylvania, Joe Trotter Sr., a thirty-seven-year veteran of Youngstown's steel industry, made the connection between the two uses of the term explicit. Picking through the rubble of the dynamited Ohio Works, he remarked about U.S. Steel, "What Hitler couldn't do, they did it for him."[1]

Although we have kept in mind the people caught in the cross fire of industrial change, the purpose of this volume is explicitly to move the terms of the discussion "beyond the ruins." While the politics and anxiety that accompanied the shuttering of the organized, high-wage manufacturing centers remains a key component of this book, the collective argument these essays make is that the time is right to widen the scope of the discussion be-

1

yond prototypical plant shutdowns, the immediate politics of employment policy, the tales of victimization, or the swell of industrial nostalgia. Rather, our goal is to rethink the chronology, memory, spatial relations, culture, and politics of what we have come to call "deindustrialization." Emphasizing a historical approach to the problem, we seek to analyze the complexity and multiple meanings of one of the major transformations of the twentieth century. Taken together, these thirteen original essays suggest that deindustrialization is not a story of a single emblematic place, such as Flint or Youngstown, or a specific time period, such as the 1980s; it was a much broader, more fundamental, historical transformation. What was labeled deindustrialization in the intense political heat of the late 1970s and early 1980s turned out to be a more socially complicated, historically deep, geographically diverse, and politically perplexing phenomenon than previously thought.

Consider, for instance, how these trends played out at Pennsylvania's Homestead Steel Works, an icon of U.S. industrial history. On the location that once hosted some of the greatest struggles in U.S. labor history—the famous 1892 strike and the Great Steel Strike of 1919—and was home to the core of Andrew Carnegie's industrial empire, now sits a strip mall featuring the same retail stores that dot the big-box outer rings of most U.S. towns. Gone are the steelworkers and their union, the United Steel Workers of America; gone are their wages, their product, and the bustling civic life they supported. On that once world-famous bend in the Monongahela River are now a Loew's Cineplex; a McDonald's; a Target; a Bed, Bath and Beyond; and other national chains displaying wares produced in an immense global network of production. They mark the completion of Homestead's move from center stage in the drama of labor and business history, to an industrial ghost town in the 1980s, and finally to "Anytown, USA," at the dawn of the twenty-first century. While the mill once supported a vibrant commercial district as workers poured out of the Homestead Works gates onto Eighth Avenue, the city itself has since been eclipsed by the faux main street created within the retail complex to simulate—in comforting and safe, if vapid and sterile, ways—the feel of a traditional old main street.

There is, however, one difference between Homestead's new Waterfront development and other generic shopping complexes around the country: towering over the cineplex are twelve ghostly smokestacks disembodied from any other reference to the old steel mill—like sentries guarding access to an already forgotten past. (See figure 1.) The strange row of smokestacks was used as the Waterfront's advertising logo, adding some place-specific color to the otherwise generic beige landscape of strip mall development. While an experienced eye might see the smokestacks as mon-

FIGURE 1. Lori Delale, *Twelve Smokestacks in a Strip Mall*, 2001. Smokestacks sit watch above a Loews Cineplex parking lot. For most visitors these structures serve more as commodified nostalgia than history, but to many these postindustrial towers are reminders that what is now a generic shopping complex was once home to the gritty and turbulent labor history of the mighty Homestead Works steel mill. Courtesy of Lori Delale.

uments to the many transformations in civil society, social life, economics, and the power relations of the workplace, for most visitors they serve no such purpose. The smokestacks are neither commemorations nor full obliterations of the industrial past—they stand merely as commodified quotations from a distant modern epoch, which do little more than offer a bit of nostalgia and character to an otherwise nondescript, postmodern retail landscape.[2]

In contrast to Homestead's strip mall present, when Barry Bluestone and Bennett Harrison published their classic 1982 study, *The Deindustrialization of America*, plant closings and capital flight presented an immediate political crisis. From the vantage of a new century, however, deindustrialization seems both less profound and more so. On the one hand, what we call deindustrialization may best be understood with hindsight as one episode in a long series of transformations within capitalism. Indeed, the industrial age is alive and well, even if the locations have changed, and even if the rules of investment have shifted. Not only has production migrated with capital to far-flung points of the globe, but many areas hit hard by "deindustrialization" in the 1980s have recently experienced a renaissance of manufacturing—though often on different terms. In many respects, the idea that we live in a postindustrial age smacks of a certain northern intellectual conceit, and using "postindustrial" to describe our current political economy and culture obscures more than it reveals.

On the other hand, the aura of permanence that surrounded the industrial culture of Europe and the United States throughout the twentieth century has made the experience of deindustrialization seem more like the end of a historical epoch. The impact on community networks and institutions wrought by plant closings, and the painful realities of job loss, appear very different on the ground to workers and their families. That we frame our historical experience of capitalism somewhat misleadingly with reference to *the* "industrial era" does not ameliorate the real hardship created by deindustrialization. The central challenge of this volume, then, is to describe a temporary, historically bound set of conditions that are experienced in terms of permanence by ordinary people in daily life. Like any historical transformation—for instance, the industrial revolution itself—the process we call deindustrialization was uneven in its causes, timing, and consequences, and the effects rippled through all aspects of society. As opposed to the changes under industrialization, however, those under deindustrialization were more disorienting than overtly political, tended toward the elusive rather than the tangible, and marked a confusion of power relations that had seemed significantly clearer under the old order. The dramatic evidence of industrial change and capital flight that litters our landscapes does, however, present a basic collective problem: How do we account for the destruction of an economic order that seemed so rooted and pervasive?

In the end, what may be most troubling about these ruined industrial landscapes is not that they refer to some once stable era, but rather that they remind us of the ephemeral quality of the world we take for granted. If Karl Marx was right in saying "all that is solid melts into air," then the industrial culture forged in the furnace of fixed capital investment was itself a temporary condition. What millions of working men and women might have experienced as solid, dependable, decently waged work really only lasted for a brief moment in the history of capitalism. Because capital was fixed in giant machines bolted to the floors of brick-and-mortar factories, the industrial culture that emerged in various places at various moments had an aura of permanence, durability, and heritage.

The rowhouse, tavern, union hall, civic club, softball field, church, and synagogue are all artifacts of a material culture made possible by the location of particular incarnations of capital in space and time. Mobilized into the service of value-added, durable-goods production, this capital provided the basis of a limited but nevertheless expanding industrial prosperity for workers, foremen, managers, and bosses. But the solidity of factories and tenements and steeples masked a fundamental impermanence; it obscured the forces that both created this world through investment and broke it apart by withdrawing investment. Working people saw in the decline of this industrial order the dissolution of their society, culture, and way of life, and the betrayal of their trust by those whose decisions shaped their fate. But owners, investors, and corporate officers did not perceive the world in quite the same terms. For them, the profitability of their enterprise, the need to stay competitive and prosper and thus theoretically serve the greater market good, trumped any considerations for the lives of working families on the ground.

What does this bode for the study of deindustrialization? To begin with, we must jettison the assumption that fixed capital investment in resource extraction, heavy manufacturing, and value-added production defines the stable standard against which all subsequent changes are to be judged. Rather, we should see this political-economic order and the culture it engendered as temporary and impermanent developments in space and time. Secondly, deindustrialization is a critical transformation in U.S. society, to be sure, but of what kind, and to what extent? What is new and old in this latest phase of history? How is it experienced differently by people in varied places, times, and circumstances? And last, our scholarship must work as hard to understand the mental and cultural frameworks of deindustrialization as it has to grasp the political, technological, and financial dimensions. What are the ideas, symbols, and images that shape our conceptions of the "postindustrial"—indeed, that undergird the very way that we think about our work lives?

The dominant method of studying deindustrialization is to trace the death of mills like Homestead and the workers' experiences of that process—an approach that has yielded an important body of research, even some classics in U.S. scholarship.[3] This collection builds on that scholarship, but pushes for a broader range of methods, frameworks, views, and conclusions. In what follows, we move the focus away from a "body count" of manufacturing jobs (a very misleading approach, since the absolute figure of manufacturing employment has actually remained fairly stable in the postwar era, though dwarfed by the rise in service sector employment).[4] Taking a cue from the changes in Homestead, we look at deindustrialization as a process, a historical transformation that marks not just a quantitative and qualitative change in employment, but a fundamental change in the social fabric on a par with industrialization itself.

None of this can be understood without reference to Barry Bluestone and Bennett Harrison's politically impassioned benchmark study, from which the actual term and political concept of "deindustrialization" entered the popular and scholarly lexicon. These authors constructed their definition of the problem in the midst of an enormous political and economic crisis two decades ago, but that definition remains the point of departure for launching a reconsideration of twentieth-century industrial history. By "deindustrialization," they wrote, "is meant a widespread, systematic disinvestment in the nation's basic productive capacity." At the core of the problem, they argued, was the way "capital—in the forms of financial resources and of real plant and equipment—has been diverted from productive investment in our basic national industries into unproductive speculation, mergers and acquisitions, and foreign investment." They explained that all of this was symptomatic of a very specific historical juncture—the end of the postwar boom—at which the old rules no longer worked and new rules would be necessary for sustainable development. The old "social contract," based on relatively high wages and on respectful working arrangements with unions formed in the New Deal era, had been abrogated by management in the face of the triple squeeze of international competition, high labor rates, and rising safety net costs for workers. The firms' response was often capital mobility—whether through the relocation of manufacturing geographically or through switching to nonproductive forms of investment—as a means of disciplining labor, fomenting regional wars for investment, and lowering the costs of doing business.

Sociologically, at the core of Bluestone and Harrison's study was a fundamental, even irreconcilable, tension between the needs of capital and the needs of communities. Capital needed to control labor costs as the postwar settlement fell apart and investors were ready and willing to build a new system on their own terms—even if it meant destroying communities in the process.[5] Communities, on the other hand, needed the wage and tax base provided by fixed capital investment in large-scale manufacturing to support their households, schools, parks, clubs, hospitals, civic and religious institutions. The higher the wages, the more robust these dense social networks became, until in certain places at certain moments a full-fledged industrial culture took root.

Today the struggle to preserve basic industry that fired Bluestone and Harrison's project is all but gone, but the legacy of deindustrialization remains. This collection both accepts and departs from the fundamental insights set forth in *The Deindustrialization of America;* it expands on the chronology, complicates the causation, draws out the complexities, and pushes the problem into previously unexplored realms. In so doing, we cover six themes, each organized to challenge our assumptions about the meanings of deindustrialization. The first part, titled "Rust," takes a new look at rustbelt cases: a carpet mill in Yonkers, New York; an auto plant in Lansing, Michigan; and the leisure industry in Atlantic City. We then move into the second part, "Environment," which draws important connections between environmental degradation and the industrial past in Anaconda, Montana, and Love Canal, New York. Part 3, "Plans," examines the range of responses from local, state, and federal government bodies meant to cope with hardships caused by industrial change. The next part, "Legacy," analyzes the ways in which the industrial past is incorporated into, or denied by, the present in three different settings. Finally, "Memory" brings us to the kitchen tables of workers and their families in two southern communities in order to learn how they perceive plant closings and pink slips, and how they construct notions of citizenship, community, duty, and survival in their efforts to carry on with their lives.

The book opens with a trilogy of essays that challenge the typical view of the causes, timing, and effects of deindustrialization in terms that are grounded in specific firms and communities. Tami J. Friedman adds to the growing literature that reconsiders the chronology of deindustrialization. Her study opens with the announcement of the Yonkers mill shutdown in 1954, at the height of the postwar boom, when the employer selected Greenville, Mississippi, as a new production site. Friedman's competitive geography of production builds on Bluestone and Harrison's tension between "capital and community," but she reorients our understanding of the problem. The mounting evidence suggests that the challenges faced by places like Yonkers had less to do with the collapse of the postwar boom than with capital mobility as a constant in U.S. industrial relations—challenges made more difficult with the globalization of industry decades later. Her analysis of the carpet company's relocation, as well as Greenville's attempts to lure industry southward, also reminds us that one town's deindustrialization might just be another town's industrialization—though the theme of labor discipline remains a constant at both sites.

The chronology in Lisa M. Fine's study of Lansing is less surprising than that in the Yonkers case, but here causation becomes the main problem. "Who killed Reo Motors?" is the question that informs her inquiry into the closing of a major manufacturing plant. Placing the plant shutdown in an analytic tension between a fundamental structural transformation that defines an era and a simpler cyclical phenomenon, she combs through multiple explanations for the death of Reo Motors. Her approach moves well beyond the binary of capital versus community by looking at key local factors, broad issues in the cold war political economy, and the geography of industry, race, and urban change, all of which underscore the complexity of a single plant closure. When the story ends with the reincarnation of Reo just outside of town—operating under very different circumstances—the complexity of causation is again brought to the fore. The new industrial regime, however, makes it seem as though labor relations have been pushed back in time, as the new firm "re-created the industrial world Ransom E. Olds began at his first Reo Motor Car Company in Lansing, in 1904." The historical slate has been wiped clean.

Next, Bryant Simon turns to a city that looks like many old manufacturing centers, but was once sustained by a very different industry—public commercial amusements. His examination of the social life of the collapsing tourist economy in Atlantic City touches on a stinging irony first aired in the movie *Roger and Me*. At the end of Michael Moore's politically charged film about the deindustrialization of Flint, Michigan, we learn that the film cannot be shown in Flint for one simple reason: there are not any movie theaters left to screen it. Simon's Atlantic City likewise lacks a movie theater today, an even more galling prospect given that the town's economy had long revolved around leisure pursuits and public amusements. He uses the movie house as a way of understanding not just the economic transformations in the tourist industry but, very pointedly, how reactions to desegregation tragically helped to destroy both a city and a service economy. The success of the earlier, glory days of Atlantic City, argues Simon, rested on racial segregation, and when court decisions removed racial restrictions from those public spaces, public life died along with Jim Crow. Like so many former manufacturing centers across the nation, Atlantic City was on the skids by the 1970s, only to be resurrected by casino boosterism. Gaming has certainly since brought money into the city, but the death of the old industry also represents the death of the (white) "public" city, as people drive in from far away, park in the acres of parking lots, and spend hours staring alone at video poker machines—a far cry from the shared, though segregated, bustling civic and commercial space of the old boardwalk.

The second part of this collection breaks new ground by bringing our attention to issues that are intimately linked but rarely considered together: industrial decline and environmental disaster. Here, the authors remind us of the dual symbolism of "smokestack industries"—part might, power, and prosperity; part pollution, waste, and toxicity. The two studies in this part, Kent Curtis's on the former mining center of Anaconda, Montana, and Richard Newman's on Love Canal enrich the broader debate about the legacy of industry by bringing the key themes of environmental crisis, regulatory politics, and community activism into the story. At these two sites the workers and their communities were left not only without jobs but with poisoned earth as well.

Before "Love Canal" became synonymous with environmental disaster, the site was called "Love's Canal," which some hoped would become a nineteenth-century industrial utopia. The failure of this industrial dream, Newman explains, would scarcely have registered in the historical record except that Love's ditch, which was to supply hydro power to the community, became a hole into which the chemical industry dumped staggering amounts of toxic waste. The famous local activism that emerged from the area in the 1970s was shaped not just by the rising environmental consciousness of the nation, Newman argues, but by the experience of working-class families faced simultaneously with layoffs and a legacy of industrial pollution. As more than two hundred firms departed the Buffalo-Niagara region, they left behind a classic deindustrialized landscape of poisoned brownfields. Working people, charged with the urgent need to make their community safe from acute toxins, could scarcely afford the luxury of nostalgia for a bygone industrial age.

A similar set of problems involving development, class divisions, postindustrial transitions, and environmental catastrophe can be found in Anaconda, Montana. When Anaconda Copper's smelters stopped running, explains Kent Curtis, the city was left not only bereft of employment but also in the midst of the nation's largest Superfund complex. As the town, the company, and the Environmental Protection Agency searched for solutions, they came up with the idea of building a golf course atop two hundred acres of smelting waste that they buried under an earthen cap. Although the sand traps are made of black slag and each of the eighteen holes is nostalgically named after an old industrial installation, Curtis concludes that the golf course essentially allowed all the parties involved—especially the company—enough cover to get out of their predicament. They were able to escape from, rather than deal with, the industrial past by figuratively and literally burying it. "It is a landscape manufactured not so much to remedy the errors of the past," he explains, "as to recast them long enough for capital to be mobilized elsewhere." The conversion of the brownfield site into a space of leisure and recreation provides a final, fitting twist to one of the worst cases of pollution in the history of U.S. industry.

Since, as Curtis explains, contending with deindustrialization is more complicated than building a golf course, the third part, "Plans," opens up a discussion of the role of city, regional, and national politics. Here the three chapters explore a variety of key issues, including suburbanization, white flight, urban renewal, taxes, investment climate, and the pursuit of high-technology alternatives. The authors argue that race, space, industry, residence, and local power are all intimately linked, and that strategies for reorganizing the city after World War II took hold, often rather ineffectually, as responses to the shifting industrial and residential terrain. This set of studies begins with Howard Gillette Jr.'s examination of the municipal politics of Camden, New Jersey. In perhaps the best and most understated summary of the problems faced by former industrial communities like Camden—or Flint or Gary or East St. Louis—Gillette writes that "disinvestment is not a one-time process. It has cumulative effects." Indeed, plans to deal with the snowball effect of industrial flight continually met the recalcitrant problem of an inadequate property tax base. As more and more industries fled Camden, the city lapsed into fiscal crisis. With less money from ratable industry, the city's physical plant and social life deteriorated, and middle- and upper-income families began to flee, taking their tax dollars with them. The larger the city's debts grew, then, the greater its problems became, but the greater its problems became, the less able were municipal institutions to attract and capture business and residence. In the absence of real support from the state or the federal government, Camden was forced to tax already poor people and already struggling businesses even more, leaving each successive generation of politicians to inherit a larger and more tangled mess from their predecessors.

The "Plans" part then moves to larger geographies of analysis. Robert O. Self's exploration of San Francisco's East Bay area reveals the tension between an old urban core and the new suburbs wrought by the flight of industry and people. The planners of Oakland, California, sought to improve their city by recruiting industry to peripheral towns, which ironically undermined the industrial growth of Oakland itself. But in the postwar era, white citizens saw in their residential enclaves a retreat from the noisome, dirty industries, and a refuge from the black and Latino families that had migrated to the Bay Area during and after the war. Such decentralizing forces fundamentally altered not simply the industrial landscape, but the political one as well. A distinct politics of "homeowner populism" emerged in the industrial suburbs, linking low taxes with growth and high property values with racial segregation. Given these complicated patterns of residential and industrial location, Self argues, Bluestone and Harrison's term "deindustrialization" obscures more than it illuminates. Self posits that we ought to think more in terms of the "spatial dynamics of industrial restructuring," which frame uneven metropolitan growth and expansion over time.

Such uneven spatial dynamics, argues Gregory S. Wilson, were the primary reasons behind the federal government's Area Redevelopment Administration (ARA). Created under the Kennedy administration, the ARA sought to build on the regional planning successes of the New Deal, but emerged in the throes of the cold war as a weakly structured and thinly funded attempt at industrial policy. Federal planners and policy makers understood the important link between regional industrial decline and poverty, Wilson explains, but they never had the funding or congressional backing to make a dent in the problem. Moreover, race, rather than uneven development or industrial decline, became more closely associated with poverty among U.S. policy makers. The weakness and ultimate failure of the ARA, then, represents an important point of transition between the structural liberalism of the New Deal and the racial liberalism of the Great Society. The emergent political discourse, which favored a racialized and urbanized explanation of broad economic problems in the 1960s, left policy makers with few tools to deal with the consequences of uneven development, regional transformation, and capital mobility.

In the fourth part, "Legacy," three chapters come to terms with the complicated meanings of place. As various cities endure the tremendous stress of industrial decline, they lose not only their industrial work but their identities as well. John Russo and Sherry Lee Linkon show the double victimization of Youngstown—first as a site of horrendous job loss and then as the national poster child for deindustrialization and political corruption. The legacy and public memory of plant shutdowns, Russo and Linkon suggest, can be just as burdensome to the community as the immediate crisis of job loss itself, reifying the symbolic weight of the city as a national site of despair. As the community drifted from its status as a shrine to industrial power to the "murder capital" of the nation, "locals internalize[d] the image of their community as a site of loss, failure, crime, and corruption." Thus, the problem is not simply that Youngstown as a place suffered a loss of identity; the larger problem is that, as yet, community members do not have the power and tools to challenge the images created about their place. The political project that remains after the mills are gone is to reclaim a positive civic identity by shunning the version of the town others thrust on it and developing ways for citizens and workers to lever their own past en route to a better future.

Similarly, S. Paul O'Hara's analysis of the image and legend of Gary is concerned with the impact on urban culture and esteem of deindustrialization. He traces several successive images of "Steel City"—a rational, planned, industrial utopia at the beginning of the century that became a hard-working, sin-filled, violence-prone, blue-collar town in the popular imagination. As black workers moved north for employment and jobs began their agonizing departure, Gary's image changed first to that of a great "black metropolis," and then to that of an "urban wasteland." Racial politics has had a particularly devastating role in shaping the city's national status, and the city finally became a poisoned symbol of everything the nation was trying to avoid—jobless, black, the other murder capital of the nation. Finally, as with Atlantic City, Gary found itself forced to embrace the casino industry as a path toward reshaping the national understanding of a place in which the words "industrial" and "utopia" were once linked.

Kirk Savage takes a different tack on the problem of imagery, representation, and legacy, exploring how the industrial past is commemorated in a city firmly committed to a postindustrial future. In his explorations of Pittsburgh, a city that hosts the Steelers football team but does not make any actual steel, he documents how industry is commemorated in much the same way war is commemorated, with monuments to generals, soldiers, and battlefields. This martial imaginary organizes the industrial past into a narrative about a collective war of technological man against the wilderness. Absent are narratives about the nature of industrial work itself, the experience of community formed by a manufacturing ethos, or the bloody conflicts between workers and bosses in the streets and factories of the city. Indeed, Savage reports, reigning strategies of commemoration manage to avoid any of the major issues of the industrial past—or the postindustrial present. Searching the landscape, he selects an enormous pile of slag (the same type of industrial refuse lining Anaconda's new sand traps) as the most fitting tribute to the industrial legacy. What some see as a worthless industrial dump to be covered over, others see an eco-monument to the industrial past. It is in the "perverse poetry" of industrial trash that Savage finds "a landscape that asks us to view our industrial legacy not as a heroic episode from a golden age but as a living challenge in the present."

The fifth and final part of the book, "Memory," moves from how we think about cities to how people think about themselves by investigating workers' intimate understandings of plant shutdowns in two southern communities. In the homes of former employees, Joy L. Hart and Tracy E. K'Meyer listen to workers in Louisville, Kentucky, and Steve May and Laura Morrison interview people "downsized" in Shelby, North Carolina. These are not the old industrial Midwest cities that we have come to associate with deindustrialization. While the large northern cities capture the lion's share of scholarly attention, the main story may just be in hundreds of small shutdowns, layoffs, and restructurings around the country. That the South, a place known to attract migrant capital, faces its own ephemeral industrial patterns reinforces the themes of the volume. Moreover, only rarely did workers have the means or drive to take action, as did the Youngstown workers who stormed the U.S. Steel building in protest of the mills shutting down. More typical of laid-off workers is a conflicted stew of emotions: betrayal and abandonment, pride and accommodation, hope and faith in themselves and their community.

Both contributions to the "Memory" part confront the pain that comes with the severance of the trust, loyalty, and security these workers expected from their employers. Workers retain their pride and willingness to struggle, but those traits are in danger of being overtaken by alienation and betrayal. We find these workers at the end of a manufacturing culture (growing out of "red neck, smokestack places" in the words of one interviewee), and entering a world of work organization largely alien to them. As Hart and K'Meyer suggest, "they find themselves navigating divergent sets of values—between the nominal solidarity and security of an industrial culture and the insecure, individualized world of service and high-tech work." Both case studies uncovered a violation of some sense of social contract or perceived norms in the interrelationships among worker, employer, community, and, in the case of factories moved abroad, nation. Bluestone and Harrison's capital-versus-community tension is developed by workers on their own, though more in terms of a bootstrap moral philosophy than in terms of political economy. Interviews with employees reveal a powerful sense of moral economy that they believe their employers violated; yet they know they have precious little leverage over their situation. Most importantly, they do not ever want to portray themselves as simple victims. Ending this collection with works about the changing realms of identity sponsored by industrial loss forces us to grapple with some of the most profound and personal aspects of this historical transformation and requires us to consider the varied and conflicting stories we tell ourselves about deindustrialization.

Taken together then, what are the "meanings of deindustrialization"? We can begin by admitting, in historian Nelson Lichtenstein's words, that the postwar settlement is a "suspect construct."[6] The decline of industry did not mark the end of a much-respected settlement between management and labor over the terms of industrial governance. It now appears that the postwar "accord" was an idea created in the face of the continued decline of organized labor in the 1970s. It allowed for the creation of a semi-imaginary historical benchmark against which very real contemporary assaults on unions and key industrial sectors could be measured. Clearly, higher levels of union density, lower rates of capital mobility, and lower levels of global competition in the postwar era suggest that things were different in the "golden age," but the industrial culture was so uneven and so poorly congealed that it hardly lives up to the quasi-corporatist notions that a later generation would apply to it. As shown in Friedman's analysis of the Yonkers mill shutdown, Self's examination of the reshuffling of investment priorities in the East Bay, the generation of neglect Gillette documents in Camden, or the efforts of the ARA described by Wilson, the postwar era can hardly be characterized by stability. In opposition to a simple, unidirectional story of political and economic stability followed by decline, we deepen an industrial history characterized by unevenness, fits and starts, and regional variance. This research reveals a history pockmarked with explosions, relocations, desertions, and competitive struggles.

Second, deindustrialization—or globalization—cannot be understood in the simplistic logic of jobs gained or lost. Other issues, often qualitative, are at stake. The numbers of jobs created and destroyed in the postwar era are very large, but the gross numbers of industrial employment are fairly stable. Quantitatively, manufacturing employment remained relatively constant—around 18 million jobs in 1965 and about 18.5 million in 2000. One person's plant shutdown may well have been another person's plant opening, whether it was the opening of a plant in Greenville, Mississippi, instead of Yonkers or one in San Leandro that some believed might have been better placed in Oakland. Even in Lansing, as Fine shows, the new was waiting to be born of the old, as new plants succeeded old ones. We must, however, be cognizant of the nature and quality of those new jobs, and the way power relations are continually reordered in the creation and destruction of employment. Although the rumors of manufacturing's demise have been greatly exaggerated, the unionization of manufacturing has in fact plummeted—by 40 percent between 1985 and 2000. What may be more significant than the decline of basic industry then is the realignment of power relations in the work place.[7] Rather than arguing that simple job creation or destruction is the key, these contributors show that fundamental long-term historical trends are very important to understanding seemingly rapid changes. We have to look at issues such as spatial relations, cultural politics, labor organization, key transformations in the urban landscape, the political and social burdens that plague former industrial communities, the environmental legacy, and changes in social identity.

Finally, as we avoid an obsession with numbers of jobs, we must also proceed with caution to prevent a creeping industrial nostalgia from dominating the debate. Those manufacturing jobs were not necessarily great jobs, it is worth remembering, just good-paying jobs. Ruth Milkman has shown in her book *Farewell to the Factory*, for instance, that autoworkers lacked "any desire to restore the old industrial system that is now collapsing around them." Such a perspective, she continues, "highlights a sad fact that is all too often forgotten in the age of deindustrialization: factory work in the golden age of mass production was deeply problematic in its own right." Workers, she explains, "mostly yearned to escape its relentless and dehumanizing rhythms."[8] This is not to deny the terror of joblessness or the reality of former industrial workers tramping the Southwest in the 1980s. It is simply to say that we have to strip industrial work of its broad-shouldered, social-realist patina and see it for what it was: tough work that people did because it paid well and it was located in their communities.

Thus "deindustrialization" can mean many varied things, like the brief sketch of Homestead suggests or Simon's look at Atlantic City helps explain. Only a small part of these meanings emerges from the loss of manufacturing employment. The broader meanings emerge from the de-linking of investment and place, the deinstitutionalization of labor relations machinery, de-urbanization (and new forms of urbanization), and perhaps even the loosening of the connection between identity and work. A still broader view suggests that deindustrialization and industrialization are merely two ongoing aspects of the history of capitalism that describe continual and complicated patterns of investment and disinvestment. These patterns respond to new politics, technology, and cultural conditions, but in the end the seeds of deindustrialization were in every instance built into the engines of industrial growth itself.

Where, then, do we take our revised frameworks for the study of deindustrialization? By framing episodes of industrialization and deindustrialization as two stages of the same process—the organization of capital on the ground in the material world—we can begin to come to terms with the politics required to bring justice to our shop floors, homes, and communities. The very set of political rules that created the industrial order that we once took to be permanent provided the means by which corporations could dismantle that order. As corporate scandal and dot-com failures have created ruins of a different sort than discussed in this volume, we must remember that, despite the institutions, networks, and habits of the heart that give us a sense of permanence in our communities, the rules that structure capitalism favor growth, volatility, and change. If our goal, in the spirit of Bluestone and Harrison's original work, is to recast capital in terms of stewardship, democracy, and prosperity broadly shared, we have to write new rules. To do this now, we will have to overcome "smokestack nostalgia" in our scholarship, complicate the industrial legacy, and assist those communities most affected by these transformations—both in the industrialized global North and the maldeveloped global South. Above all, we should strive to transform the "new American workplace" that has grown out of the industrial ashes—a place that is sponsoring spectacularly uneven levels of wealth and tremendous overwork—into a more humane and responsible place.[9]

Part I

RUST

CHAPTER 1

"A Trail of Ghost Towns across Our Land"

The Decline of Manufacturing in Yonkers, New York

TAMI J. FRIEDMAN

"SMITH TO SHUT RUG MILLS," ran the banner headline in the Yonkers, New York, *Herald-Statesman* on June 24, 1954. Some residents of Yonkers—a city of some 160,000 people just north of New York City—already had suspected that the community's largest employer, Alexander Smith, was on its way out. But most were stunned to learn that the company, one of the world's leading makers of woven carpets and rugs, planned to close its doors after operating in Yonkers for ninety years. At its peak, in the late 1920s, Smith had employed seven thousand workers; while those numbers dropped considerably after World War II, several thousand production personnel remained on the payroll that fateful day in June. Over the course of generations, a succession of newly arrived immigrant groups—first Scots and Irish, then Italians, Slovaks, Hungarians, Russians, and Poles—had been absorbed into the tightly knit world of the "carpet shop," as the mill was popularly known. The shutdown—which executives announced just ten days into a strike launched by the Textile Workers Union of America (TWUA)—not only ended a way of life for many workers and their families, it inaugurated a period of industrial decline from which, some say, Yonkers has never recovered.

On its face, what transpired in Yonkers is an all-too-familiar tale. In recent decades, we have heard much about the demise of manufacturing—so much, in fact, that the scenario seems almost mundane. A company reveals its intention to close a factory. The news sends shock waves through the community. Frantic union leaders appeal to the firm's sense of moral obligation, while local and even state politicians try to negotiate a deal—any deal—that will keep the plant in place. These efforts prove fruitless, however, for company executives, invariably citing competitive pressures, insist

19

that they simply cannot afford to stay. Once the outcome is certain, local business leaders put a brave face on the impending crisis, professing enthusiasm for the chance to diversify their community's economic base. Journalists, scholars, and other interested parties descend on the scene like vultures, chronicling each grim detail of the disaster and shadowing jobless workers and their families as they prepare for the hardships ahead. It's an American tragedy, the devastating hallmark of a postindustrial age.

Of course there are large grains of truth in this larger-than-life picture, but the reality is far more complex. First, the loss of industry is hardly a new phenomenon, as the Smith case—and others described in this volume—attest. Accounts of industrial decline tend to focus on shutdowns that have occurred since the 1970s, in such sectors as auto, rubber, and steel. But New England's textile industry began to disappear as early as the 1910s and 1920s, with severe consequences for the region's once-thriving textile towns. Plant closings persisted during the Great Depression and then became more pronounced in the early post–World War II period, in part because a series of postwar strategies—mergers, federal tax policies, and so on—made it economically expedient for firms to liquidate their mills. Textile magnates were particularly (though not uniquely) adroit at exploiting these opportunities. Most scholars of deindustrialization have missed this older story, perhaps because it departs so dramatically from the popular picture of the 1950s as a prosperous decade for the U.S. working class. Or perhaps the story has been passed over because textile workers—who were largely female, poorly paid, and nonunion—have been excluded from the standard narrative of postwar economic growth.

Second, while many U.S. factories closed down during the twentieth century, they did not always disappear from view. Rather, plant shutdowns often reflected a larger process of capital migration, in which manufacturers decided that their interests could best be served by shifting production elsewhere. This process accounted for much of the early "decline" in New England textiles. Southern boosters had been developing an indigenous textile industry since the 1880s; northern textile producers, eager to remain competitive in a labor-intensive sector, headed South largely to narrow the gap in labor costs. By the early 1920s, more than half of U.S. cotton textile manufacturing was southern based. Similarly, the cost-cutting impulse pushed many northern-based manufacturers southward (and to some extent westward) after World War II. The postwar drive to increase both production and productivity stimulated considerable capital investment. At the same time, the very techniques that facilitated plant closings also made it advantageous to channel resources into new, modern plants. Few industrialists, however, chose to build in their older locales. In some ways, residents of northern communities exerted minimal control over employers' location decisions, and there was little they could have done to stem the tide of southward flight. But capital flight did represent, at least in part, a response to postwar developments in particular settings—the rising expectations of workers and taxpayers in northern cities, the aggressive courtship of capital by southern boosters—that enlarged the gulf between regions in such areas as wages, taxes, and energy costs. Like their earlier counterparts, the corporate migrants of the 1950s carefully assessed the differences *between* locations and made their choice. Alexander Smith's departure from Yonkers was accompanied by its arrival in Greenville, Mississippi; only by drawing the connection *between* the two communities can we grasp what occurred in a single place.

The connection between regions persisted well beyond the pivotal moment of flight. In northern communities that underwent industrial losses, those who relied most heavily on manufacturing were often avid to court new employers and pacify those that remained. How they proceeded—and whether they succeeded—was profoundly influenced by their capacity to compete with their southern rivals for the favors of industrial firms. Certainly, northerners' efforts to revitalize their economies were constrained by conditions at the national level: A series of harsh recessions during the 1950s and early 1960s, for example, severely handicapped the prospects for recovery in many faltering industrial towns. Moreover, company executives continued to make location decisions based on economic factors that local people could not control. But as competition for industry escalated across the regions, northern communities came under increasing pressure to fashion favorable business climates—à la their southern counterparts—if they hoped to ameliorate their economic woes. This process was all too evident in Yonkers, where the loss of Alexander Smith shaped the course of economic development for decades to come.

The Rise and Demise of the "Carpet Shop"

For generations before the Yonkers shutdown, the Alexander Smith firm and family enjoyed considerable power and prestige. Company founder Alexander Smith, who arrived in Yonkers in the early 1860s, quickly emerged not only as the city's leading manufacturer but also as a prominent figure in community life. (He was even elected to the U.S. Congress in 1878, though he died on the night of the vote.)[1] His descendants carried on the family tradition of corporate leadership, community service, and philanthropic support. For example, in the late nineteenth and early twentieth centuries, Smith family members built a workingmen's club, a hospital, and a nursing school. By the early 1940s, the family no longer resided in Yonkers, but company officials remained active in the city's public affairs and local charitable crusades.[2] In the early 1950s, the Smith mills were still the principal source of employment in Yonkers, providing some six thousand jobs and a payroll of perhaps ten million dollars each year. Smith was also the city's largest taxpayer; on the eve of the 1954 plant closing, it accounted for about 1.5 percent of the city's annual property tax receipts.[3]

Like most corporations, however, Smith was not bound to any particular place. Alexander Smith himself had not started out in Yonkers; rather, he had begun operating in the nearby village of West Farms in 1845 and then moved to Yonkers after his factory burned down. Smith believed that his employees, apparently incensed by the introduction of the power loom, had set the plant ablaze.[4] Twenty years after moving to Yonkers, the company's management threatened to abandon that community as well. In 1885, three thousand Smith workers—mostly young Irish women—launched a spectacular strike under the banner of the Knights of Labor and stayed off the job for five months. During the walkout—which was sparked by pay cuts and other instances of what employees termed management "tyranny"—Smith executives declared that they would rather "sell the property than submit to [strikers'] demands."[5] Ultimately, company officials did give in to the strikers; they promised to hike wages and deal with a grievance committee, and they agreed not to retaliate against union members. At the same time, however, they launched an ambitious program of employee and community benefits—what one astute observer called "practical paternalism"—that helped to weaken the Knights' authority and kept the plant free of unionism for the next fifty years.[6]

In the throes of the Great Depression, Smith officials raised the specter of departure once again. Even before the stock market crash of October 1929, the Smith mills had been running on short time; after the collapse, they were operating just one or two days a week, and thousands of carpet workers were unemployed. And yet, in 1930, the company demanded that Yonkers reduce its tax obligations; if the city failed to comply with the directive, Smith executives cautioned, the firm might relocate to more receptive terrain. City officials, forced to choose between the certain loss of revenue and the potential loss of their leading industry, implemented an across-the-board tax cut for most Yonkers employers. They also granted Smith a series of annual tax reductions—and the company stayed.[7] This scenario was not unique to Yonkers. As the economic crisis deepened, businessmen throughout New York State sought to wrest concessions from workers and public officials; otherwise, they insisted, employers would be forced to migrate to other, more pliant states.

As the Depression wore on, Smith officials found community cooperation in Yonkers difficult to sustain. As company profits dipped, management dramatically scaled back operations, sharply reduced the mill's labor force, and withdrew long-standing benefits on which Smith workers had come to rely. At first, Smith employees, while chafing at the loss of economic security, were reluctant to take on the most powerful citizens of Yonkers. When pushed to the limit, however, they began to fight back. They were not alone in their resistance. In addition to the Smith mills, Yonkers was home to Otis Elevator, sugar refineries along the Hudson River, and a host of smaller manufacturing firms. Neighboring communities boasted a General Motors plant, a wire and cable company, and a large pharmaceuticals concern. Buoyed by the massive wave of organizing that swept the nation in the mid- and late 1930s, workers throughout the Yonkers area threw in their lot with the union cause. Some, especially those in the building trades, were already affiliated with the American Federation of Labor (AFL). But as representatives of the newly formed Congress of Industrial Organizations (CIO), along with their AFL rivals, launched a series of energetic campaigns in mass production, many more employees were drawn into the fray. Employers did their best to quash the labor movement, first by suppressing it directly and then, when that strategy failed, by trying to match or even exceed union demands. Smith executives in particular were dismayed by the activism; without the ability to impose "close and continuous control and discipline" over their workers, they insisted, the carpet company could not "make a profit and live."[8] Ultimately, management's resistance proved fruitless: by the late 1930s, Smith workers had formed the largest union in Westchester County—TWUA Local 122— and they stood at the center of a dense web of labor solidarity that extended countywide.

During World War II, the Yonkers labor movement gained even more ground. Smith and other area manufacturers occupied a privileged position during the conflict: in exchange for converting their operations to military use, they enjoyed government-guaranteed profits and actively participated in shaping federal economic policy. But workers also wielded considerable leverage in wartime, for without labor's acquiescence, the military effort could not succeed. For many years, company officials had claimed exclusive access to decision-making power at the plant level, insisting that they alone spoke for their employees. The outbreak of war undermined employers' capacity to exert unilateral control. At every level of mobilization—from production to salvage collection to plant protection—industrialists were forced to cooperate with workers through their unions. Moreover, federal officials conferred recognition on workers, not just employers, for the contributions they made. For example, in November 1943, Alexander Smith received its first Army-Navy "E" award for exceptional achievement. Before an audience of thousands of proud Yonkers residents, Smith president Frederick B. Klein received the accolades on behalf of the company—but Local 122 president Patrick Walsh accepted the honors for the employees.[9] In addition, when unions went after wartime improvements, they earned even greater legitimacy in the eyes of employees. As a result of these developments, by war's end, more than 90 percent of Smith workers, including clerical staff, had joined Local 122.[10] And finally, for years the local had been calling for a "union shop" (in which all workers would be required to join the union), but management had bitterly resisted the demand. In October 1945, Smith officials finally relented. By then, even "a majority of our fifty-year hands," they were forced to concede, carried union cards.[11]

Once the conflict was over, Smith tried to restore the pattern of labor-management relations that had prevailed before the war. Eager to cash in on a postwar explosion of pent-up consumer demand, most carpet manufacturers immediately invested millions of dollars to revamp their existing operations and, in some cases, to acquire or construct new plants. Smith, for example, bought Sloane-Blabon, a linoleum firm, for $2.75 million, and then launched a program to expand its facilities at a cost of about $10 million.[12] Carpet makers also committed enormous sums for new equipment, raw materials, and postwar advertising campaigns. And finally, they poured resources into perquisites for their professional and managerial staffs. In 1947, for instance, Smith purchased a luxurious twenty-room mansion, complete with domestic servants, to accommodate visiting sales and retail representatives.[13] In 1950, moreover, the company implemented profit-sharing for some eight hundred management personnel.[14] When it came to production workers, however, the spending frenzy flagged. Desperate to meet the staggering postwar demand for floor coverings, Smith and its competitors advertised widely for additional workers and begged their employees to recruit family members and friends. But they also escalated the use of techniques perfected in wartime—speed-up of machinery, use of incentive rates, heavier workloads for weavers—to stimulate greater productivity, at lower cost, among the workers they had. At the same time, carpet makers stubbornly resisted workers' economic demands. If forced to raise wages, they insisted, they would be compelled to raise prices and thus risk a dramatic decline in sales.[15]

In spite of these mounting pressures, many workers were developing new expectations of their own. The TWUA did not challenge carpet firms' productivity strategies directly in the early postwar period; indeed, in 1946, Local 122 agreed not to interfere with "any efficiencies in production that the company desires to install."[16] But in exchange for their cooperation, carpet locals went after a tangible portion of the savings they helped to secure. Their exertions paid off: between the spring of 1946 and the summer of 1948, they won a 25 percent real (adjusted for inflation) increase in minimum hourly earnings, while real average hourly straight-time earnings rose by 17 percent.[17] Moreover, while Smith officials retained considerable bargaining power inside the plant, they were forced to consult regularly with the union about wage, workload, and other concerns. And while a union contract promised some predictability, neither executives nor union leaders could always control workers' behavior on the shop floor. For example, shortly after the war ended, a group of Smith workers—one of whom had spent forty years with the company—announced their readiness to wildcat when raises went unpaid.[18]

To add to management's frustration, Local 122 extended its authority well beyond the plant gates. In seeking to secure the loyalty of both employees and community residents, the union boldly appropriated a host of management techniques. It supplanted the company-run athletic program with its own sports teams; produced a union newsletter, *Texcio News*, that rivaled the official company organ, *The News;* and even positioned union representatives alongside Smith officials in the leadership of citywide charitable crusades.[19] Local 122 also played a pivotal role in solidifying labor's power in Westchester County. By 1949, some fifteen thousand industrial workers in Yonkers, or nearly 90 percent of the city's wage earners, belonged to unions; together, TWUA Local 122 and United Electrical Workers Local 453 (Otis Elevator) represented nearly ten thousand employees.[20] Although CIO and AFL unions retained rival affiliations, they collaborated closely during strikes and other disputes.[21] Finally, unionists—in a campaign led by Local 122's business manager, Charles E. (Charlie) Hughes—began to contend for power in the political realm. Area unions formed a joint AFL-CIO Non-Partisan Committee (NPC), headed by Hughes, through which they vowed to "change the political climate in the city" and make Yonkers "a decent place for union people to live."[22] Their first effort was impressive. In November 1949, NPC-backed labor activists—including Smith carpet workers Aloysius Moczydlowski and Kenneth Grosse—won three of twelve city council seats.[23]

Yonkers unionists did not represent the only challenge to corporate control. The city of Yonkers was (and still is) a study in contradictions. On the one hand, it was an industrial metropolis; on its west side—and especially in the southwestern sector—the city's working class established richly diverse ethnic enclaves and infused vitality into the downtown area, known as Getty Square. At the same time, Yonkers was the largest city in posh Westchester County; its east side offered a haven for affluent professionals, who commuted to work in Manhattan but relished the comforts of suburban life. These commuters, despite their rhetorical support for private enterprise, were more concerned with minimizing their own tax obligations than with preserving the city's industrial base. During the Depression, they had frowned on efforts by local boosters to aid industry—through the sale of city property on the cheap, for example—that would diminish the city's available resources and require that revenue be raised by other means.[24] After World War II, the commuter population of Yonkers skyrocketed, but municipal services—schools, police stations, public transportation—remained concentrated on the west side.[25] Under pressure to expand these services, city officials began to impose greater demands on local employers. For example, Alexander Smith regularly consumed nearly a third of the city's water supply on a below-cost basis; by the late 1940s, local authorities were lamenting the loss of resources and calling for higher rates. At the same time, the city raised assessed valuations—and by extension, taxes—on most Yonkers firms.[26] For generations, Smith and other manufacturers had enjoyed ready access to municipal favors; now, it seemed, they would have to fight for the privileges they hoped to receive.

Just as conditions in Yonkers were deteriorating from the standpoint of company officials, the South's advantages surged to the fore. Although most carpeting was still made in the mid-Atlantic states or New England, one firm—James Lees of Philadelphia—had opened a branch plant in Virginia in the early 1930s. Thanks largely to lower wage rates, higher workloads, and streamlined facilities, Lees had performed admirably both before and during World War II; as the company launched its postwar modernization program, its profits continued to soar. At the same time, the carpet industry was rocked by a technological breakthrough that was indigenous to the South. Traditionally, carpets were woven on looms; the new method, tufting (which resembled sewing and originated in northwest Georgia), produced goods much more quickly and at far less cost. In response to these developments, northern carpet makers—invoking "southern competition"—pressed for greater productivity in northern factories and intensified their resistance to union demands. They also made tentative forays onto southern soil themselves. After the war, northern carpet companies had trouble attracting workers willing to accept poorly paid yarn preparation jobs. In the South, they found textile towns whose desperate residents were less choosy than their northern counterparts, as well as communities eager to put vacant defense plants to productive use. By mid-1947, Smith, along with two of its top competitors—Bigelow-Sanford and Mohawk, both based in Amsterdam, New York—had established yarn mills in small southern towns.[27]

Southerners themselves, moreover, actively promoted capital flight. Particularly since the onset of the Depression, southern politicians had been aggressively pursuing northern-based firms. In 1936, for example, the state of Mississippi had pioneered a program allowing municipalities and counties to subsidize the acquisition and construction of industrial sites. Under the "Balance Agriculture With Industry" (BAWI) plan, communities could issue tax-exempt bonds to build tax-free plants, which they rented to employers for nominal fees. BAWI even required communities to guarantee a surplus labor supply. Mississippi's industrial recruiters offered other inducements, such as short-term property tax exemptions, as well.[28] Though BAWI fell flat on the eve of World War II, it was revived in the mid-1940s, and the state went all out to "sell Mississippi," as one development official declared.[29] By the late 1940s, Mississippi's leaders were launching an ambitious promotional campaign—they even set up a Mississippi Information Office in New York City's financial district—and the leaders of other southern states soon followed suit.[30]

Alongside local and regional developments, federal policies facilitated capital flight. During World War II, congressional representatives from the South and West had lobbied successfully for greater decentralization of the nation's industrial infrastructure; after the Korean War began in mid-1950, they revived the effort to pull military contracts away from the industrialized states.[31] (Some politicians championed the practice as a cold war measure, on the grounds that, in the event of a Soviet attack, the nation's industrial infrastructure would not be destroyed in one blow.) Moreover, the federal tax code, along with other legislation, contained loopholes that eased the way for both factory construction in new locations and plant liquidation at older sites. For example, the government granted rapid tax write-offs for the cost of building new plants—as well as loans for construction—if those plants were authorized to turn out military goods. It also allowed businesses to write off net operating losses by carrying them into other tax years, and permitted parent or successor corporations to use those carryover provisions themselves. Many firms, especially textile producers, took advantage of these provisions to initiate or expand southern facilities while phasing out northern mills.[32] And since municipal bonds were exempt from federal taxes, BAWI-type financing fit nicely into manufacturers' migratory plans.

By 1950, Smith executives considered capital migration more desirable—and more feasible—than ever before. The South, of course, was not the only option. For example, Smith sent a management team on scouting trips to Puerto Rico. Harold C. Zulauf, vice president of operations and industrial relations, later rhapsodized that the island's male workers were "a dime a dozen," while the women were "taught by the nuns." He sadly concluded, however, that the potential for tie-ups by the Maritime Union made such a move too risky.[33] Subsequently, Smith signed on with the Fantus Factory Locating Service, a consulting firm whose staff typically developed an initial list of possible sites and then, after exhaustive investigation, narrowed the field to those that most closely matched a company's criteria. The preliminary Smith survey turned up numerous towns in Pennsylvania, Ohio, Illinois, and Indiana, where declining economic fortunes were apparently producing the vulnerability that often passed for business appeal.[34] But these areas soon fell by the wayside. Former Smith manager Herbert J. (Jack) Potts recalled hearing rumors of a southern operation as early as 1946.[35] Four years later, the South still beckoned, and Smith finally heeded its call.

Ultimately, Greenville, Mississippi, emerged as the ideal industrial site. Greenville was a small city in the heart of the Yazoo-Mississippi Delta, where King Cotton still reigned supreme. During World War II, many black farm workers had left the Delta in search of superior industrial opportunities in northern cities, and Greenville's planters and businessmen— hoping to augment the area's white population and strengthen its economic base—were now courting industry themselves. Greenville boasted a number of appealing attributes, including proximity to the Mississippi River, cultural amenities (garden clubs, a country club), a cheap and abundant labor supply unlikely to organize, and a local elite who enjoyed virtually uncontested political and economic control.[36] When Smith executives visited Greenville, they found precisely the conditions that, from their point of view, Yonkers no longer supplied. "The whole flavor of the town was tasty," Jack Potts, who was part of the delegation, recalled.[37] Potts had more than mere promises to go on: in January 1951, Greenville's electorate overwhelmingly approved a $4.75 million BAWI bond issue, by a vote of 2,306 to 31.[38] Once federal authorities allocated the steel needed for plant construction (with the Korean War in full swing, the government was keeping close tabs on materials needed for military use), the project got underway.

With Greenville at the ready, Smith executives imposed a new set of standards that Yonkers was now expected to meet. Greenville already possessed certain key advantages. For example, the Yonkers facilities comprised a sprawling complex of old, multistoried buildings, while Greenville Mills was a modern, efficient, single-story plant designed to employ fewer workers and turn out fewer goods.[39] In addition, Smith's Yonkers employees boosted their earnings with incentive rates and also side agreements that supplemented the union contract; in Greenville, by contrast, workers drew wages and benefits that, while attractive by Delta standards, were well below the Yonkers scale.[40] While Yonkers weavers typically tended only one loom, moreover, their Greenville counterparts operated two or three.[41] By turning up the heat on Yonkers—while escalating the commitment to Greenville—Smith sought to widen these disparities even more. While executives understood that Greenville would not immediately turn a profit, they rewarded their southern employees with wage hikes, special benefits, and lavish praise. At the same time, they blamed Yonkers for the firm's financial difficulties; Smith could not compete effectively, they insisted, unless the Yonkers workforce proved more pliant and productive, and unless local government showed greater receptiveness to the company's needs. In November 1951, company president William F. C. (Bill) Ewing warned publicly that Smith could "be driven out" of Yonkers. (See figure 2.) Only if Yonkers proved itself worthy of investment, he declared, would it make sense for Smith to "pour out the blood, sweat and tears of capital" to bring its aging facilities up to speed.[42] By the fall of 1953, Smith was ready to invest in Yonkers on a limited basis, but only as a way to "achieve greater efficiency."[43] By modernizing equipment and consolidating a portion of its operation, Smith was able to increase workloads, slash its labor force, and sell off a large chunk of its property holdings—actions that further diminished its status in Yonkers as a source of revenue and jobs.[44]

Despite—or perhaps because of—their growing vulnerability, both employees and municipal authorities found it difficult to comply with the company's demands. Over the years, Smith workers had fought for what they considered reasonable wages, benefits, and working conditions; now, they were unwilling to accept less than what they felt was their due. During spring 1952 contract negotiations, for example, leading carpet makers tried to wrest concessions from workers; in response, employees throughout the industry struck the mills for more than two months. Smith officials claimed a number of victories in the strike settlement, but they failed to achieve two major objectives: eliminating all side agreements, and restoring decision-making power to management alone.[45] Unlike locals at other carpet mills, moreover, Local 122 refused to capitulate on workloads almost to the end. And in February 1954, just after Smith completed its Yonkers modernization project, hundreds of affected workers—apparently incensed by workload pressures and the discharge of a shop steward—launched a wildcat strike.[46] Meanwhile, Yonkers was in no position to forego public funds. Historically, the city had minimized educational expenditures by re-

FIGURE 2. William F. C. Ewing, president of Alexander Smith, highlighting company concerns at a special Local 122 membership meeting in November 1951. "These are troublous times," he warned Yonkers employees. Courtesy of Wisconsin Historical Society, Textile Workers Union of America Records, image no. WHi-4227.

lying on privately financed parochial schools in predominantly Catholic west-side neighborhoods. But as the east side's population continued to climb in the early 1950s, the city's newcomers (who were largely Protestant and Jewish) began to call for adequate educational facilities of their own. In the spring of 1954, a group of Yonkers residents charged that the public schools were shockingly overcrowded and underfunded, and state education officials threatened to withdraw state funds.[47] Given the clamor for resources, city officials were understandably reluctant to relinquish the vital revenue that local manufacturers—particularly Smith—supplied.

Even if Yonkers had succumbed to the pressure, the June 1954 plant closing was probably a fait accompli. It was not clear whether Smith executives had planned all along to abandon the Yonkers facility. By the time the shutdown occurred, however, there was no real reason for them to stay. It was not that Smith could not have "afforded" to invest in Yonkers. Rather, the company now had other, higher priorities—its linoleum subsidiary, a recently acquired yarn mill, the Greenville plant, a penchant for lavish spending on executive salaries and perks.[48] The company did show losses in the early 1950s, but as top officials eventually admitted, these derived from the linoleum operation, not the Yonkers mill.[49] And yet Yonkers was expected to pay the price. "We have to do a lot that hurts some people," James Elliott, Bill Ewing's successor as company president, told shareholders in May 1954, "but like a doctor's case, if a leg has to go, you have to grin and bear it."[50] By then, new contract negotiations had reached an impasse, for Smith had presented a set of proposals that, according to union representatives, would "virtually destroy the wages, working conditions and other safeguards built up . . . over the last 15 years."[51] (See figure 3.) The June walkout might be viewed as a last desperate act of defiance, intended not to impose greater demands on management but rather to prevent the company from further rolling back workers' gains. By that time, Greenville Mills was turning out a sizable portion of Smith's total carpet production. It was easy enough to transfer what remained.

As with most conflicts between labor and capital, there were compet-

FIGURE 3.   Local 122 officials presiding at a union meeting on June 13, 1954, just before the final strike began. Picket signs refer to generous pension and stock-option plans recently granted to top Smith executives, and a wage increase just given to the company's employees in Greenville, Mississippi. From left to right: Business Manager Charles E. (Charlie) Hughes, President Carmen Rose, First Vice President John Kosorek, Recording Secretary John Hynes, and Secretary-Treasurer Mary Krupp. Courtesy of Wisconsin Historical Society, Textile Workers Union of America Records, image no. WHi-4229.

ing interpretations of what had occurred. On July 1, 1954, the international TWUA placed a sobering advertisement, entitled "A Lesson of Failure," in the *New York Times*. The Yonkers workers, the union argued, had lost their jobs "unnecessarily," for management—after stripping Yonkers of its resources—had provoked the strike in order to facilitate migration to "greener pastures." The tragedy "could have been prevented," the TWUA insisted, if Smith had felt a "sense of responsibility toward the community where it grew great." Particularly in light of the current recession, the union called on federal authorities to penalize runaway plants. The next day, the *Times* editorial writers issued their reply. In their formulation, there was an aura of inevitability about the Smith situation: it was because the carpet firm had ceased to turn a profit, they contended, that it had been "forced to close down." They acknowledged that Smith did have a "special obligation"— not to restore a drained and exhausted Yonkers, as the TWUA suggested, but to "explore every conceivable way of reducing costs." To that end, they counseled greater labor-management cooperation, and particularly greater productivity. When these measures failed, they argued, communities had to simply meet the challenge—for to impose constraints on capital would violate the "economic freedom" that "we Americans deeply prize." The TWUA had asked pointedly: "Because buildings grow old, must there be a trail of ghost towns across our land?" The *Times* writers did not exactly answer in the affirmative. Neither, however, did they offer an alternative to the scenario the union described.[52]

The Road to Recovery?

Within Yonkers, Smith's departure produced a complex and contradictory response. In the early 1950s, most U.S. carpet companies operated in small northeastern or New England communities, where gigantic mill complexes loomed over the physical landscape and dominated local economic life. Yonkers, however, was not a typical mill town, not only because of its industrial diversity but also because a large and growing proportion of its population—the east-side commuters—did not depend directly on the city's manufacturing base. The Smith shutdown deeply affected those who lived and worked in the area surrounding the carpet mills—what one observer called an "industrial city within a city"—but it did not spell disaster for the city at large.[53] As a result, Yonkers residents were divided about how to rejuvenate the local economy in the post-Smith era and, indeed, whether to pursue industrial development at all. Still, the loss of Alexander Smith remained a powerful touchstone in debates over the city's economic future—

so powerful that, when Smith-type scenarios loomed in later decades, desperate residents scrambled to proffer the very incentives that their southern counterparts supplied.

Whoever bore responsibility for the shutdown, the burden of recovery fell on Yonkers alone. In the weeks and months following Smith's stunning pronouncement, many Yonkers residents joined forces in a campaign to alter the company's plans. Yonkers was already reeling from high unemployment; in April 1954, some 4,200 people—or more than 6 percent of the city's labor force—were officially jobless, as compared to just 1,900 a year before.[54] These sobering statistics reflected not only the post–Korean War economic downturn, but also a massive wave of Smith layoffs that had begun back in the spring of 1952. Now, perhaps another 2,400 Smith workers—some estimates ran closer to 3,000—were slated to swell the ranks of the unemployed.[55] Despite the downsizing, the Smith mills still accounted for 20 percent of the jobs in the manufacturing sector of Yonkers, and nearly 18 percent of the city's total annual industrial payroll.[56] It was little wonder that local chamber of commerce chief Joseph J. Harding termed the impending shutdown "catastrophic."[57] Desperate to reverse the company's decision, city and union officials pleaded with Smith executives to reconsider, and they appealed to Governor Thomas E. Dewey to intervene.[58] But management maintained that it was an "economic necessity" to close the Yonkers plant.[59] Some hoped to salvage at least a portion of Smith's operation (the Yonkers plant manufactured two types of carpet, only one of which was produced at Greenville), but instead the company purchased a factory in South Carolina—at a cost of about six hundred thousand dollars—to turn out the rest of its goods.[60] If northerners and southerners were engaged in "economic war," as Mississippi Governor Hugh L. White had claimed publicly in 1953, then the South had won this round.[61]

Once it was clear that Smith's decision was irrevocable, Yonkers boosters—seeking to emulate their southern counterparts—launched a campaign to attract new manufacturing concerns. One of the first acts of local politicians and business leaders was to form the Community Committee on Economic Development (CCED), whose principal aim was to lure industries into Smith's sprawling factory space.[62] CCED head Thomas V. Kennedy also urged Yonkers to create a commerce department to "meet the competition of hundreds of aggressive cities" that were also seeking industry, while local authorities promised "complete cooperation" with incoming firms.[63] The taming of labor, however, formed the core of the promotional plan. In July 1954, several disputes were brewing in Yonkers—at Otis Elevator and also at Stewart Stamping, an electronics factory—and the city's daily newspaper, the *Herald-Statesman*, warned unionists to "consider the enormous need for caution against upsetting our bread-winning applecart." Otherwise, the paper admonished, workers—through their "recklessness and irresponsibility—or merely lack of cooperation"—might inflict hardship on themselves, their families, and the community at large.[64] Meanwhile, Chamber president Joseph Harding—asserting that Yonkers now had a "bad labor name outside the city" as a result of the Smith situation—stressed the need to "correct that impression" if Yonkers hoped to draw new firms.[65]

Industry courted under duress, however, came at a price. Just after Smith's shutdown announcement, union leaders urged that industrial prospects be carefully screened so that "maximum benefits would accrue to the city," while state employment officials identified a litany of occupations—not yet available in Yonkers—that former carpet workers might be able to perform.[66] But these plans soon fell by the wayside. In mid-1955, a private syndicate of area businessmen purchased the Smith mills and took over the task of attracting new employers.[67] With that transaction, the marketing of the Smith mills metamorphosed into a series of disparate deals between private parties, in which the property was sold or leased to any entrepreneur who showed up with cash in hand and promised to fill some space. The facility did attract dozens of diverse employers, including makers of plastic furniture, advertising displays, leather goods, paper boxes, car batteries, and briefcases, as well as a tea-packing company and a pharmaceuticals concern. Nearly all of the newcomers were fleeing other places—most often New York City—in search of reduced tax obligations, low-wage labor, and other perquisites not as readily available in, say, Manhattan or the Bronx.[68] Some complained that former Smith workers expected too much money, while others declared bankruptcy soon after they arrived.[69] The availability of the old factory buildings produced a kind of free-for-all for footloose industry—a way for companies to cash in on the city's vulnerability by cutting their own payroll and revenue costs. Technically, many of these migrants were moving northward—if only slightly—but they were motivated by the same factors that had pulled Alexander Smith south.

In addition, "industrialization by desperation" gave new leverage to firms that had functioned in Yonkers for many years. In mid-January 1955, just as the Smith mills were falling silent, Otis Elevator president L.A. Peterson invited thousands of employees and their spouses to gather at Brandt's Theater on South Broadway. He stunned his audience by announcing that, unless the company could reduce expenses in Yonkers, it would "have no choice" but to relocate—not to the South, but to "a new mid-Western plant." There was no evidence of financial hardship—indeed, Otis was posting record sales and profits—but management insisted on workers' "active cooperation" to raise productivity and cut costs.[70] Frightened union members quickly accepted the firm's proposals by a nearly three-to-one margin, and the *Herald-Statesman* praised their action as "a case of common sense, serving the common good."[71] Otis also wanted tax relief, and while many were incensed by the company's audacity—one small factory owner accused Otis of "kicking a city when it's down"—an unhappy city council eventually complied with the demand. Even more controversially, Otis insisted that the city turn over portions of four public streets. This proposal produced an odd shift in alliances, as local chamber leaders and Otis workers united to support the measure, while businesses directly affected by the property transfer—including the *Herald-Statesman* itself—vigorously opposed the scheme. After the city council agreed to give the streets to Otis (there seemed to be no alternative), the *Herald-Statesman* lambasted local officials for doling out public property with no conditions attached. The newspaper also led a campaign to hit the city with millions of dollars in damage claims, and even took the council to court. In defense of the city's actions, union attorneys were forced to argue that the giveaway would "advance the general welfare"—precisely the justification that southern boosters used for subsidizing industrial plants. Ultimately, the city won the state's approval to consummate the deal.[72]

Even those who were most committed to industry, however, had trouble succumbing to manufacturers' demands. Since both losing Smith and retaining Otis carried costly consequences, Yonkers relied heavily on its industrial newcomers to help compensate for the loss. As a result, by the late 1950s, executives who had moved into the Smith mill complex were complaining bitterly that Yonkers had lured them under false pretenses. Instead of offering a friendly business climate, they contended, the city was forcing them to pay large sums for unreliable services such as trash collection, and had boosted their property assessments sky-high.[73] Moreover, while local boosters insisted that Yonkers labor had been "sobered" by the Smith and Otis crises, many area workers did not readily relinquish the expectations they had developed over the years.[74] One occupant of the mill complex, lamenting that his labor costs were higher in Yonkers than in New York City, complained that "the former Alexander Smith employees consider themselves skilled." Moreover, some tenants in the mill buildings found the construction trades—a particularly powerful force in Yonkers—to be a special source of grief.[75] As the level of frustration mounted, the businessmen formed a committee to air their grievances. The newcomers, as one plastics manufacturer put it, had "reached the saturation point of being pushed around."[76]

At the same time, Yonkers public officials—in contrast with their southern counterparts—did little to facilitate industrial growth. Some observers hoped that the New York State Thruway, built just as the Smith mills were closing, would draw manufacturing to Yonkers and enhance the value of the Smith site. But there was no easy roadway access from the Thruway to the principal industrial properties in Yonkers, and the city did not try to establish new routes.[77] Boosters floated a range of ideas for achieving economic progress—issuing bonds to develop industrial properties, forming a task force to coordinate the movement of new businesses into Yonkers—but these never got off the ground.[78] Nor did local politicians address the lack of industrial land. By the late 1950s, planning officials understood that, for Yonkers to support manufacturing, it would have to provide what many southern communities offered—space for modern, one-story plants. But while the amount of acreage reserved for residential and commercial purposes skyrocketed during the 1950s, only 2.3 percent of the land in Yonkers was available for industrial use. For years, city planners and chamber leaders called for enlarging the pool of land zoned for industry, but until the late 1960s, their pleas were ignored.[79]

Alongside these limitations was the open hostility of many Yonkers residents toward economic growth. Since the city's east side remained less congested than its industrial enclaves, businesses often sought to locate or expand there. But east-side residents—who tended to be much wealthier and more highly educated than their west-side counterparts—regularly railed against any type of development, industrial or otherwise, that they felt would interfere with their pristine suburban way of life. Throughout the late 1950s and 1960s, east-side homeowners mobilized against a number of proposals, including a Western Electric distribution center, a Consolidated Edison substation, several bids for expansion by Stewart Stamping, and various department stores. Chamber leaders generally threw their weight behind these projects, on the grounds that they would provide much-needed revenue and jobs. But angry east-siders regularly thronged City Hall to denounce the proposals, arguing that they would alter the character of their neighborhoods and drive property values down. At times, residents even sued to prevent the projects from taking place. Although they often lost these battles, their contentiousness sent a clear message that many in Yonkers did not welcome new enterprise with open arms.[80]

Despite the ambivalence toward industrial development, however, the threat of a Smith-type exodus was still potent enough to compel action on industry's behalf. In 1963, for example, during one of Stewart Stamping's appeals for expansion, the company's employees turned out in force to counter residential opposition to the plan. One worker, Philip Battaglia, pointedly recalled his eighteen years of service with Alexander Smith as he "begged the [City] Council not to let Stewart move away."[81] A year later, Sau-Sea Foods, a shrimp processing firm, also sought a permit to expand. It was council member Aloysius Moczydlowski—a former Smith worker— who warned that "the city might lose Sau-Sea if the Council barred the move."[82] Most troubling of all was the announcement, in the fall of 1963, that Otis Elevator was building a plant in Bloomington, Indiana. Yonkers Mayor John E. Flynn—a former Smith mill superintendent—immediately appointed a committee to promote economic development. Otis executives claimed that they contemplated no "serious cutbacks," but in the spring of 1965, they admitted that 550 of nearly 2,000 Yonkers workers would lose their jobs.[83] As the move westward got underway, city and chamber officials called not only for increased industrial zoning but also for tax relief to firms that razed old buildings to construct new plants.[84] (In part, these proposals reflected concerns about deteriorating conditions in the Smith complex, the handling of which, civic leaders now acknowledged, had been a "clear case of missing the boat.")[85] Of course, these measures would neither solve Yonkers's short-term revenue problems nor deter Otis from moving to the Midwest. But they did reflect a growing recognition that Yonkers could not attract industry unless it offered incentives that more competitive locations supplied.

By the late 1960s, though, commuters' interests had come to dominate the terms of debate. By then, the lack of industrial growth had contributed to serious deficits in the city budget, and the need for revenue was urgent.[86] But local boosters, even as they called for more manufacturing, were increasingly anxious to appease the affluent east side. Chamber officials, for example, argued that industry—since it yielded substantial revenue while requiring little attention and few services—was the perfect way to keep property taxes down. They also expressed a preference for "clean, well-regulated industrial users," whose presence would not be "offensive to residential areas."[87] The *Herald-Statesman*, too, adopted a conciliatory approach. In a series that analyzed the city's dismal record of recruiting and retaining industry, the newspaper lambasted public officials for failing to either increase industrial zoning or link the Thruway to Yonkers's industrial sites. At the same time, the paper chastised anti-industry homeowners for selfishly subordinating the city's interests to their individual neighborhoods' needs. And yet the *Herald-Statesman*, like the chamber, promoted "clean type" industry that would serve taxpayers' interests.[88] In the wake of the exposé, there were signs of progress—the city approved some major construction projects and finally altered its zoning ordinance—but the changes reflected a greater commitment to commerce and light industry than to manufacturing growth.[89] While these forms of development proved more acceptable to the city's well-to-do residents, they did little to stimulate economic revival in the working-class districts of the west side.

Still, the need to prevent other Smith-style departures remained a powerful rallying cry. In the spring of 1970, Otis executives issued yet another warning to Yonkers: the firm would have to go elsewhere unless it had room to expand. Shaken by this latest threat, city officials proposed to purchase a parcel under the auspices of urban renewal, demolish hundreds of homes and businesses, and sell Otis the land. The U.S. Department of Housing and Urban Development (HUD) agreed to provide financing—but only if the city built a public housing project as well. As in the mid-1950s, unionists and business leaders launched a campaign to "save" the company. More than twelve hundred Otis employees signed petitions favoring the proposal, while chamber officials cautioned that "Yonkers cannot afford to lose Otis at this time." The pro-Otis bloc faced fierce resistance from community groups on the west side (where the proposed project would be located) as well as from Republican mayoral candidate Angelo Martinelli, whose printing business was slated for the wrecking ball. Over the years, growing numbers of black and Puerto Rican residents had been moving into west-side neighborhoods, and the debate over HUD's proposal was racially charged. Some opponents claimed that subsidizing black people's housing would drive the country into "economic bankruptcy," while proponents suggested that the Otis plan—by revitalizing the city's declining industrial section—might bring back older (read: white) people who had moved away after Smith shut down. The pro-Otis sentiment proved overwhelming, and the city accepted HUD's offer in the fall of 1972. The opposition then sued the city on the grounds that the project, by subsidizing private interests, represented an unlawful use of public funds. Then-Mayor Martinelli pursued the legal challenge all the way to the U.S. Supreme Court, but the high court refused to hear the case. That was a relief to the plan's proponents, who had rejoiced that "the prospect of losing another major employer will no longer loom over us"—a pointed reference to the Smith mills.[90]

Like their counterparts in southern communities, however, the people of Yonkers found that industrialization by inducement did not ensure stable economic growth. The campaign to "keep" Otis cost taxpayers at least $11.4 million (later estimates reached as high as $16 million), with the federal government covering two-thirds of the expenses, and the city and state sharing the rest of the cost. Otis paid just $1.39 million for the property, or 20 percent of its worth.[91] Otis employed about fourteen hundred people, and company executives intimated that the plant modernization might result in another six hundred jobs.[92] Instead, the public financing scheme supported a program that—as with Alexander Smith's partial revamping of its

Yonkers operation in the early 1950s—ultimately led to the elimination, not the expansion, of jobs. Within a year of the October 1974 ground-breaking, Otis had laid off 250 employees. By early 1977, there were 900 workers on the payroll, and the local union president predicted that Yonkers had "another Alexander Smith Carpet Shop" on its hands."[93] In 1982, United Technologies Corporation (UTC), which had acquired Otis in 1976, began preparations to close the Yonkers facility. By then, only 375 workers remained.[94] Given Otis's historic importance to the Yonkers econ-omy—particularly after Alexander Smith's departure—it was not surpris-ing that local people tried, at various stages, to meet the company's terms. But acquiescence had not ensured economic security; indeed, the latest aid package probably facilitated the phaseout of the Yonkers plant.

While Yonkers was suffering industrial losses, Greenville, Missis-sippi—once a center of cotton processing and marketing—was becoming solidly a manufacturing town. In luring Alexander Smith, Greenville's boosters had vowed not to go after other industry that might interfere with the carpet firm's labor supply. Between the late 1950s and early 1960s, how-ever, they brought in five more manufacturers, all based in the Midwest, whose products included screws, boilers, saws, and auto parts. To a great extent, these successes reflected Greenville's capacity to offer the sort of fa-vorable business climate that Yonkers no longer supplied. Greenville's lo-cal elite, since they wielded near-total economic and political power, were ideally positioned to assist industrialists in every conceivable way. More-over, since the mechanization of agriculture was sharply reducing employ-ment opportunities, area residents were eager to secure new factory jobs. In addition, as competition for industry escalated throughout the South, Greenville's boosters extended their probusiness efforts statewide. For ex-ample, arguing that unionism would diminish Mississippi's industrial at-tractiveness, they succeeded in passing a "right to work" law (which outlawed the "union shop") in 1954, and a "right to work" amendment to the state constitution in 1960. While the state's tiny labor movement op-posed these measures, its position was seriously undermined by both its own enthusiastic endorsement of industrial development and—particularly in the 1950s and 1960s—the rising tide of white solidarity across class lines.[95]

As had been the case in Yonkers, though, the very process of industri-alization produced tensions that threatened Greenville's business appeal. First, when the civil rights movement swept through Mississippi in the early and mid-1960s, black people in the Greenville area (who were excluded from all but the most menial industrial jobs) began to press for equal op-portunity in the economic realm. Instead of bowing to corporate interests, they openly attacked local manufacturers—particularly Greenville Mills—for partaking of the public treasury while failing to serve the "public good." Second, as industry moved to Greenville—and to the South generally—northern-based union organizers followed suit. At first, most workers—grateful for a steady paycheck at subsistence wages—resisted the call. Over time, however, as they adjusted to the rhythms of industrial employment, many grew disaffected with the status quo. The TWUA made few inroads at the carpet factory, which remains unorganized to this day. But unions with greater financial resources and organizational capacity, such as the United Steelworkers of America, proved far more effective—so much so that, by 1966, local boosters were lamenting Greenville's reputation as a union town! And finally, by the late 1960s, area residents were wondering whether the benefits of luring industry were worth the cost. Despite boosters' insistence that industrialization would bring progress and prosperity, their inducement strategy virtually assured that corporate migrants would pay low wages while adding little to the revenue base. During the 1960s, population growth in Greenville sparked greater demand for municipal spending; by the end of the decade, moreover, economic hard times were setting in nationwide. In response to these pressures, taxpayers and even city officials began to demand more from employers—just as their northern counterparts had done a generation before.[96]

In comparison with Yonkers, however, Greenville was still the more attractive site. Ultimately, neither civil rights activism nor labor organizing significantly altered the prevailing balance of power, either within the city or on the factory floor. Black workers did win access to production jobs from which they had been excluded—but on employers' terms. And while organized labor did make some progress in Greenville, it was too weak to dislodge the antiunion apparatus that boosters had built up over the years. Meanwhile, in the absence of alternative models of economic development, there seemed little choice but to continue courting and conciliating industry—or else risk having no industry at all. As a result, even in periods of severe recession, such as the mid-1970s, Greenville remained sufficiently enticing to draw new manufacturing firms.[97] Of course, these "successes," like earlier ones, were limited in number and brought only limited returns. And in the face of continued poverty and unemployment, civic leaders simply stepped up their use of accommodationist schemes. In 1986, for example, Washington County, of which Greenville was the seat, was reeling from a jobless rate of 14.3 percent (fully twice the national rate). That year, the county won official state designation as an "enterprise zone." This proved to be a bonanza for the county's manufacturers, who received tax credits for job creation, along with sales and construction tax abatements for buying new equipment or expanding their plants.[98]

With Greenville as the standard, Yonkers had trouble measuring up. Since the people of Yonkers remained deeply divided over industrial development policy, city officials could not act as a unified force on industry's behalf. Moreover, as the area's industrial base diminished, even those most reliant on manufacturing still found it difficult to yield to employers' demands. During the 1960s, as the Vietnam War was stimulating economic expansion, many manufacturers sought to increase workloads, reduce staffing levels, and otherwise roll back workers' gains. In turn, workers—emboldened by their newfound leverage in the labor market, and inspired by radical movements for social change—began to fight back. In 1967 and 1968, for example, three leading Yonkers-area employers—including Otis—were wracked by long strikes. To firms whose commitment to Yonkers was already shaky, the unrest represented one more reason not to stay.[99] In addition, Yonkers officials, even when they proved willing to "sell" their city, did a poor job of it. Of course, some of Yonkers's weaknesses—such as its dearth of suitable industrial land—were not entirely the city officials' fault. Still, local politicians continued to hinder economic expansion, subjecting industrial prospects to what even the mayor, in 1974, called "a discouraging amount of red tape."[100] During the economic downturn of the mid-1970s, a number of employers phased out their Yonkers operations, in some cases shifting production to other towns.[101]

And yet, to proindustry forces in Yonkers, the Mississippi model seemed the only feasible approach. Of course, as the Otis experience ultimately demonstrated, following that model did not necessarily keep employers in place. After UTC announced its plan to close Otis, Mayor Angelo Martinelli—who had opposed the Otis bailout back in the early 1970s—sued the parent firm. By accepting millions in public funding, he contended, the company had assumed a moral obligation to stay in Yonkers for another sixty years. But that claim had no legal basis, and boosters failed to absorb the lessons of the Otis case. Otis closed in the wake of the devastating 1981–1982 recession, and, in hopes of fending off further crises, boosters established the Yonkers Industrial Development Agency, which was empowered to offer businesses property and sales tax exemptions, along with BAWI-type revenue bonds.[102] In 1988, moreover, local authorities successfully petitioned New York State to designate Yonkers's most distressed section—roughly one square mile containing the former Smith and Otis plants—as an Economic Development Zone (EDZ). Companies operating in EDZs qualified for a tantalizing array of incentives, including real estate tax exemptions, tax credits for new jobs and investment, refunds of sales taxes on building materials, reduced utility rates, and low-interest loans.[103] At one time, Yonkers and Greenville were separated by a world of distinctions. Capital migration, it seemed, had substantially narrowed the gap.

Conclusion

Even as capital fled southward, it was beginning to cross national boundaries as well. In 1947, for example, Smith's rival, Mohawk, established a small carpet mill in Mexico City. And as noted, Smith itself seriously considered opening a Puerto Rican plant. In 1955, Smith and Mohawk merged to form a new company, Mohasco; in 1962, when Mohasco acquired Firth, yet another carpet firm, it took over properties that included a Mayaguez, Puerto Rico, yarn spinning mill. In 1965, Mohasco launched a joint venture with a group of European companies to make and sell tufted carpets in Europe; the group, based in Brussels, produced its goods at a Belgian mill. (Belgium was one of the world's leading carpet exporters.) That same year, Mohasco purchased another Mexican carpet plant.[104] The very forces that drove the industry to make inroads into southern territory also motivated its incursions into foreign terrain.

Despite these early instances of foreign investment, however, much of U.S. industry's overseas exodus occurred in later years. During the 1970s, exports from other countries to the United States climbed dramatically, and the profitability of U.S. corporations declined. In response to growing global competition, many corporate executives decided to "go global" themselves.[105] As had been the case with southward migration, federal tax, tariff, and other policies made it advantageous for U.S. firms to produce goods abroad.[106] As U.S.-based capital fled to far-flung locations, domestic manufacturing employment plummeted: between 1979 and 1987, the nation lost 10 percent of its industrial production jobs.[107] Already forced to compete with their southern counterparts, places like Yonkers now confronted rivals in Third World countries, where economic vulnerability, political repression, and other features of a favorable business climate surpassed even Greenville's allure. Globalization accelerated what historian James C. Cobb has called the "southernization of the national economy," that is, the process by which places throughout the country—in desperate bids to court and keep manufacturing—ultimately reduced their standards to match the southern scale.[108] But the process of downward leveling had already been long in the making, as the history of Yonkers—and of many other deindustrialized communities—attests.

"Southernization," moreover, did not produce the economic well-being that the people of Yonkers—or the people of Greenville, for that matter—hoped to secure. Admittedly, as practiced in Yonkers, "southernization" was not entirely successful. Torn by conflicting loyalties and divergent economic interests, Yonkers residents often refused to bend to the will of employers. But in moments of crisis, certain sectors of the community did manage to compel compliance with employers' demands. In doing so, however, they typically incurred economic losses—in the form of reduced revenue, for example, and fewer, less desirable jobs. And in the absence of constraints on capital mobility, accommodation was not enough to keep employers from leaving—if the desire to maximize profits dictated a change in locale. The same dynamics prevailed in Greenville, where it was arguably easier to forge a consensus around serving industry's needs. In 1985, for example, Boeing selected Greenville as a site for repairing military aircraft, in exchange for which it received about twenty million dollars in municipal, state, and federal aid. Boeing packed up in 1989, leaving Greenville to lure other industry in its wake. At times, firms abandoned Greenville in favor of overseas locations. In 1981, Schwinn left Chicago for the more appealing Greenville; ten years later, the bicycle manufacturer headed for an even more enticing location—Taiwan.[109] Ultimately, no matter how much local people relinquished—whether in Greenville or in Yonkers—their sacrifices brought no guarantees. In the end, capital was the real winner of the competition, and communities, states, regions—indeed, the entire nation—paid the price.

CHAPTER 2

The "Fall" of Reo in Lansing, Michigan, 1955–1975

LISA M. FINE

In 1975, after seventy-one years, operations at the Diamond Reo truck plant came to an end. Established by Ransom E. Olds, the famous automobile pioneer, inventor, and founder of the Reo Motor Car Company, Diamond Reo ended its long life bankrupt and broken apart, sold to a liquidator that stripped the plant bare. Three years later, the city of Lansing oversaw the destruction of the plant, the administrative offices, and the Reo clubhouse, during which a fire of suspicious origins ripped through the factory. The complete destruction of Reo created unemployment, dislocation, and depression, both economic and psychic, in a community whose identity is still passionately tied to the production of automotive vehicles.

At the start of the twenty-first century, the story of Reo seems to follow a familiar script. We have grown accustomed to hearing how the mobility and flexibility of capital takes its toll in plant closures, unemployment, and dislocation, leaving communities with withering infrastructures and bereft of tax revenues. In automotive history, the Reo story is but one among thousands about manufacturing plants transformed by the oligarchic structures and global corporations of the late twentieth century. The Reo story can also be read as the failure of unionism in the late twentieth century to pose a meaningful, progressive challenge to mounting globalization and domestic pro-business policies. The closing of the plant in the mid-1970s can be seen as a harbinger of the deindustrialization and creation of the Midwest rust belt characteristic of the last two decades of the twentieth century.

These were my working hypotheses until May 1999. As I was trying to sort out all of these ideas for a book on the Reo Motor Car Company of Lansing, an article in the *Lansing State Journal* revealed that GM was planning to open four new production centers in Lansing within the next five years. These centers would create four thousand jobs and double production of GM plants in Lansing to approximately 850,000 autos a year, making Lansing GM's largest vehicle-making center in North America. These contemporary events challenged my assumptions about deindustrialization, postindustrialism and the future of capitalism.[1]

Certainly the closing of the Reo plant is part of a larger story of deindustrialization, which brought about what is often referred to as the postindustrial economy. Aside from a smaller number of works that try to explain the relationship between postindustrial and postmodern,[2] much of this literature represents the late-twentieth-century phenomenon of deindustrialization as a macropolitical/-economic issue with micropersonal/-economic consequences.[3] While scholars debate the role that the government should play during this period of economic transition, they tend to agree that multinational corporations are essentially free to put their balance sheets above the lives of their workers. Moreover, scholars argue that mobile capital and high technology allow corporations to do this more often and more thoroughly.[4] The large body of literature that builds on case studies of particular plant closings provides poignant, ground-level views of the demise of individuals, families, and communities.[5]

Though is it very useful to understand the post–World War II economy as transitional, I have found that the literature that makes use of this insight often does so ahistorically.[6] Consider, for example, two excellent works in this genre: Thomas Sugrue's *The Origins of the Urban Crisis* and Ruth Milkman's *Farewell to the Factory*. Sugrue sees the process of "deindustrialization—the closing, downsizing, and relocation of plants and sometimes whole industries"—as having "accelerated throughout the twentieth century." The "decentralization" of the auto industry prompted by the need for space and automation, and the desire to weaken unions, "reconfigured the landscape of the most prominent industrial cities across the region that came to be know as the rust belt." He poignantly argues that "the bleak landscapes and unremitting poverty of Detroit in the 1970s and 1980s are the legacies of the transformation of the city's economy in the wake of World War II, and of the politics and culture of race that have their origins in the persistent housing and workplace discrimination of the post war decades."[7] Ruth Milkman, in her sensitive account of the effects of downsizing in one auto plant in New Jersey during the late 1980s, describes deindustrialization as a phenomenon of the 1970s and 1980s. "In the 1970s and 1980s, deindustrialization ravaged the U.S. economic landscape as millions of workers lost their jobs to plant closings or permanent layoffs. Among the causes were increased imports, corporate decisions to relocate production outside the nation's borders, new labor-saving technologies, and work reorganization."[8] Both works discuss the auto industry. Both focus on the effects of macroeconomic factors on personal lives, resistance, and community. Both come up with similar causes and consequences, and yet their narratives point to different eras as the locus of decline. It is not that either of these scholars is wrong; rather, they are describing phenomena that unfolded at different moments in different places, but that have common causes at their core. The concept of deindustrialization, then, should be used as a point of departure for further work, rather than to provide explanatory closure.

There are scholars who challenge some of the basic assumptions associated with late-twentieth-century deindustrialization and the postindustrial economy. Scholars dispute whether late-twentieth-century economic changes are cyclical or structural. Scholars contest assumptions of sunbelt industrial gains at the expense of the rust belt. Conservative scholars hostile to any regulation curtailing the movement or activity of corporations assert that most "runaway firms" are not running as often or as far as many fear.[9] And Stephen Cohen and John Zysman, in their book *Manufacturing Matters: The Myth of the Post-Industrial Economy*, argue that "we are experiencing a transition not from an industrial economy to a service economy, but from one kind of industrial economy to another."[10]

Plant closings of the late twentieth century are episodes that by their very definition involve the intersection of global, national, regional, and local causes and consequences; therefore, the reasons for and outcomes of the plant closings may be unique in different times and places and not simply by degree. Understanding the phenomenon of plant closing only as a scenario of remote, global, mobile capital inflicting pain and suffering on local workers and their communities overlooks the fullness of the stories. While economists, urban planners, and sociologists certainly use different methodologies to identify the causes for individual or clusters of plant closings, in exploring this particular plant closing from a historian's perspective, three overlapping, interrelated, and historically contingent explanations seem most plausible. First, Reo's decline started in 1955 when the plant was absorbed by a larger, remote corporation and the factory's production was devoted almost entirely to producing trucks for the military. Remote ownership and overreliance on one product for governmental contracts at the expense of diversification seemed a logical step in the early years of the cold war, but spelled disaster in the 1970s. Second, in the early 1970s, the corporate owners of the Reo plant were unsuccessful in their attempts to avail themselves of federal urban renewal dollars to move the plant to newer, up-to-date facilities outside the city. The story of Reo's demise is bound up with efforts by both city and federal officials to rid municipalities like Lansing of their urban blight. Finally, aging and unproductive, the factory was purchased by a private entrepreneur (a very old-fashioned capitalist, not a large, powerful, multinational corporation) who squeezed out whatever value was left in the people and facilities, for his own gain.

Reo in Lansing

Between 1904 and 1975, on a now polluted site on the south side of Lansing, Michigan, one could find a complex of offices and factories committed to the manufacture of motor vehicles. Over the years the names and faces of the workers, managers, and owners all changed many times. Only one symbol united the experience and provided continuity for the events that occurred at this place—the name Reo, an acronym for the name of the founder of the company, Ransom E. Olds. If you lived in the city of Lansing during these years and someone told you he or she worked "at the Reo," not only would you know exactly what that meant, but you would probably associate that name with a pride of place.

During its first two decades of operation as a producer of automobiles and trucks, Reo and its community prospered: consumers would have had a hard time predicting which of the two most prosperous Lansing-based companies, Reo or Oldsmobile, would last one hundred years. (Oldsmobile marked its one hundredth anniversary in 1998, although, as of 2001, the Oldsmobile line has been discontinued, even as GM builds new assembly plants in Lansing.) Reo's success until 1929 owed a great deal to its welfare capitalism program—a well-developed and popular array of services and activities coordinated through a personnel department and the Reo Clubhouse. Through its managers and company newspaper, the *Reo Spirit*, Reo disseminated to a workforce of overwhelmingly native-born, rural-rooted, white, working-class men an ideology of respectable working-class masculinity. This ideology, which stressed the importance of cross-class cooperation, home ownership, responsible family values and wholesome leisure, was also suffused with intense anti-radicalism, and anti-unionism, and "Americanism." Both the company and the workers recognized the rhetorical expression of this welfare capitalist program and its ideology when the company evoked the idea of the "big factory family." On the eve of the Great Depression, Reo produced a line of very popular cars and trucks, employed over five thousand workers, and was considered an important and progressive (in its technological innovations, production techniques, and labor-management relations) local employer.

The events of the 1930s, however, took their toll on the company. Reo introduced expensive luxury models just as it became impossible for the vast majority of Americans to afford them. The UAW-CIO staged a successful, month-long, sit-down strike in the spring of 1937. The company almost failed as poor management floundered. A major corporate reorganization, a scaling back of production to focus on trucks only, as well as an infusion of capital from the Reconstruction Finance Corporation coincided with the first of many government military and ordnance contracts that would keep the company afloat.

World War II and the Korean conflict breathed new life into the company. Not only did Reo Motors successfully compete for a variety of government contracts as both a prime and subcontractor, but it also tentatively began to diversify its product base to include consumer goods and civilian trucks and buses. As a leaner, smaller, locally owned corporation making products with a good reputation, Reo was vulnerable to buyouts and what we would now call corporate raiding. From the middle of the 1950s until the company's demise, what was still called Reo was taken over many times. After an abortive takeover attempt by Henney Motors of Freeport, Illinois, Bohn Aluminum bought Reo. White Motors of Ohio acquired the vulnerable company, and then combined with Diamond T of Chicago for its last incarnation as Diamond Reo. Diamond Reo was then taken over by a shady individual named Francis Cappaert, who rekindled some hope that Reo would be restored to its former health and vitality. In 1975, the same year Vietnam "fell," so did Reo, only two years after its last owner had begun gutting the plant and selling off its inventory, depriving loyal employees of their pensions.

It is probably a coincidence that the Vietnam War and Reo ended in the same year, but it is a meaningful coincidence. Because the company's records from the last fifteen years of its existence are less complete than earlier records, it is difficult to prove what I believe is a reasonable hypothesis: Reo failed because it could not make the transition to civilian production and became dependent on military truck contracts for survival. Reo revived as a result of both World War II and the Korean Conflict, making a variety of products for the army and navy, from bomb fuses to a popular and successful amphibious vehicle called the Eager Beaver. Reo positioned representatives in Washington, D.C., and at any military base in the United States or overseas that had Reo products. Reo was involved in the constellation of national governmental agencies overseeing military production and prices, and the procurement and rationing of resources. By 1952, the end of the Korean War seemed imminent, and the MIT-trained engineer who was the president of Reo, Joseph Sherer, began to plan for the new era of the cold war. What he called a diversification plan suited the company's new orientation toward consumer goods. Adding to an already healthy division producing lawn mowers, Reo launched a new industrial and marine engine division, a children's wheeled goods division, and two new initiatives in marketing—truck sales branches, and a truck leasing division.[11] Already the company had begun producing interurban and school buses, and civil defense vehicles as well. (These armored vehicles, designed to provide assistance to communities in the aftermath of a nuclear attack, were called Calamity Janes.) A great deal of this expansion was fueled by the large orders for trucks the company had received during the Korean Conflict; despite the gearing down that followed the hostilities, the future seemed bright.[12]

Nevertheless, Reo's dependence on the military continued. Even as the company was declaring its diversification into the civilian consumer market a success, 70 percent of its business volume was defense business, and the health of the company's future was still tied to procuring diminishing defense contracts.[13] In September 1953, just a few months before Sherer left, it was announced that Reo had scored a major truck contract, becoming one of just two producers of a two-and-a-half-ton military truck through its successful public relations in the Pentagon.[14] It is impossible to know for certain, but there is some evidence to suggest that there was a decision made to pursue this line of defense work at the expense of other, high-tech, defense-related work.[15] It is not entirely clear whether Joseph Sherer decided to leave Reo because he felt he had accomplished his goals there, or whether this industrialist—who always lived in Detroit while he ran the company—decided that he had reached the limits of what he could do.

During Sherer's last year, 1954, things began to look bad: workers experienced layoffs, shutdowns, and short weeks;[16] at work, they encountered little red tags tied to the die settings all through the plant. Ed Wright wrote, "it means their job is done. 'Final' is the word written across the card. It means that particular die has made it last run on the part it was built for. It means the contract for Uncle Sam that has kept our shop so noisy and so busy for so long will soon come to a close."[17] Henney Motors Company of Freeport, Illinois, began the process of purchasing the company. Henney, recognizing that the basic activity of the plant was the manufacture of trucks, sold the lawn mower division to Motor Wheel (another long-time local manufacturer), relieved itself of the children's toy division, received another government truck order, and pledged to shoot for the number one spot among truck independents.[18] Reo remained in limbo as the deal stalled. By the end of 1954, it became clear that the president of Henney (who also happened to be an official of Diamond T, another important truck independent) had decided against the deal. He transferred the entire arrangement to Bohn Aluminum and Brass of Detroit in a complicated financial deal that benefited the stockholders and board of directors, but no one else.[19] John Tooker, who had worked at Reo since the mid-1920s and had been second in command under Sherer, assumed the reigns. He was an appropriate choice, since for many years he had been Reo's main man in Washington, D.C., and was known in ordnance and defense circles throughout the city.[20] The rebuilding of the company was oriented toward truck production, sales, leasing, and research and development work, utilizing the expertise of the new parent company.[21]

Defense contracts trickled in, the union obliged the company with begrudging concessions, and the company limped along.[22] What ended the turmoil was the buyout of Reo by White Motors of Cleveland, Ohio, which even union members hailed as a good thing.[23] When it purchased Reo, White was one of a number of small, struggling truck independents in a market dominated by Mack Trucks. The leadership at White had decided not to wait for the competition to fail or combine; instead, they decided to engage in an aggressive merging spree that would continue throughout the 1960s. It made White one of the largest truck producers, as well as one of the top one hundred defense primary contractors, in the country.[24] In this national corporate environment, Reo was purchased to play a specialized role: it would manufacture trucks—a large percentage of which would be for military purposes—and would lease, sell, and service those trucks wherever they might be found. By the start of the 1960s, Reo was part of an organization that held one-quarter of the growing truck market and was the second largest truck producer in the United States.[25]

Between 1960 and 1969, Diamond Reo (as it came to be called, from the combination of Reo and Diamond T) filled millions of dollars worth of orders for two-and-a-half-ton trucks for military ordnance. It can be tentatively surmised that military contracts earned the company an average of $13.5 million each year. (See table 1.) Zenon C. R. Hansen, a forty-year veteran of the truck industry, remembers his years as the president of Diamond Reo in Lansing and the executive vice president of the White Motor Corporation, ending in 1965, as "extremely successful."[26] There are a variety of reasons why this flush period came to an end.

The corporate tactics that brought Reo into the White Motor Company and brought initial success and prominence eventually began to weaken White Motors. By the late 1960s, as a result of endless merging, particularly with farm equipment companies, White began to show losses.[27] White's slumping performance was also attributed to the leadership, which emphasized marketing and "let manufacturing take a back seat."[28] To ac-

Table 1. Military Contracts Awarded to Lansing Division of White Motors Announced in Newspapers

Year	Amount ($ millions)[a]
1960	13.5[b]
1961	22.0
	1.4[c]
	8.3[d]
1962	7.0[e]
1963	12.3[f]
1964	—
1965	1.2[g]
1966	10.0[h]
1967	10.4[i]
	9.8[j]
	18.3[k]
1968	5.8[l]
1969	3.5[m]

[a]Rounded to nearest tenth. Listed separately if separate orders.
[b]"Reo Awarded Large Army Truck Contract," *Lansing Labor News*, 7 July 1960, 1.
[c]"White Motor Unit Contract," *Wall Street Journal*, 5 July 1961, 3.
[d]"Pentagon Awards Over $120 Million in Defense Orders," *Wall Street Journal*, 9 November 1961, 7.
[e]"Pentagon Awarded More Than $236.2 Million in Defense Contracts," *Wall Street Journal*, 2 January 1962.
[f]"Army Gives White Motor $12,278,464 Truck Order," *Wall Street Journal*, 6 May 1963, 8.
[g]"Defense Contract," *Wall Street Journal*, 4 March 1965, 7.
[h]*Wall Street Journal*, 10 May 1966, 17.
[i]"Army Gives White Motors a $10,433,090 Truck Job," *Wall Street Journal*, 15 March 1967, 5.
[j]"White Motor Gets $9,844,869 Army Contract for Trucks," *Wall Street Journal*, 9 June 1967, 9.
[k]"Pentagon Awards $575 Million Jobs as Fiscal '67 Year Ends," *Wall Street Journal*, 3 July 1967, 2.
[l]"Borg Warner Division Gets $6 Million Navy Bomb Order," *Wall Street Journal*, 23 May 1968, 3.
[m]"Air Force Gives TRW Satelitte Work Valued At Up to $37.7 Million," *Wall Street Journal*, 4 March 1969, 16.

complish the needed corporate housekeeping, the CEOs turned to familiar tactics: they proposed a merger with White Consolidated, another Cleveland-based industry that produced consumer goods. In the summer of 1970, the merger seemed a possibility, scuttling some preliminary negotiations that were underway with Francis Cappaert regarding the purchase of the Reo plant.[29] By the start of 1971, the Anti-Trust Division of the Justice Department had ordered an injunction to block the merger as being in violation of the Clayton Anti-Trust Act, and, rather than go to court, White abandoned the merger and sold Reo to Cappaert.[30] It is important to try to identify when White singled out Diamond Reo as the plant to sell and why the capital gained by the sale of Reo was used to improve the efficiency of other White plants.

During early 1971, when the stockholders of White Motors and White Consolidated had signed off on the merger and it appeared that it would go through, W. L. Peterson, the president of the White Motors truck division, called for a delay of the merger, because, he claimed, the truck division, identified as a drain on White Motors, was financially healthy. For his efforts, Peterson was fired, while the company claimed that a division would need to be liquidated to restore the company's financial health.[31] News releases after the sale explained that the trucks made at Reo were in direct competition with other lines made by White Motors.[32] But this competition became a problem in the late 1960s only because the demand for the trucks was shrinking. There were two factors that contributed to softer demand: the decrease in productivity due to the deteriorating plant and equipment and the cutbacks in military contracts.

Scholars of the cold war industrial economy have pointed out that the Midwest did not benefit during that period to the same extent as other regions of the U.S. "gunbelt," losing the prominence it had held in the World War II and Korean Conflict eras as military dollars shifted to high-technology industries. In their seminal study of defense contracting and regional development, Ann Markusen, Scott Campbell, Peter Hall, and Sabina Deitrick assert, "The industrial heartland never captured a sufficient share of the cold war aerospace defense contracts." They conclude, "Midwestern habits of making and selling were better suited to the car dealer and the housewife than to the Pentagon colonel."[33] Because it had specialized in ordnance trucks, the Diamond Reo plant was decidedly low-tech and not competitive for making products with more sophisticated technologies. If Diamond Reo was no longer pulling its weight by bringing in sought-after government contracts, it might be considered expendable. In fact a *Forbes* article describes White's new CEO, "Bunkie" Knudsen, fresh from

Ford, as justifying the sale of Reo for exactly those reasons. It stated that "when Diamond Reo truck division, which had been losing money for five years, lost a key U.S. government order, Knudsen sold it off."[34] For what became Diamond Reo, the combination of remote ownership and the specialization in military truck production spelled doom.

Not pulling its weight in military contracts was not Diamond Reo's only problem. The aging, inner-city plant was starting to become a corporate liability, requiring "significant investment in new equipment to bring its facilities up to optimum productivity."[35] By the 1960s, both the Reo plant and the city in which it was located were in dire need of an infusion of capital and energy to restore infrastructure. Reo's demise in Lansing was also tied to White Motors' unsuccessful efforts to procure both federal and municipal funds to modernize and relocate Diamond Reo. It was not simply White Motors' inability to procure military contracts from the government that sealed Diamond Reo's fate; White Motors also failed to get a share of the corporate welfare being administered by Housing and Urban Development to update the Diamond Reo plant. Without either of these federal supports, White decided it would abandon Reo. Lansing's municipal history helps to explain the context (although not necessary the exact causes) of this unfortunate outcome.

The Plant, the City, and Urban Renewal

By the early 1960s—which was late compared to efforts by larger industrial cities—Lansing began vigorously and successfully to pursue federal funds for highway construction and a variety of Great Society programs designed to create "model cities."[36] What began as an effort to "modernize" and "destroy urban blight" ended up destroying downtown businesses and residential districts, mostly inhabited by poor and/or African American families. Until the 1940s, Lansing was essentially a "white" city, but after World War II, this began to change. During the 1950s, the nonwhite population of Lansing grew from 3,046 to 6,794 by 1960. By 1970 the African American population was 12,232, a significant numerical increase but still barely over 10 percent of the population of the city. Compared to cities like Flint and Grand Rapids and Kalamazoo, Lansing was still quite homogenous, but its African American neighborhood, which had existed since the beginning of the century, was growing faster than its traditional boundaries could maintain. (See table 2.) One scholar of residential patterns in Lansing claimed that "residential segregation or spatial concentration of black fam-

Table 2.   Percentage of Nonwhite[a] Population in Michigan and Selected
           Cities in Michigan, 1950, 1960, and 1970

Place	1950[b]	1960[c]	1970[d]
Michigan	7.1	9.4	11.7
Detroit	16.4	29.2	44.5
Flint	8.6	17.7	28.6
Pontiac	9.5	17.0	27.5
Saginaw	9.3	17.0	25.0
Grand Rapids	3.9	8.3	12.0
Kalamazoo	4.4	6.7	10.6
Lansing	3.3	6.5	10.1

[a]Nonwhite in all three censuses included African Americans, Indians, Japanese, Chinese, and people of other Asian nationalities. It did not include people of Mexican descent and other Hispanics.
[b]*Report of the 17th Decennial Census of the United States, Census of the Population: 1950*, vol. 2, *Characteristics of the Population*, part 22: Michigan (Washington, D.C.: U.S. Government Printing Office, 1952).
[c]*18th Decennial Census of the United States, Census of the Population: 1960*, vol. 1, *Characteristics of the Population*, part 22: Michigan (Washington, D.C.: U.S. Government Printing Office, 1963).
[d]*1970 Census of the Population*, vol. 1, *Characteristics of the Population*, part 24: Michigan (Washington, D.C.: U.S. Government Printing Office, 1973).

ilies represents the most obvious and extreme expression of racial prejudice in Lansing."[37] It was in this traditionally African American neighborhood that the "removals" began.

The first assault on Lansing was the building of an interstate highway right through the heart of the city itself. Interstate 496 allowed for easier access across the city and the state as it replaced east-west-running Main Street, just south of the capitol, and the main business district on the north/south-running Washington Avenue. The interstate separated the downtown from one of the large Oldsmobile plants and Diamond Reo, both located south of the highway. Interstate 496 cut through much of the African American community, destroying 890 dwellings and displacing many more families.[38] The destruction of the neighborhood and the removal of families against their will (not to mention the financial hardship) was the most serious consequence of this highway. There was another, ironic, outcome—the destruction of the Ransom E. Olds mansion on the corner of Main Street and South Washington Avenue. Once a testament to the heterogeneous mixing of classes (although certainly not races) in the downtown neighborhoods, Olds's house was within walking distance of the plant he owned and the downtown business district, as well as more modest workers' homes and boarding houses.[39] By the early 1960s, these once sumptuous mansions had begun to be broken up into apartments and become rundown. Despite some efforts to designate the home as of architectural and historical importance and to move it to another site, the house eventually came down, another victim of urban renewal and the desire for traffic flow.[40]

During the mid-1960s, the city of Lansing identified three urban renewal projects to clean up and modernize what were considered the most blighted and depressed areas of the city's business and residential areas.[41] Urban Renewal Project 1 focused primarily on a business district near the capitol with turn-of-the-century, two- and three-story buildings with locally owned, small businesses but also including about 130 homes primarily occupied by African Americans. These were bought and razed; tall glass-and-steel boxes were put in their place. Urban Renewal Project 2 included a variety of residential and business areas west and east of the capitol. This urban renewal created a large, impersonal, glass-and-steel capitol complex—a series of office buildings for use by federal, state, and local government—as well as a number of buildings for Lansing Community College, clearing 372 dwellings, again in the largely black neighborhood.[42]

Understandably, by the middle of the 1960s, Lansing had developed a "housing problem." And it certainly may have been true that many understood this "housing problem" as a "race problem," since one of the very few riots that occurred in Lansing, in June of 1964, took place on the west side.[43] Local plants such as Olds and Motor Wheel were adding to the problem. Not only were they experiencing labor shortages, fueling inmigrations of workers requiring low-cost housing, but also they were expanding production. As production increased, plants had to expand, generally doing so by razing more houses, apartments, and businesses, putting additional pressure on existing stock.[44] The removal of these businesses and homes coincided with the building of scattered-site housing projects designed to provide an alternative to low-income housing in the city, projects that were certainly inadequate in both quality and quantity.[45]

The last project in this push to revive the city was Urban Renewal Project 3. It focused on a corridor extending southward from the capitol, past the highway, to the businesses and neighborhoods beyond. Diamond Reo and the neighborhoods and commercial districts surrounding it were designated as blighted and slated for drastic change. J. N. Bauman, the president of White Motors, proposed a novel way of funding corporate welfare and community development simultaneously.[46] His plan would provide for moderate- and low-income housing on the deteriorating south side without a single removal, while at the same time providing the old and cramped

Diamond Reo plant with the land and capital for retooling. The deal involved appealing to the U.S. Department of Housing and Urban Development (HUD) for funds to buy the existing Diamond Reo factory and site from the parent company, White Motors. City officials joined with officials from White Motors to make the application to HUD.[47] With HUD money and a generous land and tax deal from the city of Lansing, Diamond Reo would relocate its plant to a site in the northern part of the city, with a new and improved facility as well as additional space to grow. The old site would then be razed and become available for private development of moderate- and low-income housing. (Needless to say, there were probably some real estate developers and agents who were happy about this arrangement as well.)

In 1968 and 1969, all of the pieces began to fall into place. White Motors, still enjoying some success at its Lansing plant, announced its plans to build a new manufacturing plant in the city.[48] It appeared willing to work with the city council as well as with the Citizen's District Council for District Area 3, created to provide community input on the urban renewal process.[49] After some delays, funding was obtained for a feasibility appraisal, the first step in obtaining HUD approval for the final funding.[50] By the start of the new decade, Local UAW 650, the Citizen's District Council, the *Lansing State Journal*, and even the township and county of Diamond Reo's new home had all approved of the arrangement.[51] The success of the project hinged on HUD's appraisal of the worth of the factory and site. Independent appraisers had calculated that it was worth between four and five million dollars, an amount that would have been acceptable to White Motors and put the whole plan into action. HUD, however, would provide only $1.8 million for the project, and after White Motors executives and a local congressman engaged in eleventh-hour meetings with the secretary and undersecretary of HUD, George Romney and Richard Van Dusen, it became clear that the amount would not be increased. White Motors rejected the deal.[52]

In the history of White Motors, the summer of 1970 was significant because it was then that the merger with White Consolidated was possible. With that merger and the money from HUD and the city of Lansing, the corporation believed, a new and improved Lansing division was truly feasible. But the poor offer from HUD and the injunction against the merger dealt two serious blows to the Lansing division. Urban Renewal Project 3 was never funded, probably a casualty of changing policies of HUD at the national level.[53] The very mechanisms designed to facilitate HUD's new urban vision rendered local city planners dependent on money from the federal government. Just like the dwindling of military contracts, the lack of cooperation on the part of HUD to facilitate Reo's retooling spelled disaster. Reo remained in an area designated as blighted.

The Demise of Reo and Lansing

There was nothing left for White Motors to do but to sell the Diamond Reo plant in Lansing, which they did in 1971, to a man who had been a shadowy figure in the injunction against the merger between White Motors and White Consolidated—Francis Cappaert. (He had, in fact, tried to buy Diamond Reo before.) When he bought the plant, Cappaert pledged to restore Reo to its former glory as an independent truck producer, but he would be Reo's last owner.

Ironically, both the former employees, many of whom lost a great deal of their promised pensions, and student activists of the New Left, identified Francis Cappaert as the reason for Diamond Reo's demise. There was certainly no love lost between these two groups. In what was undoubtedly one of the first antiwar demonstrations in the region, the *Lansing Labor News* reported on a picket line of approximately 150 Michigan State University students around the Reo plant on October 16, 1965. Apparently some student group had become aware that Reo filled military contracts, and that the trucks they were producing were destined for Vietnam. Fred Parks, the writer of the column for Diamond Reo, suggested that the "government . . . set up an induction center on Baker Street [near the plant] and draft each one as they stroll by."[54] Writers for East Lansing's underground papers, perceptively revealed that urban renewal, allegedly destined to help the poor, was really only thinly veiled corporate welfare, funding retooling and new plants for aging companies like Reo.[55]

By 1971, when Francis Cappaert purchased White Motors' Diamond Reo division, the alternative papers had begun to change their tune. Here was a man whom it was easy to hate, an almost formulaic capitalist villain. When Cappaert bought Diamond Reo, he was a fifty-year-old Mississippian (although he was born in Michigan), the father of the mobile home business in the United States, an oil investor, and the owner of numerous holding companies in electronics. He also invested in land in Las Vegas and throughout the southern United States, on which he herded twenty-five thousand Black Angus cattle. A free-wheeling, intensively private, and independent entrepreneur, he was considered to be one of the richest men in the United States, with a reputation for either making a big profit fast or dumping the whole project. Cappaert affected a "good ol' boy" image, insisting on drinking Schlitz instead of cocktails, while he visited his various business operations in his sumptuous flying home, a $3.5-million BAC-11 jet that normally would hold seventy to eighty passengers.[56] Progressive elements had no trouble attributing the financial hardships of the company and its workers to this man.[57]

One spring day in 1975, Diamond Reo workers arrived at work to find their plant padlocked. Even though this event was twenty years in the making, the several hundred workers remaining in the plant were shocked. Former employees offer vivid and painful recollections of the plant closing. Doris Dow, who worked at Reo between 1950 and 1975—an office worker, a union member, and a leader in the retiree group before she passed away in 2000—switched between present and past tense in her recollection of the troubles. They were still quite real to her.

> I'm walking down the street, there down Washington Avenue, and I'm, why there is this a crowd of people out there in front. Why aren't they going in? Well, it was, it was April, it was the spring of the year so you're thinking, well, it's nice out; [it] was quite common to see people standing out in front with a cup of coffee or something like that in the spring of the air, if it was a nice day, you know, and it was nice that day. But that was too many people and then, as you get there closer, you see the chains on the door. You know something has happened and, of course, you're looking at the chains on the door and you say, why?[58]

Dow and many others spoke about suicides and other problems after the shutdown. Calvin Chamberlain, an engine worker and time-and-motion specialist between 1950 and 1975, who "helped turn out the lights," "got to drinking" right after the closing.[59] Raymond Fuller, who worked on truck repair between 1943 and 1975, claimed he had sensed the end was near but took it hard.

> Oh yes, I know it was coming. I was on repair for it. I stayed until all the trucks was gone. Sure I know exactly when I was going to leave. You know, I was fifty-eight years old when that thing closed, now where do you go to look for a job when you are fifty-eight years old? I sat around here. I guess we went to Florida, I remember, that winter, and then I come back [and] went ice fishing. Come along the first of March I told my wife I got to find something to do, this is driving me crazy.[60]

Undoubtedly, the remaining employees and many in the Lansing community hoped that somehow the factory could be saved. Writing in the *Lansing Labor News*, Lee Magielski stated, it was during moments like this when Diamond Reo seems to be going down like a sinking ship that we remember we once were and still are a people of class, manufacturing one of the greatest trucks on the road. Whatever happens from here on in, it is important that the few of us that are left at work go about our tasks with [the] dignity and class that made us great. Let's keep that dignity and class to the very end like a captain going down with his ship.[61]

After the final sale, Cappaert stated, "they have finally buried the body."[62] Those left at the plant certainly felt that *they* were the captains of this failing ship. Abandoned by the managers and the community, only those left clinging to the sense of history, purpose, and pride long associated with Reo felt sadness at the prospect of the plant's passing. That the workers chose the metaphor of a regal but flawed and failing ship, while Cappaert evoked a diseased, dying body, reveals the perspectives of the various players in this long unfolding drama of the closing of the Reo.

Former Reo workers who were in the plant in the final years also identify Cappaert as the reason for their factory's closing.[63] Most informants who cared to offer an opinion on why Reo closed stated quite baldly that Francis Cappaert ruined the company and deprived them of their pensions in the process. Of course, these informants, drawn from the various Reo retiree groups that still exist in Lansing, would be inclined to do this, since these groups formed in the aftermath of the closing in an effort to pursue the pension money. These individuals had collectively discussed and formulated their version of the narrative of the plant's demise. The persistence of a common story suggests that this group reenforces it at retiree luncheons that still occur monthly. Arthur Frahm, who worked in accounts payable and purchasing between 1947 and 1972, claimed that Cappaert's "prime interest was to just liquidate the place." Herbert Heinz, who worked as an electrician and in truck repair between 1951 and 1974, also stated, "the old Cappaert, he is the one that bankrupt[ed] the company. . . . When Cappaert took off, when he went bankrupt in that place, he took six million dollars of our pension fund." Wayne Nunheimer, a mechanic and spot welder between 1945 and 1975, passionately asserted, "Reo could have been operating today if it hadn't been for Cappaert." There was one worker who wasn't hostile to Cappaert, Louis Garcia, but even he claimed that Cappaert had confided to him over drinks that he was going to close the place down.[64]

Informants suggested that the many buyouts had weakened Reo before Cappaert arrived, but none saw this as the cause of Reo's demise. When pressed regarding the changing nature of the labor force, the labor process, the company culture, the downtown community, and so forth, they gave be-grudging monosyllabic answers, if anything at all.[65] Pinning the blame on Cappaert is not wrong; he probably had no intention of making a go of Reo, certainly not of restoring the company to its former glory. Moreover, he did deprive these workers, many whom had worked at Reo for more than twenty-five years, of any decent retirement. But identifying only Cappaert as the reason for Reo's demise, while an understandable rhetorical device, is misleading. It allows former workers to retain a rosy gloss on their mem-ories of the Reo before Cappaert, and obscures the negative effects of in-numerable decisions made over the preceding five decades by company executives, policy makers, elected officials, and urban planners.[66]

Reo's plant closing was certainly the result of the relentless and care-less pursuit of profit by a greedy, solitary entrepreneur. Cappaert, however, was able to prey on Reo the way that he did only because the plant was al-ready faltering and vulnerable. Even though the outcome was not neces-sarily inevitable (despite national trends), multiple and interlocking causes for Reo's demise had been at play at the company since the middle of the 1950s. The business climate of the 1950s and the cold war found Reo, a lo-cally and privately owned corporation since 1904, bought up by a series of remote corporations. This hindered the ability of local business, municipal, and union officials to have a say in the workings of and plans for the plant. Ironically, the Reo plant's over-reliance on federal dollars for a single, mil-itary product probably kept Reo afloat longer than other truck indepen-dents—but ultimately, when the cold war began to wind down, challenged the parent company, White Motors, to make a decision about Reo's future. Funds from HUD had been used in Lansing for almost a decade to allevi-ate urban blight, often in small, African American neighborhoods; White Motors officials attempted to use this source of revenue, combined with generous tax and land deals from local governments, to underwrite a re-tooling and revival of Reo. For reasons that remain obscure, however, fed-eral funds were not forthcoming, and the Diamond Reo plant closed. On October 20, 1975, everything of value was auctioned off for eleven million dollars to an automotive liquidator, Consolidated International of Colum-bus, Ohio, and the plant was stripped to its bones.

Postscript

In an industrial park twenty minutes southwest of Lansing, surrounded by forest and farms, near the village of Charlotte, stands the reincarnation of Reo, Spartan Motors. Spartan was founded in 1975 by George Sztykeil, a former engineer at Reo, along with a number of other refugees from Diamond Reo management. The plant closing was as traumatic for Sztykeil as it was for other Reo workers, and it taught him important lessons that he applied to his new business venture. The experience of the last years at Diamond Reo provoked in Sztykeil a profound distaste for bureaucracy and waste. "We had the luxury of having our house burn down at Diamond Reo. . . . We had the power of poverty." Sztykeil explains his bare-bones setup: "I have used furniture in my office. How much production do I get out of a one-thousand-dollar desk? . . . We are here to make money. A solid-gold watch does not keep better time than a Timex. Luxury must be dumped."[67]

The company produces mobile home chassis, school buses, and fire engines. With additional facilities in Mexico, the company did very well in the 1990s. Spartan Motors is in many ways a worthy successor to Reo. There is the populist philosophy of its founder, and the fact that Spartan's workforce and personnel policies are eerily like those of the company that spawned it. The company prides itself on having a workforce that is "home-grown," workers and management alike. In 1992, "of 380 employees at Spartan, only eight have college or advanced degrees. The preponderance come from inside the county, off the farm, and out of the local high school." Spartan's chief financial officer and personnel manager "calls the Spartan work force 'vocationally literate' and 'not afraid to work.' Many grew up on farms, tending—from an early age—not only livestock but to broken tractors as well. Many still rebuild car engines in their spare time. Many come from families in which generations have worked at GM's big Oldsmobile plant in Lansing."[68]

Labor relations at Spartan resemble those at Reo in the 1920s. This nonunionized plant prides itself on management's hands-on relationship with the workers. A reporter for *Inc.* described how Sztykeil makes a point of talking to the workers each quarter. At one of these talks, "Sztykeil took his windbreaker off and laid it on top of the cardboard box in the corner of the room. He climbed a small stepladder, sat on the top step, and . . . began, 'Welcome. We think this is a good corporation. It's run on the same principles that a family is, because we think that's the most effective way human beings have managed to get along.'" Spartan Motors "distributes 10% of pretax profit quarterly among it workers" and in the 1990s committed itself to not laying off its workforce. Sztykeil explained, "You wouldn't do that in your family. If you have 10 children and times get tough, you wouldn't send the three youngest ones out the door. It's not only immoral, it's stupid. Why? Those who have been let go are soon forgotten—screw them—and the ones who stay haven't learned anything from the experience." "We don't recognize the terms *labor* and *management* here. I am not the boss. I am the number one servant of this corporation."[69]

On March 25, 1992, I and a number of others interested in Reo's history had a chance to tour Spartan Motors. The gentleman who gave us a tour of the plant described the supervisors, even Sztykeil, as willing to get their hands dirty: "It is not uncommon to find him working out in the shop." There was no assembly line, although progressive work stations with computer terminals were evident. The representative took a great deal of pride in the custom work the company performed, saying, "if a customer wants ten pounds of coffee in a one pound can, we'll figure out a way to do it." As far as I could tell, all of the 360 to 370 workers employed were white men. The workplace was filled with the loud sound of country western music and the various work stations contained pictures of babies and babes— the offspring of the worker as well as the worker's favorite female form. One work station featured a Confederate flag. In the offices, there were, of course, female secretaries. Not too far from their space a male employee's cubicle contained a sign that read: "Sexual harassment in this department will not be reported—however, it will be graded." If Reo lives on at Spartan Motors, then it re-created the industrial world Ransom E. Olds began at his first Reo Motor Car Company in Lansing, in 1904—a small workplace in a small community with a white labor force drawn from the surrounding farms, a workplace where everyone is said to belong to a big factory family.

Spartan's story is not over. In October 2000, the company had to lay off one hundred employees in a discontinued division, a part of a consolidation effort to save money.[70] In March 2001, when George Sztykeil retired at age seventy-one, the company still had a reputation for treating its workers right; production workers' pay was $12.50 an hour with quarterly bonuses that averaged about 10 percent of base pay, and the company had low turnover. (This was less than union wages.) Proud of his active and engaged employees and the quality of the product, Sztykeil waited until the company had recovered before he retired, claiming, "we want to grow, we will grow, but we must know our place. . . . I don't want to be the biggest. I want to be the best."[71]

The resurrection of Reo and the return of GM to Lansing is attributed not only to tax abatements but also to a "well-qualified labor force," and "very good labor relations."[72] If the reviving GM plants and Spartan Motors are harbingers of reindustrialization or restructuring, then global, national, and intensely local factors are all at play. If Spartan Motors, a small, independent, rural, nonunion automotive producer is the wave of the future, then it is important that we uncover and recognize the ways in which it is also powerfully rooted in its past. In light of the Reo and Lansing example, then, we cannot stop after we understand why a particular plant closed at any given time and place in the late-twentieth-century United States. We also need to understand historically why some communities are experiencing reindustrialization and why some communities are not. The padlocking of Reo was not the end of the story for the workers or for manufacturing activities in the region; it was the closing of one complicated chapter. To understand fully the meaning of plant closings, scholars need to understand what happens to work, workers, and industry beyond the ruins.

CHAPTER 3

Segregated Fantasies

*Race, Public Space, and the Life and Death of the Movie
Business in Atlantic City, New Jersey, 1945–2000*

BRYANT SIMON

In 1990, Caesars Hotel and Casino bought a run-down pizza parlor with a shabby-looking karaoke bar in the back on the Atlantic City Boardwalk. Soon after, they announced plans to tear down the structure. It turned out that the building's facade was part of the Warner Theater. Although it had been thirty years since standing-room-only crowds poured into the movie house, the building's aging shell still reflected the grandeur of the city's heyday as the "Queen of Resorts." Five stories high, the Warner's gilded front blended Egyptian themes with Spanish motifs and references to classical Greece. None of this mattered to Caesars's accountants. They wanted more space for cars and video poker machines. But after the local fine arts commission rallied its forces to stop the destruction, Caesars reconsidered its plans and left the Warner's ornate facade up on the Boardwalk.[1]

A few years later, the pizza parlor and karaoke bar were gone, but the Warner's facade remained. By then the Bally Corporation had purchased Caesars. Inspired by the theme park–sized casinos sprouting up in Las Vegas, they planned a dramatic makeover of the property. In 1996, Bally's broke ground on the Wild, Wild West Casino. Built to create the illusion of a different time and place, the $110 million complex, covering an entire city block, promised visitors a slice of the Old West on the East Coast. Painted in cheery whites and yellows, the casino's Boardwalk frontage was designed, according to Bally's promotional literature, to evoke "an elaborate Old West townscape complete with hotels and a general store as well as a wagon perched on a simulated rockscape." Making it look more like television's *Bonanza* than the grizzled mining town of Cripple Creek, set de-

64

signers painted checked curtains and flowers pots over false windows. In between the fake, two-dimensional saloon doors and blacksmith shop, an observant eye can still see the outlines of the Warner, painted over but still there.[2]

Despite its transformation, the Warner remains a silent monument to the city's busy past, when it served as the "nation's playground." Tens of millions of visitors poured into town every year from the 1920s to the 1960s. What they got in Atlantic City, beyond the pleasures of the beach and the Boardwalk, was a place to go out to restaurants, nightclubs, amusement piers, and the movies, and have a good time in public with other people. Of course, the towns and cities the visitors came from had restaurants, clubs, amusement parks, and movie theaters, but in Atlantic City, the attractions, like the Warner, were bigger, brighter, and brasher. The city specialized in offering a "luxury experience at a middle-class price," one that was meant to be consumed in public.[3]

Atlantic City's heyday and the heyday of the city's movie business coincided with a now lost era when most women and men lived their lives in public. They walked to work, spent evenings on their front porches, and spent nights out dancing, drinking, and watching movies. During this time, people consumed their leisure in public in front of crowds of strangers, not at home or in private. Across the country, the taste for public entertainment turned the movies, clubs, and ballrooms into big business, and in almost no other place was that business bigger than in Atlantic City.

Well into the postwar era, Atlantic City had fifteen movie theaters. Together they were large enough to seat a small town of twenty thousand people. Locals and tourists alike, in fact, went to the movies with even greater regularity than to the piers and nightclubs. The movies, in many ways, anchored the city's bustling public entertainment industry. Moviegoers packed the Boardwalk and sidewalks, headed off to the clubs after the show, wandered around in the nearby stores, and went to get something to eat before and after the film. But when the movie houses closed up—as they did one by one in the 1960s—the public life of the city died with them.

As in Larry McMurtry's beautifully sad *The Last Picture Show*, the closing of the theaters marked the end of an era.[4] But in Atlantic City the story had a twist. When the screens go dark in Anarene, Texas, the setting for McMurtry's novel, the town dies, and it stays dead. With only a couple moldering theaters still open, Atlantic City, too, was a dying town in the late 1960s, but in the late 1970s, casinos came and reindustrialized the city's entertainment industry. Today the resort hosts thirty-five million people a year, making it one of the most visited places in the United States, yet it does not have a single movie theater in operation. All that remains of the city's movie business past are the rough outlines of the Warner at the Wild, Wild West. But even those tell only part of the story.

No matter how hard you look at the front of the Wild, Wild West, you cannot tell that during the Warner's glory days segregation prevailed at the theater and just about every other public space in the city. You cannot see old man Jim Crow lurking anywhere. You cannot tell that African Americans had to sit in the "crow's nest" of the balcony if they wanted to see the picture. The Warner's facade does not reveal that the color line played the central role in the making and unmaking of the theater business and indeed Atlantic City itself. The glory years of the picture shows and the city's public entertainment industry corresponded with the age of segregation, their decline with desegregation. The inability of the casino-driven reindustrialization to revive the movie business speaks to the refusal of local officials and investors to acknowledge the city's bitter legacy of racism. While the casinos have brought people back to town, they have failed to revive the city's once vibrant world of going out in public. As a result, the casinos stand along the Boardwalk like skyscrapers on the moon, but the city behind them is barely surviving, and the movie business is as dead in Atlantic City as in McMurtry's fictional Texas town.

The story of the complete demise of Atlantic City's movie business highlights the larger story of the rise and fall of the public entertainment industry in the United States. It is, of course, a story about the changing tastes of tourists and shifting patterns of urban investment. Above all, however, it is the story of how race and race thinking shaped an industry and molded the way investors constructed and later destroyed public spaces. The extent to which public space and the public entertainment industry rested on exclusion complicates the narrative of postwar industrial change. Manufacturing has been at the forefront of our understanding of deindustrialization, but the history of Atlantic City's picture shows opens up new questions, forcing us to think about the connections between social life and capital investment. This story of decline resonates with the prototypical narrative, while broadening our conceptualization of industry and the reasons for industrial collapse. Like other narratives in this book, the shifting fate of Atlantic City's movie theaters in the postwar era speaks to the torturous process of deindustrialization and the brutal shortcomings of current urban renewal schemes.

The Segregated Heyday, 1945–1968

The millions who came to Atlantic City each year during its reign as the "Queen of Resorts" liked to do what most middle-class people did when they had time off at home—go to the movies. The beach town's heyday, in fact, overlapped with what scholars have dubbed "the golden age of American cinema." From the middle of the 1930s to the early 1950s, men and women from California to the Carolinas spent more money going to the movies than on any other recreational activity. Theater tickets accounted for 80 percent of all spectator amusement expenditures. During this time, 90 million Americans—the nation's population stood then at between 100 and 125 million—went through the picture show turnstiles each week.[5]

Visitors to Atlantic City, along with local residents, bought tens, and probably hundreds, of thousands of movie tickets each year. With almost one theater seat for every adult resident, the beach resort offered a wide range of movie choices. Film fans could go to the Astor, a smaller neighborhood theater on Atlantic Avenue, or the Plaza in Ventnor, open only in the summer. Downtown, between Blatt's Department Store, Kensington Furniture, and the other Main Street shops, there were a handful of bigger, dressier theaters. A block north of Atlantic Avenue stood the Alan, a Northside theater for African Americans.

Well into the postwar period, the Warner remained the brightest and showiest picture house in Atlantic City. On those Saturday nights that couples went to the colossal theater at the corner of the Boardwalk and Arkansas Avenue, they put on their opera clothes, their mink stolls and razor-creased linen pants. The evening began with a walk down the Boardwalk, past the rolling chairs pushed by black men; the Conventional Hall, a building big enough for football games and helicopter rides; the Steel Pier, where cats boxed cats, women led horses to dive forty feet into shallow pools of water, and Benny Goodman and Gene Krupa played swing; and hotels that looked like French castles and Byzantine temples. Finally the couple arrived at the Warner. The line in front of the box office stretched two blocks down the Boardwalk past the throngs going north and south. Standing there with the other white couples dressed in ties and coats, flowered hats and linen dresses, the moviegoers let the anticipation of the evening build up inside them.

Before the Warner and the other movie houses could deliver on their promises of fantasy, they had to create a sense of trust. This was particularly important for the movies. Theaters had to assure audience members that they would be safe in the dark next to strangers. To manufacture this sort of trust, movie house owners erected an overlapping network of confidence builders in and around their showplaces.[6]

Ushers played a key role in the trust-building process. Early in the twentieth century, picture house attendants did little more than take tickets and quiet unruly patrons. But as picture houses turned into movie palaces, theater owners made ushers over into cast members. Managers held auditions for the parts, and usually only tall, handsome, white college and high students got the roles. From there, they were sent to wardrobe to be fitted. Typically ushers dressed in red jackets with yellow epaulets, creased black pants, and white gloves, making them look a bit like soldiers from Napoleon's army. Then they had to learn their lines, so that, according to a trade journal, they could make a "steam fitter feel like the owner of 10,000 slaves." Managers instructed them to speak sparingly and in hushed tones, addressing patrons as "sir" and "madame," never "mister" or "girl." The ushers had yet another function. Armed with flashlights, they served as theater companies' in-house security forces. They took tickets and looked over the crowds. They marched through the lobbies and paraded up and down the aisles shushing teenagers and keeping sexual contact on the safe plane of handholding and the occasional kiss. Managers taught them, moreover, to handle "degenerates, intoxicated persons, [and] morons" with swift "vigilance." But the policing—even in its most hawkish forms—was as symbolic as it was real. The staging told customers that theaters like the Warner were places of aggressively enforced middle-class decorum.[7]

The crowds, moreover, reassured themselves. Cashmere sweaters with mink collars and monogrammed tie clips marked the movie houses as places filled with leading members of the respectable middle class. As they stood in line waiting to buy a ticket or in the lobby waiting for the program to begin, the moviegoers looked around and saw people dressed just like them. Assured that the crowd consisted of the right kind of women and men, they felt comfortable taking the next step of going into the dark. The crowd reassured itself in yet one other way—it appeared to be all white.

African Americans, however, were never completely absent from Atlantic City theaters. They scrubbed the floors, scrapped gum off seat bottoms, and polished bathroom fixtures. They appeared onscreen as well. Playing mammies and servants, they stuffed their faces with watermelon and served white bosses fancy dinners on silver trays, always with a smile. The Boardwalk itself became the stage for one of these reassuring Jim Crow performances in Republic Pictures' 1944 film *Atlantic City*. In this light melodrama about an overly ambitious businessman reformed by love and marriage, African American rolling-chair pushers stand in the backdrop of every scene. As they dig in, launching hundreds of pounds of steel wheels and human flesh, they never grimace or strain. Like characters out of *Gone With the Wind*, they grin and nod, and happily answer to "George." When they do speak, they mumble "yes sir," and "thank you sir" as kindly white men toss tips at their feet.[8]

Exclusion defined a night out at the movies in Atlantic City. The Warner's owners offered the illusion of opulence only to women and men who passed as white. The Warner's army of ushers steered those few African American patrons who risked cold stares and disapproving looks to the crow's nest at the very top of the balcony. A few blocks away at the Stanley Theater, African Americans had to sit on the left side of the auditorium. The manager of the movie house in the 1930s told an interviewer that if it were up to him, "Negroes would sit anywhere they like." But the movies were a business, he said, adding that "95% of the Theater goers . . . are whites." "They object," he observed, "to close association with Negroes, especially the transient tourists that come in the summer." So the Stanley manager reported that he found "it expedient for the 5% of Negroes to be put on the left hand side."[9]

To most of the couples visiting the Warner or the Stanley before 1965, the separation of blacks from whites was natural, just another part of their "special night out."[10] Although a ticket for a show at the Warner wasn't cheap, it wasn't expensive either. The picture houses offered white visitors a coveted luxury experience at a middle-class price. Matching the Warner's ornate facade, its interior looked like a palace. After buying their tickets, theatergoers walked down a long vertical hallway with a vaulted ceiling that recalled an old English manor. From there, they funneled into the lobby. A piano man sat in front of a baby grand playing sweet melodies. Chandeliers threw gentle streams of light onto oriental rugs and antique sofas with clawed feet. The marble sinks and gold ashtrays in the restrooms and parlors glistened and smelled fresh and clean. And the main auditorium, with its balconies, retractable orchestra pit, red velvet seats, and sparkling, atmospheric ceiling, drew "oohs and ahs" from the crowds. When the last star dimmed and the low hum of the pipe organ faded, the screen started to glow, first with a newsreel, followed by a long line of trailers, and finally, the featured attraction. Films at the Warner were part of the show, but never the whole show.

Although they lacked the Warner's over-the-top glitz, the other Boardwalk movie houses, like the Stanley, still offered, well into the postwar era, a luxury experience for a middle-class price. White couples headed to the Strand and the Virginia for a night out, and they got at these showplaces an evening of live music, movie trailers, and Hollywood's best and gaudiest offerings in a plush, segregated setting. The buildings were part of the attraction at the other Boardwalk theaters as well. All of them had lavish lounges and sitting rooms, solicitous ushers and gracious attendants. Egyptian themed murals lined the auditorium walls and crushed red velvet covered the seats.

Catering to locals and tourists, the ten movie houses along Atlantic Avenue stayed open all year long. But like the Boardwalk showplaces, they also sold a night's indulgence in luxury, and here too the experience started with exclusion.[11] Up and down Atlantic Avenue, uniformed ushers guided white couples in jackets and dresses to their seats, while they steered African Americans to the left side of the auditorium or to the top of the balcony.

Although less spectacular than the Warner and the Strand, the movie houses on Main Street shared more in common with the beachfront show-places than the cramped viewing rooms of today's strip malls. Opened in 1934, the Hollywood Theater, a typical downtown picture show, featured heavy, ornamented bronze doors. Inside, it had a barrel-shaped vaulted ceiling and a mural that told Arabian Nights stories. All the lighting fixtures were aluminum with colored etched glass shades. The theater, its owners bragged, had a well that pumped what they called "spring air" into the auditorium every seven minutes, clearing away noxious odors. For added comfort, the Hollywood offered extra-large couch seats "so couples could sit closer together."[12]

Providing a luxury movie experience at a middle-class price made Atlantic City's Boardwalk and Main Street theaters into anomalies in the golden age of U.S. cinema. The Great Depression initially devastated the theater business. Between 1930 and 1933, movie houses lost a third of their audiences. By 1936, however, the crowds had come back to watch gangster films and other items on Hollywood's escapist menu. Even though business rebounded, studios and theater owners remained cautious about the future and looked to trim costs. Companies shelved plans to build movies palaces on the scale of the Warner after 1932. In their place, film executives erected smaller, more austere theaters. Most of the new picture houses came without orchestra pits, prosceniums, hanging balconies, atmospheric ceilings, lavish lobbies, or marble-floored bathrooms. Streamlined modernism replaced exuberant eclecticism as the dominant architectural style across the nation. Many theaters, at the same time, got rid of their battalions of ushers, retaining just a few untrained high school students to collect tickets and turn the lights up between shows so customers could seat themselves.[13] Together the changes stressed "the movie" over stained glass facades and Spanish Baroque interiors. Well after these trends took hold in Philadelphia and Chicago, Atlantic City movie managers clung to the old way of doing things, selling luxury and making a night at the movies still a night of fantasy and spectacle, of seeing and being seen.

Along Atlantic Avenue—to look at one of the city's movie-dependent public business spheres—patrons of the Strand, the Hollywood, the Shore, the Beach, the Lyric, and the other picture houses filled the sidewalks. Families from Vineland, a farm town thirty miles east in the sandy flatlands, came to Main Street to shop for bar mitzvah clothes for their sons. After roaming up and down the avenue buying a suit, tie, shirt, and shoes, they took in dinner and a movie. Young couples from the suburbs of Margate and Ventnor, a few miles south of Atlantic City, rode the bus or drove to town for a movie. Before the show, they walked arm in arm down the street thick with other women and men on their way to the movies. After the film, friends met at Kornblau's Deli for overstuffed sandwiches of corn beef, coleslaw, and Russian dressing. Others ambled the avenue stopping in the U-shaped enclaves in front of the furniture showrooms and shoe stores to check out ever-changing seasonal window displays.

Trusting that the police, merchants, and ushers would keep "undesirables" at a distance, whites spent their leisure time out on the streets and in the dark with strangers in the postwar years. Well aware of their customers' sense of security, Atlantic Avenue and Boardwalk theater owners regularly scheduled midnight shows. Before the 1960s, being downtown or by the ocean at two o'clock in the morning did not scare white women and men. Filled with the right kind of people, the streets around the movies seemed safe and alive. As long as they did, the public world of going out to the theater and to clubs and restaurants, strolling and eating, and acting like rich people thrived, but when middle-class perceptions of these urban spaces changed, this world collapsed.[14]

The Fall of Atlantic City's Movie Business

In the summer of 1956, fifteen theaters with segregated seating for nearly twenty thousand customers operated in Atlantic City. Most of the movie houses appealed to a large, undifferentiated, white, middle-class audience by playing Hollywood's latest mainstream offerings. Steel Pier featured three "first run selected motion pictures each day." All of them, the owners assured customers, "are chosen by a special board of review with the purpose of providing the finest entertainment for all members of the family." Adhering to the same booking policy, the Warner, a few blocks down from the pier, featured Marilyn Monroe in *Bus Stop* that summer. On July 4, the peak of the season, *The King and I* ran for its fourth consecutive week at the Virginia, while *High Society* with Bing Crosby, Grace Kelly, and Frank Sinatra played at the Apollo, and Paul Newman and Pier Angelli starred in *Somebody Up There Likes Me* at the Strand. Main Street moviegoers had the choice that summer of seeing Tyrone Power and Kim Novak in *The Eddy Duchin Story* at the Beach or Gregory Peck in *Moby Dick* at the Astor. Every

Saturday morning, the Hollywood, the Earle, and other Atlantic Avenue theaters presented matinee double bills for children. Later, they ran midnight shows for couples and night owls.[15]

The crowds still lined up in front of the theaters well into the postwar period, and cinema owners still used some of the money from gate receipts to fix up their properties. The Strand and Embassy installed expensive new air-conditioning systems in the mid-1950s. In 1953, the Steel Pier spent $150,000 on a state-of-the-art Astrolite Screen and a brand-new stereophonic sound system.[16] George Hamid, the owner of the Pier, made an even bigger investment in the city's movie business two years later, when he purchased four theaters—the Colonial on Atlantic Avenue, and the Strand, Virginia, and Warner on the Boardwalk. "The key factor" in this decision, the public amusement entrepreneur told the local paper, "was a rebirth by Atlantic Citians in their hometown."[17]

The next summer—the summer of 1956, when Marilyn Monroe starred in *Bus Stop*—turned out to be the high-water mark for Atlantic City's cinema business. Just after the crowds went home in September following the annual Miss America Pageant, the wrecking ball knocked down the Earle Theater to make way for a parking lot, a development repeated again and again over the next two decades.[18] At the same time, the Warner, the Versailles of Boardwalk movie palaces, began to show signs of wear and tear. From the time he bought the theater, Hamid practiced fiscal restraint, as if he was waiting to see what would happen. Under an arrangement with the previous owners, he agreed to change the theater's name. Yet rather than buy a whole new marquee, Hamid saved money by transposing a couple letters, calling the thirty-year-old theater the Warren. When things didn't turned around quickly, Hamid moved to cut his losses. He eliminated two-thirds of the theater's seats and started to book live acts like Ricky Nelson, Mel Torme, and Ella Fitzgerald. At one point, he had the chance to bring Elvis Presley to the Warren, but thinking that no one would pay good money to hear someone named Elvis, he turned down the offer. Searching for other ways to generate earnings, Hamid began to stage Broadway previews at the theater, reviving an Atlantic City tradition that had waned. But this strategy didn't work either. Patrons complained that they couldn't hear the actors' lines. Designed for movies, the Warren turned amplified voices into garbled noise. But Hamid's real problem wasn't acoustics; it was the first signs of a drop in tourism in Atlantic City.[19]

By the winter of 1960, the Warren lay vacant, its marquee dark at night. City leaders complained that the building once tagged the "Wonder Theater of the World" now represented a business-draining eyesore. After months of wrangling about what to do, Hamid applied for a permit to raze the entire structure except for the front façade. "We feel very sad about tearing down this beautiful showplace," Hamid said, "but there is nothing we can do about it. We have tried everything for the past four years, but it wasn't a practical building for a private operation."[20] Several business leaders thought about buying the building, but in the end, they all agreed with Hamid, that it was too expensive to operate. Eventually the owner of the Steel Pier sold the old theater to a bowling company.[21]

In the summer of 1963, teen idols Frankie Avalon and Annette Funicello went out on the road to promote their new film, *Beach Party*—"It's What Happens When 10,000 Kids Meet on 5,000 Beach Blankets."[22] Along the way, cameras flashed as they tossed a few frames to celebrate the opening of the Boardwalk Bowl on the site of the old theater. Apparently no one noticed the irony of film stars marking the destruction of a movie house. Behind the Warner's facade now stood thirty-four fully automated bowling lanes. But even they would not last.[23]

The Warner's closing was just the start of what was to follow. Between 1960 and 1970, the city's movie business lost its mass audience and fantasy feel. Throughout the decade, most theaters still opened on Good Friday and played first run films until the weekend of the Miss America Pageant, just after Labor Day. But the crowds steadily shrunk, creating fiscal problems for the Boardwalk and Main Street theaters. Providing a luxury experience at a middle-class price required constant upkeep and a steady stream of people going through the turnstiles. Crystal chandeliers and marble sinks needed daily polishing and scrubbing. When gate receipts dropped, the owners cut back on repairs and skimped on improvements. Because of the theaters' showy appearances, the signs of decline were glaring and obvious. Peeling paint and broken air conditioners made a mockery of the movie houses' productions of splendor.

When the Apollo Theater, located on the Boardwalk, opened in 1934, it exuded the up-to-date lavishness typical of the city's theaters. The owners equipped the 1,700-seat auditorium with a new Western Electric sound system. Even more impressive, they promised patrons a perfect seventy-degree temperature no matter what time of year it was. "There is not the slightest possibility of deviation from this mark," they boasted, "because automatic 'policemen' do nothing else but watch that one point." Along the walls, designers installed a florescent mural of Apollo standing with Virgil, Plato, Socrates, Homer, Aristotle, Dante, and Shakespeare. When the lights dimmed, the painting took on another life. A yellow moon rose up over the luminaries of Western thought, making them look like three-dimensional wax figures. Twenty-five years later, however, the cooling system rattled and Dante need a little touching up, and the Apollo gave up pretending to be a grand theater. In the early 1970s, the movie house changed its name to the Apollo Burlesque Theater. Each night strippers shared the stage with "baggy pants comics." The days of the first-run movie in Atlantic City were running out.[24]

By the time the Apollo turned into a burlesque house, those couples who used to walk to the movies couldn't help noticing the changes on the Boardwalk. Each summer when visitors opened up their shore houses or checked into a hotel, they saw that another restaurant or shop had gone out of business. Again and again, in the late 1960s and early 1970s, Boardwalk jewelry stores closed, and T-shirt shops took their places. Some of the new stores crammed their front windows full with shirts emblazoned with Mickey Mouse and Charlie Brown in sexually suggestive positions. Borrowing from carnivals, some placed loudspeakers in front of their shops blaring messages about ninety-nine-cent sales and two-for-one specials. Others hired pushy barkers who badgered passersby about unspeakable bargains. Tripping over T-shirt displays and hot dog wrappers, *New York Times* correspondents started to complain about the Boardwalk's "crass vulgarity," while locals feared that the city had lost its middle-class sheen and become a replica of Coney Island.[25]

It didn't take long for the changes on the Boardwalk to make their way over to Atlantic Avenue and its theaters. One by one, in the late 1960s and early 1970s, the movie houses along Main Street either went out of business or lost their middle-class audiences. The Liberty, which had been the Astor, closed in 1969. Four years later, a discount furniture store owner bought the Shore and turned it into a parking lot. About the same time, the Center cut back its schedule, opening only for the summer season. Then in 1976, the Center and the Capital went under for good.[26] The handful of other downtown movie theaters still operating rotted from neglect. Porcelain toilets and sinks turned an ugly shade of yellow, stuffing oozed out holes in worn-out red velvet seats, and book-sized chunks of paint dangled from the walls. On-screen, a few theaters continued to show blockbuster films, like *M*A*S*H* and *Love Story*. But others, like the Embassy, started to specialize in slasher flicks, Kung Fu movies, and blaxploitation films aimed at the emerging consumer publics of teenagers and African Americans.[27] Catering to yet another crowd, in this case the male only crowd, other Atlantic Avenue theaters like the Beach and the Hollywood began featuring X-rated and XXX-rated motion pictures running on a loop twenty-four hours a day. By 1970, *The Curious Female* and *Cherry, Harry, and Raquel* played in the same picture houses that had once featured *The Philadelphia Story* and *Singing in the Rain*.[28]

Most middle-class residents and tourists saw the theaters' new offerings as clear, unmistakable signs of decay. When a local group complained that Atlantic Avenue picture shows no longer presented anything for kids, a couple of cinema owners agreed to revive the tradition of showing Saturday children's matinees. But not many, it seems, came for the Hollywood's screening of *Godzilla vs. the Thing* and *The Time Traveler*, so the once regal theater and the ones nearby pulled the G films and went back to showing pornographic and B movies from morning to night.[29]

The decay of the downtown movie scene moved in lockstep with the decline of the middle-class public realm along Atlantic Avenue. Nightlife— the backbone of the public entertainment industry of the past—depended on a careful balance of density, a sense of safety, and the production of fantasy. Yet as the theaters shut down and changed their marketing strategies, they took away the lights, sounds, and energy from Main Street. With fewer people on the streets, stores and restaurants closed earlier, even on Saturday nights. Then some shut down altogether. Paralleling what was happening on the Boardwalk, with each passing year in the late 1960s and early 1970s another venerable Atlantic Avenue shop went out of business or moved out of town. With commerce in retreat, stores laid vacant for long stretches. When the family-owned Shirt and Tie Shop closed, for example, the building remained unrented for over a year.[30]

With department stores and small shops closing, taking people off the sidewalks, the few middle-class patrons who did come downtown to see a film hustled back to their cars when it was over and raced home. They no longer lingered to shop or grab a sandwich. Increasingly shopkeepers were not around, either. In the past, many merchants lived above their stores, but as businesses closed and nightlife disappeared, more and more shopkeepers moved to other parts of the city and surrounding areas. Without customers milling around, storeowners locked up before dark and turned their shops into fortresses. The few window shoppers left had to peer through thick metal gates. German shepherds barked back at them as they glanced at shoes and cabana wear. The dogs and bars replaced the eyes of the street, the free-form dance of people that the influential urbanist Jane Jacobs has argued kept traditional mixed-use urban areas, like Atlantic City's Main Street, safe and alive.[31]

As growing numbers of people stayed away from Atlantic Avenue, the street started to look dead and lifeless, but as the snarling German shepherds made clear, it also started to seem dangerous. The world of going out to the movies—like the rest of the public entertainment industry—depended on trust and a sense of safety. Atlantic City, by the late 1960s, could no longer reassure theatergoers.

On the Boardwalk, there was still some life. The Strand still showed first-run films in its slightly shabby auditorium in 1970. (A few years before the Virginia had been torn down in the city's urban renewal campaign.) Conventions still came to town, but after 1970 they brought delegates without fat expense accounts.[32] While the mass gatherings of free-spending teamsters and doctors met in Miami Beach and Las Vegas, penny-pinching evangelicals and blue-collar Shriners in gaudy fezzes came to Atlantic City. In the early 1970s, the Eastern General Conference of Charismatic Revival brought thirty thousand born-again Christians to the motels, hotels, restaurants, and movie houses of the "nation's playground." The president of the Atlantic City Convention Bureau wasn't impressed. "We had the Charismatics on the Boardwalk," he scoffed, "buying hot dogs and sleeping five to a room at very low rates."[33]

Standing next to the faithful in line at the food stands were women and men wearing those cheap T-shirts for sale along every block of the promenade. Couples in their opera clothes started to stand out on the Boardwalk. Mink-collared sweaters got harder to find as each year the well-dressed crowds thinned, especially after dark. Many visitors now came just for the day. They drove into town, parked, changed into bathing suits in the public bathrooms, ate sandwiches they had brought from home, and then left before dark. Overnight visitors started to stay in their rooms watching TV, rather than risk a chance encounter with disaster or someone unfamiliar. "I don't see as many people on the Boardwalk at night anymore," noted a local commentator. That was bad news for the movie house owners and others in the public entertainment industry.[34]

Explaining Flight

Just about every picture house in town was within walking distance of the three hundred block of Melrose Avenue. In 1955—the high point of the city's movie business—white families occupied every house on the street. The next year, when the Earle Theater was turned into a parking lot, a black man, Jacob Downing, and his family moved into a house in the middle of the block. Someone planted a "crude five foot cross" on Downing's lawn to welcome him to the neighborhood. Others tossed rocks through his windows. Most, however, protested with their feet. By 1961, Downing had only one or two white neighbors. The rest bolted to the virtually all-white suburbs located downbeach or offshore. The pattern of black settlement and white flight was repeated again and again in the postwar era as African Americans desegregated the city street by street, movie theater by movie theater.[35]

The picture shows followed Downing's neighbors to the suburbs and away from African Americans. As early as 1950, the Atlantic, the area's first "open air drive-in," started showing films in a field ten miles west of the city, not far from several burgeoning all-white residential developments. With speakers and parking spaces for nine hundred cars, a playground with swings, a merry-go-round, pony rides, and a bottle-warming service, the new drive-in looked like a one-stop entertainment center for baby boom parents. At the same time, it was a safe extension of the living room. Customers watched films encased in their cars. They didn't have to rub elbows with strangers in the dark if they didn't want to. Private, convenient, and centered on the automobile, the drive-in hinted at the quieter, less public entertainment world to come.[36]

When the Atlantic Drive-In first opened, there were few other businesses around. By the time the Warren became the Boardwalk Bowl, ten years later, the area near the drive-in had changed. Nearby stood Keningston Furniture's new home. For two generations, the Grossmans had sold bedroom sets and love seats to families from far and wide from their showroom in the heart of Atlantic City's central business district, near the Hollywood Theater. But in the late 1950s, looking for more space and parking and perhaps sensing the changes to come, the family opened a store in the suburbs.

Keningston was one of the first businesses to flee the city.[37] Not long after the furniture showroom left Atlantic Avenue, construction began on the area's first enclosed mall. Located across the street from the Atlantic Drive-In, Sears Town opened in 1967 with more than half a million square feet of retail space, making it the area's largest shopping facility. By 1973, the mall's annual sales had reached $35 million, equaling revenues on Atlantic Avenue. Trying to capitalize on that success, the Philadelphia-based Steinberg's department store chain opened a branch at the mall in May 1974. The new mall had no trouble finding other tenants as well, including companies selling entertainment.[38] Within a few years, a multiscreen movie theater with a huge parking lot opened next to Sears Town. The furniture store, Steinberg's, and the cinemas were all chasing after white flight to the growing suburbs of Northfield, Linwood, Absecon, and Somers Point.

Local residents, longtime tourists, commentators, and historians have developed all kinds of explanations to account for the flight of middle-class families—both residents and tourists—from the city and its theaters. Some will tell you that the hotels declined to the point at which, after 1965 or so, no respectable person would stay in them.[39] Others have pointed to air-conditioning as the cause. "It's always been my contention," wrote a

Philadelphia journalist, "that air-conditioning killed Atlantic City." From its earliest days, Atlantic City marketed itself as the "lungs of Philadelphia," as a healthy escape from the grime, soot, and stickiness of summer in the city. "Here at the shore," one man remembered, "you'd get the cool breeze, and you could always take a dip in the ocean." But with window units pumping thousands of BTUs of icy air into newly built suburban homes, the beach's cool breezes were less of a draw than before. Others blamed backyard swimming pools for Atlantic City's demise.[40] Like air conditioning, pools robbed Atlantic City of its natural advantages. With cool water close by, this theory posits, middle-class families felt less compelled to leave home and the security of the suburbs to go to Atlantic City and mix with strangers and possibly criminals.[41] Yet another explanation focuses on air travel. According to this theory, when airlines cut prices in the 1960s, middle-class families jumped at the chance to get further away than ever before. Only those, then, who couldn't afford to fly—by definition not the right kinds of people—came to Atlantic City.[42]

But most people stopped coming to Atlantic City because after 1970 it no longer fit their definition of "a fantasy city." After this, the city did not offer middle-class white visitors something different, exhilarating, and luxurious while insulating them, from the "lower social orders," namely African Americans. The end of segregation in Atlantic City, in other words, accelerated like no other factor the collapse of the city's movie business and larger public entertainment industry.

Beginning after World War II, African Americans launched a multi-front attack on segregation in Atlantic City. For starters, the nation's wartime and postwar prosperity helped to lift many, though certainly not all, African American families out of poverty. Like European immigrants before them, they brought their hopes and dreams to Atlantic City. They came from Philadelphia, Baltimore, Newark, and New York to swim in the ocean, twirl around on the rides, hear the jazz singers, and escape the grind of their day-to-day lives. Some of these African American tourists, inspired by the civil rights movement, refused to stay at small, black-owned, un-air-conditioned Northside—that is, segregated—hotels. They wanted to be close the action on the Boardwalk. Beachfront hotel owners at first resisted, but eventually gave in and rented rooms to African American women and men. As they changed their racial policies, they put even less money back into their properties than before. Hotel owners, it seems, did not value their new African American customers. They saw them as symbols of decline rather than as members of a new, potentially lucrative market to be exploited.[43]

As the racial makeup of the Boardwalk changed, local activists in the

NAACP, CORE, and the Afro-American Unity League hammered away at the segregation of the city's public facilities. One by one the walls of separation came crumbling down after World War II. According to local legend, in the late 1940s, Miss Sara Washington, the owner of a national beauty school chain, demanded service at Hackney's, a famous Boardwalk seafood restaurant. After hushed discussions, the owners served her the lobster dinner she ordered. Other African Americans followed Washington into the restaurants and clubs. Next came the assault on residential segregation. Beginning in the 1950s, African Americans, led by fire fighters and other municipal workers and professionals, began moving into formerly all-white areas. Then in the 1960s activists concentrated on gaining equal employment opportunities. Bowing to pressure, Atlantic Avenue supermarkets and department stores, and Boardwalk hotels and hot dog stands, eventually agreed to hire African American workers.[44]

Because the movie theaters were so central to the city's racialized fantasy landscape, they were one of the last bastions of segregation to fall. Led by Horace Bryant, New Jersey's first African American cabinet officer, local civil rights activists in the late 1960s launched a protest campaign against segregation at the movies. The Atlantic Avenue theaters were the first to bow to the pressure, allowing African American patrons to sit wherever they wanted. The Boardwalk palaces followed soon after.[45] By 1970, African Americans could sit on the right or left side of the Virginia and the Beach, and in the crow's nest or near the orchestra pit at the Strand and the Lyric. Yet the triumph against segregation turned out to be something of a hollow victory.

Within a decade and a half, Atlantic City did not have a single movie theater still in operation. The picture shows followed white families to the suburbs. During the first wave of flight following the war, many young white families, some taking advantage of the GI Bill, left the city in search of larger lawns and easier parking.[46] By the 1950s, however, most white women and men were not chasing green space; they were running away from African Americans. The change happened quickly. Many white property owners saw African Americans as invaders, as the advance guard of crime and falling property values, and blamed them—not manipulative, blockbusting real estate agents or the drop in tourism—for neighborhood decline. At the first sight of people of color, scores of white families headed out of town.[47]

The same fear of contact with "the black threat" that drove white families out of Atlantic City kept tourists away from the Boardwalk, beach, and the movie theaters. Playwright Martin Sherman's remarkable character Rose clearly understood the link between race and flight. Born into a shetl in the Russian backcountry, she ended up in war-torn Poland and somehow survived the brutal liquidation of the Warsaw ghetto and the daily assaults of a concentration camp. From there she made it to America and into the arms one of her liberators, the fresh-faced, American Jew, Sonny, whose father runs a beach chair concession in front one of the Boardwalk hotels. After a rare neurological disease seizes her husband, slowing his speech and motion, Rose takes a job running the Majestic, an aging boarding house by the beach. Year after year, the same guests stay at the hotel. At night, she watches with a cool detachment as they go out on the Boardwalk decked out in mink coats and frilly hats to ride the rolling chairs and watch the Ice Capades—"an ice show," Rose explains, "that spent each summer in Atlantic City and was thought exotic because ice-skating was one of those useless things that only goyim did." But all of a sudden, these "fortunate" Jews, as Rose called them, are gone. They left, she argues, because "there were now black ghettos surrounding the hotel strip, and since victims of prejudice seem susceptible to the disease themselves, Atlantic City just packed up and moved to Florida."[48]

Philadelphia columnist Bruce Boyle's grandmother joined the exodus to Florida. After her Atlantic City neighborhood became, in Boyle's words, "blacker and poorer," she ran to St. Petersburg "to play pinochle and talk [with new friends] about places like Atlantic City they had left." Boyle knew that the tourists fled for the same reasons as his grandmother. "It was many years ago," he wrote in 1981, "when technology and racism began to kill this place." Air travel, Boyle maintains, "made it possible to get to nice warm beaches in exotic places." Television showed longtime Atlantic City visitors pictures of clear blue water and sandy white beaches. The ad men were, Boyle noted, "careful to show only white people on these exotic beaches," and the suburban audiences bought this clever ruse, even when it was used to sell Jamaica. Yet the suburbanites knew all about Atlantic City. "Atlantic City," these people who had filled the seats at the Warner said to themselves, "had black people, thousands of them." Even worse, Boyle reported, white Philadelphians thought that Atlantic City blacks "were getting cranky, too."[49]

Few white visitors made the connection between race and flight as explicit as Rose and Boyle did. Some mumbled about "black criminals," turning, in their minds, every black man into a potential mugger or crook. Business leaders, meanwhile, spoke off the record about how they thought the new wave of black visitors to the city hurt "the white tourist trade, driving business to the smaller, quieter, whiter resort communities up and down the South Jersey coast."[50] Most tourists, however, spoke in a code. Asked why they had stopped coming to Atlantic City, many said something to the effect that the place was not what it used to be and that different people, not such "classy" people, were coming down to the shore in the 1960s. What they seemed to be saying was that Atlantic City no longer reassured them or engaged their sense of fantasy. In its heyday, the sons of Italian ditch diggers and the daughters of Jewish tailors dressed up in linen suits and cashmere sweaters and came to Atlantic City to say that they had made it in America. Making it in America, they believed, meant being rich and white. Atlantic City's architecture of fantasy—its movie theaters that intimated Egyptian ruins—allowed the children of immigrants to imagine for a moment what it felt like to be rich. Segregation fueled the fantasy. Away from work on their Atlantic City vacations, these people, who had no servants at home, sat back and let uniformed black waiters, busboys, bellhops, and maids wait on them and indulge them. Clearly, as Rose understood, these same Jewish and Italian families who had been victims of past prejudice—restricted, for instance, from most of Atlantic City's grandest hotels before World War II—seemed to be aggressive practitioners of a similar brand of racist exclusion.[51] Once African Americans gained access to the beach and the Boardwalk and the movie theaters in the 1960s, white families packed up and headed for Miami Beach and other "classy"—meaning white—resorts. Integration, they might have said, was fine, but you did not want to vacation with them. How, they must have wondered, could you pretend to be rich and have made it in America in a place that excluded no one?

By 1970, longtime tourists had abandoned Atlantic City. Tax receipts from hotels and conventions were falling. New building in town had virtually stopped. As these signs of deindustrialization set in, the city's population dropped by 25 percent, from 66,000 in 1940 to 48,000 in 1970.[52] Those left behind were overwhelmingly poor and increasingly African American and Puerto Rican. Unlike their parents, city residents in the 1970s lived in a desegregated public realm. People of color could stay at any hotel or eat at just about any restaurant. The ten tattered and aging but still open theaters on Atlantic Avenue and the Boardwalk sold tickets to anyone willing to pay and let them sit wherever they wanted. But in one of the crueler ironies of modern U.S. history, the vibrant public entertainment industry of the past disappeared once segregation ended. The crowds were gone from the Boardwalk and the picture shows were dank and sad. The city's public entertainment industry, in other words, was desegregated, but it had lost its shine and its ability to thrill.

Things only got worse for the city in the early 1970s. Each year, another movie house in the city closed down, while a new theater opened in the suburbs. The new picture shows were little more than steel-and-glass boxes, with projectors and popcorn stands, stuck in the middle of parking lots. They were bereft of style or whimsy or fantasy. But it did not seem to matter; suburbanites chose to stay close to their new homes rather than chance an encounter with people of color or the poor downtown. That left the Boardwalk to smaller and more obscure conventions and Atlantic Avenue merchants with little or no business at all. Things got so bad in Atlantic City that locals grimly joked in the early 1970s, "Will the last person out of town please turn out the lights?"

The Gamble of Reindustrialization

The proponents of casino gambling promised to revive Atlantic City. They vowed to bring back jobs and tourists. They pledged to return the city to the old days of the Steel Pier, the grand hotels, and the Warner Theater. They promised to make Atlantic City into a seashore version of Disneyland. But mostly, they promised deliverance from the ravages of deindustrialization.

Not all the promises were lies. On May 26, 1978, Resorts International Casino opened its doors to a throng of eager gamblers and anxious onlookers. Soon the crowds and the rolling chairs, and even Frank Sinatra, were back. In its first seven months of operations, Resorts earned a whopping $134 million. Today there are a dozen casinos in Atlantic City, and over the past twenty-five years, they have taken in more than $55 billion in earnings. Together, the casinos employ more than fifty thousand people, and pay 68 percent of the city's total tax revenues. Investment in the city over the last two decades exceeds the total investment over the same period in the state's four other largest cities combined. As a result of the casino boom, Atlantic City has become one of the two or three most popular destinations in the United States.[53]

All these people and all this money, however, have not saved Atlantic City. Almost in defiance of all economic logic, despite the gobs of wealth generated by the casinos, the city seems more decrepit than ever. In many ways, the lure of slot machines and blackjack tables further unraveled the city's urban fabric. Once again, the fate of the city's movie business underscores these larger trends.

Several months before Resorts opened in May 1978, a Long Island developer bought the Hollywood and Center theaters along Atlantic Avenue. He promptly razed them to make room for a huge parking lot. There was talk of building a one-hundred-million-dollar "megastructure" complete with a hotel, office building, television production studio, and movie theater on the grounds of the old theaters. Yet nothing ever came of these grand plans. The destruction of the two movie houses left the city with three screens on Atlantic Avenue and three on the Boardwalk.[54] The night that Resorts opened, the Strand on the Boardwalk played the 1970s classic *Saturday Night Fever.* The Virginia and the Apollo Burlesque Theater were also still open when the dice started to roll. However, by the time Resorts celebrated its one-year anniversary, all the Boardwalk showplaces had closed.[55]

The last picture shows along Atlantic Avenue died right along with the Boardwalk showplaces. The Embassy closed in 1978, the Charles sometime in 1979. That left only the Beach. For years, the Beach had survived— barely—as an adult movie house, with a liquor store on one side and a check cashing outlet on the other. But it too closed down. The building caught fire in November 1983. Some suspected arson as the cause of the blaze.[56] Whatever the reason, the theater's owner decided not to fix the building. Apparently, he concluded that there were not enough people willing to go out at night or leave the casinos for a couple hours to make a downtown movie house profitable. That meant that, beginning in 1983, Atlantic City, home to ten casinos and host to tens of millions of visitors each year, did not—still does not—have a single movie theater.[57]

Commentators pointed to the Beach Theater's closing as a symbol of Atlantic City's grim fortunes as a gambling town.[58] Despite all the jobs and casino revenues, Atlantic City was, they insisted, in many ways, worse off than ever. At least before, the city still had some quality stores on Atlantic Avenue, a few fine restaurants on side streets, and a handful of movie theaters, albeit aging ones, scattered in between. Five years after Resorts International opened, the city's locally owned, noncasino businesses were rapidly disappearing. "The central business district is a shambles," a local retailer complained in 1986. "There still is not one movie theater."[59]

Steven P. Perskie, an Atlantic City lawyer who as an assemblyman wrote the legislation that brought gambling to town, marveled at the seven billion dollars the industry poured into the city. The money, he said, exceeded his wildest expectations. Yet, he recalled, "We had this notion of a spillover effect that didn't happen." But again, it was not because of a lack of money. Between 1978 and 2000 the city's twelve casinos have generated, according to Robert Goodman, the director of the United States Gambling Research Commission, "over $1 million for every man, woman, and child in the city." "No city in history," he continues, "has had that kind of money poured into it. Now look at what exists, what it accomplished. There are parts of the city that look like Bosnia. To me that's the measure of it."[60]

While creating new jobs and new streams of revenue, the gaming industry hastened the decline of Atlantic City's public realm. The casinos lured millions of people back to town, but few went out on the streets. This stems in part from the nature of gambling itself. Betting, even in a public place like a casino, is an essentially private activity. Most gamblers drive to town, park, eat at the buffet, and play the slots or the tables. Six hours later, they climb back into their cars and drive home. In between, they focus with laser-like intensity on winning. Perhaps a gambler will talk to a friend or a stranger in the buffet line, but gambling does not generate a great deal of casual interaction. No casino, moreover, wants its customers on the Boardwalk rampaging through souvenir stands or out on the town watching a movie. It wants them standing at attention stuffing five quarters at a time at ten-second intervals into video poker machines. Atlantic City's casinos, like all grand casinos, have no clocks or windows. The owners do not want gamblers to know what time it is, how long they have been shoving quarters into machines, or whether the sun is out or not. They want disoriented players fixed on the game and they have been largely successful.[61] But their success does not—or has not—translated into urban renewal. Within blocks of Donald Trump's gilded Atlantic City wonderland, the Taj Mahal, lie some the poorest and starkest streets in all of the United States.

What the Atlantic City gamble does demonstrate is that casino owners are shrewd businesspeople, not social engineers or urban planners. Gambling proponents promised Atlantic City residents economic salvation, but the slot quarters and blackjack dollars have not brought deliverance. The city continues to suffer from alarmingly high rates of crime, drug addiction, teen pregnancy, and infant mortality. According to a 1989 CBS poll, a majority of Atlantic City residents would not vote for casino gambling again if given the chance.[62] A waitress at a local diner born and raised near the Boardwalk complained: "People who were scrubbing pots for $3 an hour signed petitions to bring casinos in. They are still poor. They are still scrubbing."[63] Underscoring this harsh assessment, *Money* magazine, in its 1988 survey of the best places to live in the United States, ranked Atlantic City dead last, behind Buffalo; Gary, Indiana; and every other place in the country.[64]

Lisa Johnson, a former casino spokeswoman and local television news anchor, offered a different assessment of gambling's contribution to the community. "We now have a cultural infrastructure," Johnson, who was born in Atlantic City, bragged in 1998. "When I was growing up here, there were no museums, maybe two movie theaters, no playhouse, and certainly no bookstore. . . . Now we have museums, multi-screen theaters, an Equity playhouse—everything that any major suburban community has, plus a thriving resort." In twenty years, she concluded, "we've gone from a cultural wasteland to an interesting, stimulating great place to live."

Johnson delivered her appraisal of Atlantic City's history from a Starbuck's coffee bar inside a Borders bookstore located twelve miles west of the city, next to the Macy's department store anchoring the mammoth Hamilton Mall.[65] Location is crucial here. Gambling has had the most dramatic and most positive impact on Atlantic City's suburbs. While the city has rotted from neglect, losing hundreds of shops and restaurants, and all its movie theaters, the communities around Atlantic City have thrived. Northfield, Somers Point, Egg Harbor Township, and the other suburbs are where the growth has taken place and where the movies now play.[66] Today, while Atlantic City remains without a single cinema, there are nine screens across from the Kenington furniture store, now the size of an entire strip mall. Outside of Sears Town, now called the Shore Mall, a fourteen-plex stands in a massive parking lot. About ten miles away, in Somers Point, the Village Cinema presents four movies nightly. Down the street from the Hamilton Mall and Borders bookstore, a new theater complex with stadium seating is under construction. While suburban movie houses premiere the latest releases every Friday, plans for an Atlantic City movie theater have repeatedly fallen apart. No investor or casino seems willing to build a theater that will take people away from the gaming floor for two hours at a time. They are betting their future instead on video poker machines—what one industry analyst has called the crack cocaine of gambling.[67]

Casino operators' desperate desire to keep players glued to "Joker's Wild" machines, however, does not fully explain the failure of Atlantic City's reindustrialization. While the city's fall from grace started with the end of segregation, its rebirth has been stalled by the refusal of most people—especially white middle-class Americans—to live in integrated spaces. In an all-too-familiar story, scores of longtime white residents bolted to the suburbs at the very moment when civil rights activists desegregated public facilities. White tourists, meanwhile, stayed at home or headed elsewhere—in some cases, to the essentially segregated shore towns south of Atlantic City, like Avalon and Stone Harbor, both of which still have movie theaters. Yet the casino owners seem to pretend that race does not matter. Following the lead of the builders of Baltimore's Harbor Place and New York's South Street Seaport, the architects of the new Atlantic City have tried to erect theme parks, like the Wild, Wild West, on top of a city that once had shops and buses and noise and people. They argue that more hotels, a bigger convention center, taller parking decks, and larger, more intricately themed casinos—essentially, unfettered consumer capitalism—can cure the city's ills. According to this increasingly popular model of urban renewal, suburbanites will heal the cities by traveling downtown not to live, but to visit for an afternoon or a weekend. The money they leave behind is supposed to trickle down to the poor. But this has not worked in Atlantic City or anywhere else it has been tried.[68]

Clearly, for cities to grow and resuscitate their public spaces, they need for people not just to work and visit; they need families and individuals to be there all the time, walking the streets, shopping at corner stores, and going to the movies. They need, in other words, density and activity. No city will be rebuilt until policy makers start to value energetic urban spaces and encourage people—through imaginative housing and business-incentive programs—to return to the cities for good. Before department stores and downtown theaters will reopen, families and individuals, especially white families and individuals, must show a willingness to abandon their private cocoons in suburbs and get past the racism that led so many to flee from the cities in the first place. Reinvigorated and integrated urban spaces are a potentially invaluable public resource in our racially fractious society, for, as Michael Sorkin argues, cities "based on physical proximity and free movement . . . [are] our binding agents . . . [and] our best expression of a desire for collectivity."[69]

Conclusion

Today the Warner's facade remains just about the only trace left in the city of its movie business past. The outlines of this once grand temple of cinema stand on the Boardwalk as a silent monument to Atlantic City's glory days, to the troubled era of segregation, to the wrenching limits of desegregation, and to the false promises of urban renewal through gambling. No matter how stringently the new casino tries to deny the past, the Warner remains a hushed witness to Atlantic City's industrial past, sad deindustrialization, and even sadder reindustrialization.

Like Camden and Patterson, New Jersey, Atlantic City became quieter and then more run-down as its business base moved South and West. Throughout the 1960s and 1970s, corporate board members, their eyes fixed on spreadsheets, relocated their companies to the sunbelt in search of cheaper labor, lower energy bills, and sweetheart deals with tax-starved local governments. Their decisions threw countless U.S. communities into chaos and despair.[70] But in Atlantic City, no single individual or band of accountants triggered the city's slide into deindustrialization. Unlike cities in the Northeast and Midwest with rusting shells dotting their landscapes, the "Queen of Resorts" did not lose its businesses all at once. In 1970, despite the start of white flight to the suburbs, some of the Boardwalk hotels, restaurants, clubs, arcades, and amusement piers were still there. There were still shops on Atlantic Avenue. And there were still a half dozen movie theaters in town. It was the people—the tourists—who went south to Miami Beach, Bermuda, and Disney World, and west to the Grand Canyon, Yellowstone National Park, and Disneyland. Deindustrialization came to Atlantic City, in other words, as a result of millions of individual decisions to bypass the Boardwalk. That's what makes Atlantic City's decline so vexing, so complicated, and in the end, so sinister. It reflects the refusal of so many white middle-class Americans to live or vacation or even go out for a night in desegregated public spaces.

Part II

ENVIRONMENT

CHAPTER 4

Greening Anaconda

EPA, ARCO, and the Politics of Space in Postindustrial Montana

KENT CURTIS

My father used to say that golf was the most capitalist sport—
it used more land for less reason than any other.
ORLANDO OZIO in *Primary Colors,* 1996

From the dusty parking lot behind the Cedar Lanes Bowling Alley at the north end of Cedar Street in Anaconda, Montana, it is a short climb up a path that once led to the municipal dump. For years, residents had backed their trucks and station wagons up to the foot of this path, hauled their waste to the crest of the hill, and thrown it onto ground that once held the Lower Works smelting facility of the Anaconda Copper Company. The Lower Works had been closed since 1900, when the consolidating copper interests in the region constructed a state-of-the-art smelter, the Washoe Reduction Works, three miles away across the narrow finger valley. Since the 1950s, Anaconda Copper had allowed the city to dispose of household waste in the corner of the ruins. Cresting the hill on a summer afternoon these days, however, one does not find the piles of old newspaper, random appliances, and endless humps of black and green plastic that once covered the ground. In their place, and for as far as the eye can see, are the rolling greens of a new eighteen-hole golf course. Where smelters once belched and residents once threw their trash, golfers can now pay forty dollars to play a round on one of the nation's newest professional courses.[1]

The course is striking, even beautiful. To honor the industrial history of the town, designers left the weathered ruins of the nineteenth-century smelter and many of its by-products in place, including a pile of jet black slag large enough to hold the seventh tee on its crest. The fairways cut slivers of green through the otherwise dull reds, grays, and browns of the smelter remains jutting out of the cliffs. Black slag sand traps offer even starker contrasts to the polished greens of well-watered fairways. The Old Works Golf Course, as it has been named, rests like an island of chlorophyll amidst the pale yellow bunchgrass of the semiarid Deer Lodge Valley. Cheryl Beatty, Anaconda's city manager during the planning and construction of the course, counted it among the most beautiful sites she had ever seen, boasting that Jack Nicklaus had tested the unique black slag sand traps and said that they were better than the traps at Pebble Beach.[2]

Costing $30 million—$1 million of which paid the designing fees of Jack Nicklaus's Golden Bear International—and encompassing more than two hundred acres, the Old Works Golf Course is supposed to help carry Anaconda, Montana, into the twenty-first century. City planners have pinned hopes for economic growth on its potential to draw tourism, telling the community to gear up for a significant piece of the West's growing service economy. The Atlantic Richfield Company (ARCO), which paid for the project, said that the course itself will begin to net the city an additional $250,000 a year by 2006, never mind the additional dollars golfers will spend in the city's shops and restaurants. Such assertions put local boosters into a frenzy in 1997, when the course opened to the public. Echoing the language used by course marketers, the Billings *Gazette* crooned at the development: "The course rises like a Phoenix from the ashes of nineteenth century economy, and puts light in the eyes of players and Anaconda residents alike."[3]

But, as its description and the weight of hopes pinned on it suggest, the Old Works Golf Course is not just another developer's expensive gamble, or merely an effort by a small city to build a recreational magnet. It is also, and more importantly, a technological, legal, and economic construction designed to solve several layers of problems at the same time. It is in fact one part hazardous waste dump, one part image maker, one part investment, and one part social work. Course promoters and city boosters would like visitors to look at the Old Works Golf Course and embrace the rural ideal that such landscapes often evoke—rolling pastures, purity, and leisure. It is intended to place Anaconda on a short list of communities containing world class golfing facilities. Even a cursory step closer, however, befuddles these intentions. Indeed, instead of locating Anaconda within a growing number of resort towns that cater to the new tastes of American recreationists, the Old Works Golf Course locates Anaconda within two seemingly unrelated processes of historical change, and is the unintended outcome of the intersection of these processes. It is the material inscription of deindustrialization and environmental concern as they played out in this former mineral district.

The course is contained within the nation's largest Superfund complex and is a functional part of the remediation effort. (See figure 4.) The greens and fairways grow atop earthen caps covering some 250 acres of smelting waste. Gauges and piping, embedded in the caps, electronically control saturation levels, turning on and off sprinklers and channeling excess water into holding ponds on the course itself. While the exposed slag is relatively inert, thick plastic lines the bottom of the black slag sand traps as a precautionary measure. The golf course is designed to contain the dangerous heavy metals spread throughout the former smelter site, to keep it from

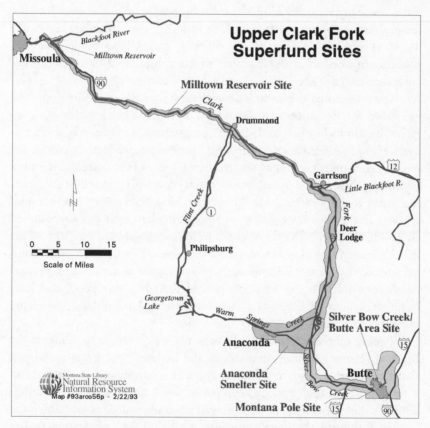

FIGURE 4. The golf course site is about 250 acres, or 1/24 of the segment of the Superfund site located in and around Anaconda, which itself is only a part of a Superfund complex that stretches all the way from Butte in the east to Missoula in the west. Courtesy of the Montana State Library, Natural Resource Information System.

seeping into water supplies, dispersing into regional ecosystems, or impacting the health of Anaconda's residents and visitors.[4]

Legally, the course has taken this segment of the ten of thousands of acres of polluted lands owned by ARCO off the Superfund list. With the completion of the course, the land has become "remediated" and thus no longer bound by the strict liability components of CERCLA, the technical acronym for the Superfund law. ARCO has done all it needs to do in order to be absolved of responsibility for the toxins and hazardous waste that remain in the soil. And, in fact, they are now the property of the town itself— unless something goes wrong before 2006.[5]

Economically, the course has come to symbolize the rebirth of the smelter city. As the *New York Times* somewhat incorrectly put it in 1997, shortly before the official opening of the course, "This company town without a company is not looking toward copper to breathe life back into the languishing economy. . . . It is looking at golf." Town planners, Environmental Protection Agency (EPA) officials, and ARCO public relations officers expressed a harmonic praise for the indisputable ability of this development to energize the local and regional economy.[6]

These contours beg us to look even closer, to ask what stories the site embodies for the history of deindustrialization. What legacies are contained within its bunkers and greens? The sequence of events *seems* to follow a Horatio Alger narrative. In 1980, the Washoe Reduction Works, the heart of Anaconda's economy and the centerpiece of the Anaconda Copper Company, then owned by ARCO, closed its doors for good. By 1983, mining had ceased in nearby Butte. Altogether, more than twenty-five hundred workers in the region were directly impacted when their employer closed shop, and thousands of others whose businesses depended on those wages felt the crunch as well. Property values plummeted. In Butte, younger miners left the city for work elsewhere, while many old-timers dug in. In Anaconda, one-third of the residents packed their bags for good, and local business evaporated. The city of Anaconda buckled under the destabilizing pressures of deindustrialization.[7]

Twenty years later, the city of Anaconda appears to be standing on the brink of recovery from its devastation and hopelessness. Promoters boast that the smelting town will bloom again as a participant in the tourism economy, the fastest growing segment of the American West's economy. There is the golf course, lined with walking trails and signs explaining the history of the site, the most prominent symbol of the new Anaconda. But plans are also underway to complete a city park around the gigantic smokestack across the valley from the course. The 585-foot masonry smokestack is the last remnant of the Washoe Reduction Works and, to retired smelter

workers, a proud symbol of the city's heritage. (See figure 5.) It is visible
from I-90, more than six miles to the north. In Anaconda, bicycle and camp-
ing stores, and fast-food restaurants, accompany dreamy neighborhoods of
parallel streets and lurching maple trees. The city bills itself as "The Gate-
way to the Pintlars," a small wilderness area whose peaks can be seen from
the town. Having redesigned sidewalks and leveled streets downtown, de-

FIGURE 5. The 585-foot-tall smokestack standing alone above the town of Anaconda is
reputed to be the largest free-standing masonry structure in the world. If city engineers
can assure its stability, community planners would like to create a park around its base.
Photograph by the author.

signed a more friendly entry point with signs and banners, and spruced up its visitor's center, Anaconda has all the appearances of a rejuvenated community.

But the history of this place and the details of these events are much more complicated and contested than the simple rags-to-riches narrative would suggest. This chapter is an attempt to reveal something of that contest. It borrows from a number of historical approaches. Environmental history informs the conceptual spatialization and localization of the story. In that emphasis there already exists a long tradition of considering the various material connections and material conditions among individuals, their environment, and their society—"where" something happens is not just a name on a map, a conceptual abstraction, but it is a real, physical, dynamic, living place.[8] The history of technology likewise sheds light on these circumstances. Technologies, whether they be roasting ovens, management strategies, or golf courses, are neither inevitable nor neutral. We need to understand technologies for the human artifacts that they are, for their tendency to embody goals and reflect and reinforce culture, and for the social order they imply. We need to see their normative intentionality, not for the vision, but for the outcomes.[9] This study also borrows tools from Kent Ryden, who suggests that every place is defined by its outward inscripted landscape and layers of personal and subcultural meanings written invisibly across those inscriptions. Often more powerful and always more meaningful than the obvious symbols on the land, these invisible landscapes often open the door to the politics of place. This chapter seeks these invisible landscapes through conversations and interviews with dozens of participants in the recent transformation of Anaconda.[10]

In the end, Anaconda, its claimed recovery, and its unusual golf course offer a rich study of the transitions involved in deindustrialization and the unforeseen outcomes of environmental policy. It provides a lens with which to view the multifaceted meanings that emerged not beyond, but literally amidst, the ruins of the mining industry in the American West.

Deindustrialization in Anaconda

The collapse of Montana's minerals industry in the early 1980s mirrored economic changes that had been rippling across the nation for several years. One by one, community by community, the stalwart industries of the United States' rise to global dominance—steel, oil, automobiles, electronics, textiles, primary metals—found their U.S. investments too expensive, risky, or otherwise undesirable. Some of these industries were suffering from excessive overseas competition and found they could not survive. Others sought the larger profits to be had employing cheaper overseas labor and operating within unregulated policy regimes. The founding scholars of deindustrialization, Barry Bluestone and Bennett Harrison, argued that greedy corporate managers sought to "restore, or preserve, rates of profit they had become accustomed to in the halcyon days of the 1950s and 1960s." While this assessment is partly true, it may be more accurate to say that United States corporate managers mobilized their capital internationally in order to find the social and ecological context of the turn-of-the-century United States. Whatever the causes and goals, the results of deindustrialization were widespread, disruptive, and transformative to U.S. society, as some 6.8 million jobs simply disappeared between 1978 and 1982.[11]

Overseas competition, rapidly declining ore reserves, and a shift in the material infrastructure had combined to stagger the United States' mining industry in the late 1960s. But many companies continued to stay afloat as untimely investments from the oil industry delayed, but could not halt, the pattern of collapse. The oil industry had become bloated with cash from the combination of the Organization of Petroleum Exporting Countries (OPEC) oil embargo and the subsequent discovery of rich new oil fields. Oil company managers believed at the time that they could use this money to revive the lagging metals industry. They mistakenly thought that a minerals mining operation was essentially the same as an oil mining operation; they were confident their business skills would transfer. The result was widespread change in ownership across the American West, as metal-producing corporations that had reigned for three-quarters of a century in the region were purchased by the giants of the oil industry. Following this pattern, in 1977, ARCO invested profits from a huge oil discovery in Prudhoe Bay, Alaska, in the Anaconda Copper Company, which by that year included mines, reduction facilities, refineries, rolling mills, and distribution networks stretching from Perth Amboy, New Jersey, to Los Angeles, California.[12]

For more than a century, "The Company," as the metal giant was known in its genesis state of Montana, had shaped the social conditions of Anaconda. The city had been planned alongside the original smelters by Marcus Daly, the West's last great practical miner, in 1880. Between 1880 and the first decade of the twentieth century, the Irish dominated both the working and the business class. Mirroring nearby Butte, Anaconda developed as one of the United States' strongest Irish working-class communities. After the 1907 consolidation of the copper interests in the region, the Irish dominance gave way to a more mixed, southern European enclave of workers. While the early ethnic connections between Daly and his workforce had given Anaconda Copper workers a sense of self-confidence, the new corporate managers sought control over, not alliance with, their workforce. The company exerted almost total control over the mining and smelting community. They owned all of the state's newspapers, the amusement park in Butte, the water company, the electric company, the street car system, the major retailer and hotel, the lumberyards, and most of the forest lands around the city. Anaconda Copper's peak production years came during World War I, when munitions demand brought full production in the region for three straight years; this was followed by a very slow decline. From the 1920s to the 1960s, the Anaconda community settled into a fairly stable rhythm of work in the factory, and social life in the vibrant downtown of movie theaters, saloons, barber shops, and bookstores.[13]

The sale of Anaconda Copper in 1977 was met with a mixture of trepidation and hope. The company had been trimming its workforce, selling off its non-metal-related holdings, and lowering its production in Montana since the mid-1960s. For a decade rumors had swirled through the mining town of Butte and the smelting city of Anaconda that the end was near. When Salvadore Allende nationalized the Chilean mines after his election, including Anaconda Copper's crucial open-pit mine in Chuquicamata, and Augusto Pinochet failed to reprivatize the same following his murderous coup, the Anaconda Copper Company tottered on the brink of bankruptcy. When news of the corporate sale in 1977 reached the Montana communities, the gloom temporarily lifted. ARCO officials promised a revitalization of operations, fresh injections of cash, and a return to the steady productivity of the two decades following World War II.[14]

Predictably, as in many of the metal industry towns that had undergone similar changes in corporate ownership, the promises of an industrial future in Anaconda soon proved hollow. First, ARCO discovered that petroleum mining and hard-rock mining were entirely different technical, economic, and management problems. Compounding the difficulties of the learning curve was the fact that Butte's ores had diminished dramatically in quality since the Anaconda smelting facility had last been overhauled, making another complete overhaul necessary; the company faced significant additional expense if it wanted to continue producing copper in Montana. Nor did the cost of labor in Montana's union-strong communities provide the oil company with much economic incentive to stay. ARCO had, in more ways than it could have anticipated at the time, purchased a lemon. On September 30, 1980, just three years after purchasing the copper giant, and in the middle of a protracted labor struggle, the fateful announcement was made: smelting would cease once and for all in the city, and the smelters would be disassembled and sold for scrap. For ARCO, this was a necessary move; corporations do not invest in that which does not bring them profit. Anaconda Copper could no longer guarantee profit. ARCO managers were so ashamed of their reversal that they forced the longtime plant manager, a resident of Anaconda, to break the news to the smelter workers after the ARCO managers fled the town in a helicopter.[15]

The closure meant sudden and radical disruption in the community of Anaconda. One thousand striking smelter workers awoke jobless on October 1. The impact of this unemployment rippled out across the community in the following weeks. Local merchants began cutting pay and hours, if they did not close altogether. By December, most local businesses had laid off an average of 20 percent of their workforce. "The closure was devastating to the community," Anaconda city manager Cheryl Beatty remembered in 1996. "Every other store was empty. We lost a lot of jobs and six million dollars from the tax base." During the dark months of early 1981, unemployment lines and food stamp rolls lengthened. Residents and laid-off smelter workers, unwilling to risk their future in the evaporating town economy, accepted up to 30-percent losses on their homes and moved elsewhere. The smelting city began a rapid disintegration under the centrifugal force of industrial collapse.[16]

Poisoned Land

Deindustrialization in Anaconda would be accompanied by another force of change whose presence would make the plant closure in Anaconda unlike plant closures in so many other communities around the United States. At the same time that company managers were debating the future prospects of Anaconda's smelter, legislators in the United States Congress were debating the merits of a new law intended to close the loopholes in existing hazardous wastes legislation. Since 1976, hazardous wastes in the United States had been monitored from cradle to grave under the Resource Conservation and Recovery Act (RCRA), a law that forced companies to identify their wastes and dispose of them in a federally approved landfill. RCRA also allowed the federal government to compel companies that had previously disposed of hazardous wastes in an unsafe manner to clean up their wastes. But RCRA could do nothing in cases in which a responsible party could not be found. This shortcoming became painfully obvious in the wake of Love Canal, and by 1980 congressional Democrats had forged a bill to deal with it. It passed Congress, and on December 11, 1980, just seventy-two days after the smelting works was closed in Anaconda, President Carter signed the Comprehensive Environmental Response, Compensation, and Liability Act (CERCLA), commonly known as Superfund, into law.[17]

Superfund created a tax-based cleanup fund (ironically for Montana's corporate situation, linked predominantly to taxes on oil production) that was to be used for hazardous waste cleanups in areas for which responsible parties could not be found. Congress, wanting to spend tax dollars on hazardous waste cleanup as a last resort only, also included provisions in the law for the EPA to attach liability for abatement to present owners of land, whether or not they had owned the land when the mess was created. While initiation of these processes and enforcement of the law was complicated by the deregulation initiatives of the Reagan administration and stonewalled by Rita Lavelle—the EPA's overseer of the RCRA and CERCLA programs—the law had a profound effect on Anaconda during the 1980s.[18]

In December 1981, one year after President Carter signed the Superfund law, well-water samples in Milltown, Montana, 120 miles downstream from Anaconda, were found to contain dangerous levels of arsenic. At first health officials took core samples of nearby earth to see if they could discover the source of the toxic heavy metal. Some theorized that a previously undetected vein of the rare mineral had been leaching into the wells. Others suggested that an old dump containing arsenic had been buried beneath the town unrecorded. But their searches turned up nothing. Milltown residents were slightly less surprised than the health officials to find their wells were contaminated. They had known for years that something was wrong with their water. "You sprinkle the lawn and the next day it's just bright red," one resident told the local newspaper. "The whole side of the house turns brown from where the water splashes." Like the health officials, residents had no idea where this pollution was coming from. An active environmental health agency in the city of Missoula eventually alerted the federal government and preliminary investigations determined that the arsenic had come from smelting wastes that had collected as sediment behind the Milltown Dam. Armed with the Superfund law, the EPA launched an investigation of the entire industrial mining complex in Butte and Anaconda as well as its river drainages as far west as Missoula. By 1983, Anaconda, Butte, and the Milltown sediments were listed on the Superfund National Priorities List as the largest single Superfund site in the nation. Almost immediately, one-third of the land area in the city of Anaconda was fenced off or otherwise restricted. At the same time, these lands acquired their new legal status: they were lands legally in need of ecological remediation, and whoever owned them was responsible. With one fell swoop, ARCO, which had been slowly but surely extracting itself from Montana, became responsible for the recovery of the community's lands.[19]

The benign intention of the Superfund framers—to protect land, air, and water in the United States while insuring that citizens' health was not compromised—was not viewed as such in Anaconda. Superfund's immediate economic impact on the community was very much like a second wave of deindustrialization. Homeowners who had not left with the first wave of economic collapse found that they could now not even sell their houses for a loss. No one was buying potential Superfund property lest they be charged for its cleanup.[20]

If this impact did not completely erode Anacondans' trust in the intentions of the federal government, the EPA's next move did. In addition to fencing and creating restrictions, the Superfund listing turned the powerful eye of federal science onto the health risks posed by the identified wastes. In 1985, following the procedures of the statute, the EPA requested that the Centers for Disease Control (CDC) investigate a small subdivision just east of the Washoe Smelter site. They were concerned that the concentrated heavy metals that would have fallen under the smoke plume of the former smelter might pose a risk to the residents of this subdivision. Through urine sample analysis, the CDC determined that the forty families living in the Mill Creek subdivision were in fact dangerously contaminated with arsenic. In May 1986, the CDC ordered the immediate removal of small children, pregnant women, and elderly adults—those at greatest risk—and recommended the abandonment of the town and the relocation of the rest of the families. By 1988, everyone had been removed and the houses demolished. A large share of the properties had been purchased by ARCO, and the remaining families were forced to move by the federal government. "It kind of sent a message," Charlie Coleman, EPA's site manager, reflected about the impact of the Mill Creek evacuation on the community: "[Is the EPA] going to come to Anaconda next, or Opportunity?"[21]

The Mill Creek evacuation not only alienated the EPA from local residents, it also sullied Anaconda's reputation outside the community, interfering with any hopes for economic recovery on its own. According to Jim Davison, president of the Anaconda Local Development Corporation, the Mill Creek closure frightened potential visitors to Anaconda. "People would literally drive into the community with their windows rolled up, coming in, getting gas, and saying, 'We have to hurry up and get out of here before we die.'" The Superfund law, aimed at environmental protection, in effect aggravated economic wounds that were already festering, bringing on more harm than good, as far as Anacondans could tell. For the community, this was a period of extreme disempowerment. As ARCO and the EPA, two enormous and economically powerful institutions, struggled to define the pollution and assign responsibility, Anaconda residents were left standing helplessly on the sidelines.[22]

Turning Brown into Green

Throughout the mid-to-late 1980s, labor advocates, community organizers, and scholars decried the painful impact of deindustrialization, or plant closure, as they called it at the time. Moderate critics claimed it was a necessary evil whose effects might be tempered through better cooperation between labor and managers and more forward-looking job training programs. The left called for legislation controlling businesses' ability to shut down, especially when they represented a significant share of a community's jobs. Proposals ranged from all-out bans on closures themselves to required prior notification (six months to a year) of an impending closure. Some activists even designed manuals with strategies for workers to monitor company behavior in order to determine whether a plant shutdown was imminent.[23]

In the same years, a host of different critics began to target the Superfund program. Within Congress, Superfund supporters and framers claimed the program did not go far enough, that it had not accomplished its cleanup mandate, and that too much time had been spent trying to sidestep its provisions rather than fulfilling them. Environmentalists made similar claims, arguing that millions, if not billions, had been spent during the decade, but only four sites had been cleaned up. Scholars who analyzed the program itself came to two related conclusions. First, they said, Superfund money had been wasted on legal expenses and research work attempting to identify and hold responsible the parties who owned the land or were liable for the pollution. Additionally, they found that the strong arm of Washington and the EPA had ignored, overlooked, or simply run roughshod over the law's provisions for community participation, failing in almost all cases to include local voices in their plans and decision making.[24]

While neither group of critics saw any common interest or connection with the other—throughout the 1980s, economic concerns and environmental concerns were still considered to be antagonistic—the groups influenced the national climate within which ARCO and the EPA operated as the 1980s came to a close. Without a doubt, the groups shaped the actions, reactions, and decision making of ARCO and the EPA during the 1990s. Curiously, however, the forces that changed the direction of economic collapse and environmental destruction were—from the perspective of Anaconda planners and boosters—wholly local. City Manager Cheryl Beatty, for example, remembered the Mill Creek evacuation as the key unifying event for the community, and the first powerful force behind changes in the EPA and ARCO activities in the region. It had led citizens to organize a community group, Beatty recalled, which then began to press the EPA for new kinds of solutions. She remembered that they demanded that the EPA remove the fences that marked off huge chunks of land as toxic zones and contributed to the generally negative image of Anaconda as a toxic community.[25]

Jim Davison remembered similar forces changing the EPA and ARCO. "By the late 1980s," Davison said, "we began asking, 'How are we going to attack this thing?' And that's sort of where the idea for the golf course came from." At the heart of the pollution problem was a valuable opportunity, Davison said; it was a matter of approaching the problem the right way. In a delicious twist of irony, the very land that had plagued the community suddenly appeared to be just the sort of local amenity the new approach required. According to Davison, during a planning meeting in early 1990, Gene Bukovich, a retired smelter foreman, jokingly suggested that the old works site be turned into a golf course, and the idea suddenly caught fire. Davison agreed that up to that point community participation in Superfund activities had been sadly lacking, and suggested that the existence of a vocal group of citizens could provide the impetus for new policy decisions at both ARCO and the EPA.[26]

In fact, the involvement of local citizens fit seamlessly into the EPA's mandate to begin paying more attention to local concerns; at the same time, it provided ARCO with a crucial tool in its efforts to escape Montana as cheaply as possible. "We not only lost an incredible amount of money while we operated the company," ARCO site manager Sandy Stash admitted. "Since then this has been nothing but a hemorrhage."

Until 1990 ARCO had been fighting the EPA and the Superfund law, but around 1990, Stash remembered, ARCO began to use a new tactic— soliciting and incorporating the views of the community. As the 1980s came to a close, the community's desire for economic recovery, a natural response to the devastation of deindustrialization, fed the new strategy of ARCO.[27] It is not entirely clear whether what became known as the MESS Committee—the active Anacondans who sought the public participation process of the EPA and sought economic development instead of fences—bubbled up from grassroots sources or was encouraged to life by local representatives of ARCO. It is clear that very quickly the group's energies were amplified and channeled by the oil giant. After Gene Bukovich jokingly floated the idea of the golf course, the whole tenor of ARCO's presence changed. Their resistance to any cleanup and consistent challenges to the solutions put forward by the EPA disappeared with respect to Anaconda. ARCO became a model environmental citizen. By 1991, the oil company had signed an agreement with the EPA to clean up the arsenic flue dust that had caused the evacuation of Mill Creek. By the end of 1992, ARCO had paid for the removal of the most dangerous material found in and around the operable unit that was to become the golf course, including beryllium, cadmium, and high concentrations of arsenic, burying the waste in plastic-lined pits near the giant smokestack. They also came up with several million dollars in assistance for Anaconda to launch a planning process.[28]

Prior to the initiation of this process, ARCO was facing a potential cleanup unprecedented in its scale. To effectively abate the old works site, some 220 acres of heavy-metal-laden ground, would involve the treatment and removal of almost a million cubic yards of material. Prior to the golf course idea, ARCO argued that their work should consist merely of removal of the most toxic metals followed by covering the site with an earthen cap. Critics charged that this would amount to a cheap, Band-Aid solution that would prevent the metals from running into the creek every time it rained, but would do little to prevent the seepage of the same metals into the region's aquifer.[29]

It is no surprise that ARCO leapt at the opportunity when the golf course idea emerged. A golf course could easily be built atop an earthen cap; it fit their desired solution perfectly. Because the idea had presumably come from the community, it also gave ARCO leverage with the EPA to forward its capping proposal. And because the end was an economic development project, the golf course idea gave ARCO leverage with the community: unlike the EPA, with its policy of fences, ARCO desired to leave behind a valuable economic property, an idea that community planners immediately embraced. "We tried to approach things on a win-win basis," Cheryl Beatty said. "The community has attempted to do this as a partnering effort to make sure that the community comes out OK and at the same time in the end it has benefited ARCO." According to EPA site manager Charlie Coleman, this option also promised to improve the EPA's reputation in the region. "By 1987, we weren't very welcome in the town," he remembered in 1996. "Now our credibility is good. They've realized we're not there to hurt them, you know, we're there to help them."[30]

With the financial assistance of ARCO, the community embarked on a planning process in which it was encouraged to imagine the ways the golf course could lift the city out of the worst ravages of deindustrialization. "We're planning trail systems to increase tourism," Beatty said in 1996, "and sprucing up the entrance to Anaconda, getting park and commercial, the residential as well as business areas looking good." The ARCO-funded vision document from which Beatty's description is derived contains drawings depicting the before and after effects of the golf course. In the before pictures, streets are empty, storefronts are barren and drab, sidewalks are decrepit. In the after drawing, not only are stores in full activity and good repair but trees line the sidewalks and people are strolling everywhere.[31]

In the months prior to completion of the golf course and its opening to the public, events looked promising to city planners. A publicity campaign had landed stories about the new course in the *New York Times* and several nationally known golfing magazines. Beatty bragged about the promising new businesses, like RDM enterprises, which used the black slag left over from smelting for sandblasting, or the ARCO foundry that produced custom metal fabrication and casting for industries in the northern Rockies. She boasted of the role the planners played in other promotional activities. "When he called to ask about the area," she said of a recent new business, "we outlined our vision document as well as our planning document, the direction the community was heading with the trail systems and the amenities we're implementing. He saw this as a good place to open a new business." She paused dramatically. "A bicycle shop!"[32]

On its opening in 1997, the Old Works Golf Course became the symbolic center of the new community. It embodied the hopes for economic recovery of the city boosters. Planners spoke of it as a magnet that would draw new people to their community, perhaps even draw back the residents who had left so many years ago. For the EPA, it was described as a model Superfund cleanup, a textbook example of community participation and corporate cooperation. For ARCO, it was the beginning of a slow retreat from the region, the first significant piece of Superfund property that the company no longer owned. Spending a few days talking with the figures spearheading the golf course left the distinct impression that this was a project that would not—indeed, could not—fail.[33]

A deep faith in the promise of the golf course lay in its seeming naturalness and beauty. Sandy Stash, for example, painted a naturalistic gloss on the golf course technology, arguing that it was "taking what was naturally there and putting it back in a more natural state." Cheryl Beatty went out of her way during a tour of the golf course to kneel over one of the slag sand traps, pick the material up in her hands, and let it trickle back to earth. "Isn't it beautiful, the way it glitters in the sunlight?" she cooed. She and the course engineer had arranged a sunrise tour of the new course, because, as they put it, "It is most beautiful in the morning."[34]

The Invisible Landscape of Industrial Change

Beneath the pomp and glitter of economic recovery and renewed land-scapes there is what Kent Ryden has called an "invisible landscape," a more personal and experiential reading of the changes in Anaconda. Many individuals in the community have not embraced the new industry that has taken hold in the town. Some of them raise serious questions about the ability of the course to do its economic duty. Others dislike the symbolic texture of a golf-based economy. Still others argue that an adequate ecological solution has been sacrificed in the name of development and corporate cost cutting. None deny the need for the community to survive, and all desire a stable economic future for the region. But considering the Anaconda story, and the golf course that remains its crowning symbol, we see an effort that is as much shaped by self-interest, politics, and power as it is by any objective desire to promote local survival or ecological health.[35]

Retired smelter workers see the golf course as only the latest stage in a long process of change that has been alienating them from their place in the community since the early 1970s. For them, the beginning of the end came a full eight years prior to the closing of the smelter, when, in the name of urban renewal, city planners gutted downtown Anaconda. Several square blocks of housing, pubs, and theaters were leveled to make space for a giant downtown mall. Community opposition eventually halted the project before completion, but most of the razed blocks were rebuilt with poured-concrete architecture or fast-food restaurants set in the middle of block-sized parking lots. This "pizzafication" of downtown Anaconda effectively removed many of the familiar places where the social life of the working community had thrived.[36]

The smelter, like the downtown, had been a place where the bonds of community developed. Joe Marusich, a Croation immigrant who settled in Anaconda in the mid-1940s, characterized the meaning of these losses after 1980 in a somber tone. "When I was working up there," he said, pointing in the general direction of Smelter Hill, "I worked in every department—painting. You know, you go paint an office, then you meet all the guys up there, and you meet again downtown. You know practically everybody down there." Urban renewal removed half of this equation, the smelter closure in 1980, the other half. "Now," Marusich lamented, looking out the window of the Old Timers' Club to the bright sunlight of Commercial Street, "I don't know nobody. Just a few older guys."

Some of the workers who stayed in Anaconda after the smelter closed and were too young for retirement found themselves working at the smelter one last time, being hired as part of its wrecking crew. Adding injury to in-sult, George Wyant, a native Anacondan and retired smelter worker, was badly hurt when he fell during this work, cracking his skull, breaking his arm, and losing an eye. Joe Marusich believed he was given a job on the demolition crew only because he hadn't sued the company after his father had been severely injured in a boiler explosion. The crew members undertook their work with a stunned disbelief. Charlie Swihart, the president of the Old Timers' Club, spoke for the group about the dismantling of the Washoe Smelting Works: "We didn't expect it, and the reason that we didn't expect it, and continue to be amazed to this day, is because there's probably only a couple of copper smelters in the United States. And I'd always thought that this one, if anything, they would mothball just in case they needed it later for war or something. I mean, where are they going to get their copper now?" Even by the mid-1990s, the global mobility of capital seemed irrational to local workers.

Unsurprisingly, the men in the Old Timers' Club held a less than favorable view of the new golf facility. To them, it was just another indication of their irrelevance to the new Anaconda, a reminder that it was no longer their town. Nevertheless, they continued to undertake small acts of overt resistance, refusing to be used by golf course promoters. George Wyant offered an anecdote to sum up this predilection. "Last Sunday they had a tour that would take you over there and show you what they've done already." By the summer of 1996, the first nine holes had been completed and promoters were anxious to show off their work and hopefully capture a few photos of former workers admiring the greens. "But me and Al," Wyant said, gesturing to a gentleman across the room, "we went fishing that day." The room full of retired smelter workers burst into a knowing laughter. None of these men had ever golfed, nor did they express any desire to learn. To them, the course was a landscape where wealthier folks than they would play. "We're not going to benefit," Wyant continued, gesturing to the others in the room. "But the town is. The town's going to benefit because people that come here, they're not on welfare if they come here to play golf."[37]

In this respect, Wyant's view of the purpose of the golf course echoed that of Cheryl Beatty and Jim Davison, both of whom claimed that the true deterrents to golf course success were residents, like the retired workers, who were not up for the new economic challenge. Cheryl Beatty stated that ARCO-funded projects, she hoped, would "inject" the community with new kinds of residents—a good thing, given the tenor of the traditional community. Jim Davison, whose job it is to plan for and encourage economic growth in Anaconda, described this critical barrier to recovery, a barrier internal to the smelting community and somehow more insidious than the moves made by ARCO and the EPA. In his opinion, development struggled against an outmoded concept of social relationships. "An interesting thing occurs in Anaconda with entrepreneurial spirit," Davison complained. "We find that a lot of people, they're looking for someone to give them a job rather than create their own jobs." In other words, there were too many working-class people in the community. Central to Anaconda's crisis, in Davison's mind, was not the economic loss or ecological impact that had torn the social fiber of the city, but a particular mentality embraced by the community. The challenges he addressed were individual, not structural, shortcomings. In order to recover, Davison claimed, Anacondans needed to develop a new attitude toward economic growth and learn to build on the amenities the city had left. He wasn't entirely sure they were up for it. While the changing global economy and concern for the environment presented a confusing and often independently insurmountable set of problems for the town, Davison and other boosters not only blamed their own citizens, they welcomed their citizens' replacement.[38]

Another point of skepticism about the success of the golf course emerged from its location in the northern Rockies. Retired smelter workers, local businesspeople, and, surprisingly, even the ARCO managers who had promoted the project were doubtful that the course would be able to sustain itself in the short summer seasons of western Montana. "Golf?" Jerry Hansen, curator of the local historical museum and former smelter worker, asked rhetorically. "In a five-week season?" The owner of a local used bookstore in downtown Anaconda expressed a similar concern. His family-owned business was almost entirely dependent on tourist traffic—the months between Memorial Day and Labor Day outsell the rest of the year several times over—yet he expressed genuine doubt that the course could operate effectively in Montana's climate. ARCO's Sandy Stash, in a moment of unguarded candor, also said she doubted the golf course would help the town recover. "We don't have a climate," she admitted. "This isn't Hawaii." In a region where it is not unusual to experience an early-season snow in August, these concerns appear well grounded. Most of the naysayers believe that city planners have been led astray by the millions of dollars ARCO is pouring into this project, allowing cash to eclipse careful planning.[39]

Also concerned about the disproportionate influence of ARCO dollars are environmentalists from Missoula who have been watching the progress of the cleanup ever since the Mill Town reservoir sediments were discovered in 1980. Peter Nielsen, Missoula's director of environmental health and formerly the director of the Clark Fork Coalition, a local river protection group, said that he supported the redevelopment goals of the project. His concern was that Anaconda had been bought out by ARCO, that the steady flow of dollars—millions each year—into city coffers had caused the planners to loose sight of the underlying ecological dimension of the effort. Environmental protection appeared to be taking a backseat to tourism development. Nielsen said he was in full support of community participation and redevelopment, but, he asserted, "you can still make it into something nice after you have cleaned it up. You don't have to do it *instead* of cleaning it up."[40]

Echoing these concerns are officials from the State Department of Environmental Quality. Andrew Young, a hydrologist for the state of Montana, has been working on projects in Anaconda for the past several years. He argued that the golf course does not fully address the ecological problems at the site. As a groundwater specialist, he was concerned about the flow of toxins into the city's drinking water. Young believed that there was a very good chance the toxins beneath the course would soon be drawn up in wells downstream and pour once again into the region's river system. Young said that, in the rush to cap the waste at the old smelter site, ARCO's engineers left too much toxic material in place. While the system of pipes and drains built into the subsurface below the course was designed to contain water flowing off the hillsides and recycle water used on the course, he argued, it was impossible to keep water from seeping through the soil cap and into the toxins below. According to Young, these ecological problems could have been prevented, but the financial relationship between ARCO and the city prevents such arguments from being heard. The project has acquired such momentum that it has become almost heresy to suggest it won't work.[41]

Young is also concerned that the course has become a lightning rod of sorts, diverting energy and attention away from the more serious environmental threats in and around the community. "All this talk about a golf course and development and it's easy to forget there are three thousand acres of tailings out there that nobody knows what to do with."[42] Indeed, despite all the attention given to the course, and its dominant presence in the cultural and physical landscape of Anaconda, most of the smelting and mining pollution remains to be cleaned up. A look at both the remediation efforts and the remaining cleanup areas seems to suggest that just below the surface, in some cases quite literally, there lurks a complex set of environmental and social issues that the new Anaconda has yet to confront head-on.[43]

Conclusion

Good judgement comes from experience,
experience comes from bad judgement.
GRAFFITI UNDER BRIDGE, Milltown, Montana

The Old Works Golf Course embodies characteristics that have come to define both postindustrial and Superfund communities around the

United States. It has redefined and repackaged its past as a commodity for the future. This is not the fantasy world of Walt Disney; the course contains real slag piles, and real rail cuts on the hillsides. It also contains real heavy metals and real dangers. The course employs RCRA-trained course attendants who will retrieve your ball if it goes too far into the exposed ruins. Golf carts are required to remain on the asphalt paths at all times, lest they speed the erosion of the soil caps where the greens and fairways are planted. Players are not allowed to wear metal spikes anywhere on the course. The plans for a new Anaconda of flourishing tourism proceed without directly confronting the ecological and social realities that linger from the old Anaconda. The worst of the ecological disaster and much of the social disruption await solutions.[44]

As the history of the community shows, the events of the past two decades have been shaped and funded primarily by two national forces, ARCO and the EPA, and neither institution has done well in abiding by the long-term environmental and human health protections intended by the Superfund framers. This is a story of social disruption, environmental engineering, and the unintended ways in which the EPA allowed environmental cleanup and social assistance to be eclipsed by the interests of a corporation and the short-term vision of economic growth. The EPA entry into Anaconda promised to change the character of deindustrialization, and indeed it did. Unlike Flint, Michigan, which continues to struggle with the social misery created by deindustrialization, Anaconda, Montana, appears to have bandaged its old wound and stopped the economic bleeding. But what are the costs for the community that made Anaconda its home for more than a century? And what are the costs for future residents along the Warm Springs Creek and Deer Lodge River watersheds, into which Anaconda's water will drain?[45]

The EPA's failure to consider and mediate the social implications of its decisions left it vulnerable to manipulation by ARCO in the early 1990s. The EPA was so singularly focused on toxic and hazardous wastes that it did not seem to notice it was operating in a social context, and thus it alienated itself from the very community whose support it would need if it was going to mandate a thorough abatement. The resulting community anger, which would have been rightfully targeted at ARCO, or the Anaconda Copper Company, or the thousands of stockholders who gained from Anaconda's loss, was instead aimed at the EPA and the federal government.

ARCO channeled this energy and anger into their own high-profile project, which cost them millions less than an actual cleanup. The golf course also gave ARCO a better image than it deserved. ARCO claimed (and city boosters did not dispute) a paternalistic relationship to the city; it presented itself as a white knight corporation that was willing to save the town from the destructive impact of environmental laws. It would end the dirty reputation of the town. It would replace the ugly smelter site, the Superfund unit closest to the town itself, with a gleaming new golf course. It would return the landscape to nature. It would, in this way, provide an end to the economic slide pulling the town into the pits, and help point it toward the beckoning new service economy in the West. At the same time, it would return local control to the community.

As the discussion above has shown, most of ARCO's image making amounts to an elaborate show of smoke and mirrors, behind which the company slipped out of its legal responsibility and its culpability in the city's economic collapse. The golf course project itself marginalized members of the traditional working-class community, who, like the ruins on the hillside, were mere props to be trotted out when circumstances seemed to demand, but who were otherwise useless to the future of the town.[46] Nor has the promise of repopulating the community been fulfilled. Anaconda's population, which had fallen steadily from its high of nineteen thousand in 1960 to twelve thousand in 1980, just prior to the smelter closure, has continued to fall, from ten thousand in 1996 to a mere ninety-four hundred in 2000. Some of the children of the retired smelter workers joined the construction crews in 1994, 1995, and 1996, but few have found permanent employment on the course, which itself has contributed fewer than fifty new jobs. Nor has an economic boom yet taken hold across the rest of the economy, where unemployment remains at just over 8 percent.[47]

The Old Works Golf Course is a gloss on a fallen community. It is an attempt to re-create the past of Anaconda, shifting the community's industrial genesis into a sanitized historical package, a valuable commodity in the tourist trade. Community politicians and economic development officials hope it will set the town on a sturdy economic foundation, allowing growth. ARCO managers are interested in the savings they will gain by turning these properties over to the city, and taking their first step toward being able to leave the region altogether. It is a landscape manufactured not so much to remedy the errors of the past as to recast them long enough for capital to be mobilized elsewhere. It is the material inscription of a story of deindustrialization.

CHAPTER 5

From Love's Canal to Love Canal

*Reckoning with the Environmental Legacy
of an Industrial Dream*

RICHARD NEWMAN

On a raw March afternoon in the year 2000—driving sleet, dropping temperatures, gray-black skies—the Niagara Frontier's industrial past came to haunt the present. With the first Earth Day of the new millennium approaching, residents of a Buffalo housing development protested toxic waste in their midst. Called Hickory Woods, the neighborhood sat in the heart of industrial Buffalo, where 250 coke ovens once fed the city's sprawling steel industry. When the last steelmaker (L.T.V. Corporation) closed in the 1980s, it sold the property to developers with the assurance that no toxic dumping had occurred. Now, in 2000, residents rebutted this claim with a "toxic tour" for politicians and reporters. The focal point of the day, however, was a guest speaker well known to Buffalo audiences: former Love Canal activist Lois Marie Gibbs. Hickory Woods, she proclaimed, "is another Love Canal." Like Hickory Woods residents, Niagara Falls citizens had lived near a toxic waste dump that they hardly knew about and that public and business officials seemingly did not care to remediate. To make the voices of Love Canal citizens heard, Gibbs continued, the community had organized a protest movement that not only sought redress of their own grievances but pushed governments and businesses to confront the environmental cost of the industrial past.[1]

Over the past decade, environmental scholars have closely reexamined the industrial backdrop of vexing contemporary issues such as smog, sewage treatment, and landfilling. As William Cronon observed in his monumental history of Chicago, "during the second half of the 19th century, the American landscape was transformed in ways that anticipated many of the environmental problems of today." That history of industrial land use, as

112

Philip Shabecoff argues in his survey of American environmentalism, has brought "a new people's army" into being, one struggling "acre by acre, dump by dump" for a cleaner postindustrial landscape.[2] This grassroots struggle, in turn, has reshaped Americans' understanding of environmentalism itself. No longer a movement concerned predominately with nature preservation—stopping rain forest development, saving endangered wildlife, slowing global warming—environmentalism encompasses the fate of postindustrial landscapes, from the siting of hazardous waste facilities to neighborhood struggles for safe playgrounds and schooling facilities.

Love Canal citizens formed one of the first environmental movements organized and run by working people.[3] "Twenty years ago the nation was jolted awake when a blue-collar community uncovered a serious public health crisis resulting from the burial of chemical wastes in their small suburban neighborhood," Lois Gibbs observed in 1998. The community made industrial waste a visible political issue and created a model for grassroots environmental activism that people everywhere could adopt. "The heroes of this new environmental movement are people of every walk of life, every income bracket, every color," Gibbs said of this newer and grittier environmentalism, people "who have banded together to protect their neighborhoods . . . [and the] right to participate in the decision making process of their government."[4] As James Schwab concludes, blue-collar and minority citizens have become "America's newest, most radical, and most committed environmentalists." Love Canal was the "landmark" for this movement.[5]

Yet, while Love Canal remains perhaps the single most famous environmental disaster in American history, it was not a singular event. Indeed, the modern-day tragedy of Love Canal evolved from a longer historical process of industrial ascent and decline along the Niagara Frontier. This history includes longtime industrial success stories—such as the creation of one of the world's leading chemical complexes along the Niagara River— as well as spectacular one-time industrial failures—like the plan to build Love's Canal, an artificial river and waterfall envisioned by a late-nineteenth-century developer. In both cases, the historical bill has come due. Deindustrialization has hit the area particularly hard, leaving many local residents to deal not only with a withering job base but with the environmental impact of years of industrial growth. In fact, western New York still contains such an array of Superfund sites (including both the area surrounding Hickory Woods and Love Canal itself) that in October 2000 the federal government named it one of only a dozen "showcase" regions for brownfield redevelopment in the nation.[6] Recounting Love Canal citizens' struggle against the Niagara Frontier's industrial past illuminates the incredible difficulty working people have had in getting business and political leaders to reckon with a troublesome environmental history. It also illustrates just how significant was the environmental battle of Love Canal citizens.

Love's Canal in the Era of Industrial Dreams

For the families who engineered the Love Canal protest movement in the late 1970s, the very name William Love represented infamy. Love was a nineteenth-century entrepreneur who envisioned creating a model industrial town of over a half million people along the Niagara Frontier. It all began with his plans to build an artificial river and falls that would feed one of the world's largest hydroelectric power plants. Just a few years after he proposed his "Model City" in 1893, however, Love's enterprise collapsed. For a few decades, the partially excavated canal stood as a monument to a failed industrial dream—"a big hole in the ground," according to one early-twentieth-century Niagara Falls resident. Government and industry began using the old canal as a dump site in the years leading into, and coming out, of World War II. Finally, Love's Canal was covered over (visitors often ask where the water is) and the land sold to developers. Between the 1950s and 1970s, Love Canal became a suburban working-class community a half dozen miles from the falls. Its residents believed they shared in the American dream of affordable home ownership. When the dump was uncovered again by investigative reporters and citizen activists in the late 1970s, Love was once again in the spotlight. "Why do we have to suffer?" resident Anne Hillis wondered in 1978. "Because in the late 1800s a Canal had been dug" by a grandiose dreamer, she answered. "It was just a Canal to nowhere," former resident Joe Dunmire remembered.[7]

Not much is known of Love, save that he arrived in Niagara Falls in the early 1890s (probably from Tennessee) with big plans. Niagara Falls was then the center of worldwide attention as industrialists, engineers, and scientists gathered to master hydroelectric power. Love proposed to go beyond any other hydroelectric power design. His artificially constructed "Model City Canal" and falls, Love claimed, would revolutionize industrial production and urban living. His megalopolis would offer free education and free electrical power; it would be free from smoke-clogged skies; workers would be pious and sober; and no matter how much it underwent industrial development, the town would guarantee residents flowing green spaces and parks.

How did Love plan to do all of this? He would build a waterfall of even greater productive power than that built by mother nature. Love's artificial canal would divert water from the fast-flowing Niagara River to an inland elevation nearly three hundred feet high, as opposed to the falls' roughly two-hundred-foot drop. With "Niagara's power doubled," as Love boasted, investors and workers would flock to his Model City. As Love confidently put it, "the plan cannot fail."[8] While some of his contemporaries balked, others viewed William Love not as a land-grabbing villain but as an up-and-coming American industrialist. Edward Williams, a longtime local reporter and industrial agent for Niagara Falls, argued that one could not study the magnificent history of the place without recalling men such as Love. "The Love Model Town project, although chimerical in some of its details, was regarded as quite feasible," Williams wrote in one history of the falls. Of course, Love failed miserably—but according to Williams, Love was part of the critical mass of dreamers who made the hydroelectric power breakthrough possible. "We dreamed of the harnessing of Niagara," he proclaimed in 1916, and "today we see the greatest electrical power development in the world."[9]

William Love hoped to do in Niagara Falls what his successful and well-known contemporaries had done in other cities around the country. This list of luminaries included Andrew Carnegie, who helped transform Pittsburgh from what had been described in the early 1800s as a pastoral frontier town into Steel City; John D. Rockefeller, whose oil-refining ventures turned Cleveland's Lake Erie waterfront into an urban jungle; and Henry Ford, whose sprawling Rouge River automobile plant outside Detroit cut away thousands of acres of prime wilderness for an industrial future. William Love wanted to become America's next Carnegie or Rockefeller.

He chose the Niagara Frontier for two reasons: first, the Buffalo/Niagara Falls region already played a key part in the United States' industrial explosion; and second, the area offered a young outsider the chance to enter the country's industrial race via the cutting-edge field of hydroelectric power. When Love first went to the Niagara Frontier in the 1890s, Buffalo was the world's leading inland port. As an east-west nexus, Buffalo was also the United States' second leading rail center. And industries such as steel, lumber, and grain milling made it the Queen City of Great Lakes commerce. The census of 1900 placed Buffalo eighth among American cities. But what about the area beyond Buffalo? Industrialists like Love viewed Niagara Falls as a natural extension of the region's industrial might. In terms of location, the city offered immense amounts of electrical power to emerging industries. But visionaries also saw Niagara Falls as a place to perfect industrial life. Scores of books and pamphlets predicted a model future in Niagara Falls. One turn-of-the-century pamphlet, entitled "1,000 Temples of Industry," captured this idealism, predicting that a great "dynamic palace over the Falls . . . would make it a capital of North America," with hundreds of factories efficiently running on hydroelectric power. Gone would be the smoky, gray, and dehumanizing environment formerly associated with industrial production. The new electrical world of Niagara would allow the human productive capacity to soar.[10]

Once the great hydroelectric power stations appeared in the last decade of the nineteenth century, Niagara Falls grew at a rapid pace. The city's population topped fifteen thousand in the mid-1890s, and by 1910 it had reached thirty thousand. Immigrants from Italy, Poland, Russia, and various Scandinavian countries settled there, as did African American migrants from the South. Niagara Falls had eleven railroads by the early years of the twentieth century, an advanced system of electric lights, phone lines and streetcars, and one of the nation's most impressive bridges, between the United States and Canada. "Niagara is not just another of the 62 counties of New York," a historian claimed in the 1940s—nor was it just another American city. Through hydroelectricity, it had become synonymous with cutting-edge industry. There were already two power plants on-line (Niagara Falls Power Company and Niagara Falls Hydraulic Power and Manufacturing Company), and plans for at least two other plants in the region. Thus had the hydroelectric revolution in Niagara, Edward Williams declared, "lessened human toil."[11]

William Love's scheme remained the most visionary of all the hydroelectric power plans. "The greatest water power in the world is THE NIAGARA," Love wrote in a pamphlet of 1895. He called the river "[s]o stupendous, that civilized man has hesitated to harness it. But this is a condition of the past; today it is harnessed, and projects are on foot for the creation of half a million horsepower from the Falls."[12] Model City, Love's company newspaper blared in February 1895, also had "an unequaled location." Sitting in the middle of the Great Lakes, it offered access to markets for timber, coal, iron, and ore, not to mention proximity to the majority of the population of the United States and Canada. "The locality possesses every advantage that can be conferred by railroads, waterways, water power, abundant water supply, attractive scenery, a productive country and good climate," the paper concluded.[13]

And because he had so much space (the state legislature granted him access to ten thousand acres, then upped the grant to over twenty thousand acres), Love promised workers land they could not get in any other city. This land-grant policy would limit strikes, for new working-class homeowners would dare not risk their mortgages by walking out on their employer. Love also guaranteed workers access to green space, declaring that development would not overrun nature. "No Lover of the beautiful in nature can fail to realize the impotence of language to portray that which lies in magnificent proportion before him," Love wrote of the falls and Niagara gorge on one occasion.[14]

But nature surely would be altered to accommodate Love's bold vision. In one pamphlet, Love printed photographs of the farmland ripe for urbanization and industrialization. All of this would be utterly transformed, he said, to make way for Model City. "What has been accomplished so far in this favored region," Love observed, "is but the advance guard of capital, enterprise and great undertakings, that in this age of rapid progress will make the Niagara section famous and prosperous as the greatest manufacturing center in the world."[15]

Ultimate success depended on the building of an artificial canal that ended with a more precipitous drop than nature had created. "We are building a Canal," he wrote, "to take water out of the upper and return it into the lower Niagara . . . which will be used to create one of the greatest manufacturing cities in America." Love's artificial canal would be about ten miles in length. Laid out largely over an old Army Corps of Engineers survey for another artificial waterway (this one connecting Lakes Erie and Ontario), the canal would be built in sections, according to Love's planners. As he proudly reported in his company newspaper, "the first sod" was turned on the canal on May 23, 1894, in the village of Lasalle. (See figures 6 and 7.) Love picked an appropriate locale: not only had Rene Lasalle built the first European commercial ship on the Great Lakes here but the Pan-American Exposition of 1901 (planned to celebrate the Western Hemisphere's industrial power) was originally to be held in Lasalle. Between 1894 and 1896, a combination of excavators, derricks, mules, and men dug out two noncontiguous sections of Love's Canal for a total excavation of about one mile. The head of the canal stretched from the banks of the Niagara inland three thousand feet. Built on farmland that had supported pear orchards and specialized livestock, Love's Canal cut a groove eighty feet wide and on average fifteen feet deep. The hundreds of thousands of tons of plowed-out earth became the canal berm that remained visible through the 1930s and 1940s.[16]

Love's Canal went no further than these partial excavations. Love's finances had fallen through by the summer of 1896. New developers held title to the canal, but it was never completed (investors tried unsuccessfully to finish Love's Canal in a different direction). Nor did Model City ever grow beyond just a few buildings. Love himself went on to manage a recently discovered gold mine in Western Ontario, while his canal sat idle.[17]

Why did Love's Canal fail? A variety of factors contributed to its demise, among them a financial panic during the 1890s, the creation of alternating current (meaning that industries did not have to be located right next to the falls), and a belief among an increasing number of would-be in-

FIGURE 6.   Forty men and women gather in 1894 at Lasalle, near the banks of the Niagara River, to "turn the first sod" of Love's Canal. The bearded William Love appears to the left of the man with the shovel. Courtesy of the Buffalo and Erie County Historical Society.

vestors that the existing hydroelectric plants satisfied industrial demands. But Love's unstable investment schemes and Niagara's skyrocketing land prices helped bring down the Model City dream too. Both factors stemmed from the often wild industrial times in turn-of-the-century Niagara. The hydroelectric power plants promised to turn water into industrialists' gold. The commercial boom in Niagara Falls also exploded land prices—from fifty dollars per acre up to three hundred dollars per acre. Love complicated matters by promising almost immediate returns of 100 percent on investments in farmland. He went bankrupt trying to keep pace with his promises. In August 1896, creditors seized what was left of his Model City office—a printing press, some tables, and copies of his company newspapers, which offered a future that would never come.[18] All that remained of his dream was the abandoned canal.

Nature's Fate along the New Industrial Frontier

Even before his Model City plan failed, William Love had stepped into the middle of an intense environmental debate in the Niagara region. In the

FIGURE 7. Nearly a century later, workers remediate the suburban development and former chemical waste dump now known as Love Canal, c. 1979. Abandoned homes appear in the background. Courtesy of the Buffalo and Erie County Historical Society.

late 1800s and into the next century, Niagara Falls played a key role in conservation and preservation movements. The speed and depth of industrial change along the Niagara Frontier spurred citizens to form local and national Save Niagara movements. Indeed, early environmental debate centered on industrialization's broad physical impact on Niagara Falls—the very type of impact envisioned by William Love. By the 1890s, industrialists had imposed a man-made landscape on one whose beauty had been extolled by centuries of poets, nature writers, and explorers. This landscape now contained dense arteries of telephone wire, miles of asphalt streets, railroad tracks crisscrossing every which way, and massive new factories. Even rural communities miles away from the industrializing town of Niagara Falls could see their environment literally being reshaped. J. Howard Pratt, an Orleans County historian based fifty miles from the falls, recalled the "wondrous" laying of the first electricity and telephone lines in his turn-of-the-century world. They symbolized for Pratt the demise of "horse and buggy" days.[19]

Newspapers from around the world covered Niagara's environmental transformation. The wheel pits (which housed the generating penstocks) amazed observers. Photographs showed the pits sinking two hundred feet into solid granite. The diversion tunnel bringing water to and from the power station stretched nearly seven thousand feet underground. To build it, workers excavated three hundred thousand tons of rock and then laid sixteen million bricks. The man-made landscape appeared to be as magnificent as the falls itself. Pictures of the time focus as much on these industrial environments as on Niagara. Yet the rush of enthusiasm for this vernacular landscape did not completely silence concerns about its new environmental hazards. On several occasions, for example, paved-over streets and railroad berms turned rainwater into fast-moving rivers and giant (if temporary) lakes. Still, Niagara's citizens hailed the creation of industrial structures that would, as the *Buffalo Courier* stated, "last for centuries."[20]

Nikolai Tesla, the famed inventor and father of alternating current, offered perhaps the most sweeping assessment of the new industrial age's reshaping of nature. Speaking before investors, technologists, and scientists in Niagara Falls in 1897, Tesla observed that the powerhouses lining the banks of the Niagara epitomized the human triumph over nature. "We have many monuments of past ages," he began; "we have the palaces and pyramids, the temples of the Greeks and cathedrals of Christendom." These relics, he continued, "exemplified the power of man, the greatness of nations, the love of art and religious devotion." But "that mighty unit at Niagara has something of its own, more in accord with our present thoughts and tendencies. It signifies the subjugation of natural forces to man."[21]

Others remained skeptical. In both Niagara Falls and Buffalo, early Save Niagara reformers opposed hydroelectric power plans, which, they argued, would sap the Niagara River of its natural energy. Although Save Niagara movements arose in the 1890s, they flowed from earlier struggles to protect the falls. Following the Civil War, railroads opened the area to more tourists than ever before. With no laws protecting the cataract from profiteers, environmentally concerned citizens organized a Free Niagara movement to protect the falls from vendors and landowners who offered their vistas for a fee. According to an 1882 pamphlet published by a member of the Niagara Falls Association (which sought to create a park at the falls), the natural beauty of the great waterfall was being "utterly ruined." The association prodded the New York legislature to purchase lands surrounding the falls and create a state park or reservation "to wrest the process of degradation now going on."[22]

In 1885, the state assembly responded by creating the first state park in the nation. After appropriating funds and securing land from private owners adjacent to the falls, the legislature hired Frederick Law Olmsted to design the park grounds. New York also created a commission to watch over the new park—which, as it turned out, proved vitally important during the industrial scramble of the 1890s. By that time, disgruntled investors and some state legislators were seeking to overturn the reservation act and exploit Niagara for all its economic worth. With the advent of hydroelectric power, they wondered, why waste valuable space on a park? Reservation president Thomas Welch, along with other members, rallied support for the park and in no small measure saved it from ruin.[23]

The reservation's triumph spurred industrialization's critics to confront the hydroelectric power plans themselves. Going beyond the "Free Niagara" movement (which sought to protect views of the falls, not prevent the cataract's industrial exploitation), a new wave of dissenters worried that hydroelectric power plants would reduce the raging Niagara to a trickle. "The American capitalist is quite merciless to the natural beauty of the Falls," a British newspaper exclaimed, echoing the more radical anti-industrial strains of American nature preservationists. Niagara already appeared "disfigured," the paper continued, the wheel pits and mighty generating plants creating environmental scars on one of nature's most pristine areas. "If the people act, the Falls can be saved," Horace McFarland challenged in the *Ladies Home Journal*. Theodore Roosevelt, a Free Niagara advocate, heeded this call, and, as William Irwin argues, the president "stepped-up federal efforts to pass national legislation limiting water diversion" at the falls. A treaty with Canada came in 1906, preventing further power schemes.[24]

Both the Free and Save Niagara movements were part of the first wave of environmental activism in U.S. culture. By the end of the nineteenth century, conservationists and preservationists had mobilized to protect the environment from the excesses of industrial growth. Conservationists sought to use natural resources more efficiently—that is, they sought to meld environmental concern with industrial growth. As president Theodore Roosevelt himself proclaimed in a 1908 meeting with state governors, if

Americans did not adopt wise use policies, they would exhaust natural resources altogether. Nature preservationists such as John Muir and John Burroughs attempted to protect the American landscape from industrialization itself. Calling nature "the people's cathedral," John Muir blasted attempts to industrialize trees, water, and land. In one of his most famous, albeit losing, causes, Muir opposed the damming of the Hetch Hetchy Valley in Yosemite (to supply hydroelectric power to the burgeoning city of San Francisco). "This grossly destructive commercial scheme has long been planned and urged," he wrote in 1912, "because of the comparative cheapness of the dam and of the territory." Muir accused "the devotees of ravaging commercialism" of having "a perfect contempt for nature."[25]

Turn-of-the-century environmentalism also included progressive reformers who began focusing on the public perils of industrialization, from the "evils" of smoke belching out of factories to the dangers of industrial sludge being flushed into rivers. As Martin Melosi has shown, urban reformers began pressing local and state governments for laws dealing with "problems of epidemic disease, lead poisoning . . . air, water and noise pollution." Many progressives believed that industrial technologies themselves would alleviate environmental degradation. "One of the greatest needs of any community is a supply of good water," Harvard professor and sanitary engineer George Whipple wrote in 1911. And one of the greatest benefits of the industrial era was the creation of "the filter plant . . . [which produces] water that is clean, and acceptable, as well as safe." In Niagara Falls during the 1890s and early 1900s, civic leaders touted their efforts to keep Niagara clean with new filtration systems. In Buffalo, urban reformers sought new smoke abatement codes. The federal Rivers and Harbors Act of 1899 tried to stop lumber mills from disposing of their refuse in rivers.[26]

Despite this increasing consciousness about industrial pollution, progressive-era environmental laws often remained "symbolic," according to Anthony Penna, particularly at the federal level. Indeed, "until the new environmental movement of the late '60s and 1970s," Penna writes, "federal agencies considered [industrial] pollution only when it threatened navigation of the nation's waterways." Public health issues remained state and local concerns. And even then, as John Cumbler has observed, many progressive-era reformers favored a "conflict-free environmentalism": a more efficient running of industrial society, in which governments would intervene in business operations only in cases of the most dire public health threats. Otherwise, reformers called on businesses and governments to strike the right balance between industrial efficiency and environmental concern. Within a few years of passing the Rivers and Harbors Act of 1899, for example, Congress told federal officials to limit their investigations to the most blatant offenses.[27]

In Niagara Falls, early environmentalists had set at least some limits on industrial growth by the early 1900s—that is, as far as that growth's effect on nature was concerned. As William Irwin concludes, the Save Niagara movement had made it unacceptable to use nature "for limitless techno-logical" development. "The Glory of the Falls," as one group put it, must be preserved for the edification and inspiration of future generations. In short, power development schemes would not overrun Niagara's natural landscape. But this brand of environmentalism also had limits. It did not seek to build a mass movement among working people. Rather, both con-servationists and preservationists appealed to people with leisure time, those who might view nature as a release from industrial civilization. In ad-dition, environmental movements closest to working people (such as urban sanitation efforts) were often run by Progressive reformers (professionals or members of the middle class) who spoke on behalf of distressed city dwellers—those people who lived in degraded circumstances and needed someone to take up their cause. Early Progressive reformers, Melosi notes, were not above blaming "certain classes of people for the spread of disease [or] filthy surroundings." Progressive-era environmentalism, he concludes, thus "provides [only] a partial legacy for modern environmental justice movements." Love Canal activists would go a step further, providing an in-depth environmental critique of industrial pollution from working people's perspective.[28]

A Chemical Reaction at the Falls

Love's Canal might have remained a footnote to history had not a series of interrelated events propelled it to environmental prominence during the next several decades. Among the most significant of these occurrences was the phenomenal growth of Niagara's chemical industry during the early twentieth century. By the 1930s, over three dozen chemical makers lined the Niagara River. A 1960 survey found that Niagara Falls was the nation's second-largest producer of chemicals. In short, chemical companies came to define the economy of Niagara Falls. The chemical industry produced explosives for the U.S. government during both world wars, conducted re-search on the atomic bomb during the 1940s, and innovated products such as pesticides and plastics.[29]

No company better exemplified Niagara's burgeoning chemical indus-try than Hooker Electro-Chemical Corporation. Indeed, Hooker's suc-cess story was the flip side of William Love's failure. The Hooker company took its name from founding father Elon Hooker, who started the firm in the early 1900s. Hooker descended from one of New England's proud families—the Reverend Thomas Hooker helped to found Hartford, Connecticut. Trained as an engineer, Elon Hooker later ascended to national prominence as treasurer of Theodore Roosevelt's Bull Moose Party. In 1903, he inaugurated the Development and Funding Company to invest in new industrial technologies. By 1906, he had constructed the company's first major plant in Niagara Falls, one dedicated to chemical production. Niagara's hydroelectric plants offered Hooker cheap and abundant power to produce great quantities of chemicals. During its first decade of operation, Hooker Chemical offered two basic products: caustic soda and bleaching powder. Ironically, bleaching powder became a staple of turn-of-the-century municipal sanitation projects. Elon's brother, Albert, even produced a textbook on the product's ability to tame water-borne diseases such as typhoid.[30]

Although it would face periodic downturns, Hooker Electro-Chemical's fortunes steadily rose. Its first major production jump occurred during World War I when Hooker built the world's largest monochloral benzol plant, producing 1.5 million pounds per month for the U.S. Army. By 1945, Hooker had expanded its product line to nearly twenty chemicals. One of the most important products was "dodecyl mercaptan, which played a crucial role in the race to produce synthetic rubber." With more than a half million pounds of the substance flowing from its plants per month by the early 1940s, Hooker contributed "nearly 50 percent of the total synthetic rubber produced by the entire industry." Years later, President Jimmy Carter would tell Americans that synthetic rubber made by companies like Hooker helped win World War II. "There are other important products," a 1955 company history claimed of the over one hundred chemicals in the Hooker product line: arsenic trichloride, for use in poison gas; chloral benzene for landing flares; and bleaching powder, still "urgently needed for decontamination."[31]

Disposal of these chemical wastes became an increasingly pressing issue to Hooker and most other large-scale producers by the time of World War II. According to J. R. McNeil, the chemical industry increased production by about 2,000 percent in the second half of the twentieth century.[32] "Until Hooker began its wartime production," a federal court would declare in 1994, "it was able to sewer and dispose of chemicals on-site." The vast scale of production made such in-house disposal problematic. Yet flushing chemical wastes into streams—a common practice of the industry earlier in the century—was becoming increasingly unpopular. Another alternative, incineration, was deemed too expensive and still problematic, for it projected particulate matter into the atmosphere. Hooker began searching for landfill sites in the 1940s for what it termed "in-ground disposal." In 1942 it leased and then bought the old Love Canal site.[33]

Until then, the canal had remained the property of Love's original firm. Generations of young children utilized it "as a recreation space," as former resident Joe Dunmire once explained. "The configuration was just an open ditch. There was dirt excavated from the original canal on either shore. Beyond that [berm] was a swampy, bushy area." Griffon Manor, a federal housing project built in the 1930s, stood near "the open Love Canal." "We swam in the canal," continued Dunmire, "and used the swampy area just outside of it for ice skating in the winter. We used the hills along the canal for biking and sledding. We used that area quite a bit." The canal waters were muddy, and murky, "more like a pond" than a running body of water. The bottom gave a little—it was not rocky or firm.[34]

Roughly equivalent in size to ten contiguous football fields and rich in clay deposits,[35] the canal seemed to answer Hooker Electro-Chemical's immediate needs for waste disposal. After securing the property, it drained successive parts of the canal and collapsed the berms, creating a series of dams in between dumping pits. From 1942 to 1954 the company dumped nearly twenty-two thousand tons of chemical refuse there. Amazingly, area children swam in the canal during early dumping. "We did that until you could really smell those chemicals," Dunmire stated. "You couldn't tell from appearances, but it started to permeate the air. It smelled identical to driving past the Hooker chemical plant."[36]

Some Hooker officials registered immediate concern over "in-ground disposal." One executive even wrote that Love Canal dumping "is creating a future hazard." He noted that the chemical DDM, used in synthetic rubber production, had already leaked out of some buried drums and surfaced. Hooker continued filling the canal. As another company official observed, as long as Hooker owned the property (and alone dumped waste there), it would not be culpable in the future. The company finished dumping and covered the canal.[37]

The continued industrial growth of Niagara Falls created still another chapter in the life of the canal. World War II brought the city's employment to an all-time high of forty-seven thousand jobs. Between 1942 and 1944, thirteen thousand workers joined the industrial labor force. The overall population of the county swelled to over one hundred thousand. By the 1950s, Niagara Falls officials were planning to build new schools, pave new streets, and make housing available to baby boomers.

Lasalle, which had been officially incorporated into Niagara Falls during the 1920s, became the focal point of these demographic pressures. In a now infamous land deal, one that would generate long-standing debates over culpability, Hooker Electro-Chemical deeded the canal property to the city school board for one dollar. The contract had two key stipulations: the land on the dump was not to be disturbed; and Hooker would not be liable for any future claims resulting from the breaching of the dump. The land was then transferred to the city in 1953. The school board built the Ninety-ninth Street School on the buried canal and sold the remaining land to developers. Housing units went up over the next few decades and neighborhoods took shape. By 1970, over two hundred homes lined the old canal. According to studies done in the 1990s, over five thousand people lived in the ten-square-block Love Canal area at some point between the 1920s and 1980s. It was, however, the over nine hundred families that lived there during the 1970s that provided the most well-known chapter in Love Canal's history.

The Love Canal Citizens Protest Movement

The citizens who mobilized for environmental justice in the late 1970s changed forever the meaning of Love Canal, transforming it into a symbol of environmental activism. From the summer of 1978, when Love Canal homeowners organized against the leaking dump, through December of 1980, when the federal government guaranteed the purchase of all families' homes, citizen action framed every part of the Love Canal saga, including congressional investigations, presidential declarations of emergency, and state and federal health studies. Without the citizens' movement, Lois Gibbs writes, "we would still be living there today."[38] While protecting their own interests, Love Canal activists represented something larger—an indigenous environmental protest from working people.

By the 1970s, the Love Canal dump was no secret to area residents, although many citizens did not know of its precise dimensions or toxic contents. During the late 1950s and into the 1960s, pungent smells filled the air, barrels laden with chemicals occasionally surfaced, and, on more than a few occasions, fires flared spontaneously from holes in the dump. In the mid-1970s, nature intensified toxic circumstances. Successive rainy seasons and a massive thaw following the "Blizzard of '77" raised the water table to new levels. The buried canal already sat in a poorly drained area, but now more disposed barrels surfaced, chemicals migrated into sewers and basements, and families complained of worse than normal smells. More distressing, an increasing number of families reported miscarriages and illnesses such as asthma, not to mention other serious ailments (including liver and kidney disease). Some residents complained; others felt they were just unlucky. Some local, state, and federal officials actually began examining complaints at Love Canal in the mid-1970s, but they did not move swiftly enough for alarmed residents.

Citizen mobilization brought matters to a head in 1978. In the face of seeming government lethargy (and corporate apathy), resident Karen Schroeder headed initial efforts to investigate the Love Canal dump. *Niagara Gazette* reporter Michael Brown subsequently ran stories on the canal, raising awareness and energizing other residents to investigate matters. Concerned citizens then became environmental activists. They changed local circumstances first, as their public meetings and petition campaigns forced New York State health officials to closely examine the contents and impact of the Love Canal dump. This led to an initial evacuation decree in the summer of 1978: New York State purchased the nearly 240 homes immediately surrounding the covered canal. For the seven hundred families in the surrounding ten-square-block neighborhood, however, state officials offered no such remedy. Citizens fought for two more years until all were evacuated and compensated for their homes.

Formal organizations headed the Love Canal protest movement. The first and most significant group was the Love Canal Homeowners Association, formed in August 1978 and encompassing nearly five hundred families. Led by Lois Gibbs and Debbie Cerrillo, it quickly gained incorporation as a legal entity. The second major group was the Ecumenical Task Force, ETF, which combined personnel from area religious organizations as well as Love Canal activists. Founded in March 1979, the ETF grew to nearly two hundred members. Both organizations had short-term and long-term goals: most immediately, they sought to get all homeowners evacuated from the Love Canal area; for the future, they hoped to raise awareness of the hazards of toxic waste dumps such as Love Canal and to inform other endangered citizens of the efficacy of organizing an environmental justice movement.[39]

Two broader trends framed Love Canal activism—Americans' rising environmental consciousness and deindustrialization. As Samuel Hays famously observed, American environmental politics shifted dramatically following the second world war. Where early movements such as Save Niagara had focused primarily on resource conservation or nature preservation, the so-called new environmentalism of the 1960s and 1970s revolved more than ever around quality of life issues such as clean air, clean water, and access to park space. As the economy boomed after World War II, Americans became increasingly interested in their country's environmental well-being, from national parks to local playgrounds. Membership in organizations such as the Sierra Club expanded during the 1970s; state and federal governments passed a wave of environmental laws; and publishers rushed to print books on the environment. The first Earth Day, in April 1970, heralded what many environmentalists hoped would be a new era of earth-friendly policies.[40]

One major hope of the burgeoning movement was that environmental groups would build a broad-based coalition of citizens that could compel governments and industry to act in a responsible manner. This idealism was captured in *Eco-tactics*, a 1970 pocketbook produced by the Sierra Club. Dedicated to "ecology action," the slim volume called on U.S. citizens "to reverse the horrifying specter of pollution and waste that hangs in the air, seeps into our waters, and destroys our land." As the Sierra Club put it in a blurb, the book provided "a guide to every individual who wants to give earth a chance." Yet outside of advice on holding teach-ins and conferences, the book had little advice for grassroots activists. "There is this to be said of eco-tactics," the book stated; "you won't find it in the dictionary—not yet. Give it time."[41]

Despite the general growth of the movement, American environmentalism fragmented during the 1970s. Working-class activists and people of color in particular came to believe that the major environmental groups cared less about local causes such as neighborhood toxic remediation and more about national lobbying efforts on global nature-preservation issues such as ozone depletion and rainforest destruction. In response, local activists formed their own environmental justice groups. These organizations focused on the daily environmental hazards faced by citizens in inner cities, industrial neighborhoods, and former mining towns—for example, the disproportionate number of toxic waste dumps located in communities of color. Borrowing both language and tactics from social justice movements (in addition to environmental groups), environmental justice advocates sought to speak out for aggrieved citizens who had little political voice or societal influence. "Our movement represented the farmers, workers, and mothers," Lois Gibbs writes of those who felt voiceless in groups such as the Sierra Club or Nature Conservancy, which gathered people largely from the middle-class, professional, and academic ranks.[42]

Deindustrialization also played a critical role in the rise of Love Canal activism. On the one hand, it prompted local activists to think about the decaying industrial landscape that remained after companies began to leave the once mighty Niagara Frontier in the 1960s, 1970s, and 1980s. More than two hundred companies had departed the region by the last decade of the twentieth century. Carborundum Corporation, one of Niagara's signature companies and a leading producer of industrial abrasives, slashed an entire division during the 1980s. Bell Aerospace, which employed twenty thousand workers during World War II, had only 150 employees by the early 1990s.[43] Quite simply, Niagara Falls residents could see the physical toll exacted by deindustrialization, as once thriving plants became hollowed-out versions of their former selves. The hulking Bell Aerospace building—a 1.85-million-square-foot structure dedicated to aviation research and technology—stood virtually idle by the 1980s.

On the other hand, Niagara's industrial downturn haunted Love Canal activists, who were quickly accused of hastening the region's deindustrial skid. Luella Kenny recalled that Lois Gibbs received several death threats, and that other activists became the targets of intimidation. "They believed we were trying to take jobs away from them," Kenny said. Joe Dunmire remembered that some of his neighbors worked at Occidental or DuPont Chemical, "and they didn't want to hear about it." For many residents of the Niagara Frontier (which at one point in the middle of the twentieth century saw over 50 percent of its workforce employed by industry), Love Canal protests seemed to pit jobs against environmentalism—and the latter would always place a distant second. According to reporter Michael Brown, deindustrialization even shaped the local government's response to citizens' complaints about toxic waste. Niagara Falls' "reluctance to address the issue directly," Brown wrote in his celebrated book *Laying Waste*, flowed from "trepidation of a political sort: the fear of distressing Hooker." "To an economically depressed area the Company provided desperately needed employment—as many as 3,000 blue-collar jobs in the general vicinity in certain periods—and a substantial influx of tax dollars." In addition, the company planned to build a new multimillion-dollar headquarters in Niagara Falls, which government officials hoped would stimulate the local economy.[44]

When Love Canal citizens began mobilizing in 1978, then, they stepped into a sensitive arena of deindustrial politics that affected their every activity. Neither that influence, nor mainstream environmentalism's cold shoulder, deterred them. "These people just kept at it," the brother of one activist commented twenty years later. "They were persistent."[45] They also had a conception of grassroots politics that transcended citizens' lack of political clout or economic status. Lois Gibbs has consistently compared Love Canal activism to other twentieth-century social movements that began with a grassroots struggle for justice, particularly those of civil rights reformers and labor unions. "The most valuable assets of grassroots groups are people power and common sense," she writes. With few monetary resources, and facing a political culture attuned to corporate interests, civil rights and labor activists mobilized themselves and then use their grassroots identity to sway society. The ETF agreed with these tactics: in March 1979, it vowed to provide "direct aid" to residents and to serve as a citizens' "advocate," thereby "put[ting] the problem in perspective for the nation."[46]

Over and over, Love Canal citizens emphasized grassroots action as the key to their success. "This was a new type of catastrophe not borne of wind, water, or fire," Pat Brown recalled. "It was mostly hidden beneath the ground." But "residents turned to each other for support," Brown continued, and then pushed the issue into the public consciousness.[47] "The Love Canal is fortunate to have a fine team of residents," Grace McCoulf told Congress in 1979, "who have educated themselves and are able to travel to other areas to lecture on the problems of hazardous waste sites." In short, residents quickly came to believe that they alone had to define, and organize to defend, their environmental interests. No one else would or could. As Lois Gibbs now tells other grassroots environmental activists, "the only thing you have is your story. But your story is powerful."[48]

The protest tactics of Love Canal residents ranged from classic social justice initiatives—such as marches, public demonstrations, and protest essays—to unique methodologies developed during the struggle. In one of the most infamous incidents, activists took two EPA officials hostage to demonstrate their frustration with the slow pace of buyout efforts at Love Canal. In another well-remembered example, residents refused to leave their temporary evacuation locales in the summer and fall of 1979, forcing the state to accelerate permanent relocation plans. Calling themselves "motel people" (a takeoff on the Cuban "boat people"), residents-turned-activists remained in local motels even after temporary funding ran out and state officials warned them that they would be arrested. Citizens stayed put, calling family members and speaking to reporters. "We grew from 2 to 25," Anne Hillis wrote in her journal after the first day of the motel siege. "I began phoning others . . . the press started calling me. I told them we would not return to Love Canal." State officials, she noted, were in a "tizzy" and motel managers complained that they had prior bookings for Labor Day. Soon after, the state legislature passed a resolution to purchase the homes of those not initially evacuated the year before. A year later, however, when state funds proved insufficient for the buyout, Love Canal activists protested at the Democratic National Convention in Atlantic City. Hoping to pressure President Carter into signing a federal relief bill, citizens carried signs, spoke to national reporters, and chanted, "two, four, six, eight, help us before it's too late." By the end of the year, President Carter had signed a final buyout agreement. "We won," Lois Gibbs declared.

Love Canal activists recognized the absolute centrality of the media to their cause. "We had to keep the media's interest," Gibbs argued. "That was the only way to get anything done. They forced New York State to answer questions. They kept Love Canal in the public consciousness. They educated the public about toxic chemical wastes." To cultivate media attention, activists carefully planned events. In one case, residents marched on the state capital in Albany with coffins which they planned to present to governor, Hugh Carey. (SWAT teams checked the boxes for explosives.) On another occasion, residents marched effigies of the governor and other elected officials through the Love Canal neighborhood, chanting, "thanks to New York State, death is our fate."

The citizens maintained a high profile by writing letters, corresponding with activists in other parts of the country, and speaking before community groups, churches, and schools. Scholars and institutions have recently begun collating the prodigious amount of material written and collected by Love Canal activists.[49] Lois Gibbs earned her reputation as a tireless and relentless advocate by pestering state health officials, congressmen, the president of the United States, and even the secretary-general of the United Nations. Gibbs often wrote multiple letters to the same person or agency in a single day. Perhaps her most consistent target was New York Health Commissioner David Axelrod. On May 24, 1979, for example, she issued three separate letters to him on matters ranging from state health tests to citizens' questions about chemical toxins discovered in the canal. "This memo is to confirm our phone conversation last week," she stated in her first letter, reminding Axelrod that he had agreed to send information on toxic waste sites in New York. "I would also like to make a request," she continued, "because of misinformation, gossip, and not knowing which department handles what, many times just not knowing what has and has not been done, I would like to ask if the Love Canal homeowners could be included in the circulation of memos from departments to departments." A second letter of the same day proposed "the creation [of] a central file or library of copies of all information gathered through the Love Canal [health] study. . . ." This would allow both citizens and officials easy access to information. On July 12, 1979, Gibbs sent three more letters to Axelrod, in addition to the weekly ones she forwarded to him from the Homeowners' Association. More than she sought to pester such figures, Gibbs sought to establish a paper trail by which citizens could monitor government responses to their complaints.[50]

Like Gibbs, ETF activist Ann Hillis wrote an autobiography that personalized the experience of living in a toxic waste dump. Entitled *Love Canal's Contamination*, Hillis's unpublished memoir expresses what she labels her own toxic feelings. "When you live in hell," she notes in one section, "you have no fear of death! It's the living that you fear." Both Hillis and her husband, a furnace repairmen, experienced ill health; she had a miscarriage and their son, Ralphie, came down with successive diseases. In addition, the family's external environment appeared almost surreal. Trees rotted from the top down during the summer (health officials called this winter kill), friends and neighbors had a variety of sicknesses, and a massive chain-link fence warned people not to cross the covered canal, even though state representatives claimed that residents need not fear the dump. As Hillis states, even the state health commissioner told residents, "Don't worry. Life is a chancy thing, you know."[51] Hearing such statements, she writes, "you want to scream out! I don't want to be a Love Canal victim— but, oh God, I AM!" Even selling her home would not suffice, Hillis concludes, for she could not in good conscience transfer its toxicity to another family. "Chemical contamination surrounds us."[52]

Hillis repeated many of these observations in letters to the editor and in correspondence to citizens faced with similar environmental challenges in other parts of the country. "Spring will be here soon and trees will bud, crops pop out of the ground, a new surge of life for survival," she observed in a letter to the *Niagara Gazette*, June 30, 1979. "For me, spring has a new meaning." Spring thaws would leach chemicals to Hillis and her family. "Who knows what the water contains? Is dioxin already here or will it come out with the flowers?" Unlike Rachel Carson, scientist and author of the famous environmental warning *Silent Spring*, whose work Hillis cites, Hillis's story is not hypothetical. "In the future," she wonders, "will we the people of the Love Canal and the Niagara frontier know what a silent Spring sounds like? God help us." To citizens fighting a similar battle in Tennessee, Hillis writes that they must persevere like Love Canal activists. "Are we not the same all over? Yes, we are the first but we will not be the last, so we must cry out the loudest to be heard by all."[53]

As the work of Gibbs and Hillis suggests, women formed the nucleus of Love Canal activism. Described at the time as "housewives-turned-activists," local women used their daily experiences as a guide to environmentalism. As part-time workers and/or stay-at-home mothers, they noticed possible links between their family's illnesses and their local environment. From this grassroots basis, Love Canal's female residents began building a movement. "I'm a housewife and mother of two small children," Grace McCoulf testified at a Senate subcommittee hearing on April 5, 1979. "I live in the Love Canal . . . a chemical dumpsite used by at least one major chemical company to dispose of hazardous wastes." From this simple fact, she continued, "hundreds of problems have occurred," with families encountering "mental, physical, and psychological problems." Residents like her fought back, knowing that their struggle had "opened many eyes across the country."[54]

"Women are more likely than men to take on such issues," Cynthia Hamilton has observed of grassroots female activists in places such as South Central Los Angeles, "precisely because the home has been defined and prescribed as a women's domain." In the 1980s, South Central women organized against the placement of a hazardous waste incinerator in their neighborhood after officials ignored residents' wishes. Feeling that their playgrounds and backyards—the very places where families lived and played—were threatened, mothers formed a movement that stood up to the political and economic interests ranged against them. In so doing, they defied the conclusions of industry consultants who claimed that, while "certain types of people are likely to participate in politics," citizens with lower levels of education and lower socioeconomic status would not hinder the siting of hazardous waste dumps via political activism. So too did Love Canal residents fight against stereotypes of politically invisible women.[55]

Indeed, gender politics played an important role in Love Canal activism, for female residents' tenacity in seeking redress of their grievances stemmed from politicians' dismissiveness. In one infamous example, state health officials told a woman who was afraid to do laundry (because of chemicals leaching into her foundation) that she should simply "throw her wash in the basement" and speedily run upstairs. "Go home and tend your garden," state officials chastised Lois Gibbs after one Albany demonstration. Instead, she helped organize her neighbors.[56]

Like other residents-turned-activists, Grace McCoulf expanded her views to encompass issues of democratic governance and civic environmentalism. "We, the people, have been very patient in our efforts to obtain basic human rights," she told Congress. Because no government seemed willing to address citizens' complaints, she and others felt that they had no choice but to organize, protest, and dissent. Indeed, "while the industries and local governments who created this problem stall and pinpoint the finger at the next guy, the victims suffer. It is time for the government to serve its primary function—the interests of the people." She ended with an appeal to home and family: "Our children are sick, our homes valueless. . . . We can wait no longer."[57]

The New Meaning of Love Canal

By 1982, federal and state officials had agreed to evacuate all remaining Love Canal families. The story does not end there, however, for many former residents remained dedicated to the cause of grassroots environmentalism. "After I was relocated, I volunteered with the ETF," Patricia Brown observed. "I receive calls from other toxic waste victims across the United States and Canada, and I listen." Luella Kenny speaks at conferences and schools, and she helps administer health funds to Love Canal families. Lois Gibbs founded the Citizens' Clearinghouse for Hazardous Waste, which evolved into the Center for Health, Environment, and Justice. Dedicated to aiding grassroots environmental groups, the center has worked with over eight thousand activists and organizations, most of them from blue-collar and minority backgrounds. Even residents who tried to leave painful memories behind have found themselves speaking about the cause in the new millennium. "I didn't consider myself an activist," Joe Dunmire told a world conference in August 2000. "I've spent twenty years trying to distance myself from Love Canal." Yet, as he put it, Love Canal "got people involved in a number of things they never would have gotten involved in, like protests. Anyone faced with a similar situation would do the same."[58]

In aiding others, many Love Canal residents (not just Lois Gibbs) have dealt with people very much like themselves—members of working-class and/or minority communities who feel both environmentally threatened and politically marginalized. Indeed, one major reason that the Love Canal struggle reverberated with local environmental activists around the country (and around the world) is that it was not unique. As deindustrialization accelerated in the late 1970s and 1980s, more and more citizens grappled with those issues confronting the Niagara Frontier—brownfields, leaking dumps, polluted water. As Michael Frisch has written, the Buffalo/Niagara saga seemed to be "the epitome of Rust Belt America" in the last few decades of the twentieth century. Like those of other regions (only perhaps with more intensity), the Niagara Frontier's once vibrant industrial fortunes spiraled downward. And alongside the problem of "displaced industrial workers," the region has had to confront the environmental scars of "closed facilities."[59] Old Pennsylvania coal towns, Chicago's formerly thriving industrial neighborhoods, and hundreds of other communities around the country witnessed similar trends. What could they do?

In this sense, Love Canal activism encompassed much more than "housewives-turned-activists," and it aimed at a broader target than the relocation of residents. It provided a model for grassroots environmental action—action led by working people. As James Schwab has observed, in the post–Love Canal world, "workers, long accustomed to the adage that jobs are more important than preserving the environment," have begun to realize that they too have environmental rights, as well as the right to mobilize for environmental justice. Love Canal citizen protest also lead to important environmental legislation. To take one major example, Love Canal activists' testimony decisively shaped the passage of Superfund, a tax on oil and chemical companies for hazardous waste cleanup. As Senator Edmund Muskie of Maine told a group of engineers in the early 1980s, "until recently, this nation's attitude was out of sight, out of mind . . . [but] names like Love Canal . . . have become synonymous with pain, suffering, and the shabby management of industrial waste." The "penetrating" testimony of Love Canal activists convinced him that the federal government must become more vigilant in the matter. Even chemical industry representatives heeded Love Canal protesters' environmental call. "We used to think of the earth as a big sponge," one Union Carbide official noted; "perhaps now it was time for a clean land act." Today companies such as Occidental Petroleum pledge to protect a community's environmental health. Needless to say, many activists remain wary of such claims, noting that chemical production continues to increase, as do the number of hazardous waste sites.[60]

As Alice Stark of the New York State Health Department commented, at an international meeting of environmental epidemiologists in Buffalo in August 2000, Love Canal protesters also helped create "right to know" statutes. Citizens now have a right to know what companies dispose of and how.[61] That was not the case in 1978. Few environmental agencies work on cases now, Stark and her colleagues agreed, without an understanding of local residents' needs and concerns. "That was certainly a lesson to take citizens seriously," Stark commented.[62]

Indeed, to the extent that business leaders, government officials, and society at large have confronted the painful environmental legacy of the nation's industrial past, it is very much the work of grassroots environmentalists. Love Canal citizens were at the forefront of that movement. They showed Americans of every class and color that, no matter the economic circumstances or lack of environmental precedents, a group of local citizens could rise up and be heard about a cleaner, safer environment.

Part III

PLANS

CHAPTER 6

The Wages of Disinvestment

*How Money and Politics Aided the Decline
of Camden, New Jersey*

HOWARD GILLETTE JR.

In July 1999 the mayor of Camden, New Jersey, Milton Milan, entered federal court to declare that the city he had presided over for the previous two years was bankrupt and he wanted the state to take it over. The response from the governor's office was anything but cordial. Having been locked in a dispute with the city for over a year as to how it should meet its obligation to balance its budget, the state retorted that the mayor had no authority to declare bankruptcy and that he ought to set about cutting expenditures.

National news outlets seized on the bitter exchange, focusing on the obvious contrasts between parties: Camden's first mayor raised in the tough streets in the aftermath of the city's industrial collapse, a Democrat, confronting the patrician Republican governor with national ambitions, Christine Todd Whitman. Here too was one of the nation's poorest cities caught at a fiscal impasse at a time of unparalleled prosperity in the state and nation. The story made for good drama, even when Milan backed down after accepting a small concession that the state would not immediately increase its control over city finances through the fiscal review board it had instituted a year earlier. But Camden's problems continued to mount, and a year later, even as Governor Whitman was attempting to showcase her commitment to improve the city for the Republican national convention being held in nearby Philadelphia, she was seeking authority to take over Camden's operation. Calling on outside consultants to offer a plan for recovery, the governor declared that the people of Camden deserved more effective leadership. Supporting her critique was a grand jury indictment delivered

in the months following Milan's declaration of bankruptcy, accusing the
mayor of accepting Mafia payoffs and laundering money from drug dealers. That, plus the city's inability to close its budget gap, was enough to
move the state to declare a "crisis" worthy of an extraordinary level of intervention.

The state's intervention in Camden's day-to-day financial operations is
an extraordinary occurrence, but it cannot be explained by focusing solely
on the drama of local and state party politics. If Camden faced a crisis, it
had been a long time forming. The story of Camden's decline derives centrally from uses and abuses of power that extend back more than a generation, and thus requires a full assessment of historical context. To tell this
story, we must examine the relationships between politics, urban finance,
and industrial change over time. Beneath the moments of crisis of the deindustrialized city lie decades of decisions about investment, resources, and
the means by which a city faced with industrial loss raises the money to
maintain itself.

Some broad accounts of industrial decline describe such changes as the
virtually inevitable reorganization of the market economy, as capital first
sought out lower costs at the suburban and then the regional periphery,
then extended even further to other countries as part of the process of globalization. Such forces—captured in the term "structural change"—imposed an enduring legacy of fiscal constraint on cities across the industrial
belt. The particular outcomes of deindustrialization varied, however, according to human agency.[1] Individuals made a difference, no doubt, in all
cities, but it was the collective response—captured both in the exercise of
political power and in its social context—that determined how well any one
city responded to the challenges of the postwar economy. With the highest
poverty rate in the nation of cities over twenty thousand residents, and with
the state of New Jersey currently responsible for more than 70 percent of
its operating budget, Camden appears an extreme example, and it is. At the
same time, because the city's structural deficit has been so persistent and
unrelenting, the drama of how money and power have been exercised to
meet that challenge over time offers an especially compelling story for historians. In such cities, to paraphrase Lewis Mumford, the issues of civilization are focused.[2]

Camden's Long Industrial Decline

Camden is like a number of satellite industrial cities—Flint, East Saint
Louis, Gary, and even Newark—in that the rise and fall of its fortunes was

tied to a nearby city. For much of its early history, Camden fell entirely under the shadow of Philadelphia, with which it was connected by ferry across
the Delaware River. The larger city's industrial prowess completely dominated the region through the mid-nineteenth century. After the Civil War,
however, Camden began to attract the elements necessary to achieve standing on its own, notably workers and the capital to employ them. If the
Delaware offered Philadelphia a viable port, it did so for Camden as well.
By the turn of the century Camden had become host to the booming soup
business Joseph Campbell had founded in 1869; the expansive New York
Ship yard, which employed some five thousand workers; and the RCA-Victor Talking Machine Company. Joining these giants were a host of smaller
manufacturing firms producing everything from fountain pens to cigars to
women's clothing. By 1909 Camden's board of trade could declare that the
city "within these ten bright and busy years [has] thrown off the shackles
inspired by a fear of being so near to a metropolitan city." A 1917 report
listed 365 industries in Camden employing 51,000 people.[3]

The first threat to Camden's economic vitality struck other industrial
cities, including Philadelphia, in similar fashion. The Depression curtailed
production drastically, forcing many workers to seek government assistance
to save their homes and to feed their families. Camden's municipal resources were so depleted the city had to pay its own workers for a while in
script. Where government programs were unavailable, Camden's tight-knit
ethnic neighborhoods rallied to help take care of their own. Defense contracts, to RCA-Victor as well as to New York Ship and associated facilities,
during World War II lifted the immediate specter of collective poverty, but
recovery proved short-lived. Within years of the declaration of peace, older
industries, starting with the secondary shipyards, began to close. Veterans
returning from the war, finding the housing market in Camden both tight
and old-fashioned, began to take advantage of new housing that was going
up with government-guaranteed loans in the suburbs. After peaking at
124,555 in 1950, Camden's population began to decline, to 117,159 in 1960
and 102,551 in 1970.

Throughout the postwar era, Camden, like Philadelphia and other core
cities, began to lose its regional primacy as a location for both work and residence. (See figures 8a and 8b.) Although manufacturing employment rose
briefly in the late 1940s, by the early 1950s it had fallen into an unrelenting downward trend. Both RCA and Campbell's Soup began to diversify,
placing new plants in other locations and reducing their operations in Camden. New York Ship, which had employed 47,000 workers at its height in
1943, closed in 1967, laying off the last 2,400 of its employees. Between
1950 and 1970 Camden lost half its manufacturing jobs, 22,000 in total.[4]

FIGURES 8a and 8b. Camden's streetscapes reflect its fortunes. Linden Street in North Camden is shown in 1952, when the physical and social fabric of the city was still largely intact. An unidentified row of houses in the same section of the city was photographed twenty-six years later. Philadelphia *Evening Bulletin* collection. Courtesy of Urban Archives, Temple University, Philadelphia, Pennsylvania.

Camden, it might be said, was slow to deal with the first signs of crisis. While other similarly challenged cities, most notably New Haven, generated new federal funding to deal with the problem,[5] Camden's traditionally patronage-based brand of ethnic politics delayed efforts to look outside the community for help. It took a relative outsider with a mission to change both the reaction to deindustrialization and the means to deal with it.

The Pierce Administration and Urban Renewal

Although he was born and raised in Camden, Al Pierce's religious vision while flying his fighter aircraft over Germany during World War II—that he had been destined to save his native city—set him apart.[6] His immediate entry into politics blocked by the local political establishment, in the hands of Democratic boss George Brunner, Pierce gained election to the city commission on an independent "Save Our City" coalition ticket in 1959. Instead of being named to the mayor-commissioner position he wanted, however, he was placed in charge of public safety. When rivals stripped him even of that post, he responded by securing support through referendum for a reorganization of city government to a strong mayor-council form. Achieving that goal in 1960, he was elected mayor the following year, determined to modernize the city in the effort to stem its decline.

At the heart of Pierce's program lay a bold redevelopment program that he said was crucial to Camden's survival. Released in 1962, the comprehensive plan he promised would form the city's new blueprint for recovery and laid out the vision of a revitalized Camden in the heart of a growing region. "If the functions for which the city was built cease to be needed," the plan intoned, "the city will decline or disappear." Unless civic leaders worked to replace older functions, "the processes of change and new development will take place outside of the city. If the people of a city want this new growth to occur within their city, its environment must be enhanced."

To achieve a "balanced environment," the plan proposed a "redistribution of functional elements" through a whole new network of highways to connect residential areas to places of work, new space for industrial expansion, downtown revitalization, and restoration of decaying neighborhood commercial centers. At the intellectual and physical heart of the plan was a call to rebuild the heart of Camden as City Centre. This two-level shopping mall, enclosed and air-conditioned, was to be located over the downtown Broadway station planned as part of a high-speed rail line connecting Philadelphia and Camden County suburbs. It represented a direct response to the opening in 1961 of the area's first regional mall, in Cherry Hill, and thus an effort to retain the city's premier commercial position in the area. Concurrently Pierce promoted an ambitious plan to build an expansive luxury waterfront development along the northeastern shore, popularly referred to as a city within a city.[7]

Claiming that with planning Camden could "prosper as it has seldom done before," the comprehensive plan revealed an unusually optimistic set of presumptions. The document promised that industry would continue to expand if only land were made available and automobile access to employment could be improved. It also argued that renovated commercial and residential areas could hold their own with suburban competitors. The city's planning director even claimed that implementation of the plan would improve property values by 100 percent.[8] As such, it represented a classic effort to stimulate new economic growth, where old industries had faltered, through federally subsidized physical interventions in the built environment.[9]

Pierce's grand plans required a good deal of clearance and relocation before rebuilding could begin. This had a short-term but acute impact on the city's tax revenues. Even as New York Ship was preparing to shut down, Pierce faced a significant budget shortfall. Until his last year in office, Mayor Brunner had managed to keep taxes from rising too rapidly due to continued increases in city property values. In 1959 those values dropped significantly for the first time, by three hundred thousand dollars. To balance the budget, Brunner had to boost the tax rate by $.68, to $8.64 per $100 in assessed value. As property values continued to decline in 1960 and 1961, tax rates went up again, to a postwar high of $10.12 in 1961, the first year Pierce presided as mayor. Pierce managed to reduce the rate over the next two years on the basis of a revaluation of existing properties completed shortly before he took office. He admitted some property owners would suffer the consequences of increased payments, but he claimed that the next two years would bring between ten and twenty million dollars in additional taxable properties as a result of his redevelopment efforts.

As those projects lagged and the tax rate climbed again to over $9.00 in 1964 and 1965 (see table 1), Pierce continued to claim that the city would be financially restored even as it was physically renewed. The *Courier-Post* commented sympathetically in 1966, "Looking at the broad picture, the mayor notes that City Council and the people must accept hard, cold facts—that industries of this city cannot afford financially to remain here without a great rebuilding program sufficient to add new ratables and provide the favorable tax base industries must have."[10]

Even as Pierce held out future prospects for recovery, he still had to

Table 1.   Camden Tax Rate (per $100 assessed value)

1949	5.64	1960	9.2	1971	7.38
1950	5.96	1961	10.12	1972	7.73
1951	5.96	1962	8.36	1973	7.76
1952	6.32	1963	8.4	1974	7.56
1953	6.92	1964	9.08	1975	7.86
1954	7.24	1965	9.00	1976	8.12
1955	7.32	1966	8.32	1977	7.25
1956	7.32	1967	8.92	1978	7.46
1957	7.48	1968	10.92	1979	7.5
1958	7.96	1969	12.06	1980	8.19
1959	8.64	1970	14.36	1981	12.29

Source: Camden City Assessor's Office.

balance the budget, and in 1966 he introduced the potentially dangerous strategy of selling off city assets, starting with WCAM, the city-owned radio station. As the sale of that property lagged, in 1967 Pierce drew on $1.2 million in surplus funds from separately budgeted water and sewer rents. The *Courier-Post* worried publicly that Pierce was relying too much on one-time "tricks," but it remained supportive, writing, "Many communities are enticing business and industries still located within cities to move to new areas to take advantage of what now are better tax rates. A challenge is presented to any city administration to try to maintain a tax climate attractive to business and industry while at the same time fighting to produce new sources of income and revenue so vitally necessary to a city's welfare."[11] Even so, the tax rate rose another $.60, to $8.92, in 1967 and to $10.92 a year later. It reached $12.06 during Pierce's last year in office, underscoring the damage done by delays to proposed redevelopment efforts.

Race, Neighborhoods, and the Deepening Tax Burden

For Pierce's successor, Joseph Nardi, Camden's fiscal problems were devastating. Lacking Pierce's cleverness and aptitude for finances, he was forced to accept a tax rate of $14.36 in announcing his first city budget in 1970. "I must tell you I am not proud of this budget," he told the city council. "I still have that pride in Camden, and with the budget—though it is burdensome and inadequate—I will continue to do the best I can." True to its past stand, the *Courier Post* declared, "There seems to be no escaping the conclusion that Camden taxpayers must shoulder the financial burden until, through the promise of urban redevelopment, the city hopefully makes its comeback." Nardi's announcement that Lit Brothers department store would not be leaving the city, as previously reported, allowed the paper to express hope that "[t]his could be the depth from which Camden comes back."[12] Nardi, however, never mastered a situation that was beyond his control. Although the tax rate fell nearly by half the next year, it did so only because the city increased its actual tax levy from 50 to 100 percent of valuation. A new $2.4 million Campbell's Soup research facility that came onto the rolls in 1971 softened the impact, but it could not overcome the continuing loss of businesses, which by the end of Nardi's term included both the Lits and Sears department stores.

Most accounts of urban decline have emphasized white flight, but have underestimated the ill effects of politicians dealing ineptly with growing minority populations. African Americans had lived in a largely contained area of South Camden as far back as the 1830s. As employment opportunities grew during World War II, their numbers increased dramatically, following the pattern of most northern industrial cities. Even then, labor shortages encouraged Campbell's, among other companies, to import workers from Puerto Rico. By the late 1950s, these newcomers were facing the dual problems of declining opportunities for manual labor and increasingly crowded and inadequate housing conditions in the few segregated areas available for their residence. Pierce's redevelopment plans worsened the situation by calling for uprooting as many as fourteen thousand mostly minority residents to make way for highways, new commercial facilities, and modern housing. Inevitably, these efforts provoked resistance, which grew increasingly militant in coincidence with the emerging black power movement. Determined to execute policies he believed were essential to the city's financial stability, Pierce directed his police department to root out his opposition. Not only did efforts to convict black activists and their white religious supporters under phony charges get thrown out in court, a civil rights coalition managed to bring redevelopment to a halt through court action.[13]

With hopes for recovery stalled, the exodus of the city's white residents accelerated. The transition from white to black occupancy in once predominantly Jewish Parkside was largely peaceful as Jews followed the migration of their chief social and religious institutions to the suburbs.[14] In working-class sections of North, South, and East Camden, however, changes in occupancy were resisted fiercely, as insecurities over housing values combined with declines in industrial employment to create a volatile mix. Festering resentments on both sides of the racial divide exploded in 1971 when a white policeman shot and killed an unarmed Puerto Rican.

The next three days Mayor Nardi remained virtually paralyzed while the city was wracked by civil disturbances. A barrage of For Sale signs followed. According to Alfredo Alvardo, who operated a grocery store in South Camden, "You should have seen the people flying out of here . . . there were moving trucks all over the place."[15] The man who stepped in to diffuse the crisis, Nardi's director of public works, Angelo Errichetti, did so by taking the city back in time.

Although Pierce had been keen enough to recognize as early as 1959 the need to add representatives of both the black and the Puerto Rican communities to his campaign ticket, neither he nor Nardi granted minorities positions of real power. Errichetti changed that, first by negotiating a deal whereby opponents of renewal would drop their injunction against the city in return for the city's opening a proposed luxury high-rise apartment on the waterfront to low- and moderate-income residents, secondly by bringing minorities into the power structure. Errichetti revealed this after his election as mayor a year later, when he named black and Puerto Rican activists to positions within his administration.

Bold where Nardi had been timid, flexible where Pierce had been rigid, Errichetti brought to his position political talent and a savvy use of patronage not seen since the Brunner era. But the situation he inherited as mayor in 1973 was dire. Graphically describing his view of his native city as he made his way through the old ethnic neighborhoods toward City Hall for his first day of work, he said: "It looked like the Vietcong bombed us to get even. The pride of Camden . . . was now a rat-infested skeleton of yesterday, a visible obscenity of urban decay. . . . The years of neglect, slumlord exploitation, tenant abuse, government bungling, indecision and short-sighted policy had transformed the city's housing, business and industrial stock into a ravaged, rat-infested cancer on a sick, old industrial city."[16]

After the Federal Bulldozer: Patronage, Poverty Programs, and Prisons

Errichetti's dire picture of Camden could have come from any number of fellow white ethnics, who had either already left the city or were counting on him to stem the tide before they might decide to leave too. What he offered in response was a commitment to a brand of politics that was sufficiently inclusive to diffuse social conflict and a knowledge of government capable of identifying the resources necessary to hold the coalition together. With a federally funded redevelopment strategy no longer possible in Camden, Errichetti had to rely on a brand of old-fashioned politics not present in the city since the Brunner era. Calling in favors from his support of Brendon Byrne's 1977 gubernatorial campaign, he secured an additional one million dollars in state funding to close a budget deficit in his first year in office. From the federal government he gained funds to hire extra city employees, opening patronage positions to minority constituents. Even then, Errichetti had to build on the precedent set by Al Pierce in trading off city assets. First, he transferred responsibility for parks and recreation to the school system, with its separate budget. Then, most dramatically, he engineered a sweetheart deal whereby, in return for an antiquated municipal waste plant, the county built a new facility in the city to serve the whole county. In return for hosting the waste facility, the city received $11.5 million dollars, paid out over a four-year period—enough to bridge the gap between revenues raised through local taxation and total municipal costs for that period.[17]

Errichetti's tenure had its difficulties, including further tax hikes, allegations of impropriety when he was director of public works, a long unsuccessful fight for a federally funded Veterans Administration hospital, and an eventual indictment in the Abscam scandal. But the difficulties Camden faced were not to be remedied by one mayor, however strong. Two perceptive articles in the *Courier Post* by Dennis Culnan at the time of Errichetti's departure revealed the heart of the problem. Camden's precipitous decline had weakened its political and fiscal position relative to the county of which it was a part. While Camden in 1960 cast a third of the county vote, in 1980 it cast only 16 percent. In contrast, Cherry Hill's portion of the county vote rose from 10 to 18 percent in the same period.

For a time, the city of Camden closed the fiscal and political gap with the county by positioning itself advantageously for the largesse of Great Society programs. "Everyone," Culnan wrote, "wanted to throw money at the lame, poor, blacks, Hispanics and downtrodden that Camden represented to the white middle-class psyche, guilty for abandoning cities like Camden all over the country. Errichetti was willing to play the poverty hustle and to subtly blackmail the conscience of white suburbia, meanwhile assuring it that he was keeping the poor—particularly the blacks—home on the city reservation." By 1980, however, the day of Great Society bailouts was over. The country was ready to let cities like Camden shift for themselves, and without the political strength it once had, Camden was in no position to dictate the terms of political rewards. "I tried to use mirrors to give the image of strength of the city," Culnan quoted Errichetti as saying, "but the smart people could see the real numbers. . . . Camden's no longer the hub of south Jersey or the county; it's just a spoke."[18]

This was the legacy inherited by Errichetti's successor, Melvin "Randy" Primas. Recruited at age twenty-three from his staff position in Camden's militant Black People's Unity Movement to join Errichetti's successful city council ticket, Primas had risen quickly to the position of chair. Although he broke with Errichetti in his last year in office over the need to address the city's growing fiscal deficit, Primas became the city's first African American mayor in 1981, even without Errichetti's support. Victory proved hollow, however. Without Errichetti's backing, Primas lacked the support of the city's remaining whites, many of whom left the city for good during his years in office. More immediately, Errichetti's failure to confront the budget crisis made it impossible for Primas to give priority to the most pressing social needs of the city's growing minority population. Even as he assumed office, New Jersey stepped in to take charge of city finances. As a price for funds to close the $4.6 million shortfall in the budget, the state required a staggering 88 percent increase in taxes. The state was sufficiently satisfied to return budgetary control to the city the following year, but the mayor still had to identify new funds to fill the continuing gap between local revenues and costs. Following precedents set by Pierce and Errichetti, he embraced the state's offer of $3.4 million in exchange for giving up valuable land on North Camden's waterfront, this time for a state prison.[19]

The decision had the immediate effect of alienating Primas's natural constituents. Charging that a prison would aggravate North Camden's precarious economic situation, the area's overwhelmingly minority residents picketed the mayor and actively sought to block the new building. Residents were not sufficiently organized to win that battle, as Primas held fast to the decision to accept the state offer. As he told the *New York Times*, "The prison was a purely economic decision on my part. I saw the $40 million in construction, the 400 jobs, $450,000 spent annually among local businesses outside the state bidding process and $1 million a year in taxes, and I sold it to the city through a public education program."[20] Under pressure from North Camden activists, Primas acceded to turning over abandoned homes to dispossessed members of the community who had been squatting there to bring attention to their plight. Convinced, however, that the city still needed commercial revenue as well as middle-income home buyers, he adopted Errichetti's strategy to attract high-end economic activities to cleared waterfront sites across the Delaware River from Philadelphia.

Progress remained slow, and city revenue continued to fall behind costs. Unlike Errichetti, Primas lacked the political debts he could call on for outside support, and when the state offered another subsidy in return for the location of a second prison in North Camden, Primas agreed to back the proposition. Again, black and Hispanic residents erupted in protest. A new organization, Save Our Waterfront, asserted that if the prison were built, as many as a quarter of North Camden's residents would be prisoners. The group argued forcefully for alternative uses of the land to serve the community, putting up $35,000 in earnest money within a month of its organization to buy the site itself. After sitting through a meeting that drew two hundred angry residents, Primas defended the sale by saying the prison would bring in $2.8 million in payments from the state in addition to the more than $1 million currently coming in from the first prison. "I have to deal in the real world," he asserted. "We operate a $70 million budget and collect $11 million in property taxes. A million dollars (from both state prisons) is 38 percent of every tax dollar we collect. I have to look at that. I need revenue to run a city."[21] But Primas failed to sustain his campaign for a second prison. Faced with the prospect of continually resorting to gimmicks to balance the budget, he resigned in 1990, before completing his third term, to take a position heading the state's Department of Community Affairs.

The confluence of growing deficits and shrinking political influence ushered in a new era in Camden politics during the Primas years. Inside the city, activists consolidated a fiercely defiant, neighborhood-based approach grounded in hostility to outside influence, whether in the form of city, state, or county authority. A prison in North Camden and a municipal waste plant—and subsequently a trash-to-steam facility and an interstate connector—in South Camden affirmed the dangers inherent in outside intervention. Even waterfront revitalization, which continued to captivate mayors and state officials alike as the best hope of building back up Camden's tax base, was viewed critically by most city residents as a diversion from more pressing social needs. Indeed, critics had good cause to complain. The independent Cooper's Ferry Development Association, formed in Errichetti's last years as mayor, had some success in redeveloping the waterfront, completing a $52-million state aquarium and a new entertainment center. However, because the state retained revenues at the aquarium and the entertainment center received a long-term tax abatement, neither facility generated much in the way of revenue for the city. The L-3 Corporation, a successor company to RCA-Victor and to General Electric, which assumed ownership of RCA-Victor in 1987, in 1993 completed an $80-million facility on the waterfront. Its payment in lieu of taxes of $600,000 a year was still below market rates for its prime location. Clearly, large-scale projects were not always living up to their promises to revive Camden's crisis economy.

Amid mounting opposition, the city reverted to its early history as a collection of largely isolated ethnic communities. The difference lay in the reality of a radically altered political context. While successful politicians like Errichetti had once managed to speak for the whole of Camden, in order to bring more outside resources to the assistance of individual constituencies, now a city divided encouraged outsiders to reap the remaining spoils without coherent and independent opposition. Even though federal funding for cities shrunk during the Reagan years, Camden continued to function, generating in the process considerable expenditures for personnel and services. During the late 1980s and 1990s these fell increasingly under the control of the Camden County Democratic Party. Both of Primas' immediate successors and most of the members of the city council owed their election to the county Democrats. The rewards for party brokers included lucrative contracts for insurance, for parking, and for legal and other services.[22] With patronage so centrally concentrated, there was little room for political dissent, and such arrangements did little to revive the residential housing market, improve infrastructure, or revitalize neighborhoods.

Local Insolvency and State Politics in the 1990s

As long as Democrats controlled state government, Camden's deteriorating condition attracted little controversy. It was only late in his one term in office that Democrat James Florio, who had represented Camden in Congress, announced a plan to revitalize the city, and even then what he offered was considered too little and too late to make much of a difference. Christie Whitman's 1993 victory over Florio based on a dramatic appeal to cut taxes made her naturally cautious about spending more money than was necessary to close Camden's annual deficits. As these continued to rise, however, the Republican governor was forced to act. She first initiated a special audit, published during her first full year in office, with a scathing review of Camden's management, then suggested formal state oversight. Announced in 1998, this second, more drastic step coincided with Milton Milan's installation as mayor.

Born in 1962 and raised in a rough Camden neighborhood from the time he was eight, Milan came of age just as drugs were becoming a major national problem. Entering the Marines after graduating from high school, Milan appeared to have beaten the bad odds of his neighborhood environment by successfully building up his own construction contracting business after his release from the military. Elected as an independent Democrat to city council in 1995, he secured the votes of his fellow Puerto Rican members, and that of the one white representative, to become council chairman a year later. An apparent reformer who used the state audit as a touchstone to criticize incumbent mayor Arnold Webster's failure to close the city's deficit, he gained a high measure of media support. Aided both by a decision within the Hispanic community to hold an informal primary to select only one of their number against the incumbent and by the presence of three African American opponents, Milan emerged the victor of the 1997 mayoral race by 1,600 votes of a paltry 12,048 cast.[23]

By her own account, Governor Whitman felt she could work with Milan, who appeared to have succeeded without the usual obligations to the Democratic county organization.[24] She thus made Milan a voting member of the state oversight panel and instructed its chair, Steven Sasala, acting on behalf of Commissioner of Community Affairs Jane Kenny, to give the city enough leeway to effect a partnership in the recovery effort. For his part, Milan indicated a willingness to swallow "medicine" in the form of increased state oversight of city affairs in return for more money to balance the current and next several budgets.[25] Both sides seriously misread each other, and what followed proved but a prelude to Milan's declaration of bankruptcy.

Although guidelines adopted at the time the review board formed recognized in their preamble the presence of a "structural deficit" in Camden, subsequent text revealed that the state would rely more on internal reforms than the creation of new revenue streams. "It is hoped," the section on social impact concluded, that "more prudent fiscal management will help return Camden to its status as a strong, vibrant urban center." Similarly, the document counted on fiscal discipline to "help improve the status of Camden as a commercial center," a theme frequently repeated during the Whitman administration.[26] Not surprisingly, then, the state's emphasis from the start was on reducing the city's budget, which at $112 million was running about $12 million short, even with the state's considerable help.

For most of a year, the board and city officials sparred over expenditures and their records. As the prospect for new funding faded, Milan became increasingly uncooperative, either challenging his fellow members or not showing up to board meetings at all. While the board approved a city request for more police, it quibbled over smaller items. The board's rejection of Milan's request for additional street sweepers, for example, galled the mayor, and unleashed the full measure of defiance of external authority that had been so much a part of the Camden in which he grew up.[27] Exhausted from wrangling over the 1999 budget, Milan acted against the advice of the city comptroller to declare bankruptcy. At the heart of his action was the state's demand that he accede to further oversight as a condition of receiving the emergency funding required to balance the city's budget at the close of the fiscal year. But he was also unwilling to bend to state authority in terms of his own power, and he sought to terminate the control board in a separate suit.[28] His defiance proved a terrible mistake.

Although the governor said little herself in response, her aides made her displeasure with the mayor clear, and many Milan allies believed it was not incidental that the mayor's name subsequently was dragged into grand jury hearings organized to indict city drug dealers.[29] News leaks of the hearings not only associated Milan repeatedly with these dealers, but also with members of organized crime who testified that they offered financial favors in return for city business. Throughout this difficult period, Milan remained defiant, claiming that charges being made against him were politically motivated. The indictment that followed on April 30, 2000, detailing Milan's role in payoffs and money laundering, severely undercut his declaration of innocence. Claiming nonetheless that the charges levied by criminals turning state's evidence were worthless, Milan continued to battle the state right until his conviction in December.[30]

Whatever Milan's rationale for his defiance, his legal difficulties only encouraged the Whitman administration to act more aggressively. Following Milan's indictment, the state issued an ultimatum to the city to meet thirteen demands for fiscal information and action, including completion of the 1998 audit, or face greater oversight. While Milan supporters complained that the governor was attempting to force Milan's resignation, other city officials, following the track that had characterized exchanges with the review board the previous year, remained evasive. They claimed that the information requested was already available or was impossible to muster in such a short period.[31] As the deadline passed, the state's Local Finance Board voted unanimously to place the city under direct state supervision. Denied further time to meet the state's ultimatum, Milan denounced the decision as that of a "kangaroo court," claiming even that the decision marked his own triumph by bringing an end to the state's financial review board.[32] But in June of 2000, Superior Court Assignment Judge Francis Orlando affirmed the New Jersey Local Finance Board's powers. The *Courier-Post* observed, "The decision means the nation's second-wealthiest state now must determine how to repair and revive the country's second-poorest city."[33]

Even as the state worked under existing laws to take charge of Camden's financial affairs, it sought full control of daily operations in the city, a move that required special legislation. To bolster the state's case, Commissioner of Community Affairs Jane Kenny contracted with the National Academy of Public Administration to examine city operations and to prepare a case for Camden's recovery.[34] Making sure to provide at least the semblance of citizen input to state supervision, Kenny enlisted a citywide coalition of faith-based communities, Camden Churches Organized for People, and the Council of Concerned Black Clergy to present their own plan for recovery. At a meeting in an East Camden church attended by more than one thousand city residents, Kenny and Republican Assembly leader Jack Collins, then a presumed candidate to succeed Whitman as governor, publicly accepted the proposed plan, which had been carefully reviewed and agreed on in state offices in advance.[35]

The *New York Times* described what ensued as "the biggest city take-over in the country since the Great Depression." State-favored legislation introduced over the summer transferred powers normally accorded the mayor and city council to an appointed chief operating officer, who would retain authority for city business for a minimum of five years. The bill naturally provoked opposition, not just from Camden city government, but also from other New Jersey cities fearing a bad precedent for state interference. As debate over the measure dragged out, the state remained relentless in its effort to assert control, forcing its own choices for business administrator and director of planning and development on the city, despite Milan's efforts to name his own appointments. Once again Judge Orlando confirmed the state's authority.[36]

In November, the state released its own commissioned plan for the city's recovery. Prepared by a Philadelphia-based company, Public Financial Management, in association with the National Academy of Public Administration, the document claimed that the city's structural deficit could climb as high as $30 million by the year 2004. To meet the crisis, the plan called for considerable financial resources—$102 million in new capital investment—but only if tied to extensive management reforms and savings, afforded largely by a rollback of city employee wages and benefits. According to the plan's complex carrot-and-stick approach, the city could achieve fiscal stability within four years. Although Commissioner Kenny did not immediately embrace the plan's particulars, she indicated it could provide guidance once new leadership was in place, thus reasserting the state's continued priority of passing takeover legislation.[37] Such caution also related closely to the fortunes of the principal antagonists. A month later Milan was convicted and jailed. News headlines the same day reported that Governor Whitman was about to be named president-elect George W. Bush's administrator of the Environmental Protection Agency.[38]

Whitman and Milan's departures removed for the moment the most personally acrimonious elements of the contest between municipal and state governments over the fate of an insolvent city. Seeing an opportunity to resolve the impasse to the city's advantage, Camden's representative in the state senate, Democrat Wayne Bryant, stepped in. A severe critic of Whitman's approach to Camden's takeover,[39] Bryant prevailed on his colleague, the senate majority leader and now acting governor, Donald DiFrancesco, to support radically revised legislation. Never an enthusiast for the Whitman bill himself and a candidate for governor in his own right in 2001, DiFrancesco appeared eager to put his own stamp on the pending takeover legislation. Introduced almost exactly a year after the first bill had surfaced, the new proposal expanded the amount of money New Jersey was willing to invest in the city to $150 million in state-backed bonds (see table 2). To this was added another $50 million in funding from Camden County, which would assume responsibility for city parks and the 911 system, and make necessary investments in crumbling sewers and streets. Gone was any discussion of rolling back wages and benefits. In its place were promises for a new start and a lasting partnership between state government and the city of Camden. The acting governor was apparently confident enough in his effort to ask Mayor Gwendolyn Faison, recently elected to office, to join him for the announcement of the effort.[40]

The new legislation represented a precarious political balancing act. Each of several constituencies was to play a role. The Democratic county organization, to which Mayor Faison owed her election in a close contest, gained potential patronage through new investments in streets and sewers. The Republican-controlled Delaware River Port Authority gained the lion's share of responsibility for redevelopment. Other important city constituents—hospitals, colleges, and universities, and the Cooper Ferry Development Association, an independent agency with the mission to re-develop the waterfront—all received allocations for favored projects. Downtown and neighborhood redevelopment areas also were targeted for

Table 2.   Proposed Spending: Bryant-DiFrancesco 2001 Proposed State Recovery Bill (in millions $)

Camden Restoration Fund		*Other Parties*	
Downtown revitalization	23.5	Camden County	50
Neighborhood revitalization	12.1	Hospital fund	6
Capital improvements	21	State aquarium (Cooper Ferry Development Assn. request)	30
Neighborhood redevelopment	33.9	Higher education development	18.5
Brownfields redevelopment	5		
Subtotal	95.5	Subtotal	104.5
		Total	200

funds, following the general trajectory of the National Academy of Public Administration's report the previous fall. Had everything been worked out in advance with the interested parties, the compromise might have worked. But a sticking point remained the state's continued insistence on the appointment of a chief operating officer (COO). Under the terms of the new bill, city council would be allowed to choose between two nominees. Once named, the COO would exercise the traditional powers of mayor, with city council reserving the right to override an executive decision by a two-thirds vote. In such instances, the disputed issue would be referred to a special master, whose decision would be final, an innovation introduced by Senator Bryant. Judge Francis Orlando, who had already ruled twice in the state's favor in arbitrating the exercise of contested powers to govern, was to fill that role.[41]

Faison's show of support for an approach that clearly gave the state all it wanted was short-lived. Within days of the acting governor's announcement, she was actively opposing the bill. A seven-to-zero city council vote opposing the takeover deepened her opposition; she argued she could accept the projected $150 million in state funds as adequate, but that she would never give up her powers to an externally appointed administrator as long as she represented the people who had just elected her.[42] Without city support for the measure, the deadline for passing it before the close of the fiscal year, June 30, passed without either hearings or a vote. Camden County Freeholder-Director Jeffrey Nash joined Faison's opposition, claiming that the county had never agreed to assume responsibility for city parks. In a letter to Senator Bryant, he pointedly suggested that the matter would have to wait until after the election of a new governor in the fall.[43]

The reconvening of the legislature in September brought a new round of proposals to the table that would eventually result in takeover legislation. The bill, a compromise between a proposal by Freeholder Nash and a counterproposal from Senator Bryant, retained most of the original provisions but incorporated some of Nash's ideas—including the mayor's right to appoint members of commissions and shared responsibility for redevelopment between the Delaware River Port Authority and a separate, city-based redevelopment agency.[44] Faison opposed the new measure in the only hearing held in Trenton on the bill, describing herself as "no Milton Milan" and, as the daughter of a man who was bodily beaten in his effort to secure the right to vote, determined not to give up hard-won democratic freedoms. But now, with the county Democratic party behind it, the bill drew the support of five of the seven Camden city councilmen who had previously opposed it, to say nothing of representatives of the hospitals and universities that remained beneficiaries of the proposed legislation.[45] Even suburban

Camden County power brokers took the virtually unprecedented step, in matters concerning Camden, of holding a large rally on behalf of the proposal. The bill passed the state senate with only three dissenting votes, all by Republicans from rural areas.[46]

Conclusion

Throughout the past half century, capital flight, population loss, and persistent poverty have left Camden to face a single constant: an inadequate property base to balance its budget at acceptable levels of taxation. The method by which Camden raised revenue to maintain its existence emerged in the context of a booming industrial era, with significant fixed investment in value-added production. As capital mobilized and grew footloose, industries pulled up stakes and went elsewhere. As its wage and tax base declined with the loss of industry, beginning in the 1950s, Camden faced increasingly burdensome deficits with few tools available to alleviate its permanent fiscal crisis.

This structural constraint prompted a range of responses, depending both on what external funds were available and on the particular social context within which leadership was exercised to meet the problem. As federal assistance shrank, the state had to make up the difference. Its attitude differed according to partisan considerations, to be sure. Much more important, however, for at least the past quarter century, was the altered social context. The cumulative effect of flight—first of whites and more recently of minorities who could escape—left poverty largely concentrated in Camden. The city's isolation and the suspicions that isolation provoked inside as well as outside the city made even the best-intentioned interventions difficult to execute. Consistently principles and party counted for less than power. Jeffrey Nash was willing, for instance, to take the high ground to defend the Camden mayor's right to govern until such a time as he was given a sufficiently large role in the recovery process. Then the mayor was left virtually on her own. Even the press could downplay patronage payoffs if it appeared the larger cause of getting something done would benefit.

Can Camden's long and complicated story possibly have salience elsewhere? If one moves the focus beyond the individual personalities involved, certain more universal tendencies become manifest. Disinvestment is not a one-time process. It has cumulative effects. Local officials burdened with declining fiscal resources have to live with the consequences of what their predecessors have done. Officials' social as much as their political background has a great deal to do with what they can accomplish. But equally important are the constraints imposed by other levels of government authority. Quite clearly, a city even approaching Camden's condition cannot pull itself out of its fiscal dilemma, no matter how well managed. It needs additional resources to reverse decline. At one level, New Jersey offered in 2001 a broadly regional solution to Camden's problem, including in the process many of the stakeholders who had a vested interest in the city. What worked effectively locally, however, was hard to sell in a state facing a significant deficit itself. In this matter of having too little money, politics matters, and to date Camden has yet to be served sufficiently well to assure its long-term recovery.

CHAPTER 7

California's Industrial Garden

Oakland and the East Bay in the Age of Deindustrialization

ROBERT O. SELF

The contemporary geography of the San Francisco Bay Area is extraordinarily suggestive. Silicon Valley, an amorphous postsuburban landscape between San Jose and San Francisco, is credited with leading the new cyber-economy and redefining the relationships between technology, information, capital, and space. To the north, San Francisco sits atop a mountain of wealth, derived in equal measure from its positions as a tourist destination; a business, finance, and service center; and an entrepreneurial staging ground and housing market for the Silicon Valley boom. Across the bay lies the third pole of San Francisco's triangulated regional political economy, Oakland. Neither the cyber-development hothouse of Silicon Valley nor the bourgeois utopia of San Francisco, Oakland struggles to attract economic investment. Indeed, Oakland has endured over the last two generations the cluster of civic trials familiar as defining elements of deindustrialization and the urban crisis—disinvestment, property devaluation, unemployment, and persistent poverty—as its Bay Area rivals have boomed.

Oakland's postwar planners and booster visionaries did not imagine it this way, of course. After World War II they were optimistic that Oakland would lead a greater East Bay industrial economy and metropolis that could complement, and sometimes rival, San Francisco. But what happened in Oakland and the East Bay after 1945 cannot be summarized in the binary logic of urban success and failure or in the booster platitudes and dreams so common to U.S. cities on the make. To understand the postwar East Bay, we must dig deeper into local planning and politics than do most studies of industrial restructuring and keep in view both the broad structure of U.S. capitalism and the particularities and contingencies of place.[1]

159

This chapter explores the spatial patterns of postwar industrialization, deindustrialization, and suburban city building in the San Francisco Bay Area, focusing on Oakland and the East Bay. It seeks to understand deindustrialization as a product of local planning, civic boosterism, and politics as much as of national macroeconomic processes and broad patterns of capital mobility. There are two dimensions to the argument. First, planners and boosters in Oakland promoted a regional, metropolitan distribution of industrial investment and growth, campaigning nationally for factories, warehouses, and other facilities for the city's suburban periphery. This initially benefited but ultimately undermined Oakland itself. Second, local political projects within emerging suburban communities (San Leandro, Hayward, Union City, and Fremont especially) gave rise to a homeowner populism that linked low taxes with industrial growth, racial exclusivity with high property values, and the bourgeois amenities of "garden living" with the tax-paying responsibilities of corporate property owners. Both efforts contributed to regional industrial decentralization in California's East Bay in the 1950s and produced new metropolitan locations of residential and industrial capital. Suburban city building in the East Bay, as in the nation, called forth a contentious debate about the relationship between public and private resources that anticipated the tax politics of the 1970s and set the stage for the transformation of the physical U.S. landscape and the terrain of national politics.

This approach contributes to the reevaluation of "deindustrialization" as a term. It stands for a set of overlapping processes that vary so dramatically on every scale of analysis that the term's analytical leverage suffers. Shut factories and unemployed workers are striking symbols of what deindustrialization has wrought. But often those factories open elsewhere, employ new sets of workers, and feed investment into new places. Further, how do we understand extreme local variations, as when a city experiences deindustrialization within a region that overall seems to be industrializing at the expense of yet another region? For the purposes of this chapter, a more general concept, the spatial dynamics of industrial restructuring, will prove more helpful. This is especially appropriate for California and the West, a region that could be said as a whole to have benefited from industrial growth after World War II, but where individual cities and metropolitan regions responded very differently, and unevenly, to the opportunities such growth represented.[2]

The mid-century dynamics of industrial restructuring were complicated, overlapping, and unpredictable, but cities across the nation endeavored to shape them to local advantage whenever possible. Oakland was emblematic. Between the 1930s and the 1950s, the Oakland Chamber of

Commerce campaigned for the suburban dispersal of residence and industry in the East Bay—from Oakland and Berkeley in the north to the San Jose boundary in the south—through a national promotional vehicle, the Metropolitan Oakland Area Program. The program set forth the spatial-economic relationships around which postwar development was supposed to move: suburban industry tied to downtown Oakland and the city's port, universal home ownership in both city and suburb, the absence of industrial strife, and booming West Coast markets. The chamber envisioned an acceleration of the regional industrial dispersal that had begun before World War II. But boosters believed that as long as development occurred "with Oakland at the center," the city itself would continue to prosper even as outlying suburbs grew and became investment magnets in their own right. "Metropolitan Oakland" married boosterism to regional planning and trusted that the relationship would ensure prosperity in the emerging postwar world. All that remained was the investment to make it happen.

In the decades after 1945 this vision was realized, but not in the way Oakland boosters had hoped. San Francisco emerged as the regional center of new employment and a political-economic heavyweight that shaped regional transportation and capital flows. At the same time, new East Bay suburban communities began to compete with Oakland for industrial investment, offering property tax advantages and inexpensive land that its older neighbor could not match. Squeezed between the emerging dynamo of San Francisco and the assemblage of smaller, more flexible suburban cities of the East Bay, Oakland began a slow economic decline. Neither an aging industrial giant like Detroit, nor a sunbelt phenomenon like San Diego or Houston, Oakland, like its metropolitan neighbors, stood somewhere in the murky middle. But it is a murky middle with much to reveal about the spatial strategies for reorganizing the urban and suburban United States—strategies that took hold as both causes of and responses to the rapidly shifting postwar industrial and residential terrain. Oakland's stories reach beyond California to a national problematic of the second half of the twentieth century: in the frantic competition for private capital investment, cities, hopelessly trapped in the capitalist marketplace, entered into a savage rivalry with each other in which homeowners, as taxpayers, became the principal combatants.[3]

Imagining the Industrial Garden

Physical geography divides Oakland and the East Bay into three distinct, roughly parallel terrains. Oakland's hillside districts emerged early in this century as an upper-class enclave. Its sloping foothills to the west were by the 1920s home to residential districts of white-collar, middle-class, and lower-middle-class workers, in their single-family, stucco California bungalows. Neighborhoods in the flatlands have historically made up the bulk of the city's working-class residential and industrial space, the principal factory and warehouse belt tracing a line north and south along the waterfront. South of Oakland, the flatlands widen substantially into broad expanses of land, where truck farms, fruit orchards, and cattle ranches—the area's prewar occupants—would ultimately give way in the 1950s and 1960s to automobile plants, machine shops, and residential developments, anchors of the suburban East Bay's postwar landscape.

Industrial dispersal along the length of the flatlands had long been characteristic of East Bay metropolitan development. But Oakland dominated East Bay industry in the first decades of the century. It was home to a diverse array of machine and metal shops, automobile plants, iron works, shipyards, a regional passenger and freight rail center (dominated by the Southern Pacific), and one of the nation's largest agricultural canning industries (led by Libby, Heinz, and CalPak). By the late 1920s, industry had pushed beyond the city's boundaries, drawing residential development with it north and south along the length of the Bay. Oakland boomed between 1900 and 1930, nearly quadrupling its population (from 67,000 to 284,000) and adding tens of thousands of jobs to its industrial base. Its East Bay neighbors enjoyed similar prosperity: Berkeley, Emeryville, and San Leandro each acquired manufacturing establishments during these decades. On the eve of World War II, Oakland was no mere suburb of San Francisco, but the axis of an expanding industrial metropolis. Wartime manufacturers took advantage of this existing pattern by accelerating industrial decentralization in San Leandro, Hayward, Berkeley, Albany, and Richmond. Between 1900 and 1945, residential dispersal and suburbanization in the East Bay tended to follow, not lead, industrial decentralization.[4]

Oakland's postwar Metropolitan Oakland Area Program (MOAP) sought to amplify and extend these patterns of industrial development. Part plan, part booster crusade, the MOAP was financed by the Alameda County Board of Supervisors and designed by the Oakland Chamber of Commerce. MOAP promotional literature, part of Oakland's national campaign to lure investment, touted the East Bay as "the natural industrial center of the West," a vital hub of factories, warehouses, and rail transport facilities with an abundance of skilled labor and easy access to West Coast markets. (See figure 9.) To attract industrial capital from the East and Midwest, the MOAP highlighted the East Bay's existing "diversified industrial economy," home to a long list of "nationally known manufacturers," while simultane-

FIGURE 9. Following World War II, the Metropolitan Oakland Area Program (MOAP) promoted regional industrial growth. Advertisements like this one were designed both to encourage national industries to locate branch plants in Alameda County and to cultivate local support for MOAP's economic strategies. Courtesy of the Institute for Governmental Studies Library, University of California, Berkeley.

ously emphasizing the easy availability of inexpensive suburban land for new branch-plant investment. Chamber of Commerce advocates envisioned a first-class industrial corridor running from Richmond in the north through the unincorporated areas of Alameda County to the south, with "Oakland at its very heart." Such a scheme, planners and boosters alike imagined, would redound to Oakland's benefit and make it one of California's great postwar cities.[5]

Founders of the MOAP were animated by a vision of the East Bay as an industrial garden: a landscape of productive factories adjacent to neighborhoods of tree-lined streets and spacious lawns, the "garden-set" homes of postwar abundance. The region, promotional pamphlets emphasized, boasted "a most unusual combination of city, suburban, and country life, closely associated with, yet distinct from, business, factory, shipping." "Homes for industrial workers are unrivaled," a 1945 MOAP advertisement exclaimed, while "factories employ more than 400 persons," and "workmen find happiness in their garden-set homes . . . their children are healthy in the mild, equable climate." While drawing on standard California booster fare, the MOAP campaign adapted its claims to a postwar world anxious about the return of economic depression and open class hostilities, concerns that resonated with the city's middle class following Oakland's 1946 general strike. In the East Bay, MOAP literature explained, "employer and employee alike may have a garden-set home, with patio and vegetable garden, within easy distance of factory or office." In the metropolitan logic of the MOAP, suburbs were home to both factory and neighborhood, and though residential and industrial districts were "distinct" from one another, their close proximity was an intentional design element of suburbanization.[6]

In the concept of "metropolitan Oakland," business leaders sought a stable social and spatial order. Their program of East Bay industrial and residential dispersal was embedded in both community planning theory and class anxieties of the first half of the century. In the growth of industry, from Oakland outward into suburban districts, the MOAP imagined not a middle-class hinterland of commuters, but a series of industrial nodes and mixed-class residential developments, mutually beneficial and reinforcing. These understandings of suburban city building were strongly influenced by the modernist urban planning of Lewis Mumford and others in the Regional Planning Association of America. Believing in the coherence of the neighborhood, these urban theorists emphasized the decentralization of industry and residence in discrete units. At the same time, the promise that homeownership could be made available to ever larger numbers of workers—through a combination of mass-produced tract developments and the conversion of inexpensive peripheral agricultural land—promised a more stable class order. The notion that homeownership could be an effective sedative for a potentially troublesome working class emerged as an operating assumption of both the Federal Housing Administration (FHA) and private real estate developers, and constituted an explicit feature of American suburban planning.[7]

Oakland's postwar ambitions unfolded in a national context in which cities clamored for investment. Intercity competition for industrial capital in the first decade and a half after the war grew more intense every year. American firms looked to relocate factories, warehouses, and other facilities outside of core cities and outside of the nation's traditional industrial regions, the upper Midwest and Northeast, after 1945. They did so to escape high urban property taxes, to build spacious new facilities on cheap suburban land, to undermine high-paid unionized workforces, and to produce goods in closer proximity to expanding markets in the West and South. And when these firms looked across the American landscape, hundreds of cities scrapped for their attention, offering concrete inducements from tax incentives to "garden-set" homes for workers.[8]

Deindustrialization and industrial decentralization in the long postwar period were not, then, processes controlled solely by the nation's business elite and dictated from corporate boardrooms or by abstract capital markets. They were equally the product of a fascinating and wide-ranging movement by smaller cities, suburbs, and regions to build their own industrial economies. We must understand these places, as much as the corporations themselves, the places they left, and the shape of the national economy, if a full picture of industrial restructuring is to emerge.

Postwar suburbs may have been the nation's most conspicuous bourgeois monuments, but they have also behaved like classic urban growth machines. Characterized by an interpenetration of business and political systems for the purpose of pursuing economic development, growth machines seek to attract capital to local places. Economic growth and the accumulation of wealth drive local politics, and the city-business coalition seeks electoral allies for support and political legitimacy. But intercity competition is often a zero-sum game. Some cities win, others lose. Even as MOAP boosters promoted Oakland and the greater East Bay as a regional space for industrial investment, individual cities in the East Bay, "suburbs" of Oakland in name, practiced their own version of growth machine politics. As individual cities within the region adopted their own industrial strategies and forged their own internal political coalitions to pursue growth, regional cooperation gave way to competition. Oakland boosters could imagine that suburban industrialization would benefit their city, but the reality was finally far more complicated, contingent, and political.[9]

The Industrial Garden Realized:
Politics and Planning in the Suburbs

In the language of consummate boosterism, Fred Cox, president of the Southern Alameda County Real Estate Board, promised in 1950 that "during the last half of the twentieth century carefully selected property will increase to prices that would now seem fabulous." An exploding real estate market in Alameda County was virtually assured, Cox continued, because "a great increase in population, tremendous industrial development, and amazing commercial growth" would continue to underwrite property value increases for decades and make the East Bay "one of the great cities [sic] of America."

Beneath these familiar refrains of suburban promotion lay a strategy for and set of contentions about the nature of city building that deserve closer attention. To recover the process of suburbanization in Alameda County south of Oakland, as in American metropolitanization more generally, we must move past the giddy formulations of boosters like Cox. At the same time, however, we have to pay attention to what these boosters understood in their bones: that cities are fundamentally about the social production of markets and the leveraging of property into one version of community or another. In the postwar United States, suburban cities emerged as the central players in one of the nation's most advanced and intense efforts to harness property to a range of class, racial, and wealth-generating projects. Suburban development may have produced a physical landscape of "sprawl," but superficial sameness obscured calculated political-economic objectives in the local contest among cities for investment. Suburbanization was driven by the politics of making markets in industrial and residential property and in maintaining exclusionary access to those markets.[10]

Between the end of World War II and the early 1960s, half a dozen cities on Oakland's southern periphery, between East Oakland and San Jose, became the industrial garden imagined in the Metropolitan Oakland Area Program. By the early 1970s, one could trace a line on a map following this landscape from Oakland's southern edge through San Leandro, Hayward, Union City, Newark, Fremont, and Milpitas to San Jose's northern boundary forty miles away in the South Bay. San Leandro and Hayward alone among that group existed as incorporated cities prior to the mid-1950s. The others incorporated during the 1950s, as groups of civic entrepreneurs forged new municipalities from the scattered towns, farmland, ranches, and orchards of the East Bay flatlands. Yet while this pattern of growth elaborated the MOAP's vision, it also undermined it, creating cities and economic networks that would compete with, as much as complement, Oakland. East Bay suburban city builders responded to the logic of intercity competition and the dynamics of property markets as described by Cox, not the regional vision of the MOAP and Oakland's boosters.

Capital mobility and the extraordinary growth of California's population during and after the war propelled suburbanization. The process is not reducible to structural forces alone, however. Development of the East Bay suburban corridor in the postwar decades was the product of local politics as much as the flow of capital. City builders in the East Bay set out to create and maximize two kinds of property markets—in residential and industrial land—in order to finance public services, maintain home equity, and, in the optimistic and ultimately market-driven logic of U.S. urban and suburban development, to ensure future economic growth. This city building was political, because interests differed over exactly how those markets would be created and racialized. City building was also territorial, because the way municipal boundaries were drawn, the way the tax burden was distributed, and where people lived in relation to where they worked depended on both an imagined and a real geography. The story of East Bay suburbanization is about the relationships between large forces at work in the region and nation, especially the mobility of industrial and residential capital, and the local strategic opportunism of political projects led by homeowners, petty bourgeois entrepreneurs, real estate developers, and other property-oriented interests.

This local opportunism was itself a synthesis of two venerable traditions within U.S. political culture: antitax conservatism and booster promotion. At the core of this synthesis was the flexible and powerfully persuasive discourse of homeowner populism. U.S. strains of populism have traditionally emphasized the interests of a broad, diffuse, and not necessarily class-bound "public" or "people" against various elites and powerful economic and political institutions. Wedded to capitalism, populists in U.S. history have rarely endorsed radical prescriptions for social change, preferring reforms and compromises that restore a balance of power to local interests. In places like the East Bay suburbs, populism was reborn in the postwar decades in the form of a homeowner-centered faith in the righteousness of the "small taxpayer." Homeowner populism brought property taxes to the fore of local politics. Based on the ideal of citizens as homeowner-consumers rather than as independent producers, this populism firmly established homeownership as a formidable political identity in the 1940s, three decades before California's celebrated 1978 tax revolt. Capital mobility, national economic restructuring, federal sponsorship of home-ownership, and the extraordinary growth of California's population during and after the war encouraged and propelled the process of suburban for-mation in the East Bay, but homeowner populism was the glue that held the new cities together.[11]

Two cases in southern Alameda County, the largely agricultural area south of Oakland, illustrate the political-economic dynamics of this local opportunism and the homeowner populism that drove industrial suburban city building: San Leandro and Fremont. They help us to see the ways in which industrial restructuring as a national process was promoted and abet-ted by tax- and race-conscious homeowner movements in the suburban pe-riphery.

San Leandro embodied postwar debates about property and symbol-ized their resolution in low taxes, new industrial development, and white racial exclusivity. By the 1960s San Leandro had entered the national iconography of suburban America, when it was named a "model munici-pality" by the *Wall Street Journal*. Oakland's nearest neighbor to the south-east, San Leandro had since the 1920s served as a bedroom community and as a truck farming center that provided vegetables, fruit, and cut flowers to nearby cities and the broader region. Despite its size (22,903 in 1940) and semirural orientation, San Leandro had attracted a few notable industries—a Caterpillar assembly plant and Frieden Calculators, in particular—before the war. After 1945, the city's civic leaders, developers, and wartime new-comers added to that industrial base by converting nearby agricultural land into cheap factory and housing sites, in pursuit of what they termed "bal-anced development." Such a pursuit called forth choices. The city's civic leaders and residents chose low-tax-led industrial growth and white racial solidarity among second- and third-generation Irish, Italians, and Portu-guese, as well as WASP newcomers. But they did so only after a series of contentious debates over the role and responsibilities of corporations and industrial property within the local political economy.[12]

Historians of postwar suburbanization have emphasized that the sub-urban form privileged private over public space. The single-family home, cul-de-sac street patterns, automobile, and nuclear family have come to symbolize the suburban celebration of the private sphere. In our justifiable enthusiasm to document this dimension of postwar American life, however, we have underestimated conflict within suburbs over the boundary between private and public spaces and resources. Suburban residents and city officials contested that boundary most frequently and fiercely around the issue of taxation. No single sphere of civic activity more concretely embodies the intersection of private and public interest, indeed the very definition of private and public, than tax policy. Debates over suburban taxation in places like San Leandro, and throughout California, transformed American politics in the 1970s and brought the term "tax revolt" into the national lexicon. But these debates had important roots in the 1940s, when suburban residents and city builders shaped local economic landscapes, political cultures, and indeed the very boundaries of municipalities in order to lower residential taxes through industrial ratables.[13]

Municipal tax policy transcended the mundane in 1940s San Leandro. Civic leaders, homeowners' associations, industrialists, and politicians all understood the enormous relevance and long-term consequences of their taxation and development policies. Residential development during the war had concentrated thousands of newcomers to the city in an expansive neighborhood of ranch-style homes named East Shore Park. The area's neighborhood association, the East Shore Park Civic League, became San Leandro's most vocal proponent of using industrial property taxes to improve municipal services and the physical infrastructure of the city. In the late 1940s the East Shore Park Civic League grew disenchanted with the city council. The council was composed of a generation of San Leandro businessmen who had governed the city since the 1930s, lived in the older downtown, and, so it appeared to the newcomers, were willing to overburden new homeowners in order to accommodate local industries like Chrysler. The league was not antitax in an absolute sense, but its members believed that neighborhoods should be shielded from high taxes by the shifting of the city's fiscal burden onto those businesses and industries that could "well afford to pay." The league, one of its representatives wrote in the *San Leandro Reporter*, intended "to assure themselves of an equitable distribution of the tax dollar by the election ballot."[14]

In 1948, angered over tax breaks for the Chrysler plant, the East Shore Park Civic League turned to politics and swept the incumbent city council members from office. In their place the league helped to elect a reform slate of pro-growth fiscal conservatives who pledged to "let the people decide how their tax dollar is spent." George Thompson and his newspaper cheered. Reform politics succeeded in San Leandro, the paper declared, because the city's governing clique "forgot to remember that there are thousands of little property owners who were not impressed with the desirability of underwriting the manufacturing costs of such enterprises as the Chrysler corporation." Thompson and the East Shore Park Civic League hoped to reverse the equation: homeowner amenities would be underwritten with the property taxes paid by local industry.[15]

The league solidified a political consensus in San Leandro that carried the city through a remarkable period of industrial and residential growth after 1948. The new city council and the chamber of commerce developed an industrial strategy designed to transform San Leandro from the "city of sunshine and flowers" into the "city of industry." New businesses would henceforth locate within the municipal boundaries, and the city would annex outlying industrial property. Taxes on industry would fund city services, while the property tax rate would remain low, both to accommodate the "thousands of little property owners" who voted and to attract new industrial capital seeking entry into the Bay Area's expanding postwar markets. There could hardly have been a more ironic reformulation of the Oakland-centered MOAP than San Leandro's tax policy. Between 1948 and the 1960s, San Leandro competed for new investment with nearby Oakland, Hayward, and Fremont, as well as with the South Bay and San Francisco Peninsula, by driving its basic property tax rate to the lowest level in California.[16]

As the 1948 election had demonstrated, however, San Leandro's business community was constrained by an active, tax-conscious group of homeowners and neighborhood associations. Wary that those constraints would intensify over time, the chamber of commerce sought to sell the city's residents on the benefits of industry. Beginning in 1949, the chamber actively sought to convince homeowners of "their stake [in the city] in terms of personal benefits and in the continued growth and expansion of industrial and business firms in San Leandro." With exclamations like "San Leandro industry benefits you!" "San Leandro industry helps pay your taxes!" and "San Leandro industry puts money in everyone's pocket!" a series of chamber pamphlets and advertisements blanketed the city in the late 1940s and early 1950s, a stream of propaganda that represented politics by other means. San Leandro's homeowners did not subscribe to anti-industry, redistributive politics of a radical stripe, but the chamber nevertheless correctly perceived that the sorts of nitty-gritty concerns residents did have about taxes, city services, and quality-of-life amenities could lead them to oppose certain kinds of industrial development in the future. Here was the antidote: constant messages that industry is on the homeowners' side, keeping taxes low, schools good, and jobs local.[17]

While San Leandro's city manager coordinated with political leaders on an industrial strategy, homeowners and real estate developers articulated a related racial strategy. "Faced with the great influx of colored population into the East Bay during the war years," as the city's newspaper put it in a frank page-one story, San Leandro residents scrambled to erect spatial barriers that would protect the "thousands of little property owners" ("all white Caucasians," according to the newspaper) from African American neighbors. In the minds of San Leandro's real estate brokers and homeowners, racial restriction was a necessary companion to the city's industrial strategy and its commitment to low property taxes and high property values. According to this logic, a taxpayer's investment could be eroded as easily by racial succession as by greedy corporations that avoided paying their share for city services. Restriction was a priority for the local real estate industry because of its more general interest in a stable and reliably increasing market. Unlike many brokers in Oakland who, in the 1950s, used blockbusting tactics to increase profits, the real estate industry in South County adopted exclusion and containment as its principal strategies. The result was a virtual white wall along the city's border with Oakland.[18]

The real estate industry and anxious homeowners produced a wave of racial housing restriction in San Leandro in the years immediately after the war. Restrictions had been used in San Francisco and parts of the East Bay for decades primarily to contain the mobility of Chinese and Japanese residents. Postwar covenant schemes perpetuated such exclusions, but late-1940s efforts were aimed primarily at newly arrived African Americans. The city's major newspaper reported that the "sudden increase in the East Bay Negro population" meant that "local neighborhoods are spontaneously moving to protect their property values." San Leandro's high-profile campaign of racial exclusion earned the city a regional reputation for whiteness, and even the U.S. Supreme Court's ruling in 1948 that racial covenants were unenforceable did not halt, but only slowed, the barricading process. The East Bay real estate industry responded to the Court's landmark decision by reconfiguring San Leandro's covenant agreements into pseudocorporations of homeowners that could legally screen (through "corporation contract agreements") home buyers as long as "race and creed" were not explicitly taken into account.[19]

Between the late 1940s and the mid-1960s, two great rivers of public and private capital surged through the nation, enriching certain kinds of places, primarily suburban, and contributing to the impoverishment of others, primarily urban. San Leandro had positioned itself well in relation to these currents and stood to benefit enormously from them. The first river of capital was the extraordinary federal underwriting of private home construction through the mortgage guarantee programs of the Veterans Administration (VA) and the Federal Housing Administration (FHA). During much of the 1950s, FHA and VA housing starts accounted for one-third of the total housing starts nationwide, and mortgage guarantees represented billions of dollars annually, sums that went to suburban locations at a rate three times that to central cities. The second river had two forks. One fork was federal contracting for private companies like Lockheed, Boeing, Douglas Aircraft, and dozens of others. California received an ample share of these contracts—on which entire communities were built in places like Sunnyvale, Pasadena, and Long Beach—but San Leandro and the East Bay were relatively minor recipients of this kind of largess. A second fork, however, did flow through San Leandro. This was medium- and small-scale manufacturing and distribution capital decentralizing from the nation's older industrial heartland in the East and Midwest and seeking new, moderate-sized facilities to produce consumer products for California and West Coast markets. In what was largely a postwar extension of the branch-plant pattern of industrialization that had contributed to the East Bay's prewar growth, industries based in the East or upper Midwest opened branch plants, employing between 150 and 500 workers, in California throughout the 1940s and 1950s.[20]

Having positioned itself to intercept these postwar capital flows, San Leandro enjoyed a two-decade boom envied by its East Bay civic rivals. Between 1948 and 1957 alone, the city added fifteen thousand industrial jobs and over $130 million in capital investment in property and facilities. Caterpillar Tractor, Chrysler and Dodge parts and assembly divisions, Frieden Calculators, General Foods, Pacific Can, Peterson Tractor and Equipment, California Packing, Kaiser-Frazer Aircraft, and Crown-Zellerbach all had new or expanded factories or processing plants in San Leandro by the end of the 1950s. In just five years, between 1951 and 1956, the city's assessed property valuation nearly tripled, from $30 million to more than $85 million. By the early 1960s, industry in San Leandro paid more than one-third of the cost of city government. Prosperous and dynamic, the city had become the growth machine envisioned by its boosters and political leaders. The *Wall Street Journal* hailed San Leandro as a national model of small-scale industrial success in 1966, noting approvingly that the city "managed to get all the benefits of lavish public spending while putting a surprisingly small bite on the local taxpayers." With homeowner populism elevated to a civic creed, San Leandrans had created a white working-class city with white middle-class amenities—the industrial garden.[21]

Tax-conscious homeowner populism in San Leandro produced one version of the industrial garden. A competing version emerged in Fremont, southern Alameda County's largest suburban community and home of northern California's most celebrated automobile plant, a General Motors factory built in 1965. Incorporated in 1956, Fremont quickly developed into the county's most elaborately planned city. Its founders, an eclectic group of middle-class political and economic entrepreneurs and landholders, envisioned a tightly coordinated landscape of neighborhoods linked by broad boulevards and ample green space. Industry would, as in San Leandro, provide the tax base and support city services. But Fremont's homeowner populism did not follow the pro-growth, industry-friendly formula of San Leandro. Fremont's founders decried "runaway growth" in the East Bay, kept local developers in close check, and designed a community that for many years would be affordable only to the region's managerial and professional classes. But developers and workers alike complained about the constraints on residential land and housing. Fremont's very success in controlling growth through high property values and development restrictions became, in the 1960s, a source of political discord, as both developers and working-class activists challenged the city's homeowner populism.[22]

The drive to shape the markets of the industrial garden had propelled city-building in San Leandro. To the south lay all of the remaining unincorporated, undeveloped land in Alameda County west of the hills, a bonanza of potential factory and home sites. The resulting land rush, one of the most ferocious anywhere in postwar California, produced in a few short years three altogether new cities—Newark, Union City, and the sprawling Fremont—and an enlarged, reinvigorated older city, Hayward. In all, between 1951 and 1957, competitive incorporation and annexation converted Alameda County's prewar agricultural hinterland into a collection of cities as vast as Los Angeles. As in San Leandro, these contests reached beyond mundane, technical questions of administrative jurisdiction to fundamental questions of class, racial geography, and competing notions of the rights and responsibilities of property and capital.[23]

Fremont's incorporation offers a window on this process of land competition in South County and a view of the class fissures hidden within the industrial garden.[24] Homeowner populism in Fremont combined antitax conservatism and disdain for "runaway growth" into a potent political mix, stirred by the local leaders who managed Fremont's incorporation campaign. Local ranchers were prominent in this group, as were small businesspeople, but the various committees included judges, insurance agents, orchardists, newspaper editors, and engineers. Some among the founders had clear speculative economic interests in incorporation—a few ranchers and orchardists, for instance, could expect to receive high prices for land once the city was established. But the majority identified themselves as "homeowners" or "taxpayers" and articulated idealistic notions of what was "best for the community." "We want to see you aren't taxed one cent more than you need to be," a representative of the Alameda County Taxpayers Association told the Committee for the Incorporation of Fremont.

"Home rule" meant more than lower taxes to Fremont's neopopulist insurgents. It also meant a return to the "balanced concept of a city, one where homes, factories and stores, parks (and farms, for a time at least) all have equal place." This combination of low-tax conservatism and a pro-toenvironmentalist take on local development, hammered into the small-property-holder faith of homeowner populism, became the founding philosophy of Fremont. The township's residents voted overwhelmingly in favor of incorporation in 1956.[25]

Fremont founders steadfastly refused to show the usual deference to lo-cal developers. Instead, they produced an elaborate "master plan" to guide every aspect of the city's residential, commercial, and industrial growth. Fremont's political entrepreneurs were determined that the city would grow slowly and deliberately. With ample green space, solidly built hous-ing, and just enough industry to supply the tax base, Fremont would become a model parklike city. Its planning commission, composed of avowedly slow-growth champions from among the proponents of incorpo-ration, envisioned a community of "planned unit developments," coherent neighborhoods with homes built around parks, schools, and community centers. Planned unit developments had emerged in the 1950s as the na-tional planning profession's answer to suburban sprawl, promising instead greenbelts and pedestrian-friendly geography. Urban planning experimen-tation of the 1950s found a nearly ideal home in Fremont, which, after in-corporation, embraced an enormous ninety-six square miles, making it the third-largest city in land area in California, behind Los Angeles and San Diego. In 1955, only twenty thousand people lived in this expansive area. Fremont had achieved the ultimate homeowner populist revolt: sequester-ing nearly one hundred square miles of land within a jurisdiction now firmly controlled by low-tax, slow-growth advocates determined to place firm reigns on development.[26]

Not surprisingly, Fremont's master plan set the founding group of civic activists against local developers. Based on the prescriptions of the plan, Fremont's planning commission denied dozens of permit requests by de-velopers and turned down four large housing tracts in the city's first few months of existence. The commission subsequently increased the city's minimum housing lot size from five thousand to six thousand square feet and required developers to cede to the city a percentage of every devel-opable property to ensure sufficiently wide streets (like many sunbelt cities, Fremont planned for extra-wide boulevards to ease traffic congestion). Accustomed to civic cooperation, if not kowtowing, zoning loopholes, and generous profit margins, local developers grew hostile to the general plan and the planning commission. The conversion of property into profit, of land into capital, would proceed in Fremont under the strictest rules that homeowner populists had achieved anywhere in the San Francisco Bay Area.[27]

Plan advocates claimed their biggest victory in late 1960 when Fremont was selected as the site of a new General Motors production plant. In December of that year, GM decided to close its factory in East Oakland and construct a state-of-the-art facility in Fremont. The company's Oakland plant, dating to the 1920s, was too small to accommodate new production techniques and higher productivity goals designed to meet the booming demand for cars in the West. Fremont's plan-oriented, homeowner-populist civic leaders made the city an attractive investment as part of the automakers' strategy of national decentralization. The Southern Pacific Railroad, which owned the land purchased by GM, benefited enormously when Fremont was incorporated and the planning commission subsequently zoned hundreds of acres of relatively inexpensive property along Southern Pacific tracks, mostly former farmland, for heavy industry. When the plant was dedicated in early 1964, its payroll exceeded $42 million. A short two years later, the plant employed fifty-four hundred workers, with a payroll of forty-two million dollars. The city's mayor buoyantly declared: "There's no question about it. Fremont has arrived."[28]

Fremont's "arrival," however, yielded a landscape in which the idealized proximities and class harmony of the industrial garden went unrealized. Rapid speculation after incorporation had driven land and housing prices up, as had strict enforcement of the master plan. Developers built enormous housing tracts and sold thousands of homes to what University of California planner Catherine Bauer Wurster called "a narrow range of middle class families." Residents of these tracts, where homes sold for between $19,000 and $29,000, formed the backbone of the "pro-plan" advocates. In the master plan's prescriptions for ample green space, parks, and controls on growth and development, these homeowners found their values reflected and protected. But as the city's population increased through the 1960s (from 43,000 to just over 100,000 in 1970), and as the General Motors workforce grew apace (from about 4,000 in 1964 to 6,100 in 1969), observers and critics noted that surprisingly few workers seemed to live in the city. Commuting from East Oakland, San Jose, Milpitas, East Palo Alto, Santa Clara, Redwood City, and other communities within the Bay Area, GM workers streamed in and out of the plant's massive parking lot at each shift change. "We're creating a beautiful city where most of our workers cannot afford to live," Jack Brooks, a local developer, told the *Fremont News Register* in 1967. By 1970, out of a total population of 100,869, four hundred African Americans lived in the city; the median income ($11,933) of residents was higher than in any other city in Alameda County and almost twice that in Oakland; and median housing prices were the highest in the county.[29]

A series of studies confirmed what many already knew: the city of Fremont maintained a rigid disconnect between industrial location and working-class residence, where the taxes paid by manufacturing plants did not support the homes of those who worked there. A survey conducted by the Associated Homebuilders of the East Bay in 1964 strongly criticized the master plan for forcing up the price of homes. A report in 1967 by the Fremont City Employees Association claimed that 62 percent of Fremont city employees could not afford to purchase a home. A subsequent detailed study by the *Fremont News Register* confirmed that the least-expensive houses in Fremont in 1967 were priced at $20,000, with mortgage payments out of the reach of workers making less than $10,000 a year. "The fact is," Jack Brooks explained, "this city has no real correlation between housing and industrial development."[30]

The odd alliance between working-class activists and developers in Fremont took its most public form in 1966, when hotly contested city elections revealed deep antagonisms at the heart of homeowner populism. That year, a Committee for Change ran candidates against two incumbent council members elected on a "pro-plan" platform in 1962. On what was billed as an "economy slate," the challengers argued that Fremont "must aggressively seek industrial development" and "cut the tax rate for the homeowner." The insurgents charged that under the "pro-plan" administration, the costs of city services had increased, while the slow-growth philosophy of the council had chased industry away and kept developers handcuffed. Veteran "pro-plan" spokespersons and Fremont founders countered that the "builder-subdivider political slate," would bring uncontrolled industrial and residential development to the city, exactly what the master plan had been designed to prevent. The Committee for Change echoed San Leandro's homeowner populism of the 1950s. The plan worked in theory, they claimed, but in practice homeowners suffered because the city was not acquiring enough industry to keep the tax rate low. By speeding up the pace of industrialization, public officials could lower the property taxes on individual homeowners. This cross-class appeal was bolstered by a local newspaper poll in which "more industry" had been identified as the number-one priority of respondents. The election revealed both the relatively narrow range of civic debate and the centrality of taxes and homeownership to local political discourse. In the end, one incumbent won and the other was defeated, setting the stage for additional rounds of attacks by both developers and homeowners in subsequent years.[31]

The complaints of workers and developers exaggerated the city's stagnation, but Fremont's critics did not lack for evidence that the bloom on the industrial garden had begun to wilt. Fremont more than doubled both its population and its production workforce between 1960 and 1970. The city remained decidedly working class, with well over half of its residents employed in trades, clerical work, and as operatives or laborers. Nevertheless, in relation to other East Bay cities, especially San Leandro, Fremont was a more expensive place to live and had fewer industrial establishments. While its median income had been somewhere in the middle among Alameda County suburbs in 1960, by 1970 Fremont's median and average incomes were higher than in any other East Bay city; only the professional suburban enclave of Castro Valley boasted higher incomes. Housing prices, too, were higher. By 1970, families paid more for homes in Fremont than anywhere else in the East Bay.

But while the city had clearly grown, it lagged behind the region's model industrial community, San Leandro, by a considerable margin. Despite its notable success in acquiring the General Motors facility, Fremont in 1972 still had one-third the total number of production establishments of San Leandro and about half the number of production jobs. All of this was in a city with a population one and a half times that of San Leandro. Fremont's relative lack of industrial property translated into higher property taxes for homeowners. By the early 1970s, Fremont homeowners were paying property taxes at a rate 40 percent higher than in San Leandro. Indeed, in 1970 Fremont's total combined tax burden was higher than Oakland's. Fremont, a planned city with the potential to emerge as the East Bay's model industrial garden community, was by the mid-1970s fertile ground for the tax revolt politics of the second half of the decade.[32]

Industrial Garden/Industrial Ghetto: Emerging Relations of Power

In the late 1960s and early 1970s, Oakland shared an emerging language with the nation. When Donald McCullum, Oakland NAACP president, testified to the U.S. Civil Rights Commission in 1967 that "[h]ere in Oakland . . . we are ringed by a white noose of suburbia," he was testing the limits of this new language of race and urban form, as Malcolm X, the McCone Report on Watts, and dozens of urban commentators had before him. Mc-

Cullum and others pointed to the suburban periphery of America's largest cities, the locus of job creation and capital accumulation for a generation, and found if not always a "white noose" at least a racially-exclusive territory that seemed to thrive as the cities declined. In contemporary American discourse, this language is by now familiar if not overdetermined. But in the late 1960s, African American activists, urban politicians and planners, and critical metropolitan observers of many allegiances had just begun to give expression to little more than a decade of experience and concern. Conservative Oakland mayor John Reading told the Civil Rights Commission, "Oakland is a typical core city with the core city's typical problems, problems which to a large extent can be traced to the well-known exodus of large numbers of white and middle-class citizens to the suburbs." He added that there was a "regional responsibility" to distribute jobs and housing equally and that "it is a fact we do have a white noose." In the face of the complexities of human and capital mobility in the East Bay and San Francisco, McCullum, Reading, and others turned to the glaring contrast between city and suburb and saw in the contrast a powerful racial metaphor and explanation for their own city's dilemmas.[33]

The promise of the industrial garden, enshrined in the MOAP campaigns of the 1940s and 1950s, was realized, if unevenly, in places like San Leandro and Fremont. Working-class neighborhoods in Oakland's flatlands, in contrast, faced a steady hollowing out, as the city's small-scale manufacturing economy contracted. Gone were the hundreds of railroad jobs that had sustained an earlier generation of black Oaklanders. Gone, too, after the advent of containerization in the mid-1960s, were many of the longshore and warehouse jobs on which both black and white workers had depended in the 1930s and 1940s. The city's massive canning industry had declined by the middle of the decade. Oakland's automobile industry had simply disappeared. Between 1961 and 1966, Oakland lost ten thousand manufacturing jobs. The MOAP had helped to industrialize the county, while proving only marginally successful at developing Oakland itself. The city's slow deindustrialization over the course of the postwar decades could not be blamed entirely on the suburban periphery—the relocation of Oakland's General Motors plant to Fremont was one of only a handful of examples of major plants actually leaving the city for nearby suburbs. But the overall shift in employment from the city to surrounding areas was impossible to ignore.[34]

Such shifts inclined Oakland's critics, ironically, to overlook San Francisco as a factor in the city's economic struggles. Historically, large numbers of blue-collar workers commuted to San Francisco from Oakland. San Francisco's relatively rapid conversion, beginning in the late 1950s, from a manufacturing, warehousing, and wholesaling hub into a financial and tourist center radically transformed the regional occupational mix, eliminating many of those blue-collar jobs. The boom in service-sector jobs that San Francisco's new economy produced shackled Oakland with a barrier to mobility nearly as problematic as the suburban "white noose," because the service sector was extraordinarily slow in absorbing African American and Latino workers, except in low-paying "back of the house" occupations. Further, San Francisco planners and business interests spearheaded the drive to build a rapid transit system linking East Bay cities with downtown. That system, Bay Area Rapid Transit (BART), extended into more than half a dozen East Bay suburbs, including San Leandro and Fremont, allowing San Francisco's white-collar workforce to commute from peripheral locations, feeding commercial and residential capital into those newer cities. The "Metropolitan Oakland Area" was also the San Francisco metropolitan area, an overlapping set of restructurings whose complexities belied the simple suburban metaphor offered by Oaklanders.[35]

McCullum, Reading, and others in Oakland were nonetheless right to direct attention to the suburban form. Homeowner populism, the loose civic ideology that guided development in places like San Leandro and Fremont, proved extraordinarily effective in adapting to national trends in capital mobility between 1945 and the 1970s. Its idealized form, embedded in the MOAP's neo-utopian images of "garden-set" homes, was imagined as a sedative for volatile class relations. Its real form, embodied in the East Shore Park Civic League in San Leandro and the master plan in Fremont, produced new class and racial divisions with outlines starkly visible over the local space-economy. The small-property-holder faith on which these communities rose was effective precisely because local actors could bound property and space into political units to compete within the competitive capitalist marketplace. But those same boundaries defined the interests of homeowners and the public officials whom they elected in the narrow terms of municipal taxes and homeowner amenities. The rush of suburbanites into local civic politics under the umbrella of homeowner populism meant a retreat from other forms of public responsibility and a withdrawal from cultural and fiscal connections to core cities like Oakland.

Industrial restructuring in California's East Bay between the 1950s and the 1970s did not, in Oakland, fell a mighty giant. Oakland's experience of deindustrialization was nothing like the precipitous process visited on Detroit, Baltimore, and Philadelphia, places where hundreds of thousands of jobs were lost in a single generation and entire neighborhoods lay virtually abandoned. Unlike those cities, Oakland had never fully *made it* as an industrial capital. To tell the story of Oakland solely as one of unidirectional deindustrialization is to miss the larger truth that there was hardly a golden industrial past from which Oakland slipped. The postwar period is less a tragic story of deindustrialization suddenly tearing asunder a once mighty industrial empire than the story of a medium-sized city struggling to find its place, first in the industrial United States, then, beginning sometime in the middle 1960s, in the postindustrial United States. Narratives of national deindustrialization miss an additional truth. At the local level, industrial restructuring was the product of complicated homeowner politics and spatial-fiscal competition between cities. In the three decades after World War II, in places like California's East Bay, antitax conservatism industrialized the suburbs, but the politics those places produced would, in the second half of the 1970s, return in the form of a "tax revolt." The insurgencies against high taxes would stun central cities with a final withdrawal that made the struggles of middling cities like Oakland even more profound.

CHAPTER 8

Deindustrialization, Poverty, and Federal Area Redevelopment in the United States, 1945–1965

GREGORY S. WILSON

We tend to think of the 1950s as a golden age of industrial production, and the 1970s as an era of dramatic decline. However, throughout the postwar era, a number of basic industries began to experience disinvestment early, as capital loosened and began the long process of relocation. Indeed, while overall economic growth remained strong in the United States during the 1950s, many communities experienced high unemployment resulting from deindustrialization, especially those relying on coal and textiles. These industries were the canaries in the coal mine, and for those families caught in the wake of change, poverty and hardship loomed.

As a response to these glaring problems, in 1955 Democratic Senator Paul Douglas of Illinois instructed his staff to draft what would eventually become the Area Redevelopment Act. Those who drafted the bill drew primarily on local, state, and federal efforts from the 1930s and 1940s designed to combat the effects of declining industries. They also drew on knowledge of similar programs in Western Europe. Originally, they hoped to establish a new federal agency that would create regional planning bodies to offer financial incentives to lure businesses to areas adversely affected by deindustrialization.

After five years of political battles, the act, signed by President John F. Kennedy in 1961, created the Area Redevelopment Administration (ARA), which provided assistance to both urban areas hurt by deindustrialization and rural and Native American communities as well. Armed with some $390 million and a four-year lifespan, the ARA tried to make individuals and communities better competitors in the market through loans and grants for new facilities, job training, and infrastructure improvements.

But the ARA lacked the strong regional vision that animated its early proponents. Moreover, the economic liberalism proposed by the ARA would quickly be subsumed by the high-profile race liberalism of the welfare-oriented War on Poverty. Responding to the civil rights movement, in 1963, ARA administrators made inner cities eligible for aid. With limited funds and projects in over one thousand communities, the ARA met constant criticism from both the political left and the right for failing to do more to generate economic growth in depressed areas. As a consequence, the ARA was hampered throughout its short life in its effort to address basic problems of uneven capital flows, investment, and development as the national economy lurched toward a decline in basic manufacturing.[1]

This chapter provides evidence of the ways social and cultural issues, particularly race and gender, intersect with politics, policy making, and state building. At times, the process surrounding redevelopment evolved in a contingent and divisive manner, as various groups and individuals engaged in efforts to halt or redirect this policy. This chapter also examines the failure of the United States, at the height of a liberal political period, to respond adequately to deindustrialization in the 1950s and 1960s. Modeled chiefly on local and state programs, the ARA was designed and executed by liberals to make individuals, communities, and regions better competitors in the market. The individuals were mostly men and most of the targeted communities had been hurt by declines in mining, lumbering, or textiles, or were rural areas and Native American reservations looking to industrialize. Not surprisingly, cold war liberals perceived no fundamental flaw in the operations of democratic capitalism, only flaws in how people and areas failed to participate in the abundance offered by the post–World War II U.S. economy. In the end, the issue of deindustrialization became the provenance of the ARA, an agency with limited funding, a tenuous lifespan, and a mandate to combat poverty across the country. In this context, I argue, it is remarkable the ARA managed to create jobs; but it was a limited response to industrial decline, which remained a marginal topic until the 1970s, when liberalism lost its support and deindustrialization became more severe.[2]

Pre-ARA Federal Programs, 1933–1954

From the 1930s until Paul Douglas introduced the Depressed Areas Act in 1955, federal interest in the issue of redevelopment was intermittent. In the 1930s, as part of their effort to understand the Great Depression, New Dealers in the Federal Emergency Relief Administration and the Works

Progress Administration conducted surveys of communities experiencing long-term unemployment, which included towns and cities dependent on industries such as coal mining and textile production.[3] Then, in the summer of 1941 the Office of Production Management (OPM) initiated a certification system for what they called "distressed areas." Growing from federal efforts to manage the resources and materials needed to fight World War II, OPM classified a distressed area as one in which unemployment threatened to reach one-fifth of the community's total manufacturing employment. To remedy this, the agency authorized the army and navy to allow priority bidding to industries in distressed areas.[4]

As World War II progressed and an Allied victory seemed likely, economists and other influential policymakers in both the United States and Europe urged the development of a full-employment postwar economy. However, U.S. legislative efforts in this area disappointed those who demanded a greater role for the state in economic planning. When Congress finally passed the Employment Act in 1946, it reflected conservative efforts to amend the original proposal, for rather than full employment, the government was to promote "maximum employment."[5] Also, instead of proposing a full-employment budget, the act required the president to provide a yearly report on the nation's economy. Keeping something of the original, the act established the congressional Joint Committee on the Economic Report (which later became the Joint Economic Committee) and the Council of Economic Advisers (CEA) to advise the president on economic policy and draft an annual economic report.[6] Both agencies would become active in the issue of area redevelopment in the 1950s.

As the cold war developed, federal officials continued to rely on defense procurement as a salve for distressed communities. Unfortunately, this indirect method did not relieve the economic distress, for it required communities to have defense-related industries, which they often did not. If they did, the law did not require that procurement officers award contracts in these communities; these officers often preferred to work with established (and usually large) firms. Moreover, army and navy officials, citing national security issues, sought to disperse industry and preferred to award contracts in the South and West, away from the majority of the distressed areas in the traditional manufacturing belt.[7] This tended to exacerbate the problem of deindustrialization in the Northeast and Midwest, since industries were already leaving these regions for the South and West. Such contradictions are common, for federal policies often work at cross-purposes. Area redevelopment was in part a response to other federal programs, which included trade policy that harmed certain industries such as coal and textiles, subsidies for highway construction that fostered the decline of inner cities, and housing policy that privileged commercial construction over housing for poor urban residents. All this points to the difficulty of coordinating programs related to industrial transformation and community development and provides part of the context within which area redevelopment began.[8]

Local and State Developments, 1945–1961

Despite these proposals and overall economic growth following World War II, unemployment still plagued several areas, and the post-Korea recession only made matters worse. These areas included New England textile communities, Pennsylvania anthracite and bituminous coal towns, and railroad communities, as well as some manufacturing areas dependent on steel and automobiles. While policymakers made attempts in the federal arena, workers, union representatives, business owners, and civic leaders at the local and state levels developed proposals to revive their economies. In time, many of these individuals and groups lobbied for federal assistance and influenced the creation of national area redevelopment legislation. The efforts in Pennsylvania, especially in the anthracite coal region, played an important role in the creation of area redevelopment legislation. Following World War II, while much of America embodied John Kenneth Galbraith's description of an "affluent society," Pennsylvania lagged behind.[9] Between 1947 and 1957, when nonagricultural employment increased 21 percent in the United States, employment in Pennsylvania grew 4 percent, just ahead of Rhode Island and West Virginia, where employment declined 3 percent. By 1961, Pennsylvania had more areas of substantial labor surplus than any other state.[10]

Not unexpectedly, local business groups created the first plans that would influence the state program and in turn shape federal area redevelopment legislation. Using fund drives and working with banks, economists, and planners, local business leaders created industrial development organizations that relied on financial incentives to attract new industries. Examples in the Pennsylvania anthracite region include the Scranton Lackawanna Industrial Building Company (SLIBCO—1946), Hazleton Industrial Development Corporation (HIDC—1947), and the Lackawanna Industrial Fund Enterprise (LIFE—1950). These organizations became part of a national postwar trend that saw cities and states create public and private institutions to offer incentives attracting new industries.[11] Although organizations such as SLIBCO, HIDC, and LIFE created new jobs, they failed to arrest high unemployment and economic decline. For example, during the late 1950s, unemployment in Scranton and Hazleton averaged between 11 and 16 percent, while the national rate hovered between 4 and 6 percent. As a result, local business leaders joined with workers to demand a greater role for the state in promoting economic development in their communities.[12]

By this time, Pennsylvania was not alone in trying to create policies aimed at industrial development. In New England, textile towns had created institutions similar to those in Pennsylvania, and states such as Maine sanctioned private development corporations that sold stock in order to promote new industries. Meanwhile, many southern towns and states had created industrial development organizations as well.[13] These developments were part of what Peter K. Eisinger has called the rise of the "entrepreneurial state." He cites the emergence "sometime after the mid-1970s" of an intense "preoccupation with economic development" at the state and local levels.[14] Although evidence from Pennsylvania and elsewhere shows that this concern predated the 1970s, Eisinger's concept of activist subnational states emerging in lieu of more aggressive federal policies is useful for understanding the history of area redevelopment and shows the need to integrate analysis of local, state, and national events.

Through the Pennsylvania Industrial Development Administration (PIDA), Pennsylvanians developed the most substantial government effort aimed directly at communities experiencing industrial decline. Created in May 1956, and composed of both government officials and private citizens, PIDA offered loans to private development groups to construct or upgrade facilities in areas of high unemployment, defined as a rate of 6 percent for the preceding three years, or 9 percent for the preceding eighteen months. Conservatives made sure that local groups were required to contribute 20 percent of the project cost, while liberals required groups to show that the facility was not part of a company plan to relocate from one part of the state to another.[15] Like earlier proposals, PIDA created jobs, authorizing some $62 million in loans for a planned 61,000 new jobs between 1956 and 1965. Still, unemployment in eligible labor markets in Pennsylvania remained higher than the national average, and the same was true in other distressed communities across the country, adding pressure for a federal response.[16]

Creating the ARA, 1954–1961

Along with developments in Pennsylvania, those in two other areas influenced area redevelopment legislation. First was New England. With support from representatives in the region, Solomon Barkin, research director of the Textile Workers Union of America, played a key role in shaping the Depressed Areas Act, first introduced by Senator Douglas in July 1955. Barkin had an interest in planning dating back to his days as a New Dealer and he continued to push for greater federal involvement in regional and national economic management. Since the 1940s, he had been pushing business and labor leaders in New England to develop a response to the decline of the textile industry, and he saw in Douglas's proposal a way to nationalize his ideas. Barkin worked closely with Douglas's staff, as did William L. Batt Jr., a former Labor Department official and the secretary of commerce and labor in Pennsylvania, who would go on to head the ARA in 1961. Second, both men admired the programs developed in Europe. After the ARA's creation in 1961, Batt authorized continued study in this area. In *Area Redevelopment Policies in Britain and the Countries of the Common Market*, the ARA published accounts of Belgian, British, French, German, and Italian programs to combat persistent unemployment in areas hurt by industrial decline.[17] Despite these precedents, passage of the Douglas bill proved difficult, revealing the struggles within the New Deal coalition and between coalition supporters and those opposed to it. In the end, the process and substance of federal policy aimed at deindustrialization reflected the nature of these postwar conflicts.[18]

The first Douglas bill carried New Deal influences into the postwar period. Introduced in July 1955 and cosponsored by several key Democrats, including John F. Kennedy, Estes Kefauver, and Hubert Humphrey, the Depressed Areas Act called for the creation of a Depressed Areas Administration within the executive branch, headed by an administrator appointed by the president. The administrator would have the power to appoint a local industrial development committee to plan industrial and commercial construction. The bill also authorized Treasury funding rather than yearly congressional appropriations. The heart of the proposal was a series of programs similar to those already developed at the local level and then being considered in Pennsylvania. These included: 1) a $100 million loan fund to finance the construction of industrial facilities; 2) a $100 million fund for grants and loans to construct community facilities; 3) preference to distressed areas for government procurement; 4) dissemination of technical information to assist in community redevelopment; 5) accelerated tax amortization for plant construction in distressed areas; 6) vocational training; 7) unemployment compensation for workers in training programs; and 8) surplus food distribution. Using Labor Department guidelines, the bill defined depressed regions as urban areas with average unemployment of 6 percent for three years, or 9 percent for eighteen months. In addition, the Depressed Areas Administration was to be a banker of last resort: community groups had to show that they were unable to obtain funding elsewhere in the private sector. In effect, this was a means test for communities.[19]

Elite and local pressure forced amendments to the bill and reflected both the opening skirmishes in the coming War on Poverty and growing tension within the New Deal coalition. Because of the power they held on committees in Congress and within the Democratic party, southerners were the most significant group in terms of either forcing amendments to the bill or blocking legislation. Those who desired federal assistance for economic development, including representatives Brooks Hays (Democrat-Arkansas), Paul Brown (Democrat-Georgia), and Albert Rains (Democrat-Alabama), indicated to Douglas that they would block the bill unless it included rural areas. As written, it targeted only industrial communities, most of which were in the Northeast and Midwest.[20] Pressure also came from a series of hearings on rural poverty conducted in November 1955 by Alabama Senator John Sparkman, during which rural citizens, as well as local and state leaders, testified in favor of including aid for their communities. While southern leaders usually opposed federal intervention in social areas, some, like Sparkman, worked hard to obtain federal support for industrial development. Indeed, since the 1930s and especially after 1945, the South had been active in promoting business development just as many northern communities struggled with the loss of industry.[21] Some southerners also benefited from the Tennessee Valley Authority, whose cheap power and development loans attracted industries, many from the North. In addition, federal spending in the South and West increased during and after World War II, making efforts to combat deindustrialization outside these regions more difficult. Northern congressional leaders were quick to remind their southern colleagues of these issues during debates over area redevelopment legislation and many wanted stronger provisions to block federal assistance to firms leaving northern communities. While some southerners tried to broaden the Depressed Areas Act, others joined with conservative Republicans and fought against it. Senator J. William Fulbright of Arkansas, chair of the Senate Banking and Currency Committee, obtained the bill for his committee and then urged other conservatives to oppose the measure. He argued that the bill was "an attempt to substitute the judgment of the Federal Government for the judgment of our free enterprise system."[22] During Senate debate in 1958, A. Willis Robertson of Virginia called the bill unconstitutional, comparing it to efforts to desegregate schools under the *Brown v. Board of Education* decision of 1954.[23] In the House, Rules Committee Chair Howard Smith (Democrat-Virginia) tried to stop redevelopment legislation by refusing to grant a hearing on the bill in 1956 and 1959.

Joining southerners were others who represented the conservative opposition. For example, leaders of the National Association of Manufacturers and the Chamber of Commerce argued against area redevelopment, even though many local business leaders supported the measure. Conservatives opposed to federal involvement, such as Republican Senator Barry Goldwater of Arizona, argued that depressed conditions were "perfectly normal to the economic cycle of American industry" and that the Douglas bill would "only aggravate the problem."[24]

Meanwhile, Native Americans and their liberal representatives in Congress pressured Douglas for inclusion in the bill. The postwar boom in the West had bypassed reservations. During hearings in 1956 and after, Oglala Sioux, Apache, Blackfeet, and Navajo leaders lobbied for inclusion to counter the Eisenhower administration's efforts to force rapid assimilation by withdrawing government aid. Under the Eisenhower plan, the Bureau of Indian Affairs tried to promote business development on reservations by advertising cheap labor and no unions. But poverty remained higher there than anywhere else in the United States, and unemployment rates ran as high as 40 to 50 percent. In this light, congressional leaders such as Senators Dennis Chavez (Democrat–New Mexico) and Mike Mansfield (Democrat-Montana), and Representative Lee Metcalf (Democrat-Montana) joined Native Americans to lobby for area redevelopment as a way to end poverty on reservations.[25]

Moderate Republicans offered a counterproposal to the Douglas bill that was drafted by CEA Chair Arthur Burns. Members of the Eisenhower administration had been studying the issue of chronic unemployment since 1953, and, like Democrats, they also responded to pressure from community and state leaders demanding federal help for industrial development. In addition, Pennsylvania Republicans in the House and Senate had drafted proposals and sought help from the Eisenhower administration. As submitted in January 1956, the administration proposal provided less federal money than the Douglas bill ($50 million as opposed to $390 million); offered less federal participation in loans, with higher interest rates; and placed administration of the program in the more conservative Commerce Department. Ironically, the Republican program exempted rural areas and remained focused on urban labor, which was suffering the most from declining industries. Still, the Republican bill showed how marginal the Eisenhower administration believed poverty and industrial decline to be.[26]

Along with economic concerns and political battles, concern over gender roles played an important part in programs to fight deindustrialization. For example, in the anthracite mining region the concern rested on the connection between traditional notions of gender roles and dependence on male miners as the chief breadwinners. In this region, men and women supported industrial development that would create jobs for men.[27] While Min Matheson, district manager of the International Ladies' Garment Workers' Union (ILGWU) in Wilkes-Barre, Pennsylvania, organized women in the textile and garment industries, she also supported redevelopment as a way to provide jobs for men. In congressional hearings in the 1950s she stated that "many of the women work in the garment factories only because the men in their homes . . . are unemployed." These men did the housework, shopped, and tended to children—"a complete reversal of the normal course of family life," Matheson argued. Male and female workers echoed these concerns. As one female ILGWU shop steward commented: "It's one thing to have an independent income if your husband is working, but it is no fun being the breadwinner."[28] A male worker testified: "It is a shame for the woman of the house to be working and the man doing the housework. It is not right."[29] Federal policy makers cited similar reasons for supporting area redevelopment and posited, as many sociologists and other experts at the time did, a connection between limited economic opportunities for men and increasing rates of poverty and juvenile delinquency.[30]

These brief examples show that gender was an important part of the cultural milieu within which area redevelopment emerged and that deindustrialization challenged traditional notions of masculinity. For women, the crisis meant that their emerging status as wage earners and union members came amidst rising male unemployment. In the case of area redevelopment, Min Matheson, workers, and political leaders used the power of the state to create jobs for men and preserve traditional gender roles. They used liberal means for conservative ends.

Other individuals and organizations lined up to support Douglas's bill as well. These included labor leaders such as United Autoworkers President Walter Reuther and United Steelworkers President David McDonald, rural interest groups such as the National Farmers Union and the National Rural Electric Cooperatives Association, and urban interest groups such as the American Municipal Association. Gathering support from a wide range of groups ensured a greater chance of passage but also diffused the original intent of the Douglas bill. By 1956, the proposal sought to combat not just deindustrialization but also poverty in general. While both goals were laudable, and the issues were connected, the problem remained that the Douglas bill was too modest to rebuild the economic base of distressed communities, and it spread its limited resources too widely.

In the 1950s, support for area redevelopment continued to grow; spurred on by two recessions, Congress passed the renamed Area Redevelopment Act in 1958 and again in 1960. However, Eisenhower vetoed both bills. Siding with the conservatives, he opposed the creation of a new agency and the combining of rural and industrial development in one bill. Eisenhower also cited concerns that overall local, state, and private initiative "would be materially inhibited" by excessive federal participation, and expressed his preference for the more modest administration proposal.[31]

The vetoes helped John F. Kennedy during the 1960 presidential race. By cosponsoring the Douglas bill, and criticizing the Eisenhower administration for not doing enough to promote economic growth, Kennedy may have generated more votes in states with large numbers of distressed areas, like Illinois, Pennsylvania, and West Virginia. On winning the presidency he worked to make the Douglas bill the first one considered by the Senate in 1961. However, sensing the need to placate southerners in the Democratic party and to show he was not antibusiness, Kennedy bowed to pressure from newly appointed Commerce Secretary Luther Hodges of North Carolina and supported placing the ARA in the Commerce Department, something Republicans had long advocated. Kennedy also stressed economy in government, and at this stage Douglas agreed to sacrifice an independent agency for passage of his bill. The Area Redevelopment Act passed Congress in April, and Kennedy signed the measure on May 1, 1961.[32]

The ARA in Operation, 1961–1965

After nearly thirty years of federal, state, and local discussion of the issue, a national program to aid distressed areas was in place. Rather than address industrial decline solely, Congress granted the ARA $390 million—which represented .39 percent of the federal budget—to begin a four-year trial of fighting poverty on a national scale through industrial loans and grants, technical assistance, public works, and job training. Scholars have criticized 1960s liberals for favoring community action programs in the Office of Economic Opportunity over rebuilding and job-creation strategies such as those advanced by the ARA.[33] The ARA had the potential to become a job-creating program that responded to the root economic causes of poverty, such as deindustrialization, but several factors prevented this. As will be seen, its small scale, weak political position, and awkward operating procedures meant that it would not generate support. The ARA was also under the gun to create jobs quickly to justify its existence. Finally, the ARA represented a minority opinion among those fighting the War on Poverty, in that liberals viewed poverty primarily as cultural and political, and paid less attention to signs of economic weakness. In the midst of an economic expansion, liberals assumed the 1964 tax cut and overall growth would provide the bulk of the jobs the poor needed. This meant that, at the height of U.S. liberalism, the issue of deindustrialization faded to the background.

The ARA was the main agency addressing the effects of industrial decline between 1961 and 1965. Many of the themes present in the ARA's development, including the inconsistency and contradictions, continued during its lifetime. These themes emerged first as the ARA established its method of operation. Using Department of Labor statistics on unemployment for urban areas, Department of Agriculture data for rural areas, and Bureau of Indian Affairs listings for Native American reservations, the ARA designated labor markets, rural counties, and reservations eligible for aid. If interested in receiving aid, communities had to form a development organization, have it sanctioned by the state development agency, and then submit an Overall Economic Development Plan (OEDP) to the ARA for approval. This was an attempt to extend the planning ideal popular in the 1930s to the local and state levels, since specific requests for money had to then fit within the approved OEDP. Adding to the complexity, the ARA used the "delegate agency" concept to evaluate programs. Essentially, loan and grant applications went first to the appropriate federal agency: plans for community facilities to the Housing and Home Finance Administration, industrial loan applications to the Small Business Administration, plans for rural areas to the Department of Agriculture, Native American applications to the Bureau of Indian Affairs, and training applications to the Department of Labor. The ARA held final approval for loans and could override an agency recommendation. Technicians in each agency did not always give priority to ARA projects, maintaining loyalty to their own agency. As a result, complaints and tension arose over the time taken to process ARA applications. Not surprisingly, local groups became confused as to which agency they should apply.

With the tools provided and the structure in place, ARA administrators did their best to combat deindustrialization and poverty. Tables 1, 2, and 3 below highlight the industrial and geographic distribution of ARA resources.

Several conclusions emerge from the data presented above. First, even excluding states in the Northwest region, the ARA spent more money, had the greatest number of projects, and created the largest number of potential jobs in the South and West. Second, the four states the ARA classified as Appalachia received the largest amount of any single region. The region contained high levels of poverty, and its local and state leaders actively sought federal assistance. The ARA developed a special task force on Appalachia, and this served as a catalyst for later federal programs such as the Appalachian Regional Commission. Both points are ironic, since many

Table 1.   Top Five Industries Supported by the ARA

Industry	Number of Projects	Investment	Number of Potential Jobs
Lumber and wood products	52	$25,875,994	5,195
Food and kindred products	42	$20,715,256	4,945
Hotels and motels	28	$21,759,200	3,095
Rubber and miscellaneous plastics	27	$14,204,154	3,185
Stone, clay, and glass	25	$14,534,128	1,915

Source: Area Redevelopment Administration, *Annual and Final Report,* 1965.

firms had been leaving the traditional manufacturing belt for locations in the South and West. Third, the ARA's priority was not high-wage, high-skill employment, but jobs in general. Also, since "blue-chip" companies did not usually need federal assistance, firms locating in eligible communities tended to be less stable, or to rely on low-skill, low-wage labor. All of this generated mixed results for communities trying to create stable employment.

Returning to Pennsylvania as an example, unemployment there dropped in many distressed communities. In Scranton, unemployment fell from 13.8 percent in 1962 to 7.6 percent in 1966; in Wilkes-Barre–Hazleton, it dropped from 13.3 percent to 7.9 percent over the same period. Building on their established activities, local political and business leaders became active in applying for ARA funding. In the anthracite region around Scranton, for example, the ARA spent some $2.1 million in loans through

Table 2.   Top Ten States Receiving ARA Aid

State	Number of Projects	Investment (in thousands)	Percent of Total ARA Investment
West Virginia	120	$42,530	13%
Pennsylvania	169	23,004	7.1
Kentucky	122	21,400	6.6
Michigan	121	19,896	6.2
Oklahoma	84	19,594	6.1
Arkansas	65	17,393	5.4
Maine	69	14,950	4.6
Tennessee	75	12,105	3.8
Minnesota	67	8,610	2.7
North Carolina	86	5,479	1.7

Source: Area Redevelopment Administration, *Annual and Final Report,* 1965.

Table 3.   ARA Support by Region

ARA Region	State	Number of Projects	Investment (in thousands $)	Number of Potential Jobs
Northeast	Conn., Del., Maine, Md., Mass., N.H., N.J., N.Y., Pa., Puerto Rico, R.I., Vt.	476 (499 including Puerto Rico)	66,105 (75,973)	20,050 (21,625)
Lake states	Ill., Ind., Mich., Minn., Ohio, Wis.	418	55,244	10,125
Appalachia	Ky., Tenn., Va., W. Va.	326	76,834	13,975
Southeast	Ala., Ark., Fla., Ga., La., Miss., N.C., S.C.	306	53,851	15,915
Northwest	Alaska, Idaho, Iowa, Mont., Nebr., N. Dak., Oreg., S. Dak., Wash., Wyo.	214	18,021	2,195
Southwest	Ariz., Calif., Colo., Hawaii, Kans., Mo., Nev., N. Mex., Okla., American Samoa, Tex., Utah	311 (316 including American Samoa)	38,875 (39,939)	7,475 (7,605)

Source: Area Redevelopment Administration, *Annual and Final Report,* 1965.

1964, creating an estimated 1,080 jobs.[34] Projects in the anthracite region included training for male-dominated jobs such as transmission specialist, machine tool operator, and semiautomatic arc welder, as well as female jobs such as stenographer and power sewing machine operator. In addition, funding from the Accelerated Public Works program (APW), which passed Congress in 1962, reached $3 million in the Scranton area.[35] In the adjacent Wilkes-Barre–Hazleton labor market, ARA officials approved five industrial projects that involved some $1.2 million in loans and nearly $560,000 in grants to add approximately eighteen hundred jobs. Besides these, the agency approved some $170,000 in training for four hundred mostly male workers. In addition, through APW, the area received nearly $2.5 million in public works grants, matched by $2 million in local funds.[36]

However, such apparent success needs to be juxtaposed with data from the U.S. Census that reveal massive population declines in all major metropolitan areas of Pennsylvania. For example, the population of the city of Philadelphia declined 6 percent between 1950 and 1970, from just over 2 million to 1.95 million. The population of Pittsburgh declined some 22 percent, from over 670,000 to just over 520,000. The ARA designated both of these as redevelopment areas in the 1960s. In the smaller urban areas, a similar story unfolded. The Scranton–Wilkes-Barre–Hazleton labor market, which encompassed most of the anthracite region, declined over 9 percent in population, from 719,863 in 1950 to 650,604 in 1970. Over the same period, the Johnstown area also declined over 9 percent, from 291,354 to 262,822, while Altoona dropped 3 percent, from 139,514 to 135,356. In addition, it is unclear how much national economic growth contributed to the decline in unemployment; and even with this growth, the unemployment rate in these regions remained higher than the national average. All this suggests that, while the ARA contributed in some way to the creation of new jobs, it certainly did not halt the process of deindustrialization, and the issue of structural unemployment still remained.[37]

In rural communities and on Native American reservations, a similar story of limited success holds true. Regarding Native Americans, the Bureau of Indian Affairs established the criteria for designating which reservations would receive aid and made fifty-four eligible during the life of the ARA. As many liberals and local tribal leaders had hoped, Native Americans became much more involved in federal policy than before; however, they did not own most of the new industries established in their communities, and thus development remained in the hands of outsiders. In addition, cultural resistance to industrialized life, low skill and educational levels, and the isolation of the reservations meant that businesses generally remained uninterested in long-term commitment to these areas.[38] While ARA administrators tried to place a positive spin on their efforts, their press releases contained elements of stereotyping and misunderstanding. "The paleface businessman is beating a path to the Indian tepee," read one October 1964 press release. Manufacturers, the ARA claimed, were discovering in Indians "the patience and dexterity which have made them famous as artisans of blankets and jewelry." The ARA noted that Indians had invested $1.3 million in industrial development and the ARA $2.3 million.[39] Evidence shows that unemployment did decline as a result of these programs, but part of the cost was a loss of the Native American culture that helped generate Native American activism of the late 1960s and early 1970s.[40]

Mixed results also were found in the rural South, which, despite opposition to Douglas's bill by many southern congressional leaders, received approximately one-third of all ARA grants and loans. Most projects involved public works development, although the ARA supported training programs as well. In the rural South and Southwest, workers, civil rights advocates, and the U.S. Civil Rights Commission fought to ensure that these programs reached minorities. Initially, the ARA approved OEDPs without regard to race, meaning that many local committees were all white, despite the minority population in the community. Also, the ARA approved loans and grants without requiring desegregated operations. Under pressure, ARA Administrator William L. Batt Jr. and other ARA officials began aggressive advertising campaigns in the African American press, encouraging black entrepreneurs to apply for grants and loans. They also began to pressure, but not require, businesses to promise integrated facilities before approving them for a loan. ARA administrators began to implement nondiscrimination under the Civil Rights Act of 1964, but these efforts came as their funds were running out and the Johnson administration was transforming the agency into the EDA.[41]

In 1963, pressure from minorities also led the ARA to make inner cities eligible for aid and brought the agency into the fight against the racial aspects of deindustrialization. However, the decision came after Congress made the agency's future uncertain by refusing to appropriate additional funds for loans and grants. The denial of funds came in June, after Governor George Wallace of Alabama resisted integrating the University of Alabama and President Kennedy responded with an impassioned speech announcing the introduction of a civil rights bill. As Batt recalled, "this routed our efforts to get Southern support for the bill." One congressman showed Batt a letter supposedly signed by every white person in the county he represented, declaring that if he went along "with anything Kennedy did but defense" he would be voted out of office.[42]

Three large cities—Detroit, Pittsburgh, and Providence—already qualified for aid, since unemployment in their entire labor markets was over 6 percent. The 1963 decision added areas in which low labor market unemployment masked higher inner-city rates. Between 1963 and 1965, Buffalo, Cleveland, Los Angeles, Miami, Newark, Oakland, Philadelphia, and Toledo became eligible for aid. With limited funds, the ARA concentrated on job training for workers and training in business operations for black entrepreneurs. These projects reflected the emerging assumption among policy makers that the poor suffered most from blocked opportunities and what they needed were new skills to enable them to compete in the market. The ARA supported forty-one inner-city training programs involving some two thousand workers, and in Philadelphia, the ARA provided technical assistance to the Small Business Opportunities Corporation, an organization begun to train African American entrepreneurs. The idea then spread to other cities, including New York, Cleveland, Pittsburgh, and Milwaukee, and later became part of federal efforts under the War on Poverty.[43]

However, providing more intensive urban-labor-market policies than these proved impossible for several reasons. First, under ARA guidelines, communities had to raise at least 10 percent of the funds for industrial development, and often city leaders could not agree on a plan to do this. Second, the point would likely have been moot anyhow, with the ARA's failure to obtain additional funds in 1963. Third, a year after these inner-city programs began, the Johnson administration began its own, larger efforts to create the Great Society, the centerpiece of which was the War on Poverty. The ARA's secondary status became clear when the legislation creating the Office of Economic Opportunity (OEO) designated the ARA to administer Title 4, part A, which provided loans to businesses in areas with a community action program. At one meeting with ARA officials, liberals in the OEO were "surprised" to learn that the ARA had been operating in the cities.[44] The OEO focused on the cities and assumed poverty was cultural and political, not economic; hence, the OEO emphasized community action instead of issues such as jobs and housing. This meant that ARA-style programs to combat urban deindustrialization with jobs and new business development became subsumed beneath the ill-fated community action programs of the OEO.[45]

The ARA's limited record of success and negative publicity, plus Lyndon Johnson's desire to have new, bolder programs under the Great Society, led Johnson and his advisers to allow the ARA to expire in 1965 and replace it with a new agency, the Economic Development Administration (EDA).[46] Congress approved the move in August and the EDA took up the banner of economic development by promoting public works projects, mostly in rural areas. The EDA kept the same eligibility requirements as the ARA, but it provided $500 million annually in public works grants, $170 million in loans, and $25 million in technical assistance.[47] The EDA continues to function, still providing aid to many of the same communities that were designated as "distressed" as early as the 1930s.

Conclusion

Although the ARA did provide jobs, like the War on Poverty itself the ARA failed to cure the problems it tried to address. Policy makers saw, correctly, the connections between deindustrialization and poverty; however, the ARA's complicated design, lack of funding, secondary status, and continued congressional opposition meant that success in fighting both problems together would be limited at best. Moreover, during the 1960s, area redevelopment was one of several policies that demanded public attention, and other programs of the Great Society eclipsed the ARA. These new initiatives, especially the community action programs, focused on the culture of poverty and not the specific issue of deindustrialization, which continued and grew worse in the 1970s and 1980s.

Emerging from a combination of local, state, and federal activity, the ARA was a hybrid institution that contained elements of reform from both the 1930s and the 1960s. Like the New Deal, the ARA promoted economic planning, provided funds for public works, and created jobs. Like the emerging War on Poverty, the ARA also sought to aid communities considered marginal by removing barriers to success through education, technical assistance, and job training, as well as promoting the involvement of residents through the creation of OEDPs.

In addition to the institutional issues surrounding the ARA, the notion of blocked opportunities had important consequences for deindustrialization and liberal reform. While the ARA did focus some attention on the issue of deindustrialization, the tone and language used by those supporting area redevelopment reflected the reemergence of the notion that the poor needed primarily "psychological assistance and other forms of counseling." In one sense, ARA administrators used economic planning, technical assistance, and job training as forms of counseling, showing residents how to become better competitors in the market. Promoting the free market was an imperative for the United States in the midst of the cold war. In this light, the ARA sought the help of the business community, which had regained the respect it lost in the depression of the 1930s. Thus, liberals did not challenge free-market capitalism and in general considered poverty to be an anomaly in an otherwise healthy industrial system. These decisions buried a focused program to address deindustrialization within a renewed effort to "reinforce commitment to the work ethic by those who were economically marginal." Such decisions came not only from federal policy makers but from workers, union leaders, business owners, and politicians at the state and local levels. These groups sought to escape growing poverty and changing gender roles by creating new jobs, which many hoped would be for men.[48]

Though both the left and right attacked the ARA and the larger poverty programs of the 1960s as inadequate, various community development programs have emerged in the decades since.[49] Recently, both Democrats and Republicans have expressed interest in developing programs to aid the same communities identified in the 1930s as "distressed." It is unknown whether these programs will be successful. However, their reemergence, combined with the history of area redevelopment, shows that Americans have yet to craft solutions to problems that policy makers and citizens identified as early as the 1930s. Institutional structures and interest group politics explain more about the failure of these efforts than do the flawed psyches and lack of initiative of community residents. Furthermore, the U.S. unwillingness or inability to exert greater control over industrial location and investment decisions, coupled with a strong reverence for private control over capital and the openness of the federal system, means that programs like the ARA will see limited success against the process and effects of deindustrialization.

Part IV

LEGACY

CHAPTER 9

Collateral Damage

Deindustrialization and the Uses of Youngstown

JOHN RUSSO AND SHERRY LEE LINKON

> From the Monongahela valley
> To the Mesabi iron range
> To the coal mines of Appalachia
> The story's always the same
> Seven hundred tons of metal a day
> Now sir you tell me the world's changed
> Once I made you rich enough
> Rich enough to forget my name.
> BRUCE SPRINGSTEEN, "Youngstown"

In a speech at Youngstown State University in 1988, Bennett Harrison welcomed a large audience by saying how proud and grateful he was to be in Youngstown. Youngstown and its steel industry had been a starting point for his book with Barry Bluestone, *The Deindustrialization of America*,[1] but that was not the reason that he was happy. That very day, ten years after Youngstown's Ecumenical Coalition had begun the first community effort to purchase one of the closed mills, the nation's first plant closing legislation was enacted.[2] As Harrison noted, that legislation was the direct result of the historic community struggle to save its steel mills. He was not the first to acknowledge that the fight against shutdowns had resulted in changes in social, economic, and religious policy. For example, the uses of eminent domain for community purposes and the *Catholic Bishops' Pastoral Letter on the Economy*[3] both emerged in part from the fight against shutdowns in Youngstown. But that history of struggle and its role in shaping the future have been all but lost following the precipitous decline of this once great steel city.

The Youngstown-Warren area in northeast Ohio became a leader in the basic steel industry in the beginning of the twentieth century. It was settled by successive waves of European immigrants and migrants from the American South attracted by the difficult but often high-paying jobs in the steel industry. From World War I through the 1960s, the area was known for its high level of home ownership and its highly skilled and hard-working labor force. But in 1977, a wave of plant shutdowns began that resulted in the loss of over fifty thousand jobs in basic steel and related industries over a ten-year period.

The legacy of the plant shutdowns in Youngstown has continued for almost twenty-five years. Youngstown has been and remains among the national leaders in unemployment, poverty rates, population decline, devaluation of housing stock, foreclosures, bankruptcies, and arsons. Neighborhoods adjacent to mills have been the hardest hit. For example, in 1999, in the city of Campbell, the former home of the Campbell Works of Youngstown Sheet and Tube, only 33 percent of city residents were working. Thirty-three percent were retired, 33 percent received some form of public assistance, 22 percent were over 65, and 56 percent earned less than $25,000. Between 1980 and 1999, Campbell's population dropped from 13,000 to 9,246.[4] While the specific statistics might vary a bit, Campbell is typical of the communities that make up the Youngstown-Warren metropolitan area. So great has been the social and economic devastation that David Rusk, the former mayor of Albuquerque and leading urban theorist, has argued that Youngstown may be "beyond the point of no return."[5]

The Youngstown story illustrates a common pattern in deindustrialized communities. Deindustrialization leads to multiple experiences of loss. At first, there is the economic loss marked by unemployment, bankruptcies and foreclosures, arson, and declines in community services and physical and emotional health. Closely associated is the loss of faith in institutions (business, unions, government, religious organizations, family) that failed to provide the economic and social protection they had seemed to promise. A sense of helplessness may develop as deindustrialization is normalized as part of the "natural" economic order of shifting capital and competition. After deindustrialization, communities face the loss of self-esteem as the population declines, efforts to attract reinvestment fail, and social and economic conditions decay.

As those who remain begin to question the community's identity, outside observers, especially the media, define deindustrialized communities as places of failure. According to this rhetoric, while other communities are sites of investment, the deindustrialized community is a place of disinvestment. Other places are resourceful in their efforts to attract new business, but the deindustrialized city is desperate. In some cases, these comparisons take on moral overtones, pitting virtuous places against corrupt ones, congratulating some cities for self-reliance while describing others as helpless and dependent. Over time, deindustrialization may be turned back on the community, which becomes a scapegoat for its own loss and comes to accept failure as its due.

Our study examines local and national media representations of Youngstown from the early 1980s through the 1990s, twenty years after the major steel mill shutdowns. We will trace media images of Youngstown as a national "poster child" for deindustrialization and discuss representations of the city as both a helpless victim and a corrupt criminal. Whether in network broadcasts such as NBC's *Dateline*, widely read newspapers such as the *New York Times*, or political journals such as *Mother Jones*—which reach fewer people but are distributed around the country and beyond—media reports created and read by outsiders almost always begin their analyses by reminding the audience of the devastating loss of jobs in the early 1980s. But in many cases, these publications associate Youngstown's failure to attract new business with political corruption, mob influence, and crime, rather than systematic structural disinvestment. Although people in Youngstown often complain about these images, many in the area have internalized this vision. By the end of the century, the community had come to blame itself for deindustrialization and the subsequent social and economic struggles.

Poster Child for Deindustrialization

The steel mill shutdowns in Youngstown drew national media attention, in part because many people recognized the beginning of a trend that would affect industrial communities around the country. The Youngstown story was told in national newspapers and magazines and on national television news broadcasts, offered up as the prototypical tale of loss, struggle, and perseverance. Initial media responses ranged from denial to pity, as reporters struggled to define the meaning of deindustrialization in Youngstown.

Some tried to represent Youngstown as a reassuring example, suggesting that the community was not deeply harmed and was recovering quickly. For example, in 1978, the *Wall Street Journal* reported that the "dire predictions about economic decline [in Youngstown] had not materialized"; steelworkers were taking jobs in nearby communities and had been aided by state and federal unemployment benefits, and unemployment was actually dropping.[6] Business and political leaders also tried to counter the perception that economic collapse was imminent. Youngstown Mayor J. Phillip Richley told *Newsweek*, "We're not as bad off as you might think." *Newsweek* agreed that "so far there hasn't been any widespread economic devastation," but it warned that the real consequences would not be felt for several more months.[7]

Other accounts were more concerned with governmental failure to protect business interests than with the effects of plant closings on the people of Youngstown. For example, *Business Week* suggested that the costs of meeting environmental regulations had contributed to the steel mill closings. In Youngstown, the federal courts had invalidated Environmental Protection Agency exemptions, thus stopping local steel plants from dumping wastes into the Mahoning River. The article quoted the director of the United Steelworkers in Youngstown, who asked, "What good's a river if the guy who used to have a job can't buy his kid a fishing pole?"[8]

By the 1980s, as the effects of deindustrialization became clear, some attempted to normalize the situation. Between 1982 and 1986, neoconservative theorists such as Irving Kristol, Ben Wattenberg, and Michael Novak were invited to speak at Youngstown State University as part of a special lecture series funded by local business leaders. To shore up the growing disillusionment and unrest in the community, these intellectual leaders echoed the ideas of economist Joseph Schumpeter, suggesting that deindustrialization amounted to "creative destruction" associated with economic development and that it was temporary. This attitude was reflected in repeated queries from such popular magazines as *Time* and *Newsweek*, who regularly called community leaders and academics to ask whether Youngstown had "turned the corner."[9]

As a national representation of deindustrialization, Youngstown also served ideological purposes, especially in the neoconservative politics of the 1980s. While some reports described deindustrialization as a normal part of the business cycle, others used it as a way to promote deregulation, personal responsibility, and the virtues of entrepreneurship and individualism. For example, in 1980 Ronald Reagan campaigned in Youngstown and lambasted the Carter administration for the mill closings. Standing in front of Youngstown Sheet and Tube, Reagan suggested that his deregulatory policies and supply-side economic theories could have kept the mills open: "These [closings] would not have happened if I were president."[10]

The emerging 1980s conservatism mirrored the community's own deep sense of institutional failure, which went beyond government to include corporations, unions, and even the Ecumenical Coalition that had attempted to save the mills. After all, these institutions appeared to be helpless in preventing mill closings and ameliorating their effects. As a deep disbelief in and cynicism toward institutions developed, it was every individual for himself. *U.S. News and World Report* quoted a steelworker who said he had learned a "bitter lesson in the layoffs. They used to tell us: 'Get out of high school, get a job in a mill and you're fixed for life.' Now I know better."[11] The combination of political conservatism and bootstrap journalism represented the first in a series of representations that shifted the blame for deindustrialization to its victims, putting the onus for recovery on the individual. Consequently, the story of deindustrialization in Youngstown both heightened institutional resentment and played into the conservative individualism of the 1980s.

Yet most of the national reports on the shutdowns in Youngstown tried to counter these apologist representations, and in doing so, they defined the city as a representative example of the social costs of deindustrialization. For example, *In These Times* used the Youngstown closings as the foundation for a four-part series later reprinted as a stand-alone booklet, *Shutdown*.[12] In this series, David Moberg describes both the short-term and potential long-term effects of the plant closings on local steelworkers. Barry Bluestone and Bennett Harrison used what happened in Youngstown as the prelude for their seminal work, *The Deindustrialization of America*.[13] Documentary filmmaker Larry Adelman used scenes from Youngstown and its former mill sites in *The Business of America* to show the effects of unregulated business enterprise and its impact on communities and individuals.[14] In *Journey to Nowhere: The Saga of the New Underclass*, the first book on homelessness in recent history, Dale Maharidge and Michael Williamson begin their story of how industrial migrant workers traveled around the country searching for employment in Youngstown.[15] In 1983, *Wall Street Journal* reporter James M. Perry described the Youngstown-Warren area as "a necropolis," citing the miles of "silent, empty steel mills" up and down the Mahoning Valley. Perry captured the community's fear and loss through interviews with laid-off workers, one of whom explained, "We're just mill hunks. . . . We can't do anything else." Perhaps most important, though, Perry recognized the community's failing sense of hope, noting the "widespread concern that the economic recovery, when it comes, will pass the valley by."[16]

In part because Youngstown had been the focus of so many news stories, by 1983 *New York Times* reporter Peter Kilborn could easily include Youngstown, along with Detroit and Akron, in a brief list of cities that represented "the clichés of unemployment and shut-down factories in the nation's depressed industrial core."[17] A 1985 "Talk of the Town" column in the *New Yorker* offered an even more dramatic assessment: "We ponder the ongoing news from yet another hopeless, sorry corner of the world. Youngstown. Chile. Ethiopia. South Africa. We're tired. Everyone's tired of their turmoil."[18] As Michael Williamson, the photographer for *Journey to Nowhere*, commented years later, Youngstown became a "poster child for deindustrialization," a symbol of the devastation of economic change.[19] Youngstown as a place of loss is probably the most enduring representation to emerge from deindustrialization in America. While many voices offered alternative stories, this one was especially powerful.

Site of Loss, Site of Failure

As the city struggled during the 1980s and into the 1990s without making a serious recovery, Youngstown was increasingly seen as a site of failure. That image was used in different ways by different groups, some offering critiques of capitalism and others defending corporate interests. Some used Youngstown's failure as a persuasive tool for projects focused on social change and liberal politics. For example, a 1999 documentary, *Michael Harrington and Today's Other American: Corporate Power and Inequality*, uses the Youngstown story to show how corporate power harms ordinary people. In a section entitled "Downsized," filmmaker Bill Donovan uses Bruce Springsteen's song about Youngstown together with images of abandoned mills, closed businesses, relief offices, and empty lots to portray Youngstown as a site of loss. Scholar and activist James Chapin explains that Youngstown's story illustrates the power of private, business-oriented decision making, noting that it was "possible for four to five people in a room to make a decision to shut down Youngstown, Ohio." Another interview, with Irving Kristol, underscores the efforts of conservative critics to erase the problem of corporate greed and to downplay the impact of deindustrialization. We should, however, also take note of Donovan's use of Youngstown's struggle to promote the issues championed by Harrington and to critique capitalism. The video defines Youngstown as a representation of how ordinary people and communities are victimized by corporations. Like so many versions of the story, Donovan's shows Youngstown only as a site of loss, completely ignoring the communitywide struggle to save the mills. Such images make Youngstown an object of sympathy, yet they also exploit the community's difficulties.

At the same time, Youngstown's continuing hardship served as a standard against which viewers were invited to measure how economic restructuring was affecting them and their communities. As white-collar workers suddenly found themselves being downsized, the Youngstown story provided a sense of shared misery but also offered an example of a place where things were *really* bad. In 1995, Bruce Springsteen released his album *The Ghost of Tom Joad*, which included the song "Youngstown." The song and Springsteen's January 1996 visit to the city brought renewed attention to Youngstown. A report on *CBS This Morning* told how Springsteen had written several songs after reading *Journey to Nowhere* one sleepless night; he later encouraged Maharidge and Williamson to retrace their journey and update their report on unemployment and homelessness in the United States. *CBS This Morning* explained that Youngstown in the mid-1990s was in much worse shape than it had been in the early 1980s, as the downtown was "just fading away." Interviews with Springsteen, Maharidge, Williamson, and the Marshall family (on whom the song is based) all emphasized that Youngstown's experience was not unique but, rather, representative of the difficulties facing the nation at large. As Joe Marshall Jr. pointed out, about forty thousand workers had been laid off from AT&T just that week—just one example of the downsizing of middle-class and white-collar workers during the mid-1990s. As Williamson put it, "Now the rest of the country knows what only Youngstown knew then."[20]

While these comments focused on the national economy and the "failure of American industry," the story's focus on Youngstown and on the Marshall family served at once to humanize the issue and to deflect attention from the role of industry. Significantly, the segment included almost no discussion of why the mills shut down, and no critique of the business decisions that led to widespread downsizing in the 1990s. American industry failed, yet the emphasis here was on Youngstown as a "symbol of failure." *CBS This Morning* host Mark McEwen commented, "For some people, having your heart in the right place is just a cliché, but for Bruce Springsteen, no cliché, it's a way of life." Youngstown was left behind, then, erased by the virtue of Springsteen's good intentions. Missing from this story, as from so many others, was any recognition of the role of corporative disinvestment or of the community's efforts to act on its own behalf.

The business media also found Youngstown to be a useful allegory. In 1998, a *Nightly Business Report* segment during the GM-Flint strike used Youngstown's history as part of a story about the potential threat to workers and communities of further economic restructuring. Reporter Stephen Aug examined the effects of the Flint strike on workers at the Lordstown GM plant outside of Youngstown.[21] The report suggested that workers and business owners who still remembered the economic devastation of the early 1980s were especially sensitive to the economic effects of layoffs. At the same time, the report emphasized Youngstown's worries that Lordstown might close or significantly reduce its workforce as the company

moved to modular production and increased outsourcing. Images of deindustrialization in Youngstown both validated workers' fears and hinted at
the dangers of workers asking too much. Indeed, viewers were reminded
that another local plant, Delphi Packard, a GM parts supplier, had already
lost seven thousand jobs to Mexico. Autoworkers in the 1990s, the story implied, were just as helpless as steelworkers at the end of the 1970s. "They
may have jobs now," Aug said, "But what about next year, or the year after?"

Site of Desperation

Once cast as a site of loss and failure, by the late 1990s, Youngstown had
come to be seen as a site of desperation, a community so hard up for jobs
that it would accept any form of economic development, even prisons. Between 1992 and 1997, four new prisons were built in the Youngstown area,
adding sixteen hundred jobs, $67 million in annual payroll, $720,000 in
taxes, and an additional $200 million in economic activity in the Mahoning
Valley. This amounted to over 7 percent of the area's total economic growth
in the 1990s. As the *Youngstown Vindicator* headline touting the prison economy ironically suggested, "Steel Bars Are Still Part of Big Business in the
Region."[22] But the prisons also brought a number of problems, including
questionable management and a 1997 escape by six inmates at a private
prison on Youngstown's north side. Not surprisingly, the growth and difficulties of the local prison industry attracted continued media attention,
much of it focused on the community's economic desperation.

Most of the stories on Youngstown's prisons open with a description of
the community that focuses on its well-known history. National Public Radio referred to Youngstown as "a rust-belt city long synonymous with steel,
more recently with unemployment."[23] NBC's *Dateline* reminded viewers
that Youngstown was "so depressed by the collapse of the steel industry it
lost half its population in just 20 years."[24] On *60 Minutes* Youngstown was
identified as "a former steel town with double-digit unemployment."[25]
While Youngstown's economic history was often used as a quick way of
defining the place, it was also, in some cases, used to portray Youngstown
as desperate and even foolish. Jane Pauley introduced the *Dateline* segment,
for example, with this comment: "How would you like to have murderers,
rapists, and thieves living in your neighborhood? It's a frightening prospect,
even if they're kept behind bars, barbed wire, and under the watchful eyes
of prison guards. But, believe it or not, some towns actually welcome prison
facilities because of the jobs they create."[26]

When one of the new prisons, the privately owned Northeast Ohio Correctional Center on Youngstown's north side, had a series of problems—including assaults, a murder, and the midday escape of six prisoners—several major news organizations came to investigate. While these reports focused on the malfeasance of the owner of the prison, the Corrections Corporation of America (CCA), they also used the familiar but incomplete conventional wisdom about Youngstown's history and its economic struggles to portray the city as a victim. In a *60 Minutes* report called "Medium Security, Maximum Problems," Youngstown's history helped to position the community as a hapless victim of yet another outside corporation. The report paid no attention to efforts within the community to fight against prison development or to improve conditions within the prisons. Rather, the story suggested that the community had come to see itself as helpless. In one segment, Mayor George McKelvey speculated that "someone in Washington obviously said 'Let's dump on Youngstown. There's nobody there smart enough to even know what we're doing.'"[27] His comment revealed resentment but also some measure of acceptance of the city's image.

While broadcast news stories emphasized Youngstown's economic desperation, a 2000 *Mother Jones* story used powerful visual images to emphasize the feeling of being at once trapped and abandoned. The article begins with a two-page spread featuring a pair of contrasting photos representing the two halves of the article title, "Steel Town, Lockdown." On the left, a full-page, black-and-white photo shows a pair of railroad tracks crossing in the empty field where the Youngstown Sheet and Tube Company once stood. Downtown Youngstown stands in the distance. The sky looks gray, and a bit of snow lies on the ground, which is scattered with a few pieces of debris from the long-gone mills. The image suggests a landscape that was once occupied but is now abandoned. On the facing page, a much smaller, more constricted image shows a scene inside a prison. In about two square inches, we see another set of converging lines, here the walls of a prison hallway, reflected in the shiny, empty floor. Running through the entire image are the vertical bars of an interior prison gate. Neither scene shows a single person, nor does either suggest a hospitable location. Each image comments on the other. The larger photo suggests that the desolation outside parallels the austerity inside; the smaller photo hints that the outside space might be just as constricted as a prison. Together, they also point to the connection between deindustrialization and the growing prison economy in Youngstown.[28] As the *Mother Jones* photos suggest, past, present, and future intersect in complicated ways in representations of economic development in Youngstown.

While these media images portray the growth of prisons in sharply negative ways, many in Youngstown bought into the idea that prisons offered economic hope. Despite difficulties with the first CCA prison, many residents were enthusiastic when Representative James Traficant began negotiations to have the company build two additional facilities, ironically on the same brownfield sites that were deemed too polluted for any other use. As the article in *Mother Jones* pointed out, "This plan suits many elected officials, who are desperate for an economic boost to a region hardened by the loss of its steel industry." If the CCA expansion succeeded, one of every fifty residents of the Youngstown-Warren area would be an out-of-state inmate. Youngstown would have become "the private prison capital of the world."[29]

Crime Town

While news stories about Youngstown as a site of economic struggle were a recent phenomenon, stories about Youngstown as a site of crime and corruption were not. The prison industry may have drawn attention from the media because they already associated Youngstown with crime, a link that dated back to a 1962 article in the *Saturday Evening Post* that dubbed the city "Crime Town, U.S.A." A series of stories appeared in the national press about crime and corruption in Youngstown, starting in the early 1990s, when the local murder rate increased dramatically. The stories were followed by tales of white-collar crime and reports on a large-scale investigation of corruption among public officials. As the prison reports had done, most stories about crime in Youngstown made use of familiar elements of the city's image. The cover of a July 2000 issue of the *New Republic* is a good example: a battered "Welcome to Youngstown" sign full of bullet holes stands before a silhouette of smokestacks, a gray building, and telephone poles, providing a background for "A Story of the Mafia, the FBI, a Congressman, and the Most Crooked City in America."[30]

Youngstown became known as a "murder capital" in the 1990s. The local paper chronicled the carnage periodically, reporting that Youngstown's per capita murder rate was in the top ten in the nation for cities larger than fifty thousand. Youngstown's murder rate was eight times the national average, six times higher than New York's, four and one-half times higher than that of Los Angeles, and twice as high as Chicago's. The paper noted that criminal justice experts define a homicide epidemic as a murder rate over three times the national average.[31] Such reports created an atmosphere of fear in the local community, presenting the city of Youngstown as a dangerous place and the rising murder rate as a mysterious trend, explainable only by the declining morality of those involved. Although the relationship between persistent high unemployment and per capita murder rates is well established, it was rarely discussed in the local media. The *Vindicator* compared Youngstown with Gary, Indiana, and Compton, California, whose murder rates were often higher, without mentioning that both of those cities had also experienced high levels of unemployment and deindustrialization.

Furthermore, the *Vindicator* failed to recognize that most of the murders occurred in the African American community, a point that was highlighted by a story in the *Cleveland Plain Dealer* in 1999. An analysis of death records from the Centers for Disease Control and Prevention from 1988 to 1997 found that black women in Youngstown were murdered before their sixty-fifth birthday at a higher rate than anywhere else in the nation. In addition, black women in Youngstown were murdered at a rate nearly eleven times higher than white women, the largest racial disparity in the country. The high murder rate was attributed to the women being "long abused by husbands and boyfriends or caught in the middle of drug deals gone bad." The study also found that "homicides, heart disease, and lung cancer—all considered preventable and treatable by public health officials—killed blacks at a much higher rate than whites." While such patterns hold true nationally, Mahoning County (where Youngstown is located) had one of the widest overall racial health gaps in the country.[32] The *Plain Dealer*'s portrayal of murder as a "black problem" fed into existing racism, reinforcing the predisposition of the local white community to dismiss the problem as not their concern. The Youngstown press had ignored what was happening in the city's African American neighborhoods, perhaps because it knew that its largely white audience simply did not care.

Deindustrialization exacted enormous social and economic costs, and the rising crime rate was one of those costs. Prior to the mill closings, the local crime rate did not stand out.[33] Six to ten years after the mill closings, as unemployment benefits ran out, families and neighborhoods were broken apart, and economic conditions worsened, nonviolent crimes and traditional domestic violence increased.[34] The most significant increase in crime came some fifteen years after the first mill closings, however, as the children from these broken families and neighborhoods became both perpetrators and victims of the wave of homicides in Youngstown. Lacking economic opportunities and access to real wealth, these young adults turned to selling drugs, especially crack cocaine, largely to suburban residents who did "drive-bys" into poor neighborhoods. Most young adults in Youngstown did not have the money to purchase drugs; rather, they had opportunities to sell drugs, purchase guns, and join gangs to protect territory and profits. No doubt, violent crime in the 1990s was rooted partly in the corporate economic violence of the late 1970s and early 1980s. Yet most representations of Youngstown as a murder capital paid only passing attention to the lingering effects of displacement and deindustrialization.

Youngstown's association with crime in the 1990s was not limited to violent crime. White-collar and organized crime also received significant media attention. Two high-profile business leaders, Michael Monus and Edward J. DeBartolo Jr., were convicted of fraud and bribery. Some reports positioned such white-collar crime in the context of local corruption, pointing out that Monus and DeBartolo had been raised in this atmosphere, and that both were seen as local heroes despite their illegal activities. For these reasons, news stories positioned Monus and DeBartolo as representatives of Youngstown. The stories made their failures appear to be failures of the wider community. As *Newsweek* suggested in one report on Monus, "the public is almost a co-conspirator."[35]

Michael Monus founded PharMor, a discount retail chain, in 1982. The company grew rapidly and soon began to rival WalMart. By the late 1980s, Monus had expanded into professional sports operations. He founded the summer professional World Basketball League (WBL) as well as several other ventures. He owned the local team, the Youngstown Pride. The team's moniker suggested courage, strength, self-esteem, and the solidarity of family and community, ideas that had powerful resonance in a town struggling to overcome the ravages of deindustrialization. In 1988, *Venture* magazine honored Monus as a top entrepreneur, and *Newsweek* reflected that Monus had become an "icon in the American cult of the entrepreneur."[36] Such accolades played well in Youngstown—a town that had become increasingly distrustful of outsiders and frantic for economic development. As a PBS *Frontline* documentary suggested, Monus became a "favorite son" whose creation of thousands of jobs, renovation of an abandoned retail store, and relocation of his national corporate offices to downtown Youngstown were seen as acts of loyalty to his hometown.[37]

But when PharMor began to falter, Monus turned to fraud and embezzlement to keep the company afloat. When the fraud was uncovered in 1992, 50 percent of PharMor stores were closed, thousands of employees were laid off, hundreds of suppliers went unpaid, and investors suffered enormous losses. In May 1995, Monus was found guilty of 109 counts of fraud, tax evasion, and embezzlement and sentenced to twenty years in prison.[38] The story was reported nationally as "a modern morality tale," some reports implicating both Monus and the Youngstown community.[39] Local newspaper columnist Nancy Beeghly explained in a *Newsweek* article that the community had had high hopes for Monus: "We were the fifth largest steelmakers in the *world*. . . . I don't think we ever got over that. People wanted something magical again."[40] As Beeghly's comment suggests, the community was betrayed by Monus, but because it was so desperate to believe in him, it also helped to make his rise and fall possible.

A few years later, when Edward J. DeBartolo Jr. was convicted of bribing the Louisiana Governor Edwin Edwards to procure a license to open a casino, Youngstown again found itself associated with white-collar crime. While Edward J. DeBartolo Sr. had long been suspected of having ties to organized crime, he was also viewed as an important local business leader, and his son was esteemed as the owner of the successful San Francisco 49ers football team. Because both DeBartolos proclaimed their Youngstown roots with pride, they and their businesses were often seen as reflective of the local community. This connection was complicated, however, as evidenced by a 1993 special Sunday section on DeBartolo in the *Pittsburgh Press*; "DeBartolo's identification with Youngstown also may be the source of the shadow over seven decades of success—persistently linking him to organized crime."[41] DeBartolo Jr.'s 1998 conviction in the bribery case added to Youngstown's image as a community that bred and even revered local "leaders" who combined toughness and entrepreneurship with touches of corruption. The fall of DeBartolo Jr., like that of Michael Monus, was presented not simply as a tale of individual avarice and greed, but also as evidence of larger-scale corruption that was supported, or at least accepted, by the local community.

Object of Ridicule

Organized crime has had an influence on the Mahoning Valley for over seventy-five years. The *Saturday Evening Post's* designation of Youngstown as "Crime Town, USA," in 1962 was based on the area's mob wars of the 1950s.[42] But except for occasional violence, the presence of organized crime seemed to fade into the constant haze that accompanied the steelmaking process and received little publicity. As the *New York Times* suggested, "When Youngstown's economy roared in the 1970s like the steel furnaces that once lit its skyline, the mob's influence became less visible. But as the mills closed and the area's economy slumped, mob influence was slowly revealed."[43]

Undergirding the strength of organized crime in Youngstown was its hold on both city hall and law enforcement. Mayors and public officials control the public assets in most communities. The ability to enter into contracts, provide services, and control who gets and keeps city and county jobs bestows incredible power, especially in a city in economic decline. In county government, the county engineer often controls major contracts involving roads, water, and snow removal. Through such oversight, mayors and county engineers control public works and can, given the right incentive, circumvent the bid process. Occasionally, this disposes politicians to corruption and to kickbacks. As former Youngstown mayor Patrick Ungaro explained to the *Vindicator,* "bribery was so common, it almost seemed normal," and this permitted organized crime to control local politics. The presence of organized crime "was so overwhelming, so ingrained. Either you are intimidated by it or you join it."[44] Mob influence and infiltration extended into nearly every branch of local government, including the full gamut of the legal system, from police to prosecutors, judges, and the bail bond industry.[45] It was not a criminal justice system, according to Mayor George McKelvey, but a "Justice for Criminals" system.

These practices had existed in Youngstown for decades, and were widely known but not openly discussed. It was not until the 1990s that a series of federal investigations fully revealed the level of mob influence on public officials. Those investigations resulted in eighty convictions by 2001; among the Mahoning County officials convicted were the county prosecutor, the sheriff, the county engineer, two county commissioners, local judges and lawyers, and top aides to Representative Traficant. The large number of convictions for various forms of public corruption contributed to another round of media stories, this time focused on Youngstown as a site of corruption. Indeed, in 1998, *George* magazine named Youngstown one of the ten most corrupt cities in the country.[46] Significantly, although many of those convicted worked in county positions and most lived in the largely white, middle-class suburbs outside the city, media attention focused on "Youngstown," ignoring any distinctions between the city, the county, and the greater metropolitan area. The media focus on "Youngstown" contributed to the predisposition of many in the Youngstown area to distance themselves from the city and to perceive the problems of corruption as happening someplace else.

Much of the media focus on corruption in Youngstown centered around Traficant, a former county sheriff who had successfully defended himself from charges of accepting bribes from the mob in the early 1980s. *U.S. News and World Report* placed Traficant at the center of Youngstown's corruption, describing the city as having a "cast of characters [that] sounds like a real-life version of HBO's popular show about a low-rent mob family, *The Sopranos,* starting with the disheveled Traficant, who is best known for shouting intemperate speeches in the well of the House."[47] *USA Today* suggested that, while his oddball appearance and one-minute rants on the House floor against government institutions, corporations, and hypocrisy have not endeared him to his House colleagues, his defiant populist sentiments and "junkyard dog" approach to politics have resonated with the media.

The media's fascination with Traficant and his populist politics brought additional national attention to Youngstown and reinforced the community's image as a place where corruption and crime are accepted parts of everyday life.[48] But Traficant's legend is based, in part, in Youngstown's struggles after the mill closings. His reputation for disdain of government and institutions began during his stint as sheriff, when he refused to enforce eviction orders for unemployed families. When charged with contempt of court, Traficant chose to go to jail. The *Plain Dealer* tells the story of how Traficant defended himself when the Justice Department charged him with accepting bribes from the Cleveland and Pittsburgh mobs. Despite enormous evidence against him, including his own written confession, Traficant was acquitted because he claimed that the bribes were part of an elaborate "sting" operation that he had planned to trap local mobsters. The Justice Department was incensed at the acquittal, but the community cheered Traficant's "up yours" attitude toward the federal government. The Justice Department continued to hound Traficant and got a measure of revenge when the Federal Tax Court found him guilty in 1984 of income tax evasion for the $163,000 in bribes and held him liable for $180,000 in back taxes and penalties. But Traficant's "legend as a hero of the little people" was launched, and he was elected in 1984 to the U.S. Congress, where he became the most visible representation of Youngstown's anti-institutional sentiment.[49]

Before his 2002 conviction on racketeering charges, Traficant represented the Youngstown-Warren area for more than fifteen years. He was seen as an iconoclastic populist who for many years had a near-perfect labor voting record, while he supported a highly conservative agenda on illegal immigration, capital punishment, and the involvement of the military in drug intervention. While many in the community vehemently defend Traficant's record in Congress, in fact the representative brought home relatively little in terms of federal dollars or significant legislation. Given his limited success, his public image, and his association with corruption, it is difficult to understand why he is still viewed as a local hero, even as he remains in prison. In order to understand why local voters continue to support Traficant even though he contributed to the community's image as a site of corruption, we need to take a closer look at local attitudes and local history.

Traficant's populist politics reflect local attitudes toward the federal government and large institutions. Resentment of government intrusion—based largely on class conflict—has a long history in Youngstown, rooted in the role of the state in protecting the interests of steel mill owners and the upper class during strikes during the first half of the twentieth century. The resentment developed further during deindustrialization, when the government was blamed for imposing environmental regulations and failing to protect the interests of the steel industry. Both Republican and Democratic presidential candidates have promised economic support for Youngstown, yet their administrations have never followed through. Other institutions also failed to provide real help during deindustrialization. Big businesses, especially after outside corporations shut down the steel mills, were clearly suspect. The Ecumenical Coalition's move to buy one of the local mills failed, leaving some doubting the effectiveness of both churches and unions as sources of support. The result was distrust of institutions and a belief that individuals and groups that challenged and even violated traditional rules were the community's best hope. Overall, this politics of resentment is best summarized by Don Hanni Sr.—a former steelworker, a criminal defense attorney, and the longtime Mahoning County Democratic chairman—who told the *Washington Post* that "a lot of people around here are hurting economically, and they're tired of a lot of phony promises from people like Bill Clinton." In Hanni's eyes, this explained Traficant's popularity: "Jim is competitive and combative, and people around here like that."[50]

In many cases, however, news reports on Traficant also link his popularity to the community's acceptance of crime and corruption, describing both as part of Youngstown's working-class culture. As the *Washington Post* noted: "In this gritty, shot-and-beer town where the mob has proved more durable than the steel industry, the prospect of being indicted by a federal grand jury does not intimidate Rep. James A. Traficant Jr. (D), the flamboyant House member who favors polyester suits and dominates politics here."[51] A *Plain Dealer* story on mob activity in Youngstown cited YSU anthropology professor Mark Shutes, who explained that Youngstown's immigrant working class saw mob leaders as heroes because—like Traficant—they "had found a way to beat the larger, more corrupt outside world." The idea that corruption close to home was acceptable because it provided protection against outside threats was, according to Shutes, part of the working-class experience of Youngstown's immigrants: "The roots of Youngstown's mob problem can be found in those old steel mills, which were largely manned by European immigrants who had grown up in small, close-knit rural villages where governments and the outside world were viewed with suspicion." In such villages, Shutes noted, "closed cultural groups encouraged the idea that it is OK to pay someone, be it business or a politician, to get a job or some benefits."[52]

The idea that corruption could be explained, in part, as a symptom of working-class culture also emerged in a 1998 book by Rick Porello, which offered a history of organized crime in northeastern Ohio. In the book, Porello cites Steven Olah, the head of Cleveland's Federal Organized Crime Strike Force, who explained that organized crime resisted reform efforts and continued to prosper in the area because gambling and political corruption were accepted by the sizeable "millworking population."[53] In fact, as Carmen Policy, former president of the San Francisco 49ers and later the Cleveland Browns, said of his hometown, "This is a working-class area and gambling is not considered a vice. In fact, gambling permeates everything. For its size, I must admit, there is no city in America like Youngstown."[54] This popular mythology of working-class culture is accurate in many ways, yet it also ignores the more complicated story of what happened in Youngstown. While some illegal activities, like gambling, were accepted as harmless, others were seen as survival strategies or ways of fighting back. Further, this version of the story ignores the active role of Youngstown's professional-managerial classes, who also participated in gambling, who were key players in other forms of corruption, and who presided over the dismantling of the industrial economy that built Youngstown. Once again, we see an account of Youngstown that privileges culture and identity, rather than key public policies and corporate decisions, in the unraveling of the steel era.

Conclusion

As the Youngstown story shows, deindustrialized communities are vulnerable to all kinds of loss—not just the loss of jobs or economic security but also the loss of identity, as outsiders interpret the meanings of deindustrialization to serve their own purposes. Over time, the focus of the story shifts, and community history is erased. Tales of corporate disinvestments and collective resistance to shutdowns are forgotten, and images of individual and communal failure gain precedence. Further, such media representations do not simply define the community in the national view. They also have power to shape the way local residents think about their past and their future. In many cases, locals internalize the image of their community as a site of loss, failure, crime, and corruption. For some, this generates a sense of despair and helplessness, while others become defensive or engage in denial.

Yet it is also possible for deindustrialized communities to reclaim their stories and their identities, as the example of Palermo, Italy, demonstrates. A United Nations conference in December 2000 explored "The Role of Civil Society in Countering Organized Crime: Global Implications of the Palermo, Sicily, Renaissance." Presentations examined the relationship between the erasure of community memory and the rise of a culture of criminality in Palermo, and they showed how the community's systematic reclamation of its past had helped build a new culture of lawfulness. For the Youngstown delegation, by far the largest in attendance, the idea that civic culture is undermined by economic, cultural, and geographic fragmentation and the loss of history had great resonance, for they had seen a similar pattern in their deindustrialized community. The symposium also suggested that a community's recovery of a positive memory of itself is the first important step toward reconstructing a sense of place, belonging, and ownership.[55] As the Palermo commissioner of education, Allesandra Siracusa, told the Youngstown delegation, in order for a city to prosper, it must recover its identity by embracing its past and refusing to let others destroy or humiliate it. Community members must understand that cities are the fruit of relations among people living together, and they must have a sense that their community, including its past, belongs to them.[56]

CHAPTER 10

Envisioning the Steel City

The Legend and Legacy of Gary, Indiana

S. PAUL O'HARA

As far as Gary is concerned, we live here because we love this place,
because we make more money here than a layman can make
anywhere else in the world . . . 'cause that U.S. Steel is open.
The doors are always open, twenty-four hours a day.
RESIDENT OF GARY, 1976

This was a vibrant community here at one time. But as you can see the
blight came in, and this is the problem that we're having: no jobs.
RESIDENT OF GARY, 1999

Introduction

In the spring of 2000, the city of Gary, Indiana, along with Trump Casinos, announced that this rusted steel town on the shores of Lake Michigan would be the next host of the annual Miss U.S.A. pageant. To the media, the "steel city" seemed an odd choice for the event. "Where will the 51 contestants frolic during the parts of the TV broadcast devoted to their nights on the town," asked *U.S. News and World Report*, "in gritty steel mills?"[1] CNN expressed similar sentiments. Gary, it suggested, was "not exactly known as a vacation paradise or everyone's perfect idea of home." Against a televised backdrop of urban decay, the report continued, "it may not look like it but Gary, Indiana, just won a beauty contest." Commenting on Gary's reputation, CNN remarked that "publicity has never been much good to Gary. Mostly it's been bad, about classic Rust Belt decay, unemployment that once hit 17 percent. As recently as three years ago *Money* magazine called this the worst place to live in the whole United States."[2]

Yet, for residents and city officials, the opening of Trump casinos on the lakefront and the acquisition of the pageant represented an opportunity to change the way people thought about their city. Civic leaders, suggested one pageant official, "have a great story to tell about how they're changing [the city's] image." After decades of national publicity for its crime rate, pollution, and urban decay, the televised pageant offered Gary a chance to redefine itself. "The people of this nation are going to have to find someone else to pick on," stated Ben Clement, the economic development director for Gary, "because they won't be able to pick on Gary, Indiana, any longer."[3] The reclamation and redefinition of the city's deindustrialized image seemed a necessary first step toward revitalization and redevelopment.

The loss of steel jobs in Gary throughout the 1980s decimated the economic, political, and civic cultures of the city. Yet, the process of deindustrialization did not occur solely in terms of job loss, nor was it the result only of economic transformations of the 1970s and 1980s. The story of U.S. Steel's Gary Works does not fully follow the traditional narrative of deindustrialization or the dying steel town.[4] During the steel crisis of the early 1980s, U.S. Steel did not close down the big mill in Gary, although it did close several small plants within the city. Rather, in 1986, it designated the Gary Works as its corporate flagship and upgraded the mill. By the mid-1990s, the mill was producing as much steel as ever. Through mechanization, however, it did so with a fraction of the people it once had employed. In 1985, after the implementation of U.S. Steel's "rationalization" plan, the mill, which once had employed over 20,000, had jobs for only 7,500.[5] Thus, while Gary Works may not have undergone deindustrialization in terms of production, the city of Gary certainly felt the effects of industrial job loss. In short, the city, itself, deindustrialized.

The timeline for deindustrialization in Gary may have its beginnings long before the deregulations, mergers, and plant closures of the 1970s and 1980s. In fact, U.S. Steel may well have established Gary Works' industrial lifespan during its construction. Between 1906 and 1909, U.S. Steel transformed thousands of acres of mostly uninhabited swampland and sand dunes into one of the largest steel-producing centers in the world. In addition to the massive mills lining the lakefront, U.S. Steel built an adjoining city, which it named after its chairman, Elbert H. Gary, to house the steelworkers. The construction of Gary was part of U.S. Steel's attempt to not only expand in terms of size and steel production capacity but also escape the labor pressure and constrictive laws of South Chicago and the Pittsburgh area. Thus Gary was born out of capital mobility and industrial efficiency; it was imagined as a kind of "disposable" city that served the expansion needs of capital. U.S. Steel created an industrial lifespan, a sort of planned obsolescence, of expansion, modification, mechanization, and ultimate abandonment for Gary.[6]

Within this disposable concept, however, there existed interpretative room for people to envision Gary on their own, to attach meaning, significance, and reputation to the city. For its scientific technology, its planned origins, and its reputation for crime, corruption, violence, and vice, Gary earned a place within the American public imagination (especially the imagination of the press) as a metaphor for progress as well as chaos. It existed as both an industrial utopia and dystopia. At the same time, Gary's residents, through the shared experiences of work, ethnicity, and race, formed a stable community that helped them shape their city's social and cultural landscape. Within this community, Gary's residents created their own sense of themselves and their city, often an identity that stressed economic possibilities. This local image often conflicted with national and regional images of Gary, which centered on its violence, crime, pollution, and racial composition. A stasis emerged that allowed for these multiple images of Gary to coexist.[7]

The physical loss of steel jobs and the following urban decay and capital flight, however, undermined this balance. Without the sense of itself as a producing steel town, Gary lost the ability not only to create or control its own urban image but also to defend itself against its harshest critics. Instead, Gary became a national example of deindustrialized rustbelt decay. This dramatic change in the composition and viability of local image is one of the strongest and longest-lasting effects of deindustrialization. It also helps to explain why present-day city officials feel a need to redefine themselves and their city, envisioning a "New Gary" based on tourism and gaming instead of steel production and industrial labor. As ABC News pointed out, "the young women competing in the pageant have a lot at stake, but their event may well mean even more to Gary."[8]

The Sum of a Thousand Short Cuts

Gary has long been an interesting place for both contemporary observers and academic studies. Gary encapsulates many of the significant trends of twentieth-century urban and labor history, including industrialization and class struggle, experiments in progressive education, the growth of ethnic communities, black migration and racial conflict, white flight and black power, and deindustrialization and urban decay. Many studies, therefore, have cited Gary as an example of larger urban and labor trends.[9] Yet Gary can be thought of in a number of different ways. While it does make a good case study, Gary also was the product of a particular kind of urbanization and represents a particular stage in capital and labor production. Gary is an industrial city created out of capital mobility and industrial relocation, whose economic, political, and cultural fortunes rest on the balance between industrial production and industrial work. One way to think about Gary, then, is in terms of relationships. Gary's history has largely been shaped by a multitude of complex relationships, including the place of Gary within a capitalistic system of expansion, the role of Gary (or the idea of Gary) within the national economy and the public imagination, and the relationship between Gary the steel mill and Gary the city. It is in examining these relationships that Gary's narrative of industrialization and deindustrialization, its role in U.S. capitalism, and the lasting legacy of job loss become clear.

Perhaps the most important relationship for Gary's deindustrial narrative is the city's relationship with capital. In *The Urbanization of Capital*, David Harvey discusses the inherent contradictions of capital and capitalism. Through constant expansion and accumulation, Harvey argues, capital is attempting to make space and distances irrelevant, yet in order to do so, capital has to create spatial structures (for instance, factories) that are immobile and implanted in the landscape. For expansion to continue, capital must abandon the very structures it has created.[10] Such a conception of the patterns of capital expansion helps us to understand not only the origins of Gary but perhaps also the predetermination of its industrial lifespan.

In 1901, the combination of J. P. Morgan's banking interests and Andrew Carnegie's steel empire created the largest steel-producing company in the world. Almost immediately, the newly minted United States Steel Corporation sought to expand its midwestern production in order to take advantage of new western and midwestern markets. The company originally considered expanding its Chicago South Works, but ultimately decided to cross the border into Indiana and build an entirely new steel mill. Being on Lake Michigan, the mill had easy access to the Mesabi iron range of northern Minnesota, and it was located on all of the major trunk lines between the East Coast and Chicago. In many ways, Gary Works was about economic location. Yet at the same time, the construction of Gary and the social control mechanisms that were part of the planning, coming as they did shortly after the 1901 steel strike, served as a warning to workers in other mill towns that U.S. Steel had the ability to move production and jobs as it saw fit.[11]

The scale of the Gary project necessitated not only a large amount of capital but a great deal of urban and industrial planning as well. The construction of the massive new mill allowed the planners to break down the steelmaking process into its smallest components and make it as efficient as possible. Because it had essentially limitless space and capital, U.S. Steel could take measures such as slowly curving its railroad tracks to allow trains to maintain speed and steam between units. Such initiatives earned the Gary Works the nicknames "Economy, Indiana," and the "sum of a thousand short cuts." The process of squeezing savings and profits out of the plant, then, was a long tradition in the Gary Works. Even during the worst of the steel crisis of the early 1980s, U.S. Steel continued to upgrade the Gary Works, including a $300 million slab caster installed in 1986. At the same time, the company closed most of its older mills and diverted its money into acquiring Marathon Oil.[12]

The reinvestment in Gary Works did mean closing down parts of the mill, automating much of what remained, and cutting thousands of steel jobs. In a 1989 article, *U.S. News and World Report* acknowledged this trend among steel companies. Calling the steel industry's recovery "a hollow comeback," it reported that, in 1982, Inland Steel Industries in neighboring East Chicago, Indiana, had operating losses of $118 million. In response, it had eliminated ten thousand mill jobs and received salary and work rule concessions from the United Steelworkers of America. By 1988, its stock price had recovered and had begun to rise; there was, however, no rise in employment.[13] The comeback of U.S. Steel had similar ramifications for Gary. While the mill continued to produce vast amounts of steel, the economic hardships of job loss remained for the city. "It's a great success story for the company," stated Gary Mayor Thomas Barnes in 1989, "but it has been a painful experience for us. The fact is, a business that once employed 21,000 people now employs about 7,500, and that number is probably never going to go any higher."[14] For U.S. Steel, which renamed itself USX Corporation after its purchase of Marathon Oil, the automation of the Gary Works was another form of reindustrialization. Much as it had done with its curving tracks eighty years before, the company cut corners to make the plant more efficient. The loss of jobs, however, meant deindustrialization for the city of Gary.[15]

"Welcome Home to Gary": Local Image and National Reputation

In 1972, the residents of Gary, tired of decades of industrial pollution, gathered to form the environmental group Community Action to Reverse Pollution (CARP). In his study of Gary's environmental movements, Andrew Hurley points out that, far from being an elite movement to protect nature at the cost of jobs and production, CARP created a broad-based coalition of diverse interests. The group included members from white middle-class suburbs, organized labor, and the black working class of Gary. In fact, since working-class African Americans faced the worst pollution, their participation was essential to CARP's success. Hurley's study challenges assumptions about the class, racial, and gender composition of environmental movements. It also showcases the struggle between a national economy that has created peripheral, and polluted, areas such as Gary and the residents of those areas—who are attempting to shape their urban image and environment.[16] When U.S. Steel created Gary, it did so with the contradictions of being both an industrial utopia and an industrial dystopia. This left interpretative room for a struggle over the city's image and a kind of equilibrium between its national and local reputation. Throughout Gary's history, the struggle over meaning has created a series of conflicting yet coexisting images of the city.

An Industrial Utopia

Since Gary was a planned city, many contemporary observers saw the possibility to begin the modern city anew. By applying the relevant scientific theories and urban plans, many thought, Gary's creators could avoid the problems that had plagued other industrial cities. "Gary, by reason of its industrial significance and the marvelous growth of its community life," remarked one observer, "is a marked place for the student of social, civic, and industrial advance."[17] Through careful planning, a stated sense of purpose, and a clear delineation of space, U.S. Steel sought to control both the construction and the city. Yet U.S. Steel's primary purpose for Gary was fast and efficient steel production. "With such a virgin site to build upon," observed *Scientific American*, "the designers of the plant were able to work with a free hand; and the component parts of this, the greatest steel plant in existence, were therefore laid out with a strict regard to the economic handling of the enormous masses of raw materials and finished product."[18] The city, however, remained an afterthought, and several urban planners and progressives complained that U.S. Steel was not putting enough effort into planning their new city.

As part of the construction of the Gary Works, the planners also tried to insure uninterrupted production in times of urban strife. Unlike the planners of cities such as Pullman, Illinois, who tried to eliminate conflict, Gary's planners assumed that urban upheaval was inevitable and built the mill to withstand an onslaught. The most overt example of this was the positioning of the Grand Calumet River. Until 1906, the river was a meandering creek that often flooded large areas of the region. However, at the onset of construction, engineers moved the river a quarter of a mile south and confined it to a concrete channel. Ostensibly, this was to give the mill room to grow and develop its own rail lines, but the river also served as a barrier between the mill and the town. The effect was not lost on observers. Commenting on the river, the lake, and the shipping channel, *Harper's Weekly* concluded, "The mills will thus be surrounded on three sides by water. This strategic position indicates a premonition of trouble. The Gary steel-mills will be an open shop, and the swarming hordes of Huns and Polacks will think twice—or at least try twice—before crossing the medieval moat to gain the industrial stronghold beyond."[19]

Within U.S. Steel's master plan, contradictions emerged about Gary. While the mill was considered a triumph of scientific planning, the city grew haphazardly. The building of the new mill suggested the opening of a new era of industrialism, yet the mill was constructed to withstand the dangers of the old. These contradictions led many to create their own story for Gary. For some promoters, Gary held the potential and promise of industrial capitalism, and they presented it as the "Magical City of Steel," "City of the Century," or the "Miracle City of Hoosierdom." Others, who saw the rapid growth of saloons, the "foreign" origins of the workers, and the sense of lawlessness, feared moral and social chaos. Still others saw limitless economic possibility. Far from constructing an industrial utopia, U.S. Steel created an empty slate on which people could transcribe their hopes and fears.[20]

Sin City, Mill Town

When, on October 4, 1919, the streets of Gary erupted in violence, many people's fears were realized. Two weeks into a nationwide steel strike, workers and sympathizers fought against police and predominately black strikebreakers in a bloody conflict that resulted, on October 7, in a declaration of martial law.[21] The arrival of over a thousand soldiers from the Fourth Division of the U.S. Army put an end to the violence and, for all intents and purposes, the strike. However, the violence in Gary changed the way people thought about the city. "The magic dream city," observed one reporter after the strike, "has become [a] weird nightmare."[22]

Especially in the sensationalist press, Gary became known for its political corruption, saloons, gambling, prostitution, and vice. The image of Gary that emerged was of a crime-ridden, violent, and morally debauched city.[23] To "Steel City" was added the nickname "Sin City." National publications focused on "cleaning up Gary stills," "Gary's bootlegging administration," and "the Gary liquor scandal." By the 1940s and 1950s, as the United States' fears shifted from political corruption and liquor-law violations to the morality of public sexuality, so too did descriptions of Gary. In a 1955 sensationalist exposé entitled "Steel and Sex," *Quick* magazine claimed that the "vice dens are hotter than the blast furnaces." Gary, Indiana, concluded *Quick*, "has been chalked up as an incorrigible sin city that probably never will change."[24]

Even through the Sin City years, the residents of Gary retained a sense of pride in themselves and their city. The riots of 1919 helped to create a culture of labor as steelworkers and their families claimed the streets as their own. The success of the Congress of Industrial Organizations (CIO) in unionizing "Big Steel" (that is, U.S. Steel) in 1937 and the emergence of Gary as a United Steelworker town reconfirmed the sense that Gary was a good place for working families.[25] In 1939, the writers' project of the Works Progress Administration classified Gary as a mill town because so much of its urban culture revolved around the production of steel. Gary's citizens even fought back against both crime in the city and the image of Sin City. In 1949, women in Gary formed the Women's Citizens Committee, which sought to pressure the mayor and the police administration to battle vice. While the actions of "the angry housewives of Gary" did expose the underworld of the city, leading many journals to report on Gary's vices, their actions also showed a citizenry willing to help shape its city.[26]

The Black Metropolis

The riots of 1919 also offered a premonition of the racial difficulties that Gary would face. Throughout the first half of the twentieth century, migrant black labor had come to Gary. Between 1920 and 1930, roughly fifteen thousand migrants from the South arrived. By 1940, another twenty thousand had joined them. As African Americans found steel jobs, the reputation of Gary rose within the black community. In 1956, *Ebony* declared Gary the top city in the United States for African Americans.[27] By the mid-1960s, however, anxieties, aspirations, and tensions in the African American and white communities had begun to play out in the political arena. In the 1967 mayoral campaign, incumbent A. Martin Katz received the endorsement of both the Democratic Party and the United Steelworkers, support that normally would have guaranteed him a victory. However, black voters' support for black candidate Richard Gordon Hatcher helped to defeat Katz in a fierce primary. In the general election, despite large numbers of white voters who supported the Republican candidate, Hatcher won. He was elected just hours ahead of Cleveland's Carl Stokes, making him the first black mayor of a major U.S. city.[28]

Hatcher's election touched off a dramatic series of events for Gary. Fear of a black city run by a black mayor led to a rash of white flight in the years after the election. Interviewed in 1976, Dorothy Gale, a white woman who lived in Gary, explained the shocked response she would receive on disclosing her residence. "I was tired of getting that reception when I said that I was from Gary," she remarked, "because people acted as if you were a leper. I have never heard anything good said about Gary, even on TV."[29] After 1967, Gary's image solidified as a black city with the inner-city problems of crime, violence, and drugs. "Gary has declined tremendously," observed a white resident of East Chicago; "the crime over there is fantastic. I haven't been to Gary in years. I wouldn't go to Gary if I had an armored guard of marines to guard me over there."[30] In his study of the folklore of the Calumet region of northwest Indiana, Richard Dorson determined that every city possessed its own image within the minds of others. "Gary," he states, "is the black city where nobody goes anymore because of crime, particularly drug crime."[31]

The residents of the black metropolis, however, created an entirely different image of their city. For many, Gary presented not only the opportunity for work and upward mobility but also an opportunity for them to define themselves and construct their own sense of blackness within their city. After detailing the white image of crime-ridden Gary, Dorson says, "Gary's black residents expressed a wholly different outlook: the sweet taste of success . . . struggles in the white world that, despite heavy odds, ended in proud achievement."[32] Within the black metropolis, the culture of steel labor and racial pride combined to give Gary's residents some control over their own lives and their perceptions of the city. "The only place I know is Gary," stated black steelworker Robert Jackson. "I love Gary; as far as I'm concerned, there's no other place in the world." On Gary's national image, Jackson admitted, "Gary has a bad reputation for vice, corruption, low-living standards. . . ." Yet, he explained, "this is all political. The same things happen in Chicago and New York, but because we are a smaller city, people pay more attention to us. We also have a bad reputation because we are 57% black and have a black administration."[33]

For black workers like Jackson, Gary offered the opportunity to take part in consumer society and join the middle class. "People in Gary aren't buying five-thousand-dollar homes; they're buying forty-five- and fifty-thousand-dollar homes," he commented. "They buy Mark IVs and Cadillacs, and they buy books, and they go on vacations and wear funny fur coats, with a motherfucking rock on their finger. They don't be stealing; they don't be peddling; they don't be pushing—they flat out be getting it."[34] To other black steelworkers, like Wilbert Harlan, the mayor was a personal hero who had created the black metropolis. Before 1967, according to Harlan, Gary deserved the title of Sin City, but "along came a guy, Richard Gordon Hatcher. He done more for the black people, I think, than any human being ever. . . . I sincerely believe God sent him, for he sure enough deliver the black people." Because of the availability of steel employment, Gary represented a promised land to Harlan; "there's more money in the black community . . . than any other city I know of in America."[35]

After interviewing several Gary residents, Dorson concluded that, while "the blighted city [was] spoken of with such fear and disgust by dwellers in other parts of the region . . . these black speakers see a shining metropolis in the inner city. . . . This is the heart of Black Gary, which teems with its own life."[36] This self-pride was evident when Gary hosted the 1972 Black Political Party Convention. The city greeted delegates to the convention with banners that read: "Welcome Home to Gary." This sense of home that residents held came out of self-governance and the shared experience of steel-production labor. Despite the national portrayal of their city, Gary's residents continued to shape their own understanding of themselves and their city. The massive loss of steel jobs, however, would undercut Gary's sense of self. Without an image of itself as a steel town, Gary had little to fall back on except its national reputation.

Epitaph for a Model City: Gary and the Steel Crisis

The recession of 1981 threw most of the world's economies into disarray. Many U.S. businesses, including the steel industry, suffered severe losses and looked to reduce their costs through layoffs and plant closings. The fiscal years of 1981 and 1982 were particularly disastrous for U.S. steel companies. During the steel crisis, U.S. mills ran at only 43.8 percent of capacity, and most companies reported record losses. Much like other U.S. industries, the steel companies decided the solution was a drastic reduction in costs through wage cuts, outsourcing, massive layoffs, and closure of plants. For many mill towns, particularly those stretching from the Monongahela Valley of Pennsylvania to Chicago's south shore, the steel crisis meant massive job loss and the deindustrialization of communities.[37]

In 1983, Thomas C. Graham took charge of U.S. Steel's chain of mills and plants. A former executive of Jones and Laughlin Steel, Graham tried to reverse U.S. Steel's economic fortunes and trim its production systems.

He chose to do so through massive layoffs and the outsourcing of steel production to cheaper outside firms, despite the union contract that forbade such actions. In December of 1984 came the masterstroke of what was called the "Graham Revolution." U.S. Steel announced the closing of parts or all of twenty-eight plants and mines, thereby eliminating 15,436 jobs. By 1987, Graham could boast that U.S. Steel, with only 18,000 employees, would match the output of 1983, when it employed 48,600. While they reversed the company's fortunes, such drastic cuts decimated steel centers such as Gary.[38]

One of the plants Graham closed was the U.S. Steel Tubing Specialties in Gary. Built in 1926, the mill thrived off the booming oil industry, which consumed most of its tubing products. However, after the collapse of both the oil and steel industries, U.S. Steel began laying off many of the employees of the plant. Explained plant manager John Benda, "The future, unfortunately, became so bleak the powers that be decided it was not in the best interest of U.S. Steel to hang on."[39] In December of 1985, the company announced the complete closure of the plant, putting 2,200 employees out of work. After losing his millwright's job in 1982, Sherman Hayes Jr. found employment in Kentucky with Mid-America Canning; however, it soon closed its doors as well. "It used to bother me, but anymore it's a way of life," remarked Hayes in a Gary *Post-Tribune* survey. "If you hire in anywhere, you just can't count on that job being there." Larry Koker expressed similar sentiments: "It's like watching a very bad movie, and you can't turn the movie off. . . . You have no control." Despite the fact that Koker earned half his old mill wage working for the Westville Correctional Center, he was determined to stay optimistic. "The dreams are always there," he stated; "you can't give up. If you give up, you end up in the garage with a shotgun in your mouth."[40]

The layoffs at Tubing Specialties affected many other workers in the same way. "Since the layoffs and shut down, we have lived through hell. We are still fighting to be independent again," said Patricia Jones. "The day they told me I was laid off, I went home and my wife told me she had good news," recalled Amos Schultz Jr. "She was pregnant; I didn't know whether to laugh or cry." Likewise, Sharon Haymon remembered the day her husband lost his job: "I was five months pregnant. It was a very emotional pregnancy for me and my husband. His job was gone, but the bills kept coming. We lost our house, car, and on Oct. 5, 1982, which is incidentally my husband's birthday, the gas company shut off our gas." Said Rudy Grasha, "It really hurt me for a long time, fifteen years of my life given to industry was now nothing." The pressures of job loss took a toll on Koker's entire family. "The children became anxious and depressed because they couldn't do the things that their friends could do," he lamented. "Their frustration would sometimes lead to tears that further depressed the wife and I." Shortly after he lost his job, Koker and his wife of eighteen years divorced. "I'm confident that if I hadn't been laid off, my ex-wife and I would still be married," he concluded. "I escaped into alcoholism. It made the hurt go away for a little while. But there's no escape for the children."[41]

In addition to the intense personal tragedies, the loss of steel jobs had a cumulative effect on the city. Economic downturns and massive layoffs were not new to the city; as early as 1973, the *Washington Post* reported white flight of both capital and population, unemployment (especially following a 1972 layoff, which sent the unemployment rate to 40 percent), and the end of federal assistance from Democratic administrations. The newspaper suggested that these factors signaled an "epitaph for a model city."[42] Yet the steel crisis of the 1980s brought permanent unemployment on a scale to which Gary was not accustomed. Beginning in 1982, Gary's unemployment rate topped 20 percent for four straight years. Downtown became largely a deserted and desolate strip of abandoned shops. By 1985, the city was in a financial crisis. A conflict with U.S. Steel over property taxes (the mill often supplied 40 percent of the city's tax base) had left the city nearly broke. Unable to fund its social programs, the city scaled back its system of welfare. Rising crime had earned for the city the title of murder capital of 1984. By 1985, U.S. Steel's "rationalization" plan had reduced the employment of the Gary Works to 7,500. According to a US Census Bureau study, in 1985 one-fifth of Gary's 49,500 households lived below the poverty line.[43] The combination of job loss, crime, and reduction of social aid led one resident to lament, "We've already been designated the murder capital and now we are headed on the road toward becoming the hunger capital."[44] Few saw any way to reverse the fortunes of the city. Lynn Feekin, the director of the Calumet Project for Industrial Jobs, stated frankly, "I haven't seen the new industry that's going to provide the stable manufacturing job base, that's going to replace the enormous job loss the region has suffered." On announcing that the Gary Works was to become the flagship of U.S. Steel, company spokesman Thomas R. Ferrall added, "I wouldn't want to suggest any hope for increased employment at this point."[45] Where, then, was the city to turn for new jobs?

On April 16, 1985, the mayor, city officials, and many others gathered to celebrate the opening of a Wendy's fast-food restaurant. "Larger cities, like Chicago, would look down their noses at a fast-food franchise," said Mayor Hatcher to commemorate the occasion, "but Wendy's represents 80 jobs." City boosters pointed to the franchise opening as a sign of economic recovery. "I absolutely believe that Gary had reached bottom and is on the way back up," expressed one. Hatcher agreed, suggesting "there really is a light at the end of the tunnel." The press covering the event, however, was less optimistic. The *Chicago Tribune* stated that the city of Gary was "grasping at rays of hope where it can," and that the opening was a major civic event because "this hardscrabble steel town of 147,532 welcomes any new businesses." Adding an ironic twist to the celebration was the fact that several of the new employees of the restaurant were former steelworkers who had traded their mill wages for $3.35 an hour. "Sure we would rather have the $15- to $20-an-hour jobs that the steel mills used to provide but that is not reality," explained Hatcher. "From our point of view, we have to get jobs first, then, later on, we can be selective."[46]

Despite his best efforts, however, the mayor could not put a positive spin on his city. His successor in 1987, Thomas Barnes, did no better. In 1988, the city published a promotional pamphlet entitled "Gary!" which it sent to thousands of companies around the world, boasting, "We're a city with a future, make no mistake." The pamphlet tried to entice prospective companies with its only photograph: a picture of downtown positioned to include the city's only national chains, a Walgreen's and its brand-new Wendy's. However, the *Chicago Tribune* observed, "the reality of downtown Gary fits uneasily with these claims." Even the environmental accountability for which Gary's residents had fought seemed to fade away. On April 14, 1987, a leak of over 27,000 gallons of hydrochloric acid at a Gary factory created a massive toxic cloud and necessitated the evacuation of thousands.[47] By the mid-1980s, the residents of Gary had lost the ability to shape and define their own city's image and landscape. Instead Gary had become a legendary example of a dangerous deindustrialized slum. Don Sullivan, spokesman for the Gary Business Development Commission, tried to separate his idea of Gary from the national image. "You have to look at Gary with the correct idea," he wrote in "Gary!"—"that Gary is an easel on which is to be painted one of the great success stories of the 20th century."[48] By the late 1980s, the officials of Gary were desperately trying to reverse the direction in which its reputation was heading. However, very few were buying the validity of Gary's self-image.

In Search of a New Gary

For cities such as Gary, the economics of urban image have had serious repercussions in terms of the city's ability to attract new jobs and industries. Despite several attempts to reinvent itself, Gary has retained the image of a deindustrialized wasteland marked by pollution and crime. The legend of

Gary, which was created by the loss of industrial jobs, serves to repel new jobs, industry, and investment, and thereby deepens Gary's negative image. Gary's residents found ways to create their own images of their city within the paradox of industrial utopia and dystopia. But attempts to reinvent Gary as an industrial city, a tourist attraction, or a gambling center have largely proven unsuccessful.

With 109 homicides in 1993, Gary again claimed the title of murder capital of the United States. "It is quite evident that there is a serious problem with violence in the city of Gary," remarked one resident. "People are being killed at alarming rates. . . . Gary is probably known all around the world for being its murder capital."[49] In their attempts to confront the national image of the city, some politicians appealed to the federal government for assistance. Writing to Attorney General Janet Reno, Representative Peter J. Visclosky asked, "Now more than ever Gary and Northwest Indiana are in dire need of federal assistance to combat crime and reclaim our streets." Likewise, Senator Dan Coates asked Reno for monetary assistance. Even the city's mayor asked for the nation's aid during a CNN interview. "Gary, Indiana, is part of America," he stated. "We need help on the national level to end this insanity."[50]

In the fall of 1994, Gary reinforced its image as a city unable to control its own streets. In order to vent their frustration over low pay and dangerous work conditions, the Gary chapter of the Fraternal Order of Police (FOP) rented five billboards at strategic locations in the city. In bright red letters on a white background, the signs read, "CAUTION!!! You are currently in Gary, Ind. 1993 MURDER Capital of the Nation. Where officers are EXTREMELY Underpaid and Overworked." The signs sparked an almost immediate response from the mayor and other city officials. Six days later, the FOP replaced their billboards with an anticrime message that did not mention Gary's murder title. Yet the FOP billboards had done their damage. "If you put wallpaper over cracked plaster the cracks don't go away by themselves," wrote the Gary *Post-Tribune*. "The Barnes administration, the police officers and the rest of Northwest Indiana would do well to remember that."[51]

By January 1995, the Gary *Post-Tribune* could declare, "Gary bashers will need to find new material. The city is no longer the nation's murder capital."[52] Many remained convinced that Gary was still a dangerous city. Even the name Gary seemed to carry connotations that many people preferred to avoid. One of the minimills that began operating in Gary during the late 1980s is Chicago Steel and Tin Plate. Although many small steel manufacturers relocated to Gary, Chicago Steel is a local business. Bruce

Mannakee, president of Chicago Steel, said that he chose the name "because it sounds much better than Gary Steel and Tin Plate."[53] Even the company literature of the city's new savior, Donald Trump, who opened a riverboat casino on Gary's lakeshore and helped bring the Miss U.S.A. pageant to Gary, calls the casino "Buffington Harbor in northwest Indiana." Gary's national reputation was also showcased by the attention received from Housing and Urban Development (HUD) Secretary Andrew Cuomo. "The strongest American economy maybe casts the greatest economic shadow," he remarked. "Gary, Indiana, tells the story here; population loss of 27 percent. Gary was also in the steel business. The steel mill is still there; it's just smaller than it was. . . . I saw that sign in Gary; it said it all. 'You have a life. Get a future.' How telling for Gary."[54]

As part of a program to attract businesses and create jobs, HUD lists the Gary Municipal Airport as a potential development site. In fact, for several decades, Gary has been proposed as the location for a third major airport for Chicago. Its selling points are the availability of inexpensive industrial land, the relative absence of residential housing, the proximity of Lake Michigan for takeoffs and landing approaches, and the existing infrastructure of freeways. Many observers, however, worry about the rustbelt image of Gary and wonder if airline customers would feel comfortable flying into such a city. Some have proposed building a new airport instead in the small town of Peotone, Illinois, south of Chicago. Although debate continues, the Gary airport is planning to expand and has begun to play an increasingly important role in the Chicago Department of Transportation. In fact, in Chicago Mayor Richard Daley's plan for the city's airports, he states that, after making the necessary investments in O'Hare and Midway, the city should "make sure that we maximize the potential of other existing airports in the region which can grow and expand, starting with the Gary-Chicago airport in Indiana."[55] O'Hare has also begun to divert many of its cargo flights to Gary. Despite these endorsements, Peotone remains a leading contender for the new airport, and many still worry about the effect of Gary's national image on the attractiveness of a major airport within the city.

Like many other cities, as well as Indian reservations, Gary has also turned to gambling and casinos to change its economic fortunes. With the addition of Trump Casinos on the lakefront and the acquisition of the Miss U.S.A. pageant, Gary has tried to recast itself as a tourist destination and a playground for neighboring Chicago. There is a certain irony in the fact that, before it industrialized, northwest Indiana did play that role for Chicago. Plus, during the twentieth century, Gary's Sin City reputation was based on the number of gambling and drinking opportunities supposedly available. As Gary seeks to rebuild itself in the image of Atlantic City, New Jersey, it is, in a way, embracing its past. As for so many other communities, gambling serves as a final alternative for Gary.[56]

Flint, Michigan, Is No Gary: The Legend and Legacy of Gary, Indiana

In 1987, *Money* magazine published its first survey of the best (and accordingly worst) places to live in the United States. At the bottom of the list, dead last at number three hundred, was Flint, Michigan. In response, the people of Flint gathered to show their anger at the magazine and defend their city. From the stage at the protest, a local deejay yelled to the crowd, "Has *Money* been to Gary, Indiana? Let me tell you—Flint, Michigan, is no Gary!" Michael Moore, who filmed the protest and included parts of it in his film *Roger and Me*, could only agree: "That was true; Flint was *worse* than Gary. Flint's unemployment rate during the early '80s had risen to 27%, vs. 15.7% in Gary." "So it seemed odd to me," Moore concluded, "that the battered citizens of Flint decided to vent their rage at *Money*."[57] An equally important question may be, why did they vent their rage at Gary? Given the similarities between the two cities—both had suffered severe job loss, capital flight, and urban decay—why did the residents of Flint take solace in the idea that they were, at least, not Gary? Moore's comments also point out one of the ironies of Gary's national reputation. Despite high unemployment and some abandonment, Gary, when compared to some of the cities hardest hit by job loss and plant closure, was not as bad off. Its unemployment rate, while high, did not skyrocket. It maintained, largely through U.S. Steel, a significant tax base. How typical, then, a deindustrial narrative does Gary provide? What can it tell us about other cities' deindustrial paths, and to what degree is Gary's national image shaped not only by industrial job loss but by racial identities and assumptions as well?

Gary's story both follows and diverges from other cities' deindustrialization narratives. In many ways, Gary's is a unique story of industrial development and urbanization. U.S. Steel conceived of the city as an industrial experiment in economic centralization and capital mobility. Gary was built in three years for the sole purpose of steel production. Yet the rise and fall (and rebirth?) of Gary demonstrate the importance of the culture of industrial labor, the value of urban image, and the effects of deindustrialization. The struggle of Gary to redefine itself is similar to the efforts of other cities that have faced economic hardship and severe unemployment.

For example, Representative Jack Quinn protested when his home city of Buffalo, New York, became the fictional site of the Broadway play *The Full Monty*. In its film version, a group of unemployed steelworkers in Sheffield, England, decides to form a strip act to earn money. For the Broadway play, however, the location moved to Buffalo. In a letter to playwright Terrence McNally, Quinn argued, "Your treatment of our city is both incorrect and irresponsible." He suggested that the play be set in a fictional location to avoid causing "undue harm to the psyche of a city on the rebound."[58] Similarly, Gary Rhoades, the head of economic development for the Flint Chamber of Commerce, remarked in 1997: "The only thing working against us is our name. . . . If people didn't know this was Flint they would probably like it."[59] Much like Gary, Buffalo and Flint are struggling to revitalize their deindustrial images.

The story of Gary also differs in important ways from those of Flint or Buffalo because of the important part that race plays in Gary's national, regional, and local image. Dorson's folklore study concluded that a vast difference existed between the way whites in the surrounding communities and blacks within Gary viewed the city. As early as 1973, the *Washington Post* argued that racial divisions, along with economic downturns, were wreaking havoc on Gary's social stability. Even the *Harper's Weekly* description in 1907 of "Huns and Polacks" suggests that ethnicity and race have long been salient features of Gary's identity. The politics of the 1960s made race one of Gary's defining elements. The deindustrial narrative, then, was shaped both by industrial job loss and racial identities; in Gary the two are difficult to distinguish. The question may be, then, how we choose to classify the story of Gary. One way to think about Gary is as an industrial mill town that relied on a single industry. With job loss in that industry came the deindustrialization of the city. In this way Gary reflects the changes in places such as Flint, Michigan; Youngstown, Ohio; or Cohoes, New York.[60] Yet its patterns of white flight, racial divisions, and decay echo the development of inner cities within Detroit or Newark. Finally, given its proximity to and relationship with Chicago, Gary resembles an industrial district or periphery much like South Chicago; Patterson and Camden, New Jersey; or East Saint Louis. Perhaps what is most interesting about Gary is that, a century after U.S. Steel created the paradox of the industrial utopia/dystopia, it retains the ability to be all of these things at the same time.[61]

The difference now, of course, is that Gary must confront its deindustrialized landscape, the ramifications of which are not only the loss of jobs and a rise in poverty, but the loss of the interpretative room for residents to create their own working image of their city. Yet city officials and citizens remain resilient in their efforts to create a new identity for Gary. Perhaps the answer lies in the reimagining of the city as a gambling center; maybe it can be found in the reworking of greater Chicago's transportation system. Or perhaps the solution lies in the way that the nation envisions the city of Gary. Instead of insisting that we are no Gary, we can, with an understanding of the place of Gary within our industrial economy and the power of urban imagery, come to the same conclusion as former mayor Barnes—that "Gary is part of America."

CHAPTER 11

Monuments of a Lost Cause

The Postindustrial Campaign to Commemorate Steel

KIRK SAVAGE

The deindustrialized landscape, like a ruined battlefield that heals over, is ripe for commemoration. As the physical traces of the industrial age—the factories, the immigrant enclaves that served them, the foul air—disappear, the urge to reaffirm or celebrate the industrial past seems to grow stronger.

Nowhere is this more true than in Pittsburgh, Pennsylvania, once the steel town to the world. Almost all the steel mills are now gone, their vast tracts of riverfront land all undergoing redevelopment in the city's transition to a new economy of "innovative research and high technology."[1] But the steel industry haunts the city, especially as a pervasive metaphor through which residents and news media still define themselves. "Man of steel," announced the local paper when the baseball team hired a new manager; "McClendon has the focus to be a good fit for Pittsburgh."[2] Steel continues to evoke a complex of moral values—toughness, hard work, pragmatism—that city boosters proclaim even as they anxiously assert that Pittsburgh has moved beyond steel into the high-tech age.[3]

In Pittsburgh, the impulse to commemorate the steel industry emerged in the 1980s at the very moment that the industry and its supporting culture were disintegrating. This is not to suggest that the steel industry had a stable "golden age" that collapsed all at once. In reality, the story of Pittsburgh's industrial development is a continuous history of transformation and displacement, with new processes replacing old ones, once valued labor skills suddenly becoming obsolete, and wrenching shifts in the labor force commonplace. The moments of cultural stability were relatively brief, if not illusory, to begin with.[4] Yet the commemorative impulse tends to obscure the processes of historical change. As I have noted elsewhere, commemorative monuments usually hope to create a stable and coherent past sealed off from the vicissitudes of change we know so well in the present. The irony, of course, is that those very commemorative projects are themselves products of specific historical forces and conflicts. Try as they may, commemorative designs cannot escape the flux of history.[5]

This chapter examines a series of commemorative projects in Pittsburgh that address the industrial past in multiple and conflicting ways, each project mediated by disparate local constituencies and agendas. Taken together, their relation to the industrial past follows a pattern that is familiar from battle commemoration. All the essential types of war memorials find their counterparts here in the campaign to memorialize steel: monuments to "generals" (the corporate leadership); to "common soldiers" (the steelworkers); and to the battle-scarred landscape itself, laid to waste by the industrial machinery of the steel mills. Like the military memorials, which usually cloak their subject in valor and hide the sheer savage destructiveness at the heart of every war, the monuments to steel mostly avoid the fundamental dilemmas of the industrial past. Only in the final project I will discuss, the least traditionally commemorative or artistic of the three, do we find the opportunity of a truly "postindustrial" cultural landscape—a landscape that asks us to view our industrial legacy not as a heroic episode from a golden age but as a living challenge in the present.

In Pittsburgh some commentators chafe at the notion that industry is a thing of the past: they point out that, even though the big mills are gone, manufacturing continues to play an important part in the regional economy.[6] It is obviously misleading to declare a postindustrial era, as if industry were dead. I want to suggest, however, that just as industry survives within the postindustrial age, the idea of the postindustrial was actually born within the industrial age. The term "post-industrialism" was coined by an art historian working in England in the 1910s, one of a group of antimodern socialists who, in the tradition of William Morris, looked forward to a time when machine-based industry would die away and be replaced by a new labor system of guilds and handicraft more in tune with nature.[7] In the United States, the dream of transcending industry was articulated not only as an opposition movement but as a spiritual yearning from within the ranks of industry itself. At the same time that big industrialists came to dominate the national economy, many of them were creating alternative universes meant to lift industrial man above and beyond the brute material world of the factory. In Pittsburgh the dream of a "postindustrial" salvation came to be embodied in the philanthropic career of Andrew Carnegie.

Carnegie spent the first part of his adult life inventing the modern steel industry, and the latter part of his life redirecting the surplus fortune he had so singlemindedly amassed toward the propagation of learning, high culture, and international peace. "Dollars are only dross until spiritualized," Carnegie insisted:

> Our mines of iron and coal have not completed their mission when transmuted into articles for use; not even completed their mission when transmuted into dollars. All is still upon the material plane. Not until the dollars are transmuted into service for others, in one of the many forms best calculated to appeal to and develop the higher things of the moral, intellectual and esthetic life, has wealth completely justified its existence.[8]

The monument that best crystallizes Carnegie's transcendental impulse is the vast civic palace of high culture—housing a public library, music hall, and art and science museums under one roof—appropriately called the Carnegie Institute, which he had built in Pittsburgh between 1895 and 1907. Erected at the height of the steel industry, from the industry's surplus wealth, the Carnegie Institute nevertheless functions as Pittsburgh's first major "postindustrial" monument.

While the Carnegie Institute might be seen as a kind of culture factory, with its systematic divisions of knowledge and creativity into various "departments," in most crucial respects the complex declares its difference from the world of industry. The classical order on the outside, the conspicuous display of colored marbles and other ornate materials within, the representations of culture heroes like Michaelangelo and Shakespeare at the entrances, the surrounding fountains and monuments all worked together to offer a vision of a higher and better world to which the factory worker and middle-level manager might aspire—a world of beauty and leisure somewhere beyond the sweat and grime of the mills.[9] Look, for example, at the lovely fountain on an axis with the library entrance. The fountain was erected in 1908 as a monument to a local political boss named Christopher Lyman Magee, who was instrumental in persuading the city authorities to accept Carnegie's gift. (See figure 10.) Its allegorical image of beneficence—a sumptuously draped female figure holding an extravagant cornucopia of fruits and flowers—stands under an oak tree framing a quotation from Shakespeare. This imagery represents everything the steel mill was not: cool and restful, not hot and busy; extravagant and luxurious, not frugal and efficient; beautiful, not utilitarian; female, not male; the bounty of nature, not the bounty of man.[10]

The building and its environs thus model Carnegie's own "postindustrial" life, as they put into concrete form his basic philosophy of converting

FIGURE 10. Christopher Lyman Magee Memorial, erected 1908 (Augustus Saint-Gaudens, sculptor; Henry Bacon, architect). Photograph by the author.

industrial capital into postindustrial beauty. It is easy to say that his philosophy was just a cynical self-justification, even self-aggrandizement, but that assessment is simplistic and ultimately inaccurate; Carnegie's moral principles and his desire to transcend his industrial self-definition were so entangled that it is impossible to know where conviction ended and self-

promotion began. The cultural palace he donated asks the city and its residents to follow in his footsteps, to leave the dross of the material world and
find spiritual sustenance in the purer realms of art, poetry, and nature. John
White Alexander's murals inside the main entrance, with their fabulous images of steelworkers flying through the clouds and smoke, give a wonderful visual expression to this early postindustrial ideal.[11] All this is not to
suggest that Carnegie's factory workers could actually get to his institute;
they rarely had the time off to make such an indirect and time-consuming
trip. But in Carnegie's dream world, his library and museum were for them.

While this great product of the industrial age evokes a postindustrial
ideal of transcendence, a monument to Carnegie erected at the beginning
of the postindustrial age deliberately evokes an industrial aesthetic and
ideal. Richard Serra's huge propped structure of rusted Cor-Ten steel entitled *Carnegie*, located in front of a modernist wing attached in the early
1970s to Carnegie's original complex, was erected in 1985 in the midst of
the local steel industry's collapse. (See figure 11.) While Carnegie's early-
twentieth-century building and its surroundings were supposed to take us
away from the world of the factory, Serra's monument is meant to lead us
back. The enormous steel plates propped against each other evoke the incredible scale of the mills and the tremendous mechanical force they harnessed. Serra's use of materials belongs to a tradition of the industrial or
technological sublime that continues strong to this day.[12] Although the
artist disavowed any content whatsoever, an examination of the work's patronage and context shows conclusively that it does function as a commemorative monument. Ironically, while the managers of the art museum
were promoting Serra's work as a symbol of Pittsburgh's industrial character, *Carnegie* actually marked the end of the big-steel era.[13]

Carnegie is a work of great artistry that offers a highly sophisticated series of perceptual surprises, but in the end still functions rather simply as a
monument. Inside the structure, accessible by a ground-level opening between two of the steel slabs, the walls close in on the spectator as they soar
upward and inward to a small square opening of sky forty feet above. But
from the outside—the way most people see the work—the profile of the
structure spreads outward, almost as if taking flight.[14] The odd vertiginous
spatial experience of the interior—a little like Alice's rabbit hole—gives
way to a very different optical experience on the exterior, so different that
the structure can become a graceful or even "uplifting" landmark when it
is seen from the museum plaza or street.[15]

Serra, the consummate modernist, refused to see his piece as a symbol
or any kind of monument. As he told a local interviewer, his works do not
"defer to that kind of literary or commemorative or topical or temporal ex-

FIGURE 11. *Carnegie*, erected 1985 (Richard Serra, sculptor). Photograph by the author.

istence. They are not about that. They have an internal meaning which is their content which is open to anyone, and their structure organizes that meaning."[16] The content of the piece, according to him, is simply the viewer's own perceptual and spatial experience of it. But the interviewer pressed further: Does the piece have a specific meaning by virtue of its location in Pittsburgh as opposed to, say, Paris? "I think for people of this town, absolutely," Serra conceded. People who have worked in heavy industry, he argued, "have a basic respect for how something is built or what the weight of something is or what the nature of steel is. So I think that in this town it becomes almost a metaphor for what the industry of the town has produced. . . . Not that I am saying it is a symbol for that, but I think that could probably be why the people are tolerant."[17] Serra was imagining his audience, the "people" of Pittsburgh, as industrial workers; for him, Pittsburgh summoned up the populist ideal of a proletarian beholder who looks at art with a no-nonsense eye practiced in the skill of seeing how things are put together in the real world. As an artist, Serra identified himself with industrial labor, especially with steel. He had worked in steel mills in his youth, and as a sculptor he continued to work with the material—so much so that he liked to call steel mills his "surrogate studios."[18] But his artistic relationship to the steel mill was rather different from the relationship a steelworker would have. Serra became a client, a manufacturer. He designed *Carnegie* by mocking it up in miniature in a little sandbox, then gave the specifications to the steel mill, much as any other manufacturing client would.[19]

Indeed, it was not the working class that commissioned, financed, or promoted the piece as a steel-town symbol. A bronze plaque near the structure informs us that Jane Holt Roesch, wife of William R. Roesch, donated the piece as a memorial to her husband, president of U.S. Steel from 1979 to 1983.[20] The piece was commissioned by her for the international exhibition of contemporary art, sponsored by the Carnegie Museum of Art, of 1985. The exhibition had been held periodically since 1896, when Andrew Carnegie founded the institution as a museum of contemporary art. But it was only in 1985 that the exhibition was renamed the Carnegie International, drawing renewed attention to the founder of the museum and U.S. Steel.[21] The museum was responsible for bringing the donor and the sculptor together, and it is clear that the museum wanted to recruit a high-profile sculptor to create a monumental "signature piece" for the exhibition.[22] U.S. Steel, in turn, was the major corporate bankroller of the exhibition. The title *Carnegie* (apparently chosen by Serra)[23] suggests the web of interconnections between the piece, the exhibition, the museum, the corporation, and its founder. Located at the front entrance of the building and the exhibition, Serra's piece functioned as a kind of cultural logo for U.S. Steel as it revived its founder's philanthropic support for high art in Pittsburgh.

Despite the minimalist claims of nonreferentiality, *Carnegie* actually celebrated the tradition of corporate leadership at the very time that the leadership was dismantling the local steel industry. This was a watershed moment in the history of labor-capital relations, when the deindustrialization of the Pittsburgh region was in full swing. Massive layoffs and plant closings began in the region in 1979, when Roesch became the head of steelmaking operations at U.S. Steel. The most recent scholarly history of U.S. Steel asserts that Roesch "pushed ahead vigorously with the program of closures and cost reduction."[24] By the time the sculpture was installed in 1985, most of the plants in the region had shut down and nearly one hundred thousand jobs had been eliminated.[25] At the same time that U.S. Steel was engaging in massive disinvestments—which shattered whole towns like Homestead, in the river valley just outside Pittsburgh—it was generously underwriting an extremely expensive international art exhibition that used *Carnegie* as its focal point.

The timing of *Carnegie's* installation is similar to that of George Segal's *Steelmakers* in Youngstown, although the form and content of the two pieces differ radically. Segal's life-size bronze depiction of two steelworkers was erected in downtown Youngstown in 1980 and promoted as a morale booster for a town battered by three major mill closings in the late 1970s.[26] Serra's piece eschewed realist representation and evoked management rather than labor. But both celebrated steel production at the very moment that actual production was drastically declining.[27]

How do we account for the seeming paradox? Normally, commemorative works try to solidify an identity for a constituency that is changing or even dying. The reassertion of industrial identity in the midst of deindustrialization is typical of the commemorative urge to fix history in one place. But in both Serra's and Segal's cases, this reassertion was specific to the needs and concerns of that particular moment. In Youngstown, a local arts agency in partnership with other local public and private sponsors used a public art initiative to glorify its labor base; in Pittsburgh the monument emerged from image-management concerns of the corporate executive class.

Carnegie puts a proletarian face on what is in every other way an elitist monument. Unlike its namesake, *Carnegie* embraces steel, glorifies it, savors its hard-edged, rusting, man-made look. Why is it that Carnegie himself would never have considered erecting a monument of rusting steel, while a new generation of civic and corporate leaders would embrace this industrial symbolism as they were in the process of shutting down that very industry? In part, the answer has to do with larger shifts in the mentality of the corporate elite, which would explain the embrace of modernist aesthetics for their office buildings, art collections, and so forth. Yet within this broader history, *Carnegie* deserves recognition as a serendipitous meeting point between modernist art and corporate image management. At a time when its corporate image was being buffeted, U.S. Steel and its executive class sought to reassert a traditional leadership role in local civic culture.[28] To do so they found a symbol that seemed to lower high culture from its elitist pedestal and give it a proletarian flavor. Serra, working in the opposite direction, sought to elevate industrial materials and processes into the realm of art. Meeting in the middle, they created a hegemonic icon—a work that maintained high-cultural distinction while ostensibly appealing to a low-cultural sensibility. Made of steel, manufactured by millworkers rather than handcrafted by artists, *Carnegie* could function at once as a symbol for an elite international exhibition catering to a rarefied art audience and for a gritty factory town of people who know how things are built. The museum was particularly sensitive to the sculpture's dual role. Press releases emphasized Serra's roots in the steel industry and the museum director went so far as to say that the sculptor "has continued to have a special affinity for the metal and for the workers and the communities that make steel." Those same press releases downplayed the role of U.S. Steel in sponsoring the exhibition and Serra's work; in one draft press release, the museum director deleted a sentence explaining that U.S. Steel had provided part of the funding for the exhibition.[29]

All this may help explain why the piece never became the target of any organized protest from the labor movement. Between 1983 and 1985, protestors did target elite institutions such as Mellon Bank and Shadyside Presbyterian Church, in an effort to publicize the social and financial dealings of the executives in charge of plant closures.[30] But the protestors did not seem to grasp the marriage of corporate patronage and high culture that had created and sustained Serra's *Carnegie*. Only a few observers in the local press seemed to connect the piece to ongoing deindustrialization. One editorial wryly noted, "Anything made out of two hundred thousand pounds of American rolled steel cannot be all bad. What with the way the steel industry is right now, we'll take just about any order we can get."[31] A letter to the editor blasted the "mockery" of naming the sculpture after Carnegie, founder of U.S. Steel, when the company was no longer even capable of manufacturing the piece; the steel plates were being fabricated "by a former competitor because U.S. Steel can no longer fabricate profitably."[32]

Today, few Pittsburghers seem to know the work at all. It has lapsed into its generic function as modernist street furniture that passersby vaguely recognize as "art" without quite knowing why. Recently the art critic David Carrier has lamented that the lack of appreciation for Serra's work is symptomatic of a broader failure of art education in the region and the U.S.[33] But this does not seem to me a problem that art education necessarily can correct. Despite *Carnegie*'s great formal interest, the piece does indeed have commemorative content. Not only does it explicitly honor the steel industry's executive class, but it implicitly reinforces the powerful role that class has played in sponsoring, and indeed defining, high culture ever since Andrew Carnegie started on his philanthropic path. And it is this commemorative content that makes it difficult, in the end, to conjure a proletarian audience for the work, however strongly the steel forms evoke the world of the factory.[34]

Not surprisingly then, several efforts arose in the mid-1990s to erect a work more specifically commemorative of labor in the steel industry. Labor historians and activists took an interest in the site of the 1892 Homestead strike—the famous Pump House where striking workers and Pinkertons clashed and fell. But the corporate landowner, which bought the entire site from U.S. Steel, was bent on redeveloping it for movie theaters, shops, and upscale restaurants, and effectively blocked various efforts to create a steel industry heritage site.[35] Today the Pump House still stands on the edge of the site, with only a small historical marker to remind visitors of its significance.

In 1998 another campaign emerged, this one initiated by the mayor of Pittsburgh (whose father worked for over fifty years in a steel mill) and organized by the city's planning department. The plan called specifically for "a work of public art that celebrates the steelworkers who labored at the South Side Works," the former Jones and Laughlin mill located on a prime stretch of riverfront land not far from downtown Pittsburgh.[36] The mill, one of the oldest in the region, had been finally demolished in the mid-1990s, and the property purchased by the city's Urban Redevelopment Authority. On this site the city has been implementing a redevelopment plan that includes, among other things, a new training facility for the Pittsburgh Steelers football team: the replacement of actual steelworkers by "Steelers" is wonderfully symptomatic of the postindustrial condition.[37]

In the heart of this ambitious redevelopment project, which is replacing the old mill with a vision of the city's techno-gladiator future, the Steelworkers Monument carries the burden of representing the past—reminding the new workforce who and what used to work there. (See figure 12.) The design was chosen by competition, with a mixed jury composed of

FIGURE 12.   Dedication of the Steelworkers Monument, April 20, 2001 (James O'Toole, architect). Photograph by the author.

arts professionals and retired steelworkers. The jury bypassed blatantly romanticized images of labor—such as a heroically nude workman shouldering a steel beam—and eventually settled on a more abstract architectural solution without any figural sculpture at all. Made by local architect James O'Toole, the winning design suggests a deconstructed "ghost mill." Located on the riverbank at the foot of the old "hot metal" bridge, it is a sequence of simple structures—shed, rail tracks, ladle for molten steel— hovering in midair above a curving "wall of memories" intended to make the steelworkers' past come alive. Thus the monument is really a conjunction of two concepts: a memorial wall akin to the war memorial walls that have become de rigueur since Maya Lin's Vietnam Veterans Memorial; and an icon of the demolished mill serving as a dreamlike reminder of the old industrial landscape.[38]

This conjunction is representative of the two different constituencies that this project served from the beginning. On the one hand there was the "veterans" organization—the Steelworkers Organization of Active Retirees—whose past lives are explicitly celebrated by the monument. Their input was an integral part of every phase of the monument campaign, including planning, selection, design, and construction.[39] Although the monument campaign appeared to put them in the spotlight, the campaign itself was a symptom of their ever increasing marginalization within the life of

the city. The impulse to commemorate steelworkers—to fix their historical identity forever in a didactic monument—arose from the demise of a
living industrial culture that could nourish such memory from within. This
living culture was decaying even before the industry itself declined, due to
suburbanization and other forces fracturing the steelworkers' communities.
Indeed it is an open question whether such a "living" memory ever existed
in the first place. Robert Bruno has suggested that steelworkers were more
interested in upward mobility for their children—in getting their kids out
of the mills rather than reminiscing about them. Only when the mills shut
down and the steelworkers began to reexamine why their industry had collapsed did they begin to construct a collective memory about their life in
the mills.[40]

The designer, O'Toole, took the labor constituency very seriously. Like
Serra, he wanted to create a design that had the look and feel of factory materials. But unlike Serra, he took the idea of proletarian manufacture a step
further by collaborating with his labor force in an extraordinary way. Re-
jecting the traditional hierarchy of architects and contractors, O'Toole
asked the contractors to teach him how to build the monument; the design
was modified by their input. In this way, he feels, the very fabric of the monument honors the working intelligence of industrial craftsmen—something
rapidly being forgotten and devalued in the shift to a high-tech economy.[41]

Yet the monument was designed to appeal not only to ex-steelworkers
but also to an entirely different constituency for "public art." Public art of
course implies a public, but that public is not in any way identifiable with a
fixed population, such as "the citizens" of Pittsburgh. It is rather a diffuse,
shifting, contested entity. In this case, that art public included—at a minimum—the new workers on the site, planning officials within the city administration, and various high-culture interests that care about reshaping
the city's "image." O'Toole's design appealed to this distinct public by
avoiding kitschy imagery and creating an interesting deconstructivist structure.[42] The monument looks up-to-date, like it belongs in the same uni-
verse as the new economy. But by evoking specific elements of the old plant,
the monument anchors the visitor's experience in the historical reality of
the steel mill. Thus O'Toole's design managed to synthesize disparate pro-
grammatic needs.

Instead of actually representing steelworkers, the monument puts the
visitor in the position of a steelworker navigating the ghostly shell of a mill.
Within the ghost mill, the most conspicuous motif is the "ladle," the open
four-sided container from which molten steel was poured. Here it acts essentially as a rain collector, directing rainwater into a small concrete pool
accessible by steps. The pool is connected to a concrete trough that has the

same dimensions—nine inches by ten feet—as the steel bars produced in the mill. Thus the design elements evoke the process of pouring and shaping the molten metal that took place inside the mill. But in the monument, the intense heat and danger of that process are transformed into an inviting, soothing experience. The water from the concrete pool will be recirculated through a pump back up to the ladle in order to create a fountain. As the project description states, "the molten steel that flowed through the mill was a 'thing that the workers could never touch.' Through reference to the pouring out of the ladle, water replaces the molten steel, inviting the visitor to run his/her arm through its flow."[43] This is what rhetoricians would call metonymy, the use of one term to stand for another, flowing water for molten steel, fountain for factory. The most terrifying, death-dealing, inhuman aspects of the industrial process are evoked but transfigured through the natural element of rainwater into a healing, playful, humanly scaled experience. Knowing that he could not and would not want to recreate the actual conditions of the plant—the heat, noise, danger—the designer converted the industrial sublime into a kind of urban pastoral, a setting for rest, reflection, and gentle play.

This brings us back to the idea of the war memorial with which this chapter began. The conversion of factory into fountain recalls the age-old idea of swords into ploughshares, turning weapons of human destruction into instruments of production. With a few exceptions, war memorials embody this idea. They do not tend to depict warfare itself—its violence, hatreds, and calamities. In the process of commemoration, these aspects of war are repressed, usually replaced by imagery of gloriously intact soldiers' bodies. Metaphorically, the battered body and psyche of the nation are healed, made ready for the next war.[44] In O'Toole's dreamlike factory-scape, a similar process of transformation takes place: the fiery energies of the industrial process, which threatened the workers inside and wasted the environment outside, are replaced by the natural flow of life-producing waters.

As objects of commemoration, war and industry present a similar paradox: death and destruction bring life and meaning. Warfare is supposed to kill and maim. Industry, of course, is not, but it does nevertheless—most conspicuously through factory accidents, which took an appalling toll in the early days of the steel industry; and less conspicuously, but more pervasively, through devastating waste products that filled the air, the water, and the soil. Yet while the battlefield and the steel mill both brought fire and smoke and waste, they also produced masculinity and power. War built "men" and nations; steel mills built "men" and the infrastructure of the modern world. The mythic qualities of the men who made steel—toughness, bravery, endurance—are the very qualities that define a warrior. Indeed, when the Steelworkers Monument was dedicated in April 2001, speaker after speaker made the connection between war and the steel industry, one even going so far as to say that "in some ways WWI and WWII were won right here in Pittsburgh because of the hard work" of the steelworkers who helped armor the United States' fighting force. The military-industrial complex was not an abstraction, but part of the living fabric of Pittsburgh.[45]

Like two sides of a coin, the destructive and the constructive aspects of war and industry are almost impossible to see at once, especially in memory. When they are commemorated, the focus is almost always the life-giving meaning rather than the destructive toll on which meaning rests. "It was a hot, dirty, filthy job, and a lot of guys died here," one ex-steelworker said at the dedication of O'Toole's monument, yet the monument does little to remind us of that.[46]

Up until the 1980s, no one would have needed to be reminded. The evidence of industry's "hot, dirty" work was almost everywhere, in the vast tracts of riverfront land occupied by the mills, in the soot-stained buildings throughout the city, in the very air people breathed. Pittsburgh, after all, was "hell with the lid taken off"—an epigraph that actually predates the heyday of the steel industry but defined the city's image for nearly a century anyway. Today, a mere two decades after the major shutdowns, almost none of that evidence remains. Gleaming office buildings and retail complexes have replaced the demolished mills; the air has cleared; even the soot stains have been blasted off most of the older buildings. City boosters actively promote the town as a high-tech center where clean "knowledge work" has replaced the dirty work of steel.[47] Yet there is one place within the city where a remnant of the old industrial "hell" still intrudes: a once lush stream valley now filled with a towering pile of slag, nearly two hundred feet high and miles long. (See figure 13.) The site is akin to a battlefield, the product of a violent collision between nature and industrial might. Unlike a battlefield, though, which grows back into field or forest, the slag pile has remained a desert. Slag is a waste product, the garbage of the steel industry. When steel is refined in a blast furnace, the impurities that are removed form slag. It comes out in molten form but then hardens into a kind of gravel, so alkaline that it kills most plant growth and poisons the water draining through it.

The steel mills in and around Pittsburgh produced millions on millions of tons of slag, and it had to go somewhere. Vast slag dumps were created throughout the region, but the most striking and tragic of these is the Nine Mile Run stream valley. Located just on the outskirts of the city, this trib-

FIGURE 13. Slag pile at Nine Mile Run, seen from adjacent neighborhood near the Monongahela River. Photograph by the author.

utary of the Monangahela River was once a meandering stream cutting through densely wooded slopes. A famous nineteenth-century feminist, Jane Grey Swisshelm, lived and died in a homestead on the banks of this stream during the Gilded Age. In the early twentieth century, the Carnegie Institute's botanists surveyed its rich flora and brought back specimens to the natural history museum. Later Frederick Law Olmstead Jr. recommended preserving the wooded slopes and turning the site into a major urban park. But beginning in 1922, the Duquesne Slag Company began to buy up the valley slopes for the sole purpose of dumping molten slag into the streambed; the slag came from the very mill on whose site the Steelworkers Monument now stands. Through various legal and extralegal means, the company extended its reach and ended up transforming the valley into a vast expanse of slag stretching for miles on both sides of the stream. Amazingly, the stream still flows and a remnant of the original riparian ecology has survived, a reminder of the power of nature in the midst of industrial devastation.[48]

In a sense, this pile of slag is the perfect postindustrial monument. It is literally postindustrial: long after the steel was produced, after the mills closed down and their physical traces disappeared, the slag is what remains. Its indestructibility, its vast scale, the clean geometry of its inorganic slopes all give it the aura of a monument. And there is indeed a certain beauty here, in the strange collision of industrial form and ancient ecosystem, of sublime and pastoral aesthetics. Stubbornly, the slag pile at Nine Mile Run resists the sweep of deindustrialization. It stays ever visible in all its shame and glory, an ironic counterpoint to the official landscapes of urban rejuvenation.

Here is the third and final project I will discuss: integrating this visible monument of the steel industry into the fabric of the deindustrialized city. Two competing visions have been offered, each driven by a different constituency and agenda. The first, officially sponsored by the city administration, offered a plan in line with the administration's larger strategy of sweeping the city clean of industry's material reminders. After acquiring the Nine Mile Run site for redevelopment in 1995, the city soon unveiled an ambitious plan to build a new residential neighborhood on top of the slag. To implement this vision, part of the stream was to be hidden in an underground culvert; the slag was to be regraded, piled on top of the culvert, and then covered by topsoil so that no one would even know it was there. In all, the plan required moving some fifty million cubic feet of slag, about 20 percent of the physical mass of the site. A "neotraditional" neighborhood of expensive houses, alleys, and yards would obliterate the "ugly" industrial dump and the old riparian ecosystem that had managed to survive in its midst. Partnering with private developers, the city explicitly aimed to attract affluent homebuyers away from the suburbs. This vision can easily be seen as part of the city's ongoing effort to create a cityscape attractive to the "knowledge workers" of the new economy.[49]

A second vision, offered in response to the city's plan, came from a group of eco-artists working in collaboration with various academic and community groups. This group, based at Carnegie Mellon University (CMU), approached Nine Mile Run with the simple assumption that it was not a worthless "dump" to be eradicated, but a place with historical and ecological value in its own right. Allied with a local foundation and some interested citizens groups, they conducted a series of public discussions and highly technical studies of water quality and biodiversity that culminated after two years in a far-reaching plan for restoring the stream and the valley.[50]

Why did eco-artists initiate and organize this process? The core group from CMU—Tim Collins, Reiko Goto, and Bob Bingham—belong to a larger movement in public art away from conventional notions of artistic "making." In the case of Nine Mile Run, they were interested in forging a new kind of public conceptual art aimed at radically changing the understanding and the discussion of the "postindustrial" landscape. Their work does have artistic antecedents, of course, for example in Joseph Beuys's idea of "social sculpture," which he carried out in political action with the Green Party in Germany (such as his famous *7000 Oaks* project in 1982). More recently, Helen and Newton Harrison have been envisioning new kinds of cultural landscapes centered around the ecological principles of diversity and interconnectedness (such as their *Future Garden* on the roof of the Kunst-und Austellungshalle in Bonn, a patchwork quilt of various ancient meadow habitats from around Europe).[51] But unlike Beuys or the Harrisons, the team of Collins, Goto, and Bingham were working not as landscape designers but as facilitators in a complex public process. Indeed much of the thrust of their work was to empower a counterpublic to take control of the site away from the forces of privatized development. They found important pockets of support in various areas: among local elites (notably the Heinz Endowments, which had been focusing on ecological initiatives); among eco-aware constituencies such as birdwatchers and hikers; and among the small municipalities and citizens groups located on the edge of the site, which were interested in improving water quality and expanding urban parkland. Ultimately the artists found support within the city planning bureaucracy as well.[52]

The plan that emerged from this process had a strong ecological focus. Its goals were to protect the stream and its riparian habitat from culverting and further damage, to improve its water quality, and to expand the habitat area through a series of ecological restoration measures. Where the Steelworkers Monument created metaphors of healing, this restoration project sought to go beyond metaphor and heal the site in an ecological sense. Much thought and discussion were devoted to the issue of how to revegetate the slag slopes. At the same time, however, the plan argued that the industrial character of the site deserved protection as well. The eco-artists' final report recommended that some of the most barren slag slopes *not* be vegetated, that instead they be left alone to expose the industrial legacy of the site. The stated goal: "Don't eradicate [that legacy] or cloak it in nostalgia."[53] In contrast to the city's earlier plan to obliterate the valley's historical character, the new plan embraced the site as a kind of living palimpsest, in which various historical strata—ancient ecosystem, industrial waste, contemporary ecological intervention—would all remain visible and evolve together.

It would be easy enough to dismiss this plan as simply a more sophisticated initiative to make the city attractive to a high-tech workforce. Routinely, local initiatives to improve city parks and riverfronts are justified on the grounds that these are the kinds of amenities "knowledge workers" crave.[54] The institutional support given to the Nine Mile Run project by the Heinz Endowments and CMU could be cited as further confirmation.

(CMU receives heavy criticism, for example, in Dale Hathaway's study of deindustrialization in Pittsburgh—for its corporate connections in general and more specifically its support of robotics research, which aims to replace human workers with computerized drones.)[55] But while there are certainly overlapping interests between eco-artists and "knowledge workers," this kind of argument is reductive. For the restoration plan did not intend to create a recreational paradise for the workforce of the new economy, as the city had originally hoped to do by hiding the slag. Rather, the plan aimed to bring an important industrial site into the public eye and raise questions about its meaning and value in the present era of deindustrialization. The Nine Mile Run restoration plan deliberately avoided the strategies of closure and erasure common to most other commemorative initiatives.

In the end the notion of artistic making here is totally unlike the heroic ideal of proletarian manufacture that underlies both Serra's and O'Toole's monuments. For what the Nine Mile Run restoration plan offered was not another human construction or "erection," as we often refer to monuments, but a set of possibilities, a set of alternative futures for a real place. These futures can only be realized by ongoing public intervention—a combination of political and ecological action. The restoration envisaged the slag pile as a kind of living memorial, with overlapping stories and no clear ending. There is the story of industry's war on nature; of nature's unpredictable adaptations; of twenty-first-century humanity's drive to heal its devastation of the life around it. Nine Mile Run reminds us that the questions posed by deindustrialization are not merely questions of labor and capital, of social and economic policy. They are questions about the ethical stance of human beings in the larger nonhuman world on which our survival ultimately depends.

In retrospect, it is easy to see why the military model of commemoration is so well suited to the steel industry. War and industry present many of the same dangers, and invoke many of the same values. The military model offers a conventionalized vocabulary for honoring *men*—whether they be veterans of the mills or the battlefields—who worked hard, made sacrifices, and helped build the modern world.

Certainly these *are* men worth remembering, and indeed, honoring. The problem with the military model is not so much what it remembers but what it forgets. Both war and industry work on the principle of domination, whether domination of human beings or domination of nature. Yet as they become objects of public memory, the violence of this act of domination becomes obscured, if not totally forgotten, replaced by visions of regeneration and progress. Wars happen only because less brutal means of domination haven't worked; yet war memorials are never about brutality or domination. Military memorials almost always seek to transcend the core facts of warfare, and by doing so they do not ask us to think about war and its costs in any serious way.

In a similar way, the Carnegie Institute, Serra's *Carnegie*, and O'Toole's Steelworkers Monument all offer their own fantasies of transcendence. The Carnegie Institute offered an outright escape into an ethereal realm of beauty and knowledge far removed from the factory that made it possible. Serra's piece seems to be precisely opposite, frankly evoking the products of the steel mill. But those industrial references are subsumed within an abstract form that demands a specific kind of art-critical attention that lies beyond the ordinary experience of the industrial laborer—and more relevant to the world of the corporate elites who sponsored the piece. Of the three, the Steelworkers Monument is the most directly representative of the steel mill, and the most explicitly pitched to a steelworker audience. Yet even here the obvious references to the mill have been transformed into life-giving metaphors through the healing tonic of memory. The contradictions within the steelworker's world—the pride in the work and the paycheck mixed with recognition of its toll on the workers and their environment—fade from view.

These acts of commemorative escapism are completely understandable. It is not easy to face the violence behind the things we hold most dear—ideals of service, nationhood, industrial might. Traditionally, it is the very purpose of commemoration to overlook this violence in order to assert a more stable and peaceful future. Commemoration, typically, dreams of transcendence: we can escape the sins of the past in order to occupy a renovated future. Unfortunately, we can't. We must face the fact that industry and its evils still live in the so-called deindustrialized world. Factories have closed, jobs have disappeared, but the consequences of industry's war on nature remain with us—in two crucial ways. First, even where industry has died, it has permanently reshaped the urban landscape, its infrastructure, and its ecology. Second, as industry withers in places like Pittsburgh, it blooms elsewhere, with global ecological impacts that continue to intensify. As I look over Pittsburgh's skyline on a hot summer day, I can't escape industry; the smoke from local factories has long disappeared, but it has been replaced by a thick layer of smog blown in from the coal-burning power plants up the Ohio River; the air conditioners humming around me make us all complicit.

This is why we need a fundamentally new kind of commemorative landscape, like the one at Nine Mile Run. Here is a landscape that cannot hide its own contradictions: it demands an ecologically minded, ethically informed encounter with the continuing legacy of industrialism. The restoration plan offered by the eco-artists and community activists articulates a new "postindustrial" ideal—radically different from the antimodern fantasies of harmony between labor and nature entertained by William Morris's followers early in the twentieth century. Rather than recreating a nostalgic landscape of "pristine" nature isolated from humanity's industry and technology, this new postindustrial ideal assumes that human intervention in nature will and must continue but that its ethics and its consequences can be changed.

It remains to be seen how the slag pile will finally be treated at Nine Mile Run. The city has embraced the idea of restoring the stream valley, and the residential development has been confined to the slag plateaus high above.[56] How much of the slag slopes will be revegetated—and whether such efforts will even work—has yet to be determined. Whatever the final outcome, it is hard to imagine that the slag will ever entirely lose its unique monumentality and its perverse poetry. If we manage to survive this era of deindustrialization, it will be not by transcending industry, as Carnegie once imagined, nor by transforming the industrial past into artistic metaphors, as more recent designers are doing, but by heeding the laments and the lessons of the slag piles.

Part V

MEMORY

CHAPTER 12

Making Sense of Restructuring

Narratives of Accommodation
among Downsized Workers

STEVE MAY AND LAURA MORRISON

It was their life, their home, their second home, their *first* home.
A DOWNSIZED KEMET WORKER

Although many scholars have sought to explore deindustrialization's general effect, our purpose is to better understand its specific impact on the "lived experiences," the day-to-day lives, of Americans seeking to make an honest wage, support their families, and sustain their communities. In this chapter, we suggest that the experience of deindustralization is firmly rooted in the personal identities of manufacturing workers, the companies for whom they work(ed), and the communities in which they live(d). We argue that, to best understand the effects of deindustrialization, in particular, we should turn to the narrative descriptions of the workers who have lost their jobs. Analysis of broader trends and statistics has provided us with a more thorough understanding of deindustrialization and its scope. It is also appropriate to listen to the narrative voices of workers who have faced the challenges of deindustrialization most directly. As a result, we used multiple methods—including interviews, ethnographic observation, and textual analysis—over several months in order to understand and, ultimately, represent the complex and often contradictory experiences of workers who were downsized at the KEMET manufacturing plant in Shelby, North Carolina, in 1998.

Deindustrialization in the United States—and the downsizing that often comes with it—is not necessarily a new phenomenon, nor is it a simple one. It is a broad, yet deeply entrenched, social, political, economic, and technological process, with unique inflections during different historical periods. Deindustralization is also a regional and a local transformation of work with profound implications for both global and local conditions. Its legacy in the United States and around the world has been wide-ranging, but, in the end, its historical significance will be framed not by broad academic arguments, but by the lingering and firmly rooted memories of workers who have lost their jobs. The varied and conflicting stories that downsized workers tell about deindustrialization provide the collective memory that will enable or constrain them as they attempt to re-create their lives, their conceptions of work, and their perceptions of community.

We argue that one of the personal challenges for downsized workers during deindustrialization has been to rethink and restructure their identifications. While workers heard public discussions about a vital, prosperous economy in the 1990s, many remained perplexed about what, in reality, appeared to be a "jobless recovery."[1] As Barry Bluestone and Bennett Harrison explain in *The Deindustrialization of America*, we have all seen "a widespread systematic disinvestment in the nation's basic productive capacity."[2] At the time, they argued, significant shifts in the global economy produced a growing contradiction between capital and community. Left behind, in the ruins of the tension between capital and community, were closed factories, displaced workers, and a growing number of industrial ghost towns.

From our research, it is clear that this trend continues, in many respects. Downsized workers, for example, view deindustrialization—at least at the local level—as a breach of the social contract between employer and employee. They believe corporate leaders overemphasize the rationales of "global competition," "customer service," and "the market" in their decision making; in turn, they underemphasize the human capital of workers and the social relations of community.[3] Downsized workers, in particular, lament that "big business" has lost its moral compass in ways that affect not only individual employees, but also families and entire communities. They explain that corporate attention to the bottom line, at the expense of human capital, violates both the economic and the psychological contract between employer and employee, corporation and community. Although they often feel helpless to directly resist this moral breach of the social contract, downsized workers also seek to retain a sense of pride in the face of the difficult realities that downsizing creates. The new social contract—based on limited commitments and short-term responsibilities—is the result of multiple cultural forces, including global competition, domestic deregulation, and technological change.[4] Yet many of these forces are accepted, without question, as justifying decisions that negatively affect large numbers of workers and, in turn, their families and their communities.

Regardless of the complex and multifaceted reasons for this new social contract, its human costs have been significant. Aside from the obvious economic effects, observers have begun to note the relationship between deindustrialization and workplace (and domestic) violence, workplace litigation, and workplace stress and injury—with the related health care costs that follow.[5] At the very least then, deindustrialization has caused us, as a culture, to consider how we should redefine (e.g., in our educational institutions, through our media, and in our public policies) the opportunities and responsibilities to millions of workers who have lost their jobs.

At its most basic level, deindustrialization has left workers (and, most certainly, their children) with lingering questions: What do I believe? Whom do I trust? To what and whom am I committed? Where should I invest my energies? How can we create organizations that are simultaneously productive and humane?

In our interviews with downsized workers from a high-tech manufacturing plant in rural North Carolina, we found them to be hurt, angry, and resentful, yet incredibly resilient in their ability to respond to, and subtly resist, their downsizing. Most importantly, their stories reaffirm their commitment to their own value of work, to their coworkers, and to their community.[6] Through their stories, for example, downsized workers begin to restructure a future away from their employer. The narratives also clarify important distinctions between the workers' identification with their company and its executives. The workers tell about the anger, frustration, and loss they experienced during and after the downsizing. They describe—in personal, familial terms—their sense of belonging with their coworkers. Finally, they remember and reimagine a more idyllic community that reaffirms their values of hard work and strong kinship ties.

Restructuring Organizations

Since the publication of *The Deindustrialization of America*, work—and the conditions surrounding it—have been given wider, noneconomic significance. In the last twenty years, work has increasingly been construed as "an essential element in individual psychological health, family stability, and social tranquility."[7] Work is now viewed by many as a personal imperative as much as an economic imperative. No longer do we necessarily work as a means to an economic end. Work is not an obligation to be met, but rather an opportunity to be pursued. Work, in this respect, has become a means to self-fulfillment; corporate profits have emerged as a path to self-actualization. It is the way we come to know the world and the world to know us. Work becomes the marker of our identity, our personalized signature to those around us. As Al Gini notes very succinctly, "To work is *to be* and not to work is *not to be*."[8] In this chapter, we contend that the work/identity relationship has strengthened not only among white-collar workers, but also among blue-collar, manufacturing workers. We have found that this is particularly true in small, rural communities in which a large, primary employer has been a focal point for employment and community networking.

In this particular historical era of restructuring and downsizing organizations, then, it should not necessarily surprise us that job loss has a profound effect on worker identity. However, while the relationship between work and identity seems stronger than ever, workers must confront faster-paced, fluid, adaptable organizations seeking to adjust to market trends "just in time" in the midst of turbulent organizational change.[9] For many organizational leaders, the method of choice for responding to these quick (and often chaotic) changes has been restructuring through downsizing.

"Downsizing," as some authors note, is a term that has evolved out of popular use rather than systematic theoretical development.[10] As a result, a variety of related terms have been used somewhat interchangeably with "downsizing," causing confusion regarding the downsizing process itself. In the past, workers who lost their jobs were "fired," "sacked," or "laid off." However, in today's popular management jargon, workers are faced with "business process reengineering," "force management programs," "slimming," "rightsizing," "rationalizing," "focused reductions," "reinventing," "reductions in force," "outsourcing," "release of resources," "redundancies," and even "career change opportunities."[11]

As organizational experts have argued that innovation and flexibility are prerequisites for success, "lean and mean" business practices have become an accepted part of organizational life.[12] For example, an American Management Association survey showed that, on average, 49 percent of all major U.S. companies eliminated 9 percent of their workforce in the last decade.[13] When the most profitable companies are examined, the percentage is even larger. More than 85 percent of the Fortune 1,000 companies reduced their workforces in just five years, affecting more than five million workers.[14] Even the U.S. labor secretary proclaimed, "The job security many workers experienced in the three decades after World War II is probably gone forever. The unstated agreement was that as long as a company was profitable, workers wouldn't be fired, but that agreement no longer holds."[15]

As a result, downsizing has exacerbated worker anxiety, particularly since only 35 percent of laid-off, full-time workers in the 1990s found equal- or better-paying jobs, which is in contrast to previous decades.[16] Many of these workers have entered the growing ranks of a less secure contract or contingent workforce, marketing their skills like vendors, with varied levels of success. Although media attention to downsizing has waned, the practice has continued at a consistent rate in the last few years. Organizations continue to rationalize the practice of downsizing as they did in the 1980s, as a response to: 1) deregulation that has blurred geographic and market boundaries; 2) new technologies that have introduced lucrative niche markets accessible to smaller, more flexible organizations; 3) globalization, which has created new competitors on an international scale; and 4) pressure for short-term gains, especially from investors. While downsizing continues, however, mounting evidence suggests that downsized organizations fail to achieve desired outcomes (e.g., higher share prices, profitability, quality, innovation) in the long term.

Regardless of whether decisions to downsize meet the intended economic ends, we must consider whether they also meet our culture's social ends. In response to the troubling trend of downsizing, this chapter focuses on the themes, or dominant patterns of sense-making and meaning, in the stories that downsized workers tell about their company, themselves, and their community. More specifically, this chapter explores workers' struggles to accommodate, through their narratives, a downsizing by KEMET Electronics Corporation in Shelby, North Carolina, in 1998, which affected 80 percent of the plant's workforce.

KEMET History, Vision, and Values

According to company documents, KEMET Electronics Corporation is the largest manufacturer of solid tantalum capacitors in the world and the second largest manufacturer of ceramic capacitors in the United States. The company, headquartered in Greenville, South Carolina, manufactures and sells solid tantalum and multilayer ceramic capacitors, and employs more than seventy-one hundred people worldwide. KEMET has multiple manufacturing sites in Mexico and the United States, with distribution centers in the United States, Europe, Brazil, Hong Kong, and Singapore. A blend of the words "chemical" and "metallurgy," KEMET was officially formed on April 1, 1987, but it began to evolve in 1919 as a Union Carbide division developing a high-temperature alloy. KEMET's first product used this high-temperature alloy for grid wires in vacuum tubes. By the late 1960s, KEMET had established itself as a major U.S. capacitor producer, with the leading market share in solid tantalum capacitors. In order to expand its product scope and to continue its growth, KEMET entered the multilayer ceramic capacitor business in 1969. As more production facilities were needed, new plants were constructed in Matamoros, Mexico, in 1969; Columbus, Georgia, in 1976 (since closed); Greenville, South Carolina, in 1979; Shelby, North Carolina, in 1981; Fountain Inn, South Carolina, in 1986; and Monterrey, Mexico, in 1991. A second manufacturing facility in Monterrey, Mexico, began production on July 1, 1996—approximately two years prior to the restructuring and subsequent downsizing at the Shelby plant.

In 1986, Union Carbide announced its decision to divest itself of businesses that no longer fit its strategic business plans, including KEMET. On April 1, 1987, the existing management group bought the company from Union Carbide Corporation and renamed it KEMET Electronics Corporation. While Union Carbide still retained 50 percent of KEMET's stock, KEMET was now legally a separate company, with David E. Maguire as its CEO. On December 21, 1990, a group of investors, including KEMET senior management and Citicorp, purchased the balance of KEMET stock; the sale severed all ties with Union Carbide Corporation. Within two years of severing its ties to Union Carbide, KEMET went public. The company's product line now includes tantalum and ceramic-leaded and surface-mount capacitors, all manufactured and distributed under the KEMET brand name. According to the company, its "capacitors are fundamental elements used in every type of electronic equipment, including computers, telecommunication devices, automotive electronics, military electronics, medical electronics, and consumer electronics." They have been used in military/aerospace projects such as Telstar, Viking, Apollo, the Patriot missile, and the International Space Station.[17]

Currently, the company's vision is to "establish a distinctive competence that differentiates KEMET as the unquestioned Best-In-Class supplier." In addition to this more general vision, KEMET identifies several core values, including: 1) best-trained and motivated people; 2) company-wide quality concept; 3) easy to buy from; 4) lowest-cost producer; and 5) leading edge of technology. Although each of these core values is undoubtedly important to KEMET, the company's focus on employees is highlighted in many of its documents. For example, according to its company website, KEMET is "committed to creating a culture that fosters growth, satisfaction, and empowerment for all employees. This includes employee involvement, teamwork, quality education and training, employee recognition, and employee well-being and morale. KEMET provides opportunities for personal and professional growth, thus enabling us as a company to advance toward our business and quality goals." Simultaneously, however, the company identifies low-cost production as a related, if not necessarily consistent, value: "In order to maintain our position as an overall low-cost producer of capacitors, KEMET is constantly seeking to reduce material and labor costs, develop cost-efficient manufacturing equipment and processes, and design manufacturing plants for most efficient production."[18] This distinction between economic capital (with its attention to efficiency) and human capital (with its attention to personal and professional growth) at KEMET vividly represents the ongoing dialectical tension of challenges and opportunities for companies and their employees.

Restructuring and Downsizing at KEMET

At KEMET, the tension between economic development and employee development is perhaps nowhere more pronounced than in the decision to restructure and, subsequently, downsize. In the spring of 1998, KEMET decided to restructure its operations, creating a "reduction in force" at its manufacturing plant in a small, rural community in the western foothills of North Carolina in order to reduce production costs. KEMET's decision to restructure its Shelby, North Carolina, plant occurred shortly after it had established a new facility in Monterrey, Mexico. According to a company press release at the time, the restructuring directly resulted from the company's efforts to "focus on production capability, accelerate cost reductions, and provide additional floor space for future expansion."[19] It specifically stated that the "lower cost Monterrey facilities" were the primary factor in the company's decision. The press release noted that, in contrast to other corporate restructuring occurring in the industry at the time, the KEMET decision was not based on financial difficulties. Rather, according to CEO David Maguire, "bookings and shipments for the fiscal third quarter [for 1997] continue to be strong and are on target" and will have "a positive effect on margin performance in the future."[20]

As a result of the restructuring, 750 of the plant's 950 workers were downsized over a six-month period.[21] Although the restructuring at KEMET may be considered small in comparison to larger downsizing efforts nationwide, it nevertheless affected a significant portion of the plant's employees; approximately 80 percent of them lost their jobs. KEMET represents the more familiar face of downsizing that affects thousands of workers via smaller, yet significant, cuts in employment. As in similar downsizings in small communities across the United States, few, if any, of the downsized workers from Shelby had comparable employment opportunities in their community, and the two hundred or so who remained at KEMET retained very little job security.

Employees and members of the community had long believed that the plant's operations were to be transferred to Mexico. This expectation first took hold because many KEMET employees from Shelby were required to train the new workers, flying to Mexico as the Monterrey facilities opened. The anticipation of downsizing, then, was based on the insider knowledge of workers who had traveled to the Mexican plant. Many of these employees understood that, in effect, they were training their replacements. However, regardless of the years of rumors that circulated within the plant and the surrounding community, most employees were somewhat shocked when the downsizing was announced.

Not surprisingly, KEMET executives explained that the restructuring was imperative in order to remain competitive. In the March 1998 issue of the company's newsletter, *Inside KEMET,* CEO David Maguire described the decision in the following manner: "This was a difficult decision. After careful consideration and weighing of all alternatives, however, this was the best course of action for the long-term health of the entire KEMET enterprise."[22] Formal explanations for the decision from company executives were limited, if not ambiguous. Discussion of the effect on the plant's employees was also limited. In a relatively terse expression of concern for the Shelby employees, Maguire noted that KEMET "regrets the hardship and inconvenience this decision will have on our affected employees in Shelby."[23] In a related downsizing of nearly two thousand employees at U.S. and Mexican plants in 2001, Maguire's comment was similarly brief: "On top of all our voluntary efforts to reduce costs, this action will also allow KEMET to bring employment levels more in line with current and projected business levels."[24]

Given the labor history in North Carolina, the stated rationale for the restructuring and, later, the downsizing, did not necessarily soften the impact of KEMET's decision—either for the employees or for the other members of the community. Nor did the short, businesslike expressions of concern for employees temper their frustration with KEMET executives. Yet, on the one hand, downsized workers seemed to understand the regular refrain of "the globalization imperative" that was all too familiar to them from both company newsletters and national news reports. On the other hand, many employees believed that the community's future rested on the success of high-tech manufacturers that offered better pay and less-arduous labor than the textile plants that had once dominated the area. As a result, KEMET's decision was both accepted—and subtly resisted—by those most familiar with its operations. While workers sought to accommodate the downsizing by making it congruous with their own values of hard work, responsibility, and community; they also juxtaposed their own values against those espoused by the company, such as profit, short-term commitment, and self-interest.

To better understand their accommodation of the downsizing requires a more thorough understanding of the community of Shelby and its people. Shelby is located in Cleveland County, North Carolina, approximately fifty miles from Charlotte, North Carolina, and seventy miles from Asheville, North Carolina, in an area referred to as the "foothills" of North Carolina by local residents. Prior to its restructuring plan, KEMET was considered, by most members of the community, to be not only one of the largest employers in the area but also one of the best. KEMET had been a source of pride and hope for citizens of Cleveland County, since it offered a high-tech manufacturing alternative to the low-tech textile manufacturing that had begun to rapidly leave the area in the 1990s.[25]

Shelby, North Carolina, and Cleveland County have a long history in agriculture and manufacturing, as "many county residents received income from farming and manufacturing, primarily textiles."[26] The county, still largely rural, was sustained by cotton until the 1950s. As one local resident explained, "Time was when everybody had a cotton patch." Cleveland County prospered, compared to many neighboring counties, because of its ability to grow an abundance of cotton and manufacture textiles from it.

However, by the 1950s, cotton no longer reigned. Insects, poor weather, "cotton controls," and federal programs for farms all converged to create a decline in the land used to produce cotton in Cleveland County. According to the county's historical documents, "The dethroning of cotton was one major change; the other was the industrial revolution that began in 1955 as a reaction to this change."[27] This belated "industrial revolution"—largely based on cheap, nonunion labor in the South—produced a significant influx of manufacturing in the area from the mid-1950s to the mid-1970s. In 1976, there were approximately one hundred manufacturing firms in Cleveland County, including film, steel, cardboard, and textiles firms. By the end of 1996, there were 154 manufacturing businesses in Cleveland County according to the Cleveland County Chamber of Commerce. These companies manufactured products from truck cabs to compact discs to aircraft parts and transmissions.

In contrast to other manufacturing plants in the area, KEMET offered good pay with little strenuous work. The work required extensive operational and mechanistic knowledge, but most positions required only a high school diploma or its equivalent. Permanent employees at the lowest level, called capmakers, made approximately ten dollars per hour. KEMET was lauded not only for its wages, which were approximately 20 to 40 percent above the average for manufacturing in the county, but for its willingness to hire permanent employees. The few companies in the area that were larger than KEMET, such as PPG Industries, Doran Textiles, and Hoechst Celanese, were more prone to hire temporary employees through agencies such as Manpower and Personnel Services Unlimited. As a result, KEMET not only offered reasonable pay for less physical labor but also provided more stable employment, with benefits such as health insurance.

The announcement that KEMET was downsizing in 1998 frustrated not only the workers but also the community. The best jobs in the area were lost. In addition, opportunities for future generations of residents who aspired to follow their parents to KEMET were lost. The industrial revolution that lasted nearly one hundred years in many other manufacturing areas of the Midwest and North had come and gone in less than half that time in the rural communities of the South, such as Shelby. As one might expect, then, the narrative responses to the fading economic opportunities offered by employers such as KEMET also took on a decidedly regional, southern inflection.

Structuring Narratives

At the most basic level, humans are storytelling beings, or *Homos narrans*. We construct stories to reflect on the past, to comprehend the present, and to anticipate the future. Stories weave the intricate and sometimes contradictory experiences of our lives into seemingly coherent accounts that often define us, simultaneously enabling and constraining our personal and collective memory. Not surprisingly, then, the stories we create for ourselves, as well as those that are bestowed on us, powerfully shape our identities and our relationships.[28] As a result, personal identity may be constituted in and through stories of self, other, and community that are told and retold, visited and revisited. From birth to death—with many years of work between—we enter into a narrative conversation that has both preceded us and will, later, follow us.

As a central feature of human experience, storytelling is also common in organizations and may have a profound effect on an organization's practices, its politics, and its culture.[29] Sometimes formal and produced at the highest levels, sometimes informal and created at the lowest levels, stories also locate workers in their "place," their location within the organizational hierarchy and authority structure. Organizational narratives, then, may both reflect and refract the situated experiences of workers and are particularly pronounced during organizational change and transition.

As anthropologist Victor Turner explains, stories are a fundamental source of creativity for personal and social transformation. They are particularly important during "lamina" moments, when persons are "betwixt and between" more stable and predictable social structural arrangements.[30] As in the case of workers seeking to understand and explain losing their jobs, narratives are moments of heightened reflexivity, during which the spectrum of social (and business) rules and norms can be reconsidered—and, perhaps, ultimately can be reconfigured.

Both hard working and strongly devoted to their families and community, residents of Shelby are also, like many southerners, avid storytellers. However, storytelling in a community such as Shelby does not necessarily carry the same functional, strategic purpose as in some other regions that have been affected by deindustrialization. Significantly influenced by the Cherokee and Scotch-Irish history of the area, many who live in and around Shelby have a long, established oral tradition. This tradition is evident in the poetic, lyrical, circular, and often indirect manner of storytelling that is common in a community such as Shelby. Storytelling, in this tradition, is less about "getting to the point" than about "connecting with the person." Perhaps more commonly than in other areas facing deindustrialization, sharing stories in small, rural, southern communities such as Shelby binds people together. In such locales, stories are the collective memory that provides the relational sustenance of kinship networks and coworker ties.

In the case of the downsizing at KEMET, the stories are also a means of organized remembering and organized forgetting. That is, downsizing stories—like so many others in the South—are wrought with subtleties and the unspoken. To fully comprehend southern stories, one must pay attention not only to what is said, but also to what is left unsaid. What is purposeful in this narrative tradition, then, often may be the strategic omission.

These omissions, or "hidden transcripts," represent a means by which workers downsized at KEMET were able to come to terms with their altered lives. As James Scott explains, "every subordinate group creates, out of its ordeal, a 'hidden transcript' that represents the critique of power spoken behind the back of the dominant."[31] Such stories are shielded from public view and are more likely to be enacted in a safer, more familial environment. Narratives, then, are a means by which downsized workers can shed light on (and bring to light) their work-related experiences and, thus, articulate their futures. In this regard, the use of narratives, imbued with thick description, in this chapter seeks to provide "detail, context, emotion, webs of affiliation, and micro-power" to our understanding of the lived experiences of downsized workers.[32] That is, by including extensive comments from workers downsized from KEMET, we hope to better understand the ways in which the performance of narratives focuses and clarifies personal, organizational, and community realities for the workers. More specifically, this chapter focuses on the themes, or dominant patterns of sense-making and meaning, in the stories that downsized workers tell about themselves, their company, and their community.[33]

Restructuring Identifications

As a subordinate group with limited access to the political, social, and economic leverage needed to resist the downsizing explicitly, the KEMET workers sought to accommodate the downsizing in more implicit, nuanced ways. One means by which the downsized workers accommodated KEMET's decision was more personal than public: restructuring their identifications. In the weeks following the downsizing, workers who lost their jobs sought to frame their experience within a narrative structure that made sense to them, identifying heroes/heroines, villains, and turning points. It is quite common, for example, for persons experiencing any type of job transition to rethink and reconsider their commitment and loyalty to their work, their company, and their community.

Narrative identification, then, is particularly relevant to downsized workers because it is the medium through which the relationships among the individual, organization, and community are negotiated. Workers can talk through their feelings of unification with, and/or separation from, KEMET, in particular. Such a major life change, though, will also cause many to reconsider and restructure their relationships to their coworkers and their community. At the most fundamental level, they will often ask themselves, "Is this what I want to do for a living? Is this the right type of work for me?"

As cultural critic and rhetorical scholar Kenneth Burke explains, "identification is compensatory to division."[34] Yet, there is always a "wavering line" between identification and division, just as there is often a tenuous link between "standing with" and "standing against" an employer that has downsized workers. The nature of downsized workers' identification with

KEMET, for example, varied over time and cannot be understood simply as being for or against the company. Rather, the sense of unification with, or separation from, KEMET must be understood against every workers' multiple and complex identifications—with self, with employer, with co-workers, and with community. To fully understand the effects of deindustrialization in general, and downsizing specifically, we must explore the conflict and contradiction inherent in these identifications.

Work and Identity

For many of the downsized workers at KEMET, the experience of job loss was characterized as a time to reflect on the relationship between work and identity. KEMET was considered to be an employer that offered good pay and working conditions. In the words of several of the downsized workers, "it was the best place I had ever worked" and "is likely to be the best place I will ever work in the future" because "it was easier work." Clara, who had worked for KEMET for eight years, readily admitted, "I feel that KEMET spoiled us." Similarly, Doris, who had also worked in a sewing plant with "pay on production," explained that not only was the KEMET work less physically demanding than other jobs in the area, but that managerial supervision was limited: "Well, it wasn't hard, wasn't hard work. . . . Easy, actually, unreal, I mean you know. When I first went to work, I was in cap—, I tested capacitors. . . . And, I mean, no set amount you had to do, no, nobody pushed you, nobody ever. . . . It was a dream job."

For most of the downsized workers at KEMET, though, the work was important not just because it was less demanding physically. Within the context of the community, it was important because a job at KEMET was a source of pride, as well. Emma, who had worked for KEMET for five years, explained that "working at KEMET in Cleveland County was a prestigious thing to say when somebody said, 'Where do you work?' When you said 'KEMET,' they knew automatically that you had a good job."

This personal pride and community prestige was based, in part, on the working conditions at the plant, which were considered to be cleaner and safer than at other plants in the area. According to downsized workers, managers were known to "put people's safety above everything else." In addition, Sue explained, "it was a clean job. It wasn't like the textile mills. . . . You didn't come home with cotton all over or it wasn't like PPG, [where] you come home with fiberglass all in your fingers." Finally, the constancy of regular shifts meant that many employees could lead more predictable, patterned lives with their families. They were not asked to "change shifts at a moment's notice, without any advance warning," as in other plants. Because workers were not required to rotate shifts, KEMET offered particularly important opportunities for working mothers that had not been available previously.

It is somewhat to be expected, then, that—even though the downsizing had been rumored for years—workers who lost their jobs experienced dramatic life changes that affected their sense of self. Nearly every worker described, in one form or another, the various challenges that ensued and their struggle to meet them with a semblance of dignity. It was, as Julie explained, "like you have just had the rug pulled out from under you." On an economic level, the workers sought to adjust to starting over after becoming "comfortable with the income" provided by a job at KEMET. Claire's comment typified many from the downsized workers: "You know, I'm not saying that money is everything, but when you get used to making a certain amount of money. . . . I mean, you know, you do your life around it, you be wanting that money. . . . I have to adjust to what I'm bringing home now." In some cases, though, the loss of benefits was even more troubling than the loss of income. As Emma, who has two children, explained, " . . . it was a major thing just realizing we were going to lose all our *benefits*. You know, so that was a major deal. I told somebody last week, I said, 'I don't want the job back, but I would sure like to have my benefits [back].'" One of her coworkers similarly noted that "we're up a creek" if "anybody gets sick or dies. There's just that little feeling in the pit of your stomach like please don't let disaster come." In short, as Helen emphasized, "Well, it's [the downsizing has] *just messed* everything *up.*"

Certainly, the financial and health-related risks that follow a downsizing cannot be underestimated. However, in the case of KEMET's downsized workers, many of the narratives revolved around the emotional and relational consequences of losing one's job.

Perhaps the most dramatic shift in identity for many of KEMET's workers was the perceived "loss of family"—both literally and figuratively—that resulted from the downsizing. Although it is predictable that memory of a job loss will be tempered by somewhat idealistic recollections of one's previous coworkers, the stories told by KEMET workers are strikingly consistent and poignant in their emphasis on family.

For example, Tonya, employed for over eleven years at KEMET, explained—in a manner typical of other workers—how important her coworkers were to her: "We, to me, we became a family. We wasn't just operators. We were a family there, 'cause most of us spent more time at work with people you worked with than you did at home with your children." Lucy, in her early sixties, described how it felt to leave the plant on the last day of work: "It was like losing my children, my friends, an' it was just about as bad, not as bad as ever, but it was bad losing the people I loved. Yeah."

Jane, who was on the verge of early retirement when the downsizing was announced, clarified the relational aspect of work when she said, "I really miss all the friends I had made. I don't miss the place, but all the friends, the talking, and the gathering, and the friendship." As Emma explained, "there were people at work who knew more about what I felt about things and what was going on [in my life] than my husband or my Momma or anybody. You know, anybody." Later in her own story, she recounted that the social life of the plant was the tie that bound people together: "So it was really hard getting used to, that had been your social life [voice quivering] for so long. Then all of a sudden, you don't have it anymore. So, I think that was the hardest part. . . . You just don't think about how *much* you socialize, 'cause KEMET was a very social place." Even Becky, who had been relatively new to KEMET when the downsizing occurred, described that for most workers, "it was their life, their home, their second home, their *first* home." Leaving that secure, stable environment was, then, for some of the downsized workers, like leaving home. For example, as Tonya concluded one portion of her story: "It's kind of like I guess leaving home for the first time; you don't feel like you fit in anywhere else, so. . . . We just, I mean you know, we had this group of people that would sit together [on breaks at lunch]; it didn't matter what race or whatever, you just, you were family."

These comments and many others like them punctuate the narratives of KEMET's downsized workers. On the one hand, they seem to represent a longing—a nostalgia—for a work life now past. In some cases, the stories also suggest a desire to relive, reanimate, or, at the least, reappreciate the type of life that work at KEMET provided. In this way, the company is granted a central role in the workers' identities, even as it is perceived as "abandoning the family." On the other hand, the stories also make public what is often hidden, yet known, by many of the workers: that family and social ties matter, regardless of whether they occur at work or at home. Or, perhaps more accurately, the stories also suggest that for workers in Shelby—as in many other communities—the distinctions between work and family, public and private, labor and leisure are blurred by social, affiliative networks that transcend these dichotomies.

KEMET and "Business as Usual"

Although the place of family is prominent in the narratives of the downsized workers, this does not suggest that their perceptions of KEMET are entirely positive. Their commitment to and identification with KEMET and its workers were strong, but their allegiance to the company's management was not. That is, downsized workers appeared to make clear distinctions between their coworkers and immediate supervisors—as accepted members of their community (and family)—and KEMET's managers and executives. The latter, according to downsized workers, were conducting "business as usual" with a "focus on greed," regardless of whom it might harm.

As a response to the perceived "bottom line mentality" designed to cut production costs, worker narratives position KEMET decision makers as "thoughtless bureaucrats" who are "out of touch with people's lives and needs." More directly, some workers generalized that all business owners are greedy and only focused on profit. As Sarah lamented: "I wish there was some way you do away with it [downsizing]. . . . If they are doing OK that they, instead of getting rich, they want to get filthy rich. If they could just be content with being rich and let us average people work our jobs out instead of taking them away from us and sending them somewhere else." The downsizing decision made by KEMET's owners was even less palatable because, according to the company itself, the Shelby plant remained profitable. Wanda, a capmaker who had been with KEMET for seventeen years, explained: "I think I was hurt because I felt like we, none of us deserved, you know, what they did, and it was just because of greed that it was takin' place. They just wanted to make money and they could hire people down there in, in Mexico, uh they could work for fifty cents to a dollar, seventy-five cents doing the same job I did." Wanda was certainly not alone in her frustration about cheaper, global labor displacing her job, but others viewed the downsizing decision as merely a means to move hardship and control elsewhere. The company, then, was portrayed not only as a poor community citizen but also as a poor global citizen. For example, feeling "used" by KEMET, in retrospect, Lucy declared her concern for the Mexican workers who "don't need to be used [either]; they're paying them so little amount of money." Still others felt vindicated by the decision because the company had "made a mess out of it" by moving operations to Mexico. They claimed that both quality and quantity of production were lacking at the Monterrey plant. With even greater satisfaction, though, Jen reported the following: "They went to all the expense to bringing a lot of those young Mexican guys over there that was training—you know like the superintendents, plant managers, supervisors. . . . See, the ones that we really trained and that was good at what they were doin', they didn't keep their knowledge and keep it with KEMET. They went to another to better their selves." From this narrative perspective, then, "KEMET lost all the way around, really, 'cause they lost a lot of good people from the Shelby plant and then a lot of guys from Mexico."

Still attempting to come to terms with what many considered a heartless decision, Becky said, "I guess that's the only part that I can't digest, other than that you know because they didn't, they couldn't care less about us." Put most bluntly by Henry, the goal of the executives was "saving money instead of saving lives." He later asked, "Where did our lives take part in you making this decision or did you even think of us at all?" These comments and many others like them suggest that, although downsized workers retained their identification with the company, its goals, and their coworkers, their loyalty to company executives was ambivalent, if not weak. The few workers who retained a sense of loyalty to the company's leaders appeared to reason that the workers' hardship might not be fully understood by management. As Amy, a relatively new employee, claimed, "I don't think that top management knows that we're struggling. . . . They don't know how hard it hit us."

Most, though, came to characterize the decision to downsize as merely economic, devoid of heart and soul—and "guts," as one worker described. Perhaps most troubling to the workers, though, was the company's unwillingness to give them an opportunity to prove their worth. The importance of the relational ties such an opportunity would represent was explained by Martha, who had been with the company for eleven years: "If they had come to KEMET [in Shelby] and gotten to know the people and saw how things run, they would have never moved it." Workers believed that, if they had been given the opportunity to work alongside management to find ways to reduce costs, a more cooperative decision would have benefited employer and employees alike.

Not surprisingly, then, downsized workers were quick to blame KEMET management for making a self-serving, bottom-line decision. In some regards, this served as a protective mechanism whereby responsibility could be clearly laid at the feet of KEMET executives and not the more familiar supervisors and plant manager. Lucy noted, for example, "It is Dave McGuire, the CEO [who downsized the Shelby plant]. . . . And he is the one that'll have to answer to God, not me." The overall sentiment of many workers was stated succinctly by Doris: "It was a *corporate decision.*"

In addition to blaming KEMET executives in their narratives, downsized workers communicated emotions of anger, frustration, and resentment. Emma, for example, expressed her anger about the manner in which the downsizing occurred: "I was just so mad [with emphasis] because they were sooooo insensitive. They announced the layoff and then like the next week they put the earnings up." Such actions by the company, according to several of the workers, confirmed for them that, in fact, the decision to downsize was not necessary. To them, the decision was a reflection not only of management's greed, as noted earlier, but also its arrogance.

Perhaps the greatest frustration for KEMET workers, then, was that they perceived that the downsizing was not necessarily related to job performance. They felt they had done "honest, good work" for the company and, in turn, "deserved a degree of respect." Tonya conveyed how hard she took this realization: "They said we did a good job, that they never com— — for one minute said that we were not doing a good job, that it had nothing to do with our work. . . . So here, you're telling me I worked for twelve years, I've done a good job. There's nothing wrong with what I've done but you don't need me anymore. . . . I worked hard and I took pride in what I did, but that wasn't good enough. They still sent my job to another place." Henry complained that the workers were "let down" by the company; they had "done their part," such as gaining safety and productivity awards for five straight years, yet the company could "take something that we've, you know, we've worked here so long . . . And why?"

Workers' frustration was not limited to the downsizing decision itself but was also associated with the manner in which that decision was communicated. For example, Clara stated, "I mean when you have people working for you, I feel like you have to be up front with 'em." Amy was especially hurt that the downsizing was on the news before she had been told about it by the company. Other workers expressed similar frustrations, noting that they no longer trusted KEMET because of the way the decision had been announced. Wanda's comments are indicative of the feelings of distrust: "As far as KEMET, personally . . . I don't trust 'em. . . . If I went back to work there for whatever reason, I would never trust 'em, because I—I don't feel that they, I don't feel that they earned people's trust. I *don't*. I just don't like the way they did things . . . but that's corporate . . . that's business." She, like many of the other workers, felt a sense of resignation that the decision "was just business," yet they directly rejected that such decisions are "the right way to do business."

Resentment was also another common emotion communicated by workers in their narratives about the downsizing. In particular, downsized workers who were asked to train Mexican replacements at the Monterrey plant felt that they had been "used" and "betrayed by the company." As one worker explained, downsized workers did not necessarily resent the Mexican workers, since they were merely attempting to make a living. However, downsized workers did resent management's blatant "slap in the face." As Sarah said, she was asked to "train somebody else to . . . take my job away from me."

The cumulative effect of the emotions after the downsizing was, for many of the workers, a sense of death—not just the death of a plant, but the death of friendships and relationships, too. In some respects, the language and imagery of death is to be expected after such a life-changing experience. The comparison to death offers a vivid method of coming to terms with the sense of loss that downsized workers experience.

The physical, visceral experience of being downsized—like death—can only be understood if you have been through it yourself, according to Emma. In their narratives, downsized workers described the plant itself as "a morgue," a "morbid place" that felt "like a funeral" was in process. Sarah portrayed the stark emptiness of the experience and the plant itself: "You know the plant used to be full of all these machines and now they just have these big departments that there's nothing there. It's just like a . . . well, what's the word that I want to use. I guess in one respect it's sorta like a death. It is, it's just sorta like a death. It's just something that's gone and it won't never be there again." Cleansed of its interior objects, the plant is described in nearly human terms by the workers, which gives credence to the importance of physical space to manufacturing workers. It is not their office that they associate with, as in white-collar work; it is "the floor" that is meaningful. Their last days were not spent boxing up books and mementos from an office, but rather were spent looking at a nearly empty hull of a plant. In addition to the funeral-like attitude of the employees, then, was the impression of a casketlike workplace created by the plant's interior.

Taking the funeral comparison a bit further, Doris noted that, in contrast to other funerals, this one lasted for six months. After the downsizing was announced, many workers were given several months until their final day on the job. Some workers were thankful for the additional time to prepare for their eventual layoff. Nevertheless, it felt "like somebody's going to die in a certain amount of time." The length of time between the announcement and the last day of work may have actually exacerbated the workers' grief and made the experience surreal for some.

What made the experience vividly real again, though, was the workers' acceptance, in the final days, that many of them would not see their coworkers again—particularly those from surrounding counties. For example, Jane, who was close to early retirement, expressed her sadness at leaving her coworkers, who had been a source of comfort and inspiration during difficult times: "You talked to them every day at work and you took them your trouble and their family was sick and you talked, and now a lot of them I haven't seen." This experience of coworker support was evident in many of the workers' stories, as they attempted to come to terms with a loss of job and a loss of friendship. Martha described it as a "heartbreaking time," and

Sarah seemed to remind herself of the finality of losing coworkers: "It was a sad feeling. . . . A lot of them were closer to you than your own family members. You were leaving some of them people behind . . . and some of them you will never see again."

Limited Opportunities in a "Mayberry" Community

In addition to the ways in which worker narratives frame personal identity and KEMET as an employer, they construct a new, yet recurring, vision of community. For workers downsized at the KEMET plant, community was understood in the broadest sense; they spoke of a failed spirit of patriotism following on the heels of the North American Free Trade Agreement (NAFTA). Downsized workers spoke of "companies shuttin' down and most of 'em sending things to Mexico." Because of NAFTA, "we are going to see so much more downsizing. . . . And, in fact, we have." Sue, a sixty-year-old worker with twelve years at KEMET, characterized the community's future as so many other workers did, as a "leaving": "So much is *leaving*. You have Dora Mill, which is closing down; you have Cone Mill which is moving to Mexico. You have KEMET which is moving. Practically every day you see in the paper another manufacturing company that is *leaving* or cutting down on their help." For a community with strong kinship networks among families that have lived in close proximity for generations, leaving is not taken lightly, nor is it necessarily accomplished easily. A company's decision to leave such a community, then, conveys a dual message: "We neither need your help nor want it." "Help," as used by Sue and many other workers in their stories, may describe, at a literal level, one's employment status. Yet, at a relational level, it may also describe one's spirit of cooperation during hard times. "Help" doesn't leave because life is better or easier elsewhere.

Given the community's view of leaving, then, it is not surprising that several of the workers described the transfer of labor to Mexico not just in community terms but also in more nationalistic terms. Workers explained that KEMET's decision typified how companies are "letting the people of America down" in ways that will "eventually come back to 'em." Jen, an employee at KEMET for seventeen years, concluded, "If they keep this up, the United States is going to be the poor country and Mexico and a lot of other places are gonna be . . . the rich countries." Julie, who worked for KEMET for over ten years, went further and connected job loss to a loss of national pride: "I am not proud of where I live anymore. I can't look at the American flag the same way. . . . If I wrap it all up . . . Before all sports games, they always sing the national anthem. And I go practically every week and I stand there and seven thousand or eight thousand people get up and we look at the flag and they sing. And it used to bring tears to my eyes because I was proud of where I lived. It doesn't *anymore*. It's just not there anymore." Like many southern narratives, Julie's story concludes with a lingering, ambiguous line, leaving us to wonder what has gone: her job, her company, or her pride in the country.

Beyond these more general themes of leaving and loss, the community after the downsizing was defined more specifically as a locale with increasingly limited employment opportunities. Downsized workers talked about "finding new ways of making money" that require "leaving Cleveland County" or "commuting to nearby counties to find work." Lucy, a sixty-year-old widow and grandmother, referred to the textile-driven history of labor in the county when she noted that "manufacturing is about all we got now. Textiles is about gone. And I do not believe that textiles will ever build back up. 'Cause they can make 'em cheaper in Hong Kong, overseas, anywhere and everywhere, so . . ." Mary, a KEMET employee for twenty-five years, explained that manufacturing is vital to the area, repeating, "but we're losing it . . . but we're losing a lot of it, you know."

Others reflected less on the county's past and more on its future, acknowledging, in a resigned manner, "that's the way the economy is going." Greg, who had just begun working for KEMET when he was downsized, explained that, "since I've been in school, you know, they have been teaching us things like, you know, the United States is going to a service economy or service country. And there is a lot of manufacturing around here and, ah, it's something that people are going to have to deal with." As one might expect, though, KEMET workers preferred to "deal with" these economic changes on their own terms, in their own time. Perhaps most troubling to many of the downsized workers was the seeming necessity to travel further and further from Shelby and Cleveland County for work. Tina's story of a discussion between an employee and a manager during a meeting announcing the downsizing is typical: "A woman in the meeting asked, 'Where am I going to work?' Apparently, the man conducting the meeting said something about, 'Well, there's plenty of jobs around in neighboring counties, a couple of counties over and all.' The woman who asked the question responded, 'Well, what do you expect me to do? Just uproot my whole family and move?'"

Unfortunately, this is, in fact, what younger generations from Shelby will need to do in order to make a reasonable living, according to many of the older, downsized workers. Helen, for example, talked about her children and grandchildren, declaring, "There's not opportunities here for them. And they are going to have to go elsewhere to make a good life for themselves." While many workers lamented that they would "prefer to keep their children at home" in Shelby, they understood that doing so meant they would "have to find something besides Wal-Mart to come into the community."

Even within these more cynical and less hopeful depictions of community, however, many downsized workers also portrayed Shelby and Cleveland County as an idealized place to live and work—similar to the "Mayberry" depicted on *The Andy Griffith Show*. It is a decidedly nostalgic, yet important, representational image for many of the downsized workers. To them, Shelby is a "safe place," a "quiet, slow-paced community," "a place where people have close bonds," and a "clean, ideal-sized town with good schools." In short, as Amy, a longtime resident, proclaimed, "It's a good community. . . . It's a down home place."

In many respects, employers such as KEMET allow Shelby to retain its local qualities, according to the downsized workers. It is a place where people "don't bother to lock their doors," and "nobody is afraid to stay at home alone" because "neighbors are always close by and ready to help." Put simply, by Martha, "It's a better place to live than Charlotte or the bigger places. I think it's, ah, you know, slower pace[d]. . . . It's quiet." Even after the downsizing, Helen asserted that "Cleveland County is still a good county and you can't find no better people. Everybody's real friendly and nice, you know everybody." Similarly, Sue, commented, "You know all your neighbors and they're the first ones to know if you have a problem and they're all there to help you out."

For most of the downsized workers, then, the economic conditions of Shelby limit opportunities, yet they do not necessarily change the fundamental features of the community: the stability and longevity of its people and their social networks. Although KEMET's absence will create a significant economic void in the community, Shelby is still, according to Helen, "just home. We have lived here all our life and you feel safe and secure when you're with people around and your neighbors and your home."

Accommodation and Memory

As one might expect, many of the preceding comments from downsized workers' narratives suggest that they experienced a loss of control during and after the downsizing. Some were resigned: "There was nothing I could do about it," Sarah explained. The narratives contained common refrains: "We had no choice," "There was nothing we could do," and "They had us over a barrel." As Amy summarized the sense of powerlessness caused by the downsizing: "We weren't in control anymore."

Other workers, like Mary, felt that it might be possible "to ride it out" and hoped for work at KEMET in the future. Some, like Dana, were given a choice "to stay on for a while or leave immediately." According to her, "they offered an incentive [to leave] and that was sort of, do I take it now and run or do I stay and get nothing. . . . So, I took mine and ran." Lucy explained, "I could have stayed. They didn't make me leave. It was my choice." Similar comments were made by many of the other downsized workers, whose sense of pride and dignity was evident in the decision to leave on their own terms. Although it was a relatively minor form of resistance in the face of losing their jobs, these workers were able to reconstruct a narrative that placed them in the role of decision maker. This reframing of "choice" when confronted with downsizing undoubtedly served as an important face-saving device for many workers who, as noted earlier, had to manage their job loss not just in front of friends and family, but also in front of a tight-knit community.

In addition to choosing to leave early and retain a sense of dignity, some workers engaged in more typical slowdowns characteristic of many plant closings. Most of the workers acknowledged that they lost their pride in their work after the downsizing was announced. Becky observed that "morale went all the way down" and, as a result, "nobody cared about coming to KEMET anymore." Greater playfulness—and its implied disrespect for the company—developed over time. Anonymous poems began to emerge in various locations throughout the plant, offering coping mechanisms to survive the downsizing in addition to pointed jabs at KEMET. A strand of jokes also made its way throughout the plant. The most common joke was perhaps the simplest, yet most telling, one, noted by Tina: "After they announced it [the downsizing] . . . it was terrible. Their attitudes just went phhhhh, you know like I don't care. I'm not going to do anything. I don't care if I work and then this was the joke, 'What can they do? Fire me?'" Similarly, when describing her last night at KEMET, Amy explained: "I worked half a night. We had a farewell party for everybody. I had enough days left that it wasn't going [to] count [against me] and there again, what were they going to do? Fire me on my last night?"

Still other workers challenged the company's moral authority through their unwillingness to contribute to auxiliary activities promoted by the company, such as holiday events designed to assist those in need and highlight the civic responsibility of KEMET. Somewhat surprisingly, no workers talked about outright sabotage, as a form of resistance, but they did describe paying less attention to quality control or "letting mistakes slide through." Only Emma spoke directly about revenge against the company, and in her case it was future oriented: "If I go out and I have a better life and my goal is, this is my goal. . . . I want to go on to get my accounting degree and I want to get my CPA and I want to become an auditor and I want to audit KEMET. That would just be my dream. To be able to go in, and get to audit them and strike fear in their hearts. You know, that would be the ultimate revenge."

Like Emma, though, many workers felt there was little they could do to directly resist KEMET's downsizing decision. As a result, they articulated their accommodation into the future, around a theme of learning and education. Several of them emphasized the importance of using provisions in NAFTA to their advantage to gain a higher education and, thus, avoid similar circumstances in the future. More specifically, they suggested that the Trade Adjustment Assistance (TAA) and the Trade Readjustment Allowance (TRA) provisions would provide them with better opportunities and greater control over their future working conditions. The eighteen months of education provided in the TAA and the TRA were, for many, a "chance to improve" themselves and "better [their] lives." The educational opportunities provide new alternatives for workers suffering in the midst of deindustrialization, making plant closings seem like "blessings in disguise." As Jane noted, "There's not any high-paying jobs that hires a plan person. You have got to have a college degree." Similarly, Michelle noted the reality of life for manufacturing workers: "They used to have some good-paying jobs for skilled workers . . . but those seems to be going out faster than they are coming in." Beyond their desire to educate and empower themselves, most workers felt it was important to provide a model for their children. They believed that the downsizing might not only offer them a second chance but also offer a new opportunity for the next generation of Shelby citizens. As one worker put it, "I don't want my children to find themselves in this position. They will need to have more control over their lives—and more schooling will do that for them."

Finally, it is also evident that workers resisted the perceived KEMET philosophy of "business at all costs." Their persistent reiteration of the importance of coworkers, family, and community suggests the truth of one worker's claim: "Big corporations can stay here for a while, but they can't change our way of life." Even in the midst of such a significant life change and the stress, frustration, and loss of control that ensued, the downsized workers found stability and permanence in steadfast "traditions and values that sustain" them. This form of narrative accommodation is certainly less political, less visible, and, ultimately, less unified. It is not an organized protest or a sustained movement, but it is, nevertheless, a means of adapting to the downsizing experience in varied, immediate, and idiosyncratic ways.

Resistance to deindustrialization and the downsizing that has followed it cannot be reduced only to public behaviors such as sabotage or rebellion. Rather, in the case of KEMET, it is to be found in the narrative appeal of improvised performances of self, company, and community. Workers at KEMET sought to accommodate the downsizing by reframing their experience as a breach of the social contract between employer and employee, company and community. Although never directly resisting KEMET, the workers nevertheless drew on a moral economy that they believe will persist long after the company's departure from their community. While violating the local, interpersonal ties that bind, according to the downsized workers, the KEMET downsizing also reaffirmed workers' ability to sustain themselves in adversity, drawing on coworkers and community as sources of pride and strength.

In all likelihood, the KEMET downsizing will be yet another southern tale whose moral will be left largely unstated, yet fully understood by future generations in Shelby and Cleveland County. The telling and retelling of the stories of KEMET will no doubt provide the memory, the history, and the moral to restructure workers' multiple and complex identifications for years to come—empowering those willing to listen.

CHAPTER 13

Worker Memory and Narrative

*Personal Stories of Deindustrialization
in Louisville, Kentucky*

JOY L. HART AND TRACY E. K'MEYER

When Johnson Controls closed its battery plant in Louisville, Kentucky, in 1995, Danny Mann lost his job. He described his experience thus:

> The Louisville plant always got the hardest batteries to run. If the other plants couldn't run them, they sent them to the Louisville plant, and the Louisville plant would make them work. . . . We had awards from Nissan and Ford and Toyota for zero defects. So that means everybody was doing their job. . . . Our plant was a good plant to work at, but Johnson Controls stunk. Their upper management, they could care less. But I guess that's probably true in all industrial environments; you're a number, and as long as you produce, you're a good number. If you don't produce, then you're a bad number and we take you out.
>
> [Other people] didn't think they was ever going to close the Louisville plant. "Too strategically located." That's what everybody kept saying. I kept trying to tell them it wasn't true. . . . We all thought when they brought him [a new plant manager, Jim Dibiagio] in that he was the hatchet man because he had just shut a plant down. . . . I told him, I said, "You go out and look on that calendar out there. . . . I'm marking that calendar when y'all are going to do this." This is when it's going to be, they're going to shut this plant down. . . . "The writing's on the wall, man." I'm not an optimist. . . . I was one of the ones who saw this coming and I started socking it back. Some of them, some old people out there, that's all they did all their life was work there and now what are they going to do? . . . I don't think Johnson Controls gave us a fair shake. . . . I feel like . . . I gave them 110 percent. They paid me for 110 percent but they did everybody out there wrong.
>
> I didn't want to go back into a—not unless I had to—an industrial

284

environment; that place had beat me to death. I couldn't find anything
that paid anything, nothing near what I was making. . . . I need a challenge. I don't like to go in and do the same thing. I can fix things and
make them work. I like that pretty well. I mean, I don't like the pay [at
my new job], but I think that will grow a bit in time. . . . I enjoy this a
whole lot more than I did production work. . . . I found out that there's
more in life than money. There for a long time I was consumed with the
buck. . . . I thought money was the key to happiness. Then I found out
that it didn't matter how much money I had. I might have more things
but I wasn't going to be any happier. So I decided to stop and smell the
roses some.[1]

Danny Mann's experience was part of the broader phenomenon of
deindustrialization. Although the roots of this economic change had been
established earlier, by 1980, stories of plant closings frequented the nightly
news and popular press.[2] The early scholarly response sought to document
the reaction to, and consequences of, this economic change by relying heavily on survey research, statistical analysis, and aggregate data from the social science and medical fields.[3] As a result, the process and social impact of
deindustrialization was often painted in broad strokes. Individual stories
were used only to add drama or portray the misery and bitterness that result when a factory shuts down.[4] Typically, these stories were presented in
brief form, not submitted to a full examination. Whether the resulting picture was relatively optimistic—a story of economic transformation that,
while unfortunately hurting some, created growth and benefits for many—
or pessimistic—a tale of individual and community despair—it did not con-
vey the complexity, ambivalence, or contradiction seen in stories like
Mann's. By the late 1980s ethnographers had begun to probe the experience of people undergoing plant closings. Using participant observation
and extended interviews, their analyses often contained composite characters and life stories. The result was a more people-centered account of the
impact of deindustrialization.[5] More recently, oral historians and folklorists
have presented the stories of workers in the form of extended, edited oral
history interviews, encouraging us to read the words of displaced workers
not just as a mine for valuable information but as a source of interpretation
by workers as they tell their own histories.[6]

Following these models, we use oral histories of workers as the starting point for understanding deindustrialization. In oral history interviews,
narrators are invited, with a few guiding questions, to tell the story of their
experience in as extensive detail as they see fit. The resulting narrative contains multiple levels of information. On the simplest level, interviews provide a wealth of first-person data regarding work tasks and conditions, the

process of a closing, and the results. In these stories narrators paint a picture of the individual circumstances, dreams, work, and family and community life shaping their experience and often place their story in the broader social context. On another level, as folklorists have pointed out, recurring themes in an oral narrative—either in a single story or a collection of stories—can be read as reflections or expressions of consciousness, identity, and values.[7] In short, oral history interviews can reveal not only what people experienced but also what they interpret their experience to mean, and how they would like the broader public, the ultimate audience, to understand it.[8]

In this chapter, we will highlight the stories and interpretations offered by individuals, keeping economic and historical analyses in the background. To do so, we present themes that emerged in interviews conducted in 1997 with former workers at two plants in Louisville, Kentucky: Johnson Controls—Danny Mann's workplace—and International Harvester, which closed in 1985. The narratives contain commentary on the causes, results, and broader significance of these plant closings from the workers' point of view. If we are to write the history of deindustrialization in a way that fully accounts for its social and political outcomes, we need to incorporate how people who experienced it directly explain it. In sharing his story, Danny Mann asserted his work ethic and ability, insisted on his prescience and agency, accused the company of unjust treatment, and concluded that he enjoys life more despite making less money. We will demonstrate that, in their narratives of the experience of plant closings, workers like Mann portray themselves as agents—not victims—who demand and deserve respect and fairness, and who judge business and government accordingly. Moreover, when read closely, the ambiguities and contradictions in the interviews display the struggle on the part of the narrators to reconcile the impact of these events with their self-images as shapers of their own destinies. Finally, in the course of their narratives these workers communicate that deindustrialization changed the way they see the world and hint at the perceived violation of values and loss of trust that must be healed if workers' investment in the political system is to be revived.

The Causes of Plant Closings

In 1946, International Harvester purchased an existing Louisville plant and began compiling what eventually became a 130-acre facility housing an assembly plant, forge, and foundry. This manufacturing complex produced the company's Farmall tractors and several components of farm equipment.

The assembly plant alone was 1.6 million square feet, and Harvester was one of the largest employers in the metropolitan area. In 1973 the workforce peaked at 6,800 across the three Louisville facilities. But by the late 1970s, employment figures had slipped to 2,500. The downsizing began when the farm equipment business skidded in the late 1970s, and continued as the company reported huge losses in the 1980s. Company officials often cited a general economic recession, the collapse of the farm equipment market, and their attempts to avoid bankruptcy as reasons for decreasing the workforce. From November 1979 until May 1980, Louisville workers joined a national United Auto Workers (UAW) strike against International Harvester.[9] During this time, the company incurred huge debts that worsened its already mounting financial problems. On July 29, 1982, Harvester announced the first of three closures—the assembly plant would close in January of 1983. Following suit, the foundry shut down in August of 1984. Finally, in April of 1985, International Harvester stopped production at the last of its facilities, the forge, notifying workers by telegram not to return and sending home those on second shift who arrived for work.[10]

A decade later, as part of an effort to reduce its battery division, Johnson Controls closed its Louisville facility.[11] In April 1994, the company announced that it would lose its Sears DieHard battery contract in September. Although share prices immediately dropped $1.50, a few months later CEO James H. Keyes predicted record years for the company in 1994 and 1995. Nevertheless, in order to cut excess production Johnson Controls began closing battery plants, eventually shutting down facilities in Dallas, Texas; Bennington, Vermont; and Owosso, Michigan. Despite reporting increased dividends for the twentieth consecutive year, the company considered additional closings. According to local union president Roy Puckett, in late 1994 managers informed Louisville employees that their facility was on a list of plants being considered for closure. Employees were asked to find incentives to keep the plant open, either by securing financial support from local government or by making extra efforts to improve the relative standing of their plant in the chain. Despite signs that the plant had increased production, in April 1995 Johnson Controls announced it would close the Louisville facility. The company reported a "better than expected income of $67 million" in October, but the plant was closed on the projected date in December 1995.[12] According to former employees, production was moved to other, non-UAW plants in the United States.[13]

The men and women who lost their jobs in these closings have very specific, clear ideas about who or what was at fault. Here, as throughout this chapter, our purpose is to present what workers perceived, knew, concluded, and remembered rather than a multiperspective account of events.

While at times mentioning broad economic forces, these workers most often blamed closings on the lack of skill, poor decisions, or nefarious motives of management. It might be expected that workers would blame "the boss" in general terms, criticizing the "piss-poor management" for example. But workers at these plants named particular decisions and policies, and backed up their charges with myriad examples and authoritative sources. The decision makers at International Harvester, for example, pulled out of producing the International Scout on the eve of the Sports Utility Vehicle craze and sold off lines contributing significantly to profits. Recalled Kenneth Rhodes: "It seemed like everything that we ever were invested in turned out to be a success after Harvester got rid of it. For instance, the lawn mowers, the Cub Cadets, they were a very big, large seller, a big money maker. We turned around and sold it out and then it seemed like it turned out to be a rave all over the country. . . . We were doing the little Scout—that's the same thing as a Ford Explorer—they got rid of that. . . . That's the biggest thing going now in America is everybody wants an all-terrain vehicle. . . . So, I don't know if they just didn't have any insight or whether they just, the ball wasn't falling on their side of the net. I'm not sure."

Besides being unable to discern market trends, the management made mistakes in internal operations. Some workers, such as Rob McQueen, recalled misplaced priorities: "I remember so many days of running trash and knew that I was running trash, but yet being told to run trash so I could make my quota." Sharing McQueen's views, Kenneth Rhodes asserted, "There was some situations that I'd have to say that the things that we did over there didn't make a lot of sense as far as like running bad parts just to get numbers out, the production out. I didn't understand that. I felt like if you're going to do something, do it right or don't do it. And they obviously didn't feel that way." Other workers blamed the managers' decisions to cut maintenance, sell off inventory, and go to a just-in-time production system. As if to insist that these critiques were not idle speculation or merely unemployed workers' resentment, narrators cited authoritative sources to substantiate their claims. According to Phil Nalley, Harvester "kind of admitted that they made a mistake" in hiring a new CEO, and the stockholders were angry as a result. Thomas Rhodes invoked an established authority, saying, "I used to take *Fortune* and *Forbes*. . . . They determined International Harvester being one of the worst managed companies ever in the history of this country because of the things that they had done."

According to these interviewees, not only did managers make bad decisions but sometimes their decisions made no sense. Former Johnson Controls employees, like Danny Mann, repeatedly asserted that the closing was foolish because the plant was producing award-winning batteries of a higher quality than its competitors, while making a profit. Indeed, several narrators remembered that the company pushed them to work extra hard to improve production and profit in order to prevent a closing, and that Louisville had become the best or one of the best production facilities.[14] But the company closed the plant anyway. Similar stories come out of Harvester. Kenneth Rhodes remembered, "Harvester spent over $300 million retooling their foundry, and it was the most modern foundry, from what I read, in the United States. Instead, they closed that down . . . and moved the works to Indianapolis, which was over a hundred-year-old facility." "I'll never understand how a company can work that way, shut down a plant that produces eighty parts a day and keep another plant open that only produces twenty-five," added Don Anderson.

Because company decisions made little sense or seemed to be in conflict with stated goals, many employees concluded that executives lied about their motives. As Rob McQueen bluntly stated: "I feel there was a little bullshit there as far as why Harvester closed." "The union wasn't breaking them," he continued. "They was doing all fine with their contracts and everything like that." Considering how much money the company spent updating and refurbishing the plant, McQueen concluded, "I really feel like there was something shady . . . going on." In the same spirit, others debunked specific excuses the management gave for the closing. Johnson Controls said the closing was due to the distance of shipping. But Arthur Pugh and Roy Puckett both pointed out that the Louisville plant sold mainly to local customers. The management claimed Johnson Controls had too many workers. But "that was a barefaced lie because six months after they shut the plant down they hired five hundred people in two plants," recalled Bob Reed. Many employees concluded that Johnson Controls had made the decision to close the plant long ago. Charlie Noyes explained that in 1990 Johnson Controls International had tried, and failed, to sell the battery division and then "slowly but surely they managed to shut down a number of plants in order to 'downsize.'" In the process they simply "bled the company dry."

If the reasons publicly stated by the companies were false, what were the hidden agendas? In both cases, workers adamantly insisted that the decision to close the plant was aimed at busting the power of the union. Indeed, breaking the union, along with reaping the benefits of the North American Free Trade Agreement (NAFTA) were the two most frequent attributions by workers from Johnson Controls. Moreover, in the view of those from International Harvester, disentangling from the union was second only to inept management.[15] Johnson Controls employees recognized a pattern in which the corporation steadily closed plants within the power-

ful United Auto Workers Council. At Harvester, while several people acknowledged that the company's financial problems had some roots in the
six-month strike in late 1979 and early 1980, they insisted that the duration
of the work stoppage was the fault of the company, not the workers. Employees such as Don Anderson and Phil Nalley believed that in the strike's
aftermath CEO Archie McCardell had a vendetta against the union. Nalley gave his reasons: "In the *Wall Street Journal*—it was in 1980 or '81—it
quoted Archie McCardell saying that he would close Louisville works because of the strike that we had gone through." Further, Nalley repeated a
rumor that said McCardell had declared, "You won the battle, but I will win
the war."[16]

Beyond breaking the union, workers from Johnson Controls charge,
management was seeking to avoid environmental and occupational safety
laws and find cheap labor by moving to Mexico. Despite complaining of
worker overcapacity, the company built a factory near Torreone, Mexico.
Former workers criticized Johnson Controls for finding ways around provisions of NAFTA they believed were meant to protect them. For example,
Ron Phillips hypothesized that:

> If we could have proved that they were making our batteries down there,
> that we were making here, we could have sued. . . . When they shut our
> plant down, we were making original equipment batteries. What they
> did, they took all our batteries and they split it between St. Joe, Mis-
> souri; Toledo, Ohio; Winston-Salem, North Carolina; and three or four
> other plants. And they took their replacement batteries and sent them
> to Mexico. So, we didn't have nothing to stand on. They didn't take our
> batteries, but they did. . . . Even though they did take our business, they
> didn't. But they did, you know. They took our business to American
> plants, but they shipped their business to Mexico. . . . That's the loop-
> hole. So, we lost.[17]

The sense of being cheated out of benefits and lied to about the real
reasons for the shutdown contributed to resentment over the closing, the
treatment of workers, and the government's role in the process. Interestingly, interviewees did not blame or criticize Mexicans themselves, instead
fixing their sights on management. Indeed, management's seemingly sense-
less actions and hidden motives convinced many workers that the upper
echelon did not care about rank-and-file employees and would do anything
for the limited benefit of those at the top. As Danny Mann put it, "Johnson
Controls didn't care about nobody—but Johnson Controls." "They took
away my living," Arthur Pugh added, "for some money-making scheme."
The workers were just numbers, "just an unnecessary expense" toward

whom the company showed no loyalty and little respect. Howard Etherton was hurt particularly by the lack of respect shown for the workers who stayed at Harvester until the end, and then were sent a telegram telling them not to come in again. At Johnson Controls, the drawn-out suspense over which plant would close left workers believing the managers had purposely played games with them—lying to them, leading them on, and tricking them into working harder until the last possible moment. Running through these comments is the sense that the managers, in their ineptness and dishonesty, did an injustice to the workers and the community.

Many employees accused local and national government of facilitating this injustice. One exception is that Johnson Controls workers acknowledged that the Kentucky state government offered a helpful tax package to the company, which refused it. Earlier, International Harvester had less success in attracting local government support. A number of union officials recalled that the city and county made no effort to entice Harvester to stay. Don Anderson contrasted this situation with the help General Electric received from the county government, and Etherton conjectured, "Maybe if we had gotten help like Chrysler did" Harvester would still be there. They imply that even if the federal government would not step in, at least the city should have helped Harvester in the interest of saving local jobs. But Thomas and Kenneth Rhodes charged that city fathers, in the interest of getting rid of "these old redneck smokestack places" and ushering in a non-industrial downtown, had sealed Harvester's fate.[18]

Narrators blamed the federal government not only for not helping but for actively hurting workers by giving companies the incentive and ability to move across the border. Ron Phillips remembered, "They said there's a road down there that looks like a superhighway in Mexico. As far as you can see, there's American plants, companies." As a result of NAFTA, workers now have to "compete against everybody in the world," leading to lower wages for U.S. laborers. Howard Etherton summarized the views of many this way: "Before the free trade with Mexico, the NAFTA thing, the company wouldn't think about coming into Harvester and telling you they was going to cut your pensions or they was going to cut your benefits. But they'll tell you now, 'We're going to do it or we're going to take them to Mexico.' . . . Mexico ain't big enough to take every job out of the United States and put in there. But they've got enough hold, the companies do, to bring all the good paying jobs down to a level to where the rich man gets richer and the poor man gets poorer." Several narrators expressed indignation along with concern for the future of the country, especially working people and their children. Instead of facilitating disloyalty and injustice on the part of companies, "The United States should have a law preventing companies from moving to Mexico with high-paying jobs, for cheap labor," argued Roy Puckett.

Worker Agency, Skill, and Foresight

Although displaced workers in these two cases saw the closings as unjust, and criticized management and government policies, they did not see themselves as mere victims. Indeed, narrators presented themselves as skilled agents, able to discern the future closing and carve out ways to survive it. Their agency and foresight were based on their abilities and knowledge of the factory. While detailing work processes and plant conditions, these narrators showcased considerable pride in their work. For example, Rob McQueen explained, "I was a good operator. I was able to do any work, and the foreman knew he could put me anywhere." Bob Reed likewise claimed, "I ran the best quality I could and I was proud of what I did. . . . I got compliments from other departments saying that I did good stuff." These examples of self-esteem based on the ability to do hard work reflect a shop floor culture in heavy industry in which people are recognized, and expect respect, for their skills.

To emphasize their proficiency these workers related how hard it was to work in the dirty, dangerous conditions at International Harvester and Johnson Controls. Indeed, long passages of nearly every interview conveyed graphic pictures of sweltering heat, deafening noise, and, most dramatically, the health dangers of molten metal and flying lead. For example, Bob Smith recalled the "noise, heat, the heat and the noise" of Harvester. "It was real dusty in there." He later added, "You got metal in your eyes all the time working down in that mill room. . . . You wear goggles, but they had a nurse on call over there and you'd go in there and he'd get stuff out of your eyes. Dr. Block, he would take this little thing and pick in your eyes and take the metal out of it. I've been down there. He's done that to me several times." Of Harvester, Kenneth Rhodes said, "It was a very hot, poorly insulated or poorly ventilated, I should say, place. There were days when the temperature in the dead of summer on a day shift, which was 6:30 to 2:30, it would get up around the presses, where the steel would come through, to 130 to 135 degrees, and that was pretty unpleasant. But that was part of the job too. But I guess for the most part, I pretty much enjoyed it. . . . It was quite uncomfortable. But it was the job." Ron Phillips characterized the tough working conditions at Johnson Controls: "Summertime was hot. The machine I ran—everything I ran had to go through a flash oven, and the oven averaged about 800 degrees, so it was very hot. You go in and a half hour after you were there, you were soaking wet. That's just how it was. You get used to it." Each of these descriptions of work conditions ended with a statement that evidenced the speaker's ability to withstand them. For these workers, being able to produce under such conditions was what earned, or should have earned, them respect.[19]

The narrators often continued by pointing out that only a particular type of person—skilled, hardworking, smart, strong, and determined—could endure these conditions. Phil Nalley, taking pride in never having been injured, said that given these dangers, "You had to be fairly smart to work in there or you got hurt." The narrators attributed their ability to survive and thrive in these conditions to their strong work ethic, learned in working-class households. Danny Mann recalled that his father taught him a belief in a fair return for hard work: "I've always been a hard worker. That's the way my father was; that's what he instilled in us. You go in there and give a guy a day's work for a day's pay." Similarly, McQueen stated, "We, for the most part, of that generation, was brought up that you put in a good eight hours, you get eight hours' pay. I could never quit." In addition to demonstrating the narrators' hard-working self-images, these comments reveal their belief that this strong work ethic gave them the right to good wages. Moreover, these narrators often spoke collectively, not only about their own fortitude and skill but about those of other workers as well. There is an individual and collective portrait painted here of a certain type of person who can do this work and not give up. But while these workers forged bonds of mutual respect based on character and ability, they expected such respect, and the benefits that go with it, from their bosses.

Workers also cited special knowledge and ability as sources of foresight into the impending closing. In their stories of the plant shutdown, almost all of these narrators claimed they saw the problems in advance, even though others did not. A few workers told stories about access to authoritative information. Thomas Rhodes's friend, the plant manager, hinted he should get another job. Arthur Pugh's foreman told him no new equipment was being brought into the facility. Charlie Noyes noted, "Being involved in maintenance I had better insight into that [problems in the plant] than maybe other people did." Others read in *Fortune* or the *Wall Street Journal*—papers they said were not usually read by their colleagues—that the company was losing millions or that the division was up for sale. More generally, employees credited their intelligence and "street smarts." Danny Mann recalled some coworkers who were "just a little bit more intelligent" than others. Likewise, Frank Reinhart attributed his good sense and that of his friends to the fact that "you had people there that had been around the block like me, you know, we growed up on the streets and survived."

Several narrators noted they saw specific signs that the plant was going to close. For one, because of their knowledge of the shop floor they recognized that the plants were being allowed to deteriorate. Machinery was disconnected or not maintained, lines were being sold or periodically stopped, and there was a general lack of repairs or plans for the future. Saying he had anticipated a plant closure at least four or five years before it happened, Charlie Noyes reported, "They weren't maintaining the factory in a manner that would indicate to me they intended for it to last a significant length of time. . . . When you see that happening, you know there's something in the wind. . . . When things go bad, they have to be replaced. When you see a company not doing that, you know damn good and well somebody somewhere who makes decisions has already decided what they're going to do." For those at Johnson Controls, the clearest sign of trouble was the arrival of a new plant manager, Jim Dibiagio, who was notorious as a plant closer. When Dibiagio showed up, Arthur Pugh recalled, he told his wife, "He's here to close it." Why were workers so sure that Dibiagio's arrival was a harbinger of future unemployment for them? Dibiagio's reputation for closing another Johnson Controls facility preceded him. Besides this, Mike Reid insisted, when Dibiagio claimed he would keep the plant open, "I knew he was lying. He wouldn't look you in the eyes. He hanged his head down." These remarks demonstrate that in response to a lack of information workers accepted rumors and looked, both at the time and in retrospect, for signs to confirm those rumors.

Because they saw the closing coming, these workers were able to take steps to prepare themselves. When he heard rumors that Harvester might close the Louisville facility, Phil Nalley recalled, "I did brace for it. . . . I started refusing to spend, to buy." On hearing the Louisville plant was on Johnson Controls' closure shortlist, Roy Puckett said his family started to "get our financial house in order" and reduce bills so they could live on his wife's salary. Saving money, reducing spending, and paying off cars and homes were central to these workers' financial preparation. Like their work ethic, thriftiness was a source of pride for several narrators, and it helped to prepare them for the layoff. Bob Reed explained that he always saved money "for a rainy day" because he believed you had to think about what might happen. Phil Nalley likewise noted that he had always saved money and avoided credit cards. At times this virtue of thriftiness was contrasted to the habits of others. Winifred Shake compared his own avoidance of debt with the carelessness of other people "who lived high on the hog."

The emphasis on prescience and preparation reveals that these narrators value their ability to take care of themselves. Rather than victims who merely reacted to hard circumstances, they were agents who took proactive steps to insure the security of their families. Some people got out early; when they saw the signs they arranged for new jobs, early retirement, or medical leave. Others looked into new careers while riding out the closing. When Marilyn Reed first heard rumors of Johnson Controls' impending shutdown, she did not wait for someone to help her. She went on her own to the dislocated workers office to get training for a new, more appealing career. Inspiring these actions was a belief that, given the unsettled economy and the nature of factory work, you have to take care of yourself, and not depend on your job or other people for help.

Impact of Plant Closures

Most workers insisted that as a result of their foresightedness the closing had very minimal overall negative impact on them personally. As Don Anderson remarked, "I didn't feel devastated knowing the job was ending." In some cases, like Anderson's, workers reasoned that they were prepared because they had been laid off before and knew how to save money for hard times. Phil Nalley claimed he "didn't lose nothing" because of savings, having his home paid off, and having his children raised and out of the home. In other cases, the workers felt protected against hard times. Some men had wives with well-paying jobs. Others believed they could easily find employment because of special skills or training. Those who took early retirement and medical leave said they could just readjust their budgets and get used to living on less. When Marilyn Reed's father expressed concern over her substantial cut in pay, she replied to him, "You just give things up. I mean, you don't need that money to live." She and her husband, fellow employee Bob Reed, did OK because: "We're not real big spenders. Like I've had my car for ten years and things like that. We're not really spendthrifts and things. We go to flea markets. If I saw something I wanted I bought it. So that kind of changed. But, I mean, we didn't really change our lifestyles as far as eating beans and potatoes, you know, or things like that."

Most narrators argued assertively that the closing had had a positive impact on their lives, concluding, "I'm really glad I lost my job there." While acknowledging that the loss was a financial blow, several simply saw it, for one reason or another, as a "blessing in disguise."[20] In part, this was a result of their determination to "look at the positive things that could happen out of this," but they also justified their perspective in specific personal terms. For Winifred Shake, the closing presented the opportunity to take early retirement and care for his wife as she was dying of cancer. "At that time I regretted not going sooner because she had cancer, but if everything, if her health had been good and everything—I'm sorry I didn't stay longer, you know. But no, I don't regret retiring when I did. Of course, it's always nice to have money, but money's not everything." Kenneth Rhodes found the closing of International Harvester to be a good learning experience. More specifically, the combination of being laid off and discovering a congenital heart problem revived his religious faith. He explains: "I think it's probably made me a better person. . . . As far as losing everything and the job and everything, like I said, it was just a learning experience. I wouldn't recommend it for everybody, but like I say, I'm better for it. I don't begrudge International Harvester or anything else for it." He continued, "I believe there was a reason for all these things to happen. . . . Maybe I was going the wrong direction or something." But, he added, "We're survivors and we'll figure out a way to get though it. We trust God and we believe He'll work with us and we'll work with Him." These stories are not generalizable and obviously do not explain why the majority of narrators found a silver lining in their unemployment. But the stories' very specificity highlights the ways in which unique personal circumstances shape individual reactions.

Dislocated workers most commonly attributed their satisfaction to their preference for their new jobs and relief over health concerns. Like most people who lost jobs in major plant closings, former employees of Harvester and Johnson Controls had trouble finding jobs and ended up in positions that are less secure, are nonunionized, pay less, and have fewer benefits; nevertheless, they insisted they preferred their new positions.[21] Jobs such as doing maintenance for hospitals and schools, repairing recreational vehicles, or working for the park service allow them to use diverse skills, vary the pace of work, and have a more congenial social environment. For example, in his job as a recreational vehicle repairman, Ron Phillips says, he gets to travel, meet customers, and make them happy when he fixes their trailers. Danny Mann likes setting his own pace and developing new skills. Phil Nalley accounted for his satisfaction by saying: "Harvester shutting down was a setback and yes, it was a major, what I felt at that time, a major blow, but it has turned out for the good. It's just, you know, I really enjoy this lifestyle. I get to use my hands at Jewish [Hospital] plus I get to use my mind. . . . My boss gives me a lot of leeway. He trusts my judgment. He allows me to think versus just follow. Yeah, it's really, I'm glad now that it's happened." In their new jobs, the workers are rewarded for the skill and work ethic they were proud of, but not recognized for, in the plants. In their narratives these displaced workers portray the trade of lost income for greater autonomy and a chance to use their skills as not only acceptable but as the key to the improvement in their work lives.

Another factor contributing to the workers' happiness with their new jobs was the lack of health concerns. As Rob McQueen dramatically stated, "No way I would go back to work there, even for twice as much. I don't know if I'd still be alive if I worked there." In nearly every interview, narrators described at length, and with little prodding, the extensive health hazards in the factories, including clogged lungs, chronic lead poisoning, disfiguring acid burns, broken limbs, and even deaths by accidents. The closing was a relief to some because they were not sure how much longer they could survive. Marilyn Reed recalled: "By the time they closed I was glad they were closing because I don't know how much longer I would have been able to work there doing that type of work. It was really physical work, and I would come home from work and I couldn't hardly lift my legs up I was so tired, and it was just exhausting." She continued, "I was getting to where my hands were going numb and things like that. So, I thought this is my chance to do some of the things that I've wanted to do that I wouldn't be doing if they had stayed open because I would have stayed there until I was either handicapped or retired maybe at fifty-five."

Contrasting his new job with the Parks Department to his old one at International Harvester, Rob McQueen explained,

> Although I don't make nearly the money or have near the benefits . . . it's clean. I'm outside on a golf course. I'm at work at daybreak. A lot of times at daybreak I've got a big cup of coffee, and I might be riding out turning on water on different fairways or greens or tees. I look over and there might be a groundhog or a deer or rabbits. And there's times that I might pull over for a minute and reminisce and say, boy this is a lot different from Harvester. I really enjoy myself at the golf course. I do wish it was a little bit more money cause I can only imagine if Harvester was still open, there's no telling what I'd be making now.

These expressions of relief reveal that workers were acutely aware that factory work, despite efforts by the Environmental Protection Agency and Occupational Safety and Health Administration, was dangerous. While many admitted they would have "stuck it out" for the money, and were proud to say they "could take" the conditions, they saw the happy ending of the plant closing in their longer, healthier lives.

While people declared positive personal consequences, the stories are also laced with resentment and indications of personal loss. Although at times narrators were hesitant to move beyond vague statements, or were prone to bookend their losses with positive outcomes, still they provided a wealth of information about the negative financial and emotional impact of the closing on them and their families. Some of the older workers had trouble finding new jobs. Don Anderson recalled, "Here I was over fifty and I had to start over again trying to find another job and not being that familiar with what seemed to me was a new system of writing up your resume and go out here and ask people . . . 'Well, give me a resume. Well, I don't have one.' I never had to do all that; I never learned that." Another worker felt that employers would hold against him the fact that he had once made a high wage, fearing that he would not settle for less. Among all the dislocated workers in this study, the consensus is that new jobs, once they were secured, paid far less. One narrator went from $47,000 to $15,000 a year. Another dropped from $50,000 to between $20,000 and $30,000. Virginia Daniels summarized her situation and that of many other workers by stating, "It was just like I had to start all over again."

With the lower wages in new jobs, there also were fewer benefits. People lost vacation time and health insurance, but they complained the most about the loss of their secure, hard-earned retirement. "The thought that another year and a half and I'd be retired . . . ," mused Rob McQueen. "I could play golf all the time. All I would have to do is walk to the mailbox and, I'm not sure of the amount of the check but it would be more than enough to live on. It would be a lot more than what I'm making right now working. A lot more." Now, he and other downsized workers will have to work until they are sixty-five and the retirement pay will be less. "I think it messed up my retirement plans," complained Roy Puckett. "I think I would have come out much better with a retirement plan had I been able to stay there and finish out all my years. And financially, you know, I was making more money there than I am now. I guess that was the biggest thing was the pension thing. When you go to work somewhere you think you're going to be there all your life and anymore that's not true." This loss engendered particular bitterness. As Arthur Pugh put it, "you counted on the retirement . . . and they up and kick you in the face and kick you out." The reward for hard work in brutal conditions was not just high wages, which people felt they deserved, but the promise of a comfortable and early retirement. These workers felt robbed of the latter, coloring the lessons they would take from the whole experience.[22]

What is clear in the narratives is that in their stories people downplayed the hurtful consequences of deindustrialization for them as individuals. One method of accomplishing this was bracketing information about loss with positive assertions and conclusions. For example, one narrator explained:

> It wasn't that stressful on me. Like I said, I was pretty well set here. My home was probably three-quarters paid for. You know, I had twenty-five years invested in it. I guess the only thing that changed was my—I guess

my way of life some. You know, I had five weeks vacation and now I have none. I was making $50,000 plus a year and now I probably make $20,000 up to $30,000, in that area. So I took quite a cut in pay. My lifestyle has changed. I can't go like I used to; I'm not getting the vacations I used to. . . . I can't do what I used to do. I can't buy. I don't know if it was stressful. . . . If I can maintain what I got, I'll be happy. I got a decent home. I got a decent vehicle. I got a boat. I can do the things that I want to do. I can't do it as often. . . . That's probably the only part of my life that's changed. You might be looking for somebody that's had more stressful things happen or maybe lost something or maybe caused a divorce or something like that. None of that's affected me 'cause I'm done past that stressful part.

Just as this person seemed almost compelled to make repeated positive remarks, even while listing losses, after telling a story about hard times other narrators added comments such as "it goes with the territory," "it's not really your fault," or "it hasn't changed my life very much." This suggests people are uncomfortable presenting a picture of loss. Instead, the workers tried to provide an integrated summary of their experiences, complete with tidy, happy endings.[23]

At times, the tension between the recognition of loss and the conviction that they had realized a happy ending rose to the surface, as the interviewees self-consciously wrestled with their stories. Rob McQueen became emotional when he tried to explain:

I have no idea how to say this. I'll probably—whoever listens to this will think I'm nuts. I have so many mixed emotions on it. I was overjoyed. I was sad. I was hurt. Every emotion that you can feel, I think I went through it. I was relieved because I didn't have to work like that. I was hurt and sad because I, to a certain extent, was losing a lot of friends. I was losing a lot of my benefits, insurance and what have you. But at the same time, I was almost happy. I know that doesn't make sense, but for a period of time I was happy. I don't know if happy is the word, or relieved. . . . I'm almost feeling like I'm glad that I'm out of there. I'm glad that I don't still work there, but man, I wish I still worked there.

This story demonstrates that beneath the presentation of a happy ending lie conflicted emotions. For these workers there is an ongoing struggle to reconcile the impact of job loss with a positive personal story, and a need to cope with the disintegrated views and emotional turmoil this struggle brings.

The seeming contradictions in explanations of deindustrialization's personal impact should not surprise us. Experience is never simple or unidimensional. In these cases, while dissatisfied with some aspects of factory work, narrators were well compensated, good at their jobs, and enmeshed in work communities and industrial culture. Their tasks were familiar and they looked forward to retiring with security, often being able to care for their family and extended families. At times they dreamed of different possibilities, and in the end were happy for the opportunity to change. But overwhelmingly, they admitted they would likely be punching the time clock if the plant doors were still open. It is not surprising that the views of these interviewees were not fully integrated; they were both depressed and happy, resentful and grateful. They were freed, given a chance to reach for new possibilities, but they were also deprived of a comfortable identity and a secure future.[24] These stories remind us not to take oral history interviews only at face value. Scholars cannot simply dismiss these contradictions as manifestations of confusion, or worse, "false consciousness," nor can we assume the narrators were being deliberately misleading. Instead, the narratives should be read as evidence that people, like experiences, are complex and can hold multiple values and have many reactions at once.[25]

Another way these narrators minimized the significance of their own personal setbacks was by frequently mentioning that other people had been hurt worse. Quite often in the course of explaining why they themselves survived, narrators contrasted their experience to that of others. While they had had the foresight to see what was coming and the knowledge and skill to succeed in finding a job they liked better, others were not so intelligent or good at forecasting upcoming events. People worried about their colleagues who were unskilled, lacked education, had "low IQs," or did not know any other work. And in describing their own preparation, narrators alluded to the fact that other people were not as thrifty. They lived "high on the hog" or "hand to mouth," not saving or looking ahead. These narrators also voiced concern for those who were older, but not ready to retire, or who still had children in the home. They also passed along stories, perhaps rumors, about other people who had lost their marriages, cars, or homes and who had mental or physical health problems, including "two or three suicides, three or four heart attacks." With few exceptions, however, the narrators were unwilling to discuss details of such extreme consequences in their own lives. In these narratives, the workers for International Harvester and Johnson Controls expressed deep sorrow for their colleagues. But by directing their concern toward other people who were less skilled, intelligent, thrifty, these workers in effect acknowledged the impact of the plant closings while drawing attention to their own lack of victimization.

Lessons from Plant Closings

One last element in the narratives is the lessons these speakers have learned from their experience. Most important, the plant closing taught them that there is no job security in manufacturing. As Virginia Daniels summarized, "I guess I don't take any job for granted." "There is no such thing as job security any more," Roy Puckett seconded. "You keep in the back of your head that it could happen to you." Along with this conclusion comes a profound mistrust of companies and their intentions. Phil Nalley explained, "It made me wiser, less trusting, and it kind of proves today in corporate America that you are a number. . . . You can't depend on the company—as my father knew it—you can't depend on that any longer. And also, you need to be aware of what's going on outside around you. If an opportunity presents itself that would be better, don't stay just because that's what you know." While many of these workers began their careers assuming they would work all their lives at one place and there would be mutual loyalty, now they observe, "I guess it is just kind of the rule of the jungle." Because companies "can and will treat people wrongly" and will "look out for their bottom line," workers have decided, "you can't put too much trust in anybody outside yourself." They disagree about whether it is still possible to rely on other workers. One narrator fervently argued that unions are needed more than ever, but another thought that even they cannot be trusted. Many former workers concluded that they have to look out for their own interests. Thus, their stories emphasized their individual responsibility and agency, and revealed their pride in their ability to foresee events, take care of themselves and their families, and survive.

Though these lessons might seem individualistic, these narrators . showed social concern in their worry about their colleagues and in their remarks on the state of the nation. In brief, there was an undercurrent of concern about the direction of the country. The narrators fear that NAFTA is resulting in worsened working standards in the United States. Good jobs are being lost and the gap between rich and poor is growing. A number of narrators painted a dire picture of the consequences of that division. "We're going to have a serious, severe situation with welfare and people that have not in this country, and what does that lead to?" asked Thomas Rhodes. Other narrators answered—escape into drugs and violence. According to these workers, the government, by facilitating the movement of manufacturing jobs south of the border, is weakening our country and leading us into social crisis. Arthur Pugh wondered: "I don't see why the government had to lower our standard of living down with the rest of the world. . . .

That weakens our country and that's exactly what they did." He continued, "I don't have no trust whatsoever and I don't want no politicians around me. I don't have no use for politicians whatsoever. Because to my way of thinking they ain't nothing but a damn big bunch of crooks that's out to screw the working man, and they've done it."

These workers bemoan the loss of trust, loyalty, and security that, in their memories, previous generations knew. They worry about their children's and grandchildren's futures and urge them not to depend on factory work. Many of these narrators picture an idealized time when hard work was respected and committed employees were appreciated. For the most part, they do not talk about differences in the labor market, general economy, and use of technology, or about the move from production to service. Rather, they remember a time when their fathers and uncles could count on lifetime employment, good wages, and respect in the workplace and community. They are disillusioned because they cannot expect the same, which they had come to take for granted. Because of these longings and their personal experiences, they argue that the country should provide good jobs for working people. As Thomas Rhodes argued: "I think that there are things that could and should be done in this country from the standpoint of its citizens and its workforce because in my opinion manufacturing- and production-type jobs may not be the answer to all sins or all evils or all the greatest things but I think without a certain amount of them . . . everybody's not a doctor or a lawyer; they don't have the potential or desire or anything else to be." His brother Kenny added: "I would like to see our country have, be furnishing jobs for people like my son so he could get a good-paying job with decent benefits. . . . I hate to see us lose the rights and stuff that we've all grown to enjoy through our history."

Conclusion

Admittedly, we began these interviews with some preconceived notions about what we would hear. For example, we expected that workers would blame management or the government for job loss, in part because of recent debates over the passage of NAFTA. The interviews contain such information, but we were surprised when narrators insisted, "this was the best thing that ever happened to me." How should such expressions be interpreted? On one level, this project reminds us that every plant closing is unique and has roots in local decision-making. Despite broadscale economic trends, these workers believe that the closings were largely influenced by the motivations of those in power and internal company politics.

In addition, these interviews uncover specific circumstances that shape an individual's experience of a plant closing and the subsequent results. Some workers were relatively cushioned because their spouses had good jobs, their houses were paid off, or their children were grown and out of the home. Some were able to file for medical leave or transfer to other plants in the company.[26] Yet others, who were less well cushioned, lost not only anticipated income, benefits, and job security, but also homes, cars, and sometimes the respect of neighbors. Finally, looking at whole interviews, especially their contradictions, reveals the multilayered nature of experience itself. This approach sheds light on the ways in which narrators present their critiques of the business and political elite while preserving their positive self-image.

On another level, these narratives illuminate the belief systems of these workers and the impact of deindustrialization on them. These workers share a culture that is based on pride in, and willingness to do, hard work in difficult circumstances. Part of that willingness assumes an expectation of reward in the form of respect, fair wages and benefits, and security. The interviewees asserted that they had earned their high wages and attributed their willingness to "stick it out" to the promise of an early and comfortable retirement. Their expectation of respect was conveyed in their stories of foremen and others above them in the hierarchy recognizing their skill. But the plant closings violated their expectations. The management showed disrespect by treating them like numbers, lying to them, and "playing games" with them in the months before the close. When they lost their wages and benefits, most importantly, they learned that there is no security in the workplace. This violation produced resentment, bitterness, and, ultimately, a failure of trust. Indeed, many of these workers asserted that they have learned not to trust anyone—not their union, their company, or their government. They are alienated and isolated. They argued that they have to look out for themselves and their families, and were proud to be able to do that. Their response was not completely selfish, however; they expressed concern for others who had not fared as well, for working people "like me" or "like my son," and for the country as a whole. They also asserted how they think things ought to be. In particular, the country ought to be preserving jobs for "people like me."

Many investigations into the individual effects of deindustrialization focus primarily on the harmful effects in people's lives. Although many people, including those in this study, experienced significant losses due to deindustrialization, scholarly and media portrayals often paint them as passive victims. Clearly, individuals in this study emphasized their agency and stressed their active roles. Their experiences and narratives show us something about how people accommodate loss. But more importantly, these narratives show us what people really value or how they come to adapt what they value. They find compensation for the loss of high wages in the autonomy, skill, respect, and healthy conditions their new jobs offer. In part, this is a generation of people caught in a transition between heavy industrial manufacturing and a new, high-tech, service- and information-based economy. Consequently, they find themselves navigating divergent sets of values—between the nominal solidarity and security of an industrial culture and the insecure, individualized world of service and high-tech work. Finding themselves at odds with new economic realities, it is not surprising they should feel alienated. Channeling the social concern workers maintain for their fellow employees and their country in a way that overcomes this cynicism and reintegrates them into the body politic will require addressing the lack of security and trust that are at the root of this alienation.

NOTES

Foreword

1. "The Reindustrialization of America," *Business Week* (special issue), 30 June 1980, 58.

2. Organization for Economic Cooperation and Development, as reported in Leonard Silk, "The Ailing Economy: Diagnoses and Prescriptions," *New York Times*, 4 April 1982, 4E.

3. Barry Bluestone and Bennett Harrison, *Growing Prosperity: The Battle for Growth with Equity in the Twenty-first Century* (Berkeley: University of California Press, 2001), 81, figure 3.6.

4. These statistics were calculated from the Council of Economic Advisers, *Economic Report of the President, 1986* (Washington, D.C.: U.S. Government Printing Office, 1986); Council of Economic Advisers, "Economic Indicators" (Washington, D.C.: U.S. Government Printing Office, September 1986); and U.S. Department of Commerce, Bureau of Economic Analysis, *Survey of Current Business* 67, no. 4 (April 1987). The statistics also appear in table 1.1 in Bennett Harrison and Barry Bluestone, *The Great U-Turn: Corporate Restructuring and the Polarizing of America* (New York: Basic Books, 1988), 9.

5. Reported in the Council of Economic Advisers, *Economic Report of the President, 1981* (Washington, D.C.: U.S. Government Printing Office, 1981), 71.

6. Barry Bluestone and Bennett Harrison, *The Deindustrialization of America: Plant Closings, Community Abandonment, and the Dismantling of Basic Industry* (New York: Basic Books, 1982), 9.

7. Louis Jacobson, "Earnings Losses of Workers Displaced from Manufacturing Industries," in *The Impact of International Trade and Investment on Employment*, ed. William G. Dewald (Washington, D.C.: U.S. Government Printing Office, 1978).

8. Matthew P. Drennan, *The Information Economy and American Cities* (Baltimore: Johns Hopkins University Press, 2002), 9.

9. For pessimistic forecasts during the early 1990s, see Paul Krugman, *The Age of Diminished Expectations* (Cambridge: MIT Press, 1990); and Jeffrey Madrick, *The End of Affluence: The Causes and Consequences of America's Economic Dilemma* (New York: Random House, 1995).

10. Bluestone and Harrison, *Growing Prosperity*, 28, table 2.1.

11. Alejandro Bodip-Memba, "Consumer Confidence Hits 32-Year High," *Wall Street Journal*, 24 February 1999, A2.

12. For a more detailed treatment of this phenomenon, see Barry Bluestone, "Forget Bush and Gore; Our Economy Needs Another Khrushchev," *The Chronicle of Higher Education*, 5 January 2001, sec. 2.

13. It is important to recognize the critical role of the federal government in stimulating the information revolution. Underwriting the initial development costs of the new technology were investments the federal government made in basic research and in education and training beginning in the late 1950s and early 1960s. Massive computing power

stuffed into the cramped quarters of missile nose cones was needed to guide international ballistic missiles (ICBMs) and space rockets. Accordingly, the government paid for the development of the first integrated circuits and microprocessors. Software was needed for the instruction sets for these minicomputers and the government paid for this as well. The personal computer and all that followed descended directly from these federally sponsored cold war research projects. Later, it was investment by the Department of Defense in the ARPANET that led to the modern-day Internet and the World Wide Web. Without these investments, today's ubiquitous e-commerce would never have come about—or at least would have been delayed by decades. Moreover, the money the federal government poured into science and math education after the launching of *Sputnik* in 1957 was critical for preparing a generation of scientists and engineers who developed all the new technology.

14. Council of Economic Advisers, *Economic Indicators*, March 1999; and Council of Economic Advisers, *Economic Report of the President, 1998* (Washington, D.C.: U.S. Government Printing Office, 1998).

15. Council of Economic Advisers, *Economic Report of the President, 1996*, 297, table B-15.

16. U.S. Department of Commerce, Bureau of Economic Analysis, "Real Gross Domestic Product by Industry in Chained (1996) Dollars, 1987–2000" (Washington, D.C.: U.S. Government Printing Office, 2000).

17. U.S. Department of Commerce, "Real Gross Domestic Product."

18. Council of Economic Advisers, *Economic Report of the President, 1998*; and Council of Economic Advisers, *Economic Indicators*, January 2003.

Introduction: The Meanings of Industrialization

1. Dale Maharidge and Michael Williamson, *Journey to Nowhere: The Saga of the New Underclass* (1985; reprint, New York: Hyperion 1996), 17, 20.

2. For a fine discussion of Homestead's transformation, see Lori Delale's prize-winning senior honors thesis, "Twelve Smokestacks in a Strip Mall: Homestead, Pennsylvania and the Rise of the Postindustrial Landscape" (School of Industrial and Labor Relations, Cornell University, 2002); for the pre–strip mall history, see William S. Serrin, *Homestead: The Glory and the Tragedy of an American Steel Town* (New York: Times Books, 1992).

3. The literature on deindustrialization is immense. By 1985, there were 820 entries in *Plant Closings: A Selected Bibliography* (Ithaca: Martin P. Catherwood Library, Cornell University, 1987). Barry Bluestone and Bennett Harrison's *The Deindustrialization of America: Plant Closings, Community Abandonment, and the Dismantling of Basic Industry* (New York: Basic Books, 1982) remains the touchstone of the discussion for the 1980s; this work can be rounded out with the many viewpoints in Paul D. Staudohar and Holly E. Brown, eds., *Deindustrialization and Plant Closure* (Lexington, Mass.: Lexington Books, 1987). A small selection of the current historical and sociological understandings includes: Thomas J. Sugrue, *The Origins of the Urban Crisis: Race and Inequality in Postwar Detroit* (Princeton: Princeton University Press, 1996), which rethinks race and the timing of the process; Judith Stein, *Running Steel, Running America: Race, Economic Policy, and the Decline of Liberalism* (Chapel Hill: University of North Carolina Press, 1998), which takes an extended look at the politics of the problem; Ruth Milkman, *Farewell to the Factory: Auto Workers in the Late Twentieth Century* (Berkeley: University of California Press, 1997), which questions the meanings of plant shutdowns; and Jefferson Cowie, *Capital Moves: RCA's Seventy-Year Quest for Cheap Labor* (Ithaca: Cornell University Press, 1999; reprint, New York: New

Press, 2001), which looks at the timing, causation, and regional variance of plant openings and closings.

4. For a quantitative explanation of manufacturing employment trends, see Steven J. Davis, John C. Haltiwanger, and Scott Schuh, *Job Creation and Destruction* (Cambridge: MIT Press, 1997).

5. Bluestone and Harrison, *Deindustrialization of America*, 6, 11.

6. Nelson Lichtenstein, "Class Politics and the State during World War Two," *International Labor and Working Class History* 58 (fall 2000): 270.

7. Jack Metzgar, "Blue-Collar Blues: The Deunionization of Manufacturing," *New Labor Forum* (spring/summer 2002): 20–23.

8. Milkman, *Farewell to the Factory*, 12.

9. We use the term "new American workplace" broadly to refer to the many changes in work organization as documented in Eileen Appelbaum and Rosemary Batt, *The New American Workplace: Transforming Work Systems in the United States* (Ithaca: Cornell University Press, 1994).

1. "A Trail of Ghost Towns across Our Land"

1. "Old 'Carpet Shop' Plans Issue," *Business Week*, 16 March 1946, 66–67; Sophie Greenblatt, "The History and Development of the Carpet Industry in Yonkers" (M.A. thesis, Columbia University, 1937), 29.

2. For the early period of Smith involvement in Yonkers, see "For a Workingman's Model Club," *New York Times* (hereafter cited as *NYT*), 3 April 1896, 8; Rev. Charles Elmer Allison, *The History of Yonkers, Westchester County, New York* (1896; reprint, Harrison, N.Y.: Harbor Hill, 1984), 331; and "Academic Choices Plus High Standards of Excellence," in *Yonkers Chamber of Commerce Centennial Book, 1893–1993*, by Yonkers Chamber of Commerce (Wilmington, Del.: Suburban Marketing Associates, 1993), 80. For the later period, see "Dunn Lauded for Community Service," *The News* (Alexander Smith) 6, no. 5 (19 April 1950): 5, in "Employers File 1943–1952, Alexander-Smith, General (1949–1950)" folder, box 4, series B, file 4B, MSS 129A, Textile Workers Union of America Records (hereafter cited as TWUA Records), State Historical Society of Wisconsin, Madison; and "Promotion Committee Begins Work for Community Chest," Yonkers *Herald-Statesman* (hereafter cited as *H-S*), 15 September 1952, in "Community Chest" folder, Yonkers vertical files (hereafter cited as YVF), Yonkers Public Library, Getty Square Branch, Yonkers, N.Y.

3. Jack A. Tupper, "The Impact of the Relocation of the Alexander Smith Carpet Company upon the Municipal Government of the City of Yonkers, New York" (M.A. thesis, New York University, 1963), 16–17; "New York Central, Raised $3 Million, Becomes City's Largest Taxpayer," *H-S*, 1 September 1954, in "Taxation" folder, YVF.

4. "Old 'Carpet Shop' Plans Issue."

5. Susan Levine, "'Honor Each Noble Maid': Women Workers and the Yonkers Carpet Weavers' Strike of 1885," *New York History* 62, no. 2 (April 1981): 153–76 (quotes, 163–65).

6. Donald L. Grant, "A Case in Collective Bargaining: The Alexander Smith and Sons Carpet Company, Incorporated, and Local 122 of the Textile Workers Union of America, C.I.O." (senior thesis, Princeton University, 1941), 48–50.

7. For employment conditions, see "Smith Carpet Mills Resume Full-Time," Yonkers Chamber of Commerce *Yonkers Progress* (hereafter cited as *YP*) 4 (May 1929): 9; "Factory Payrolls Rise Here," *YP* 11 (August 1936): 5; and Richard A. Lester and Edward A. Robie, *Constructive Labor Relations: Experience in Four Firms* (Princeton, N.J.: Industrial

Relations Section, Department of Economics and Social Institutions, Princeton University, 1948), 20. For tax breaks, see "Relieving Industry," *YP* 5 (November–December 1930): 10; "Assessments Cut for Trade, Industry," *YP* 8 (October 1933): 9; and "Ask Lower Valuation," *Carpet and Upholstery Trade Review and Rug Trade Review* 67 (15 November 1936): 17.

8. Affidavit of Maitland L. Griggs, 5 March 1936, 4, in case no. E-82-229, *Alexander Smith and Sons Carpet Co. vs. Herrick et al.*, record group 21, Records of District Courts of the United States, National Archives and Records Administration, Northeast Region, New York, N.Y.

9. "Employees of Alexander Smith and Sons Awarded Army-Navy E November 23," *Rug Profits* (hereafter cited as *RP*) 32 (December 1943): 46.

10. Lester and Robie, *Constructive Labor Relations*, 32; minutes, Carpet and Rug Division Advisory Council, 14 January 1944, 1, in "Rug and Carpet Conference 1944" folder, box 2, series A, file 1A, MSS 129A, TWUA Records; Charles Hughes to Emil Rieve, 21 June 1945, in "Alexander Smith/General 1944–45" folder, box 96, MSS 396, TWUA Records.

11. See untitled document, Personnel Office, "Active 50 Year Employees," 22 October 1945, in "Alex Smith and Sons Carpet Co./Employees—Length of Service" folder; and "Rug Mill Grants Union Shop and General Payrise," *H-S*, 27 October 1945 (quote), in "Newspaper Clippings 1936–1956" folder; both in Alexander Smith Company Archives (hereafter cited as ASCA), Hudson River Museum of Westchester County, Yonkers, N.Y.

12. See "Sloane-Blabon Purchased by Smith Carpet," *Retailing Home Furnishings*, 6 November 1944; and Alexander Smith and Sons Carpet Company and Its Subsidiary, Sloane-Blabon Corporation, *1948 *Review and Preview* 1949*, 12; both in "Alexander Smith, Yonkers, N.Y., Financial no. 1 and General (thru 1949)" folder, box 343, MSS 396, TWUA Records. See also "Sloane-Blabon Announces $9,000,000 Expansion Program to Double Output," *RP* 41 (February 1948): 56.

13. "The Carpet Shop Will Be At Home . . . ," *The News* 4, no. 1 (19 November 1947): 4, in "Alex Smith, The News" folder, box 343, MSS 396, TWUA Records.

14. Alexander Smith and Sons Carpet Company, *Annual Report 1950*, 15, in "Industries—Alexander Smith Inc." folder, YVF.

15. Tami J. Friedman, "Communities in Competition: Capital Migration and Plant Relocation in the U.S. Carpet Industry, 1929–1975" (Ph.D. diss., Columbia University, 2001), 64–65, 66.

16. Lester and Robie, *Constructive Labor Relations*, 31.

17. Leaflet, TWUA, "Workers of the Carpet and Rug Industry," n.d., in "Carpet and Rug Conference 1946" folder, box 2, series A, file 1A, MSS 129A, TWUA Records; TWUA, "A Review of the Carpet and Rug Industry," 24 May 1946, 5, in "Industry Memorandum Vol. VI, 4. Industry Economic Analysis, C. Carpet and Rug" binder, box 4, M88-324, TWUA Records; "New Wage Increases Halt Strike Threat," *RP* 41 (June 1948): 118. Adjustments for inflation calculated by author using Consumer Price Index, in U.S. Department of Commerce, Bureau of the Census, *Historical Statistics of the United States, Colonial Times to 1970*, pt. 1 (Washington, D.C.: U.S. Government Printing Office, 1975), 210 (series E, 135–66).

18. Handwritten note, "Huddlemen and Section Hands of Narrow Vel-Wide Vel.," to [Jack] Rubenstein, 18 December 1945, in "Organizational Files, 1943–1948, Locals 96–129, N.Y. State, Local No. 122" folder, box 3, series B, file 3B, MSS 129A, TWUA Records.

19. Friedman, "Communities in Competition," 70–71.

20. "Giant of the Hudson Valley: Fourth Ranking Industrial City of State, Yonkers Leads World in Carpet, Elevator Production," New York State Department of Labor *Industrial Bulletin*, January 1949, 13, 15, in "General" folder, YVF.

21. See "A.F.L.-C.I.O. Group Assails City's New Labor Commission," *H-S*, 12 January 1949, in "Politics and Government" folder; and "County A.F.L. Seats Acropolis for New Term," *H-S*, 12 January 1950, in "Labor" folder; both in YVF.

22. "Men Meet, Vote Again to Stay Out," *H-S*, 2 March 1949, in "Labor" clippings packet, YVF; "Hughes on Political Bosses, Calls Them Tinpot Hitlers," *Yonkers Record*, 4 September 1949, in "Local No. 122, Yonkers, 1948–56" folder, box 504, MSS 396, TWUA Records.

23. See "Meet the First Ward Candidates," *H-S*, 24 October 1949; "Meet the Third Ward's Candidates for Office," *H-S*, 26 October 1949; "Meet the Fifth Ward Candidates," *H-S*, 28 October 1949; and "Elected as Members of Yonkers' Next Common Council," *H-S*, 9 November 1949; all in "Elections" clippings packet, YVF.

24. *Bulletin*, no. 19 (9 March 1940), in "Committee of 100" folder, YVF; "Annual Report," *YP* 15 (December 1940): 3; Marshall Beuick, "One Hundred Men and a City," *Nation's Business* 28 (November 1940), 68–69.

25. See Harrison E. Salisbury, "Schools Are Clue to Yonkers' Pains," *NYT*, 20 April 1955, 1. See also City of Yonkers, *Annual Report of the City Manager, 1955 . . .*, in "City Reports" folder; William J. Wallin, *Can We Have Faith in Yonkers? An Address . . . May 24, 1955*, distributed by Ralph B. Feriola, 27 May 1955, 10, in "General" folder; and William L. Bookman, "Yonkers Is Looking Ahead—And Up: How Can It Improve Bus Service?" *H-S*, 3 February 1955, in "General" folder; all in YVF.

26. See booklet, Alexander Smith and Sons Carpet Company, *100 Years of Carpeting America, 1845 . . . 1945*, n.d. [1946?], in untitled folder [Business—Alexander Smith], YVF. See also "Higher Water Rates Loom Here and in County, Parley Decides," *H-S*, 12 December 1947; and "Lighting Company, Carpet Mill Assessments Raised Sharply," *H-S*, 1 September 1948; both in "Taxation" folder, YVF.

27. Friedman, "Communities in Competition," 156–58, 196–97.

28. Ernest J. Hopkins, *Mississippi's BAWI Plan: Balance Agriculture With Industry: An Experiment in Industrial Subsidization* (Atlanta: Federal Reserve Bank of Atlanta, 1944), 9, 19–20, 29; James C. Cobb, *The Selling of the South: The Southern Crusade for Industrial Development, 1936–1990*, 2d ed. (Urbana: University of Illinois, 1993), 15, 21–22; Jack Edward Prince, "History and Development of the Mississippi Balance Agriculture With Industry Program, 1936–1958" (Ph.D. diss., Ohio State University, 1961), 153–54.

29. "Ads Dispel False Notions about Mississippi," *Sales Management* 61 (10 November 1948): 166.

30. David Markstein, "Advertising Helps to Balance State's Agriculture with Its Industry," *Printers Ink* 214 (1 March 1946): 78, 80; Agricultural and Industrial Board, *State of Mississippi: Balancing Agriculture with Industry: Second Report to the Legislature . . . (Biennium 1946–1948)*, 12–13, in Mississippi Department of Archives and History (hereafter cited as MDAH), Jackson, Miss.; "How to Sell a State via New York Office," *Sales Management* 59 (15 July 1947): 94.

31. For World War II, see Friedman, "Communities in Competition," 122–23, 137–38. For the Korean War, see U.S. Congress, Joint Committee on Defense Production, *Defense Production Act: Progress Report—No. 18: Hearing . . .*, 82d Cong., 1st sess., 6 February 1952, 899–933.

32. "Defense Production Act of 1950," *Congressional Quarterly Almanac* 6 (1950): 624; "Revenue Act of 1950," *Congressional Quarterly Almanac* 6 (1950): 574–75; "Tax Write-Offs, Defense Loans," *Congressional Quarterly Almanac* 7 (1951): 496–97; TWUA, "Statement of the [TWUA] . . . before the House Committee on Ways and Means on the Need for Revision of the Internal Revenue Code of 1954 Relating to Carryovers of Net Operating Losses . . . ," F-96, supp. 4 (rev.), 30 January 1958, 2–6, 8, in "Research Dept 1958" folder, box 606, MSS 396, TWUA Records.

33. Harold C. Zulauf, interview by Rosalie Flynn, draft transcript, Yorktown Heights, N.Y., 20 April 1983, in "Alex. Smith and Sons Carpet Co./H. Zulauf Oral History 1983" folder, ASCA.

34. Leonard C. Yaseen, Fantus Factory Locating Service, to William F. C. Ewing, Executive Vice-President, Alexander Smith and Sons Carpet Company, initial survey of sites, 22 June 1950, photocopy in author's possession, courtesy of Deloitte and Touche, Chicago.

35. Herbert J. Potts, interview by author, tape recording, Fair Hope, Ala., 2 and 3 March 1996.

36. Leonard C. Yaseen, Fantus Factory Locating Service, New York, N.Y., to William F. C. Ewing, Executive Vice-President, Alexander Smith and Sons Carpet Company, report on Greenville, Miss., 2 August 1950, 5, photocopy in author's possession, courtesy of Deloitte and Touche, Chicago; Washington County Chamber of Commerce, Industrial Committee, "Presenting Greenville, Mississippi . . . Its Facilities and Resources," n.d. [1947?], in MDAH.

37. Potts, interview.

38. "Officials Exuberant at Overwhelming Vote Given to Bond Issue," *Delta Democrat-Times* (hereafter cited as *DD-T*), 16 January 1951, 1, in *Scrapbook, 1950–1953*, vol. 2, George F. Archer Papers, William Alexander Percy Memorial Library (hereafter cited as WAPML), Greenville, Miss.

39. See "Greenville [Miss.] Mills—Delta Civic Achievement," *America's Textile Reporter*, 30 September 1954, 10; "Greenville Mills," *Textile Age*, January 1955, 6, 10; and Kenneth Bache, "Smith Output 50% Capacity in Greenville," *Retailing Daily*, 7 December 1954; all in "Alexander Smith, Inc., Greenville, Miss." folder, box 343; and Dewitt C. Morrill, "Alexander Smith Expects to Be in the Black by July for First Time in Five Years, after Overhauling Operation," *Wall Street Journal*, 9 February 1955, in "Alexander Smith—Newspaper Clippings" folder, box 96; all in MSS 396, TWUA Records.

40. For Yonkers, see TWUA, "Survey of Key Jobs in Carpet and Rug Industry, Hourly and Base Rate and Average Straight-Time Piece Work (a) Earnings, December 1951," W-42, in "Carpet Industry Negotiations 1952" folder, box 139, M86-019; minutes, Carpet Conference, 27 March 1953, 7, in "Carpet Conference—Fri., March 27, 1953, 6–7, TWUA Headquarters—2nd Floor—N.Y.C." folder, box 608, MSS 396; and "Agreement between Alexander Smith, Incorporated, and Textile Workers Union of America (CIO) (Production and Maintenance Workers)," 1 August 1952, in "Alexander Smith and Sons Carpet Co. Contract File," box 96, MSS 396. For Greenville, see "Wage Schedule, May 26, 1952, Greenville Mills . . . ," attached to memo, Solomon Barkin to Jack Rubenstein, 29 August 1952, in "Economic Statistics" folder, box 507; and Boyd E. Payton to William Pollock, 14 July 1953, in "Alexander Smith, Yonkers, N.Y., Labor IV, 1951–53" folder, box 343; both in MSS 396. All in TWUA Records.

41. Albert Shirley, interview by author, tape recording, Greenville, Miss., 24 January 1996.

42. "Ewing Tells Rotary What Smith Needs to Survive, Prosper, Grow," *H-S*, 16 November 1951, in untitled folder [Business and Industry—Alexander Smith], YVF.

43. "New Smith Mill Modernizing, Ties Plant to City's Future," *H-S*, 4 December 1953, in untitled folder [Business and Industry—Alexander Smith], YVF; "Where Do We Go from Here?" *The News*, April 1953, 2, in "Employee Newsletters 1950s" folder, ASCA.

44. Friedman, "Communities in Competition," 210–11.

45. Alexander Smith, *Financial Report for the Six Months Ended June 30, 1952*, 11 August 1952, in "Alexander Smith, Yonkers, N.Y., Financial and General II, 1950–" folder, box 343, MSS 396, TWUA Records; minutes, Carpet Conference, 18 October 1952, 10, in "Carpet and Rug Conference 1952" folder, box 2, series A, file 1A, MSS 129A, TWUA Records; "Major Company Objectives in Current Contract Negotiations," 26 May 1952, in "Alexander Smith and Sons/Yonkers, N.Y. (Local 122, unaffiliated)" folder, box 96, MSS 396, TWUA Records; untitled document [Smith's 1954 contract proposals for production and maintenance workers], in "Alex. Smith and Sons Carpet Co./Walkout, Strike, and Closing, 1954" folder, ASCA.

46. See "$500,000 Project Gives Smith Company Straight-Line Production in Velvet Mill," *H-S*, 23 February 1954, in "Business and Industry—Smith Carpet" folder, YVF. See also "225 Quit Work at Smith Mill after Union Steward Is Fired," *H-S*, 26 February 1954; and "Smith Mill Absentees Going Back," *H-S*, 4 March 1954; both in "Labor" clippings packets, YVF. See also "Deadlock Continues in Rug Mill," *H-S*, 1 March 1954, in "Alex. Smith and Sons Carpet Co./Walkout, Strike, and Closing, 1954" folder, ASCA.

47. "Yonkers Schools Called 'Shocking,'" *NYT*, 25 March 1954, 31; Harrison E. Salisbury, "Changing Economy Jars Yonkers, Unprepared for Swift Transition," *NYT*, 18 April 1955, 1; Salisbury, "Schools Are Clue to Yonkers' Pains."

48. For spending, see TWUA, "Alexander Smith Inc., Notes on Stockholders' Meeting of 4/15/52," 15 April 1952, in "Alexander Smith, Yonkers, N.Y., Financial and General II, 1950–" folder, box 343, MSS 396, TWUA Records; and "Ewing Predicts Gains in 1952, Profit-Wise, for Carpet Mills," *H-S*, 16 April 1952, in "Business—Alexander Smith" folder, YVF.

49. See Alexander Smith Incorporated, *Annual Report 1951*, 3; *Annual Report 1952*, 1; *Annual Report 1953*, 1; and *Annual Report 1954*, 3; all in "Alexander Smith, Yonkers, N.Y., Financial and General II, 1950–" folder, box 343, MSS 396, TWUA Records. See also "Sale Nets Smith Firm $9.1 Million," *H-S*, 14 May 1953, in untitled folder [Business and Industry—Alexander Smith], YVF.

50. "Alexander Smith Drops Common Stock Par to $5," *H-S*, 21 May 1954, in untitled folder [Business—Alexander Smith], YVF.

51. "Hughes Breaks Off Talks with Smith Conferees," *H-S*, 13 May 1954, in "Industry—Labor" folder, YVF; "Resolution of Carpet Conference," 14 May 1954 (quote), in "Carpet and Rug Conference 1954" folder, box 2, series A, file 1A, MSS 129A, TWUA Records.

52. Advertisement, "A Lesson in Failure: The Story of Alexander Smith Inc." (TWUA), *NYT*, 1 July 1954, 16; editorial, "Industrial Shut-Downs," *NYT*, 2 July 1954, in "Local No. 122/Alexander Smith, Inc., Yonkers, N.Y." folder, box 609, MSS 396, TWUA Records.

53. Tupper, "Impact of the Relocation," 1 (quote).

54. See "Unemployed in Yonkers Up 125% in Year," *H-S*, 2 April 1954, 18, in "Elections" clippings packet; and "Labor Force Here 67,621," *H-S*, 13 March 1953, in "Labor" clippings packet; both in YVF.

55. See "State Employment Service Places 2,400 Former Smith Employes in Jobs," *H-S*, 4 December 1954, 14, in "Business—Alexander Smith" folder; "Four Syndicates Bid for Purchase of Smith Mills Here, Kennedy Says," *H-S*, 15 October 1954, in "Industries" folder; and "Program Framed to Help Idled Smith Workers," *H-S*, 29 June 1954, 1, in "Business and Industry—Smith Carpet" folder; all in YVF.

56. Tupper, "Impact of the Relocation," 14, 17.

57. "Smith Carpet Concern Is Unyielding on Plan to Close Its Plant in Yonkers," *NYT*, 26 June 1954, in "Business and Industry—Smith Carpet" folder, YVF.

58. See "Union Plea to Mill Fails," *H-S*, 26 June 1954, in "Business and Industry—Smith Carpet" folder, YVF; "Yonkers Will Push Carpet Plant Fight," *NYT*, 27 June 1954, 56; "State Acts to Keep Factory in Yonkers," *NYT*, 29 June 1954, 27; and TWUA Local 122, "Petition" (to Board of Directors, Alexander Smith, Inc.), attached to news release, 30 June 1954, in "Local No. 122/Alexander Smith, Inc., Yonkers, N.Y." folder, box 60, MSS 396, TWUA Records.

59. "Smith Officials Reiterate Plan to Close Plant," *Retailing Daily*, 1 July 1954, in "Alexander Smith, Yonkers, N.Y., Labor No. 5, 1954–" folder, box 343, MSS 396, TWUA Records.

60. See William Pollock to R. L. Waterman, 11 August 1954, in untitled accordion file, box 96; and "Alex. Smith Paid $597,609 for New Mill," *Retailing Daily*, 23 July 1954, in "Alexander Smith, Inc., Liberty, S.C." folder, box 343; both in MSS 396, TWUA Records.

61. Hugh White, "Address of Governor Hugh White at the Daytona Beach, Florida, Chamber of Commerce," 29 January 1953, 2, in "Speeches, 1953" folder, series 960, Governors Records, RG 27, State Records, MDAH.

62. "Community Committee Is Organized to Help City through Smith Crisis," *H-S*, 15 July 1954, in "Business—Alexander Smith" folder, YVF.

63. See "Early Sale of Smith Mill Forecast by Kennedy," *H-S*, 17 February 1955, in untitled folder [Business and Industry—Alexander Smith]; and "Syndicate Buys Smith Plant," *H-S*, 3 June 1955, in untitled folder [Business—Alexander Smith]; both in YVF.

64. Editorial, "Let's Try to Head Off an Industrial 'Forest Fire,'" *H-S*, July 1954, in "Business and Industry" folder, YVF.

65. "Smith Set to Open for 3-Month Wind-Up," *H-S*, 8 July 1954, 1 (quote), in "Business and Industry—Smith Carpet" folder, YVF.

66. See "5 Rockefeller Sons 'Interested' in Smith Mills, Kennedy Reveals," *H-S*, 16 September 1954, in untitled folder [Business and Industry—Alexander Smith]; and "State Study Shows Smith Workers Have Varied Skills for New Jobs," *H-S*, 28 September 1954, 8, in "Labor" clippings packet; both in YVF.

67. See "Syndicate Buys Smith Plant," *H-S*, 3 June 1955, and "120 Inquiries Reported on Rug Mill Space," *H-S*, June 1955, both in untitled folder [Business—Alexander Smith], YVF.

68. See "Hill Mfg. Corp. Moving to Yonkers," *H-S*, 2 August 1955, in "Business" folder. See also "Factory of 125 Employes Buys 2 Smith Buildings," *H-S*, 22 September 1954; "Big Smith Building Sold," *H-S*, 6 October 1955; "Auto Battery Makers Lease Rug Mill Space," *H-S*, 8 March 1956; "Brief Case Makers Buy a Carpet Shop Building," *H-S*, 8 February 1956; and "Tea Firm Buys Building in Former Smith Plant," *H-S*, 14 October 1955; all in untitled folder [Business and Industry—Alexander Smith]. See also "Pharmaceutical Co. Rents Two Floors in Carpet Mill," *H-S*, 18 April 1955, in untitled folder [Business—Alexander Smith]. All in YVF.

69. See "Firms Which Moved Here See Red in Carpet Shop," *H-S*, 12 October 1957, 5, in "Business and Industry—Smith Carpet" folder; and "Bassons Plastic Firm Here Folds," *H-S*, 28 January 1958, in "Industries" folder; both in YVF.

70. See "Otis Says It Wants to Stay in Yonkers but Can Do So Only If Its Costs Are Cut," *H-S*, 15 January 1955; "Otis Sets a New High Record in Selling Its Products," *H-S*, 26 March 1954; and "Otis '55 Profits at All-Time High," *H-S*, 23 March 1956; all in "Business—Otis Elevator" folder, YVF.

71. See "Workers Adopt Otis Plan 3 to 1," *H-S*, 22 February 1955; and "Editorial Comment . . . Otis Management and Union Give Us a Lift," *H-S*, 24 February 1955 (quote); both in "Business—Otis Elevator" folder, YVF.

72. Friedman, "Communities in Competition," 292–94.

73. "Firms Which Moved Here See Red in Carpet Shop"; "Bassons Plastic Firm Here Folds."

74. Wallin, *Can We Have Faith in Yonkers?* 10 (quote).

75. "Firms Which Moved Here See Red in Carpet Shop."

76. "Firms in Old Smith Plant Form Unit to Fight Abuses," *H-S*, 17 October 1957, 11, in "Business and Industry—Smith Carpet" folder, YVF.

77. Harrison E. Salisbury, "Choice of Future Is up to Yonkers," *NYT*, 21 April 1955; Wallin, *Can We Have Faith in Yonkers?* 10.

78. See William I. Bookman, "Yonkers Is Looking Ahead—And Up: Does It Need a Housing Act for Industry?" *H-S*, 5 February 1955, in "General" folder; and "Big Task Faces Yonkers Getting Sites for Industry," *H-S*, 13 January 1956, in "Business" folder; both in YVF.

79. Yonkers City Planning Board, *General Guide Plan for the City of Yonkers, New York*, 31 January 1958, 25–26, in "Planning" folder, YVF; Yonkers City Planning Board, *Land Use and Community Facilities Plan for the City of Yonkers*, 21 June 1961, 14, 16, 4; Oxie Reichler, "Yonkers Young Again," *Westchester Commerce and Industry*, 18 January 1966, 32A, in "Economic Conditions" folder, YVF.

80. Friedman, "Communities in Competition," 323–24.

81. "Stewart Stamping Wins Go Ahead for Extension," *H-S*, 13 December 1963, in "Zoning" folder, YVF.

82. "Shrimp Firm Granted Right to Expand Here," *H-S*, 8 July 1964, in "Zoning" folder, YVF.

83. See "Otis' New Plant at Bloomington to Be Built on a 150-Acre Farm," *H-S*, 16 October 1963, in "Industries—Otis Elevator Co." folder; and "Yonkers—Big, But Tax-Balanced," *H-S*, 21 January [1964], in "General" folder. See also "Otis Rumor Reaches City Hall," *H-S*, 8 July 1964; "Indiana Plant Won't Replace Yonkers One, Otis Tells City," *H-S*, [10?] July 1964; "Otis to Lay Off 550 in Yonkers," *NYT*, 16 March 1965; and Eileen Campion, "The Big Move," *H-S*, 15 October 1965; all in "Business—Otis Elevator" folder. All in YVF.

84. See "Chamber and City to Discuss Zoning, Taxes for Industry," *H-S*, 30 November 1965, 4; Dave Hartley, "Industrial Revolution Here?" *H-S*, 9 December 1965; and Dave Hartley, "Chamber Warns City to Attract Industry without a Tax Break," *H-S*, 26 November 1965; all in "Business" folder, YVF.

85. "Yonkers Trying Hard to Get New Industry," *H-S*, 18 November 1965, in "Business" folder, YVF.

86. See Elder Gunter, City Manager, to Honorable Mayor and [City Council] Members, 15 November 1968, in City of Yonkers, *City of Yonkers Budget, 1969*, 7, 8, 13; and

James Andover, "Will 70s Widen City's Industrial Tax Base?" *H-S*, 10 February 1970, in "Industries" folder; both in YVF.

87. Hartley, "Chamber Warns City"; Reichler, "Yonkers Young Again."

88. See Gwen Hall, "Is Yonkers a City of Empty Dreams?" *H-S*, 6 March 1968; and Gwen Hall, "New Zoning Map Could Foster Growth," *H-S*, 7 March 1968; both in "Business and Industry" folder. See also Gwen Hall, "City Offers No Inducements," *H-S*, 8 March 1968, in "Industry" folder. All in YVF.

89. See James Andover, "'New Age': 15-Story Building Approved," *H-S*, 11 April 1968, in "Business and Industry" folder; Howard Smith, "Gestetner Rezone Okayed," *H-S*, 3 July 1968, in "Zoning" folder; Carmel Marchionni, "Gestetner Breaks Ground for Future Headquarters," *H-S*, 21 October 1969, in "Industries" folder; and James J. Andover, "Master Plan Opposed by Large Firms," *H-S*, 24 May 1968, in "Zoning" folder; all in YVF.

90. Friedman, "Communities in Competition," 339–340.

91. See Brian Gallagher, "City Renewal: $11.4 Million," *H-S*, 26 May 1972, in "Urban Renewal" folder. See also "Otis Will Sign Pact with City," *H-S*, 5 June 1972; and Jennie Tritten, "Otis to Unveil Expansion Plan," *H-S*, 6 June 1973; both in "Business—Otis Elevator" folder. See also Franklin Whitehouse, "Yonkers Woos Jobs but Ends Up Jilted," *NYT*, 21 August 1983, in "Industries—Otis Elevator Co." folder. See also Katie Schmitz, "Agencies Grant Approval of 9-Acre Site Expansion," *H-S*, 28 August 1974; and James Feron, "Yonkers Hails Otis as Man Who Gave City a Lift," *NYT*, 25 September [197?]; both in "Business and Industry—Otis Elevator" folder. All in YVF.

92. Franklin Whitehouse, "Yonkers' War over Otis Gathers Force," [*NYT*?], 12 December 1982, in "Industries" folder, YVF.

93. See Katie Schmitz, "Otis Plants New Future," *H-S*, 17 October 1974, in "Business—Otis Elevator" folder; and "Otis to Lay Off 100 Here," *H-S*, 8 January 1975, in "Employment" folder. See also Jennie Tritten, "Otis, CPC Plan to Fire 183," *H-S*, 22 September 1975; and "Otis Elevator Co. to Lay Off 78," *H-S*, 12 January 1977; both in "Business—Otis Elevator" folder. All in YVF.

94. Franklin Whitehouse, "Yonkers' War Over Otis Gathers Force."

95. Friedman, "Communities in Competition," 139–149, 160–65, 212–35, 375–86, 417–19.

96. Ibid., 386–95, 407–15, 421–35.

97. Ibid., 395–403, 415–21, 435–37.

98. See Mary Dixon, "Greenville's Largest Employer May Close," Jackson, Miss., *Clarion-Ledger*, 4 June 1986; and Mary Dixon, "2 Washington County Firms Planning Major Expansions," *Clarion-Ledger*, 21 March 1986; both in "Greenville—Commerce and Industry" folder, subject files, MDAH. See also "County Designated as Enterprise Zone," *DD-T*, 21 February 1986, 1, in "Washington Co.—History" folder, vertical files, WAPML.

99. Friedman, "Communities in Competition," 320, 335–336.

100. Jennie Tritten, "Business Unit Hits 'Red Tape,'" *H-S*, 13 February 1974, in "Business and Industry" folder, YVF.

101. See "Company Announces Layoffs," *H-S*, 10 January 1975, in "Employment" folder. See also Carolyn Weiner, "Mayor Asks Klein's Meeting," *H-S*, 12 June 1974; "Western Electric Site for Sale," *H-S*, 8 March 1976; and "Anaconda Loss Latest in Series of Area Setbacks," *H-S*, 21 May 1975; all in "Business and Industry" folder. All in YVF.

102. Yonkers Chamber of Commerce, *Centennial Book*, 101, 43–44.

103. James Feron, "Yonkers Wins State Development Zone," *NYT,* 26 June 1988.

104. Paul Olsen and Ben Lipson, "Firth to Add $22 Million to Mohasco Sales," *Home Furnishings Daily,* 25 August 1961, in "Mohasco" folder, Carpet and Rug Institute Records, Carpet and Rug Institute, Dalton, Ga.; Mohasco Industries, *Annual Report, 1965,* copy in author's possession, courtesy of Herbert Shuttleworth II, Amsterdam, N.Y.

105. Bennett Harrison and Barry Bluestone, *The Great U-Turn: Corporate Restructuring and the Polarizing of America* (New York: Basic Books, 1988), chaps. 1–2.

106. Rachael Kamel, *The Global Factory: Analysis and Action for a New Economic Era* (Philadelphia: American Friends Service Committee, 1990), 7–8.

107. Cobb, *Selling of the South,* 267.

108. Ibid., 281.

109. Friedman, "Communities in Competition," 472; Lee Ragland, "Schwinn Gears Up for Success," Jackson *Clarion-Ledger,* 3 March 1991, in "Greenville—Commerce and Industry" folder, subject files, MDAH.

2. The "Fall" of Reo in Lansing, Michigan, 1955–1975

From *The Story of Reo Joe: Work, Kin, and Community in Autotown, USA* (Temple University Press, forthcoming). I thank Jefferson Cowie and Joseph Heathcott for their skilled editorial help.

1. Tim Martin, "Plans Would Secure 'Car Capital' Status," *Lansing State Journal,* 17 May 1999, 1. The additional interesting subtext here is the story of Flint, where a very damaging GM strike was staged June 1998. Flint obviously did not share in the prospects for new plant production, but had to weather the closing of Buick City. The proposed plants in Lansing will make Cadillacs, Malibus, and a yet undisclosed small car. Cadillac production has begun, but the completion date of one of the plants had been delayed due to a softening economy and a looming energy crisis.

2. One of the first and certainly one of the most important and influential of these works is Daniel Bell, *The Coming of Post-Industrial Society: A Venture in Social Forecasting* (New York: Basic Books, 1973). See also Krishan Kumar, *From Post-Industrial to Post-Modern Society: New Theories of the Contemporary World* (Cambridge, Mass.: Blackwell, 1995); Margaret Rose, *The Post-Modern and the Post-Industrial* (New York: Cambridge University Press, 1991). The work that I have found most helpful is David Harvey, *The Condition of Postmodernity* (Cambridge, Mass.: Blackwell, 1989).

3. In Barry Bluestone and Bennett Harrison, *The Deindustrialization of America: Plant Closings, Community Abandonment, and the Dismantling of Basic Industry* (New York: Basic Books, 1982), the first chapter is entitled "Capital vs. Community."

4. The two ends of the ideological continuum in this debate over the causes of plant closings, the role of government in them, and the effects of mobile capital are represented by Bluestone and Harrison, *Deindustrialization of America;* and Richard B. McKenzie, ed., *Plant Closings: Public or Private Choices?* (Washington, D.C.: Cato Institute, 1984). McKenzie has written several dozen works on a variety of economic issues, including plant closings.

5. An incomplete list might include: Gilda Haas and Plant Closures Project, *Plant Closures: Myths, Realities, and Responses* (pamphlet 3, Boston, Mass.: South End, 1985); Charles Craypo and Bruce Nissen, *Grand Designs: The Impact of Corporate Strategies on Workers, Unions, and Communities* (Ithaca, N.Y.: ILR Press, 1993); Carolyn C. Perrucci, Robert Perrucci, Dena B. Targ, Harry R. Targ, *Plant Closings: International Context and Social Costs* (New York: Aldine de Gruyter, 1988).

6. One of the best critiques of the literature on deindustrialization, a work that asserts the importance of exploring local developments as well as national and global change, is Douglas Koritz, "*Restructuring or Destructuring? Deindustrialization in Two Industrial Heartland Cities,*" *Urban Affairs Quarterly* 26, no. 4 (June 1991): 497–511.

7. Thomas J. Sugrue, *The Origins of the Urban Crisis: Race and Inequality in Postwar Detroit* (Princeton: Princeton University Press, 1996), 127, 128, 271.

8. Ruth Milkman, *Farewell to the Factory: Auto Workers in the Late Twentieth Century* (Berkeley: University of California Press, 1997), 93.

9. Many articles in McKenzie's *Plant Closings* speak to this issue. See, for example: McKenzie, "Business Mobility: Economic Myths and Realities"; James P. Miller, "Manufacturing Relocations in the United States, 1969–1975"; Robert Premux and Rudy Fichtenbaum, "Labor Turnover and the Sunbelt/Frostbelt Controversy: An Empirical Test"; and Bernard L. Weinstein and John Rees, "Sunbelt/Frostbelt Confrontation?" This volume, published by the Cato Institute, evidently in response to repeated efforts to pass a bill in Congress to establish a national policy regarding plant closings, is obviously a profoundly political piece. I have found more useful to my thinking Lloyd Rodwin and Hidehiko Sazanami, eds., *Deindustrialization and Regional Economic Transformation: The Experience of the United States* (Boston: Unwin Hyman, 1989), especially Ann R. Markusen and Virginia Carlson, "Deindustrialization in the American Midwest: Causes and Responses," 29–56.

10. Stephen Cohen and John Zysman, *Manufacturing Matters: The Myth of the Post-Industrial Economy* (New York: Basic Books, 1987), xiii.

11. Joseph S. Sherer Jr., "Reo's Future As I See It," unpublished and undated talk, probably mid-1953, folder 29, box 1, Reo Papers, Michigan State University Archives and Historical Collections (hereafter cited as MSU Archives and Historical Collections), East Lansing, Michigan.

12. See "Let a Power Mower Do It," *Business Week*, 22 March 1953, 33; and "Reo Motors Shows New Products to Be Made When War Work Ends," *New York Times*, 29 January 1953. See also "Reynolds and Company, Stock Department: Daily Statement," *Reo Motors, Incorporated*, 1 May 1952, and 23 July 1952, folder 11, box 3, Reo Papers, MSU Archives and Historical Collections.

13. See Frank Drob to Joseph Sherer, "The Value Line Investment Survey," 15 April 1953, and response from Sherer to Drob, 17 May 1953, folder 50, box 1, Reo Papers, MSU Archives and Historical Collections.

14. Clipping of *New York Times* article, 11 September 1953, folder 9, box 122, Reo Papers, MSU Archives and Historical Collections.

15. In 1953, Reo was apparently a serious competitor for a government rocket project and only needed to establish a rocket research department to get the contract. This would have positioned the company to compete for more high-tech and aerospace contracts, but apparently was never accomplished. See W. M. Walworth to Joseph Sherer, memorandum, "Re: Dr. C. O. Harris, Michigan State College, as an advisor on Rocket Project," 8 January 1953, folder 30, box 4; George Kramer to Joseph Sherer, memorandum, 20 March 1953, folder 35, box 2; and George Kramer to Al Zimmer, memorandum, "Re: Resignation," 26 August 1953, folder 35, box 2; all in Reo Papers, MSU Archives and Historical Collections.

16. See Dollie Beadle, "Reo News," *Lansing Labor News*, 22 April 1954, and 13 May 1954; and "Reo Local Awaits Plant Sale Verdict," *Lansing Labor News*, 1 July 1954, 1.

17. Ed Wright, "Small Press," *Lansing Labor News*, 15 April 1954, 2.

18. *Automotive Industries News Letter,* 1 November 1954, 1, in folder 5, box 1, Reo Papers, MSU Archives and Historical Collections.

19. The high finance involved in this deal was strange and confusing, even for the reporter at *Barron's.* See Walter Mintz, "The Reo Story: It's Recent Sale Is a Puzzling Piece of Corporate Finance," *Barron's,* 10 October 1955, 9.

20. There is ample evidence of this in the Reo Papers. Tooker and all of those who reported to him and to whom he reported in Lansing kept good records. For example, when Tooker became president, Colonel W. A. Call, the office chief of ordnance, Department of the Army, wrote to congratulate his friend in a handwritten letter from the Pentagon. He signed off, "Love to the Family." (Call to Tooker, 9 December 1954, folder 46, box 1, Reo Papers, MSU Archives and Historical Collections.)

21. "Promising Prospects for Independents in Truck Field Shown by Reo Comeback," *Automotive Industries,* 15 January 1956, folder 56, box 23, Reo Papers, MSU Archives and Historical Collections.

22. See "Supplemental Agreement between Reo Motors, Inc. and Local 650 UAW for April 1956": "It is to the mutual benefit of the parties and to the benefit of the employees that the proposal be as competitive as possible and to that end, the Union agrees that the rates to be paid for direct and indirect labor to be performed on this contract for military vehicles resulting from such proposal shall be reduced by 10% from present level" (UAW Local 650 Papers, "Misc. Agreements" folder, box 12, Reuther Library, Wayne State University, Detroit, Michigan).

23. "Reo Items," *Lansing Labor News,* 12 July 1957, 2.

24. "White Motor: 'A' for Agility," *Forbes,* 1 December 1961, 19. White bought and either combined or liquidated Sterling Motor Truck, Autocar, Reo, and Diamond T. See Seymour Melman, ed., *The Defense Economy: Conversion of Industry and Occupations to Civilian Needs* (New York: Praeger, 1970), 400, chart.

25. "White Motor," 21.

26. Zenon C. R. Hansen, *Legend of the Bulldog* (New York: Newcomen Society, 1974), 32. Hansen went on to be the head of Mack Trucks. See also "Heavy Duty, High Gear Merger," *Business Week,* 5 October 1963, 94; and "White Molds the Parts," *Business Week,* 16 October 1965, 159.

27. "White Motor Unit Sold to Industrialist: Price Said to Be $15 Million," *Wall Street Journal,* 16 July 1971, 26.

28. "Knudsen Returns in a White Truck," *Business Week,* 1 May 1971, 22.

29. "White Motor Unit Sold."

30. "White Motor to Merge," *New York Times,* 18 August 1970, 47; "U.S. Will Oppose White Motor Tie," *New York Times,* 27 January 1971, 41; "White Motor's Merger Plan Is Abandoned Following Preliminary Order against Tie," *Wall Street Journal,* 26 February 1971, 26. The *Wall Street Journal* described it this way: "White Motor was negotiating with Mr. Cappaert last year. Those negotiations were terminated when White reached an agreement to merge into White Consolidated and Mr. Cappaert filed a suit seeking damages and restitution for the expenditures he allegedly incurred during the negotiations. The suit never went to trial. After the merger was blocked by a government anti-trust action earlier this year, negotiations were resumed between White Motors and Mr. Cappaert" (16 July 1971, 26).

31. See John Bryan, "White Truck Chief Urges Delay of White Consolidated Merger," *Plain Dealer,* 14 January 1971, 1; John Bryan, "White Corporation Orders Peterson Away after He Refuses to Quit," *Plain Dealer,* 15 January 1971, 1; John Bryan,

"White Merger Wins Overwhelming Vote," *Plain Dealer*, 19 January 1971, 1; Brian Williams, "U.S. Judge Blocks White Merger Plan," *Plain Dealer*, 25 February 1971, 1; John Bryan, "White Drops Merger," *Plain Dealer*, 26 February 1971, 1.

32. See "White Motor Unit Sold"; "Bunkie Knudsen Redesigns White Motors," *Business Week*, 30 October 1971, 44; "Galahad to the Rescue," *Forbes*, 15 November 1972, 30; "How Bunkie Knudsen Took On the Bankers," *Business Week*, 13 December 1976, 72.

33. Ann Markusen, Scott Campbell, Peter Hall, and Sabina Deitrick, *The Rise of the Gunbelt: The Military Remapping of Industrial America* (New York: Oxford University Press, 1991), 25, 12–16, 13, table 2.1, 238.

34. "Galahad to the Rescue," 30.

35. "White Motor Unit Sold."

36. While there is no critical historical account of this era in Lansing's history, there is a good-sized literature on the Great Society in U.S. history in general. I have found helpful William Lee Miller, *The Fifteenth Ward and the Great Society: An Encounter with a Modern City* (Boston: Houghton Mifflin, 1966), which is about New Haven, Connecticut, and, while not "objective," is very helpful for the parallels to Lansing. Also, in a more scholarly vein, see R. Allen Hays, *The Federal Government and Urban Housing: Ideology and Change in Public Policy* (Albany: State University of New York Press, 1995.)

37. Douglas K. Meyer, "The Changing Negro Residential Patterns in Lansing, Michigan, 1850–1969" (Ph.D. diss., Michigan State University, 1970), 114. Rose Toomer Brunson, "A Study of the Migrant Negro Population in Lansing, Michigan, during and since World War II" (M.A. thesis, School of Social Work, Michigan State University, 1955) describes a meeting of the Real Estate Board of Lansing in 1943, when it was debated whether to set aside a neighborhood where black migrants could buy homes. The board could not agree to do so (11).

38. Richard G. Crowe, "The Lansing Housing Problem," *Michigan State Economic Record*, July–August 1971, 3. Homer Chandler Hawkins, "Knowledge of the Social and Emotional Implications of Urban Renewal and the Utility of This Knowledge to the Practice of Social Work" (Ph.D. diss., Michigan State University, 1971), is a study of the effects of removal on a sample of African American families displaced by the construction of Interstate 496. See also Lansing City Demonstration Agency, *Mid-Planning Statement: Model Cities Program* (Lansing, November 1969); Meyer, "Changing Negro Residential Patterns"; and Brunson, "Study of the Migrant Negro Population." Brunson interviewed black residents of Census Tract 18 in the city of Lansing, a neighborhood where the majority of the black migrants during the 1940s had settled. In 1950, the total black population of the tract was 2,125 when the total black population of the city was 3,290. While crime and other urban problems were not common, the neighborhood was overcrowded. Interstate 496 went directly through Tract 18.

39. This residential mixing of the white classes is described in chapter 1 of my book *The Story of Reo Joe*.

40. See articles in the *Lansing State Journal* on 6 June 1966; "Loses Bid to Save Mansion," 26 August 1966; and "Famous House Crumbles," 20 October 1966.

41. "City Urban Renewal Director Starts Job," *Lansing State Journal*, 16 May 1962; Lloyd Moles, "New Look for Downtown Lansing: Urban Renewal Plans Outlined," *Lansing State Journal*, 17 May 1964, C1; Lloyd Moles, "Plan Community Renewal Study," *Lansing State Journal*, 15 June 1965, C1; Lloyd Moles, "Downtown Urban Renewal Progresses toward Goal," *Lansing State Journal*, 14 February 1965; Curt Hanes, "Pin Hopes on U.S. Aid," *Lansing State Journal*, 19 April 1967.

42. I am using Crowe's numbers, but other sources support the basic statistics. Crowe, "Lansing Housing Problem," 3.

43. "700 Riot; Police Chief Hurt," *Lansing State Journal*, 20 June 1964, 1.

44. "City Housing Mess Seen Getting Worse," *Lansing State Journal*, 5 March 1966; Lloyd Moles, "Rental Homes Scarce in City," *Lansing State Journal*, 11 December 1966; and Crowe, "Lansing Housing Problem."

45. This is obviously not a thorough evaluation of public housing in Lansing. See Lloyd Moles, "Homes Sought for 592 Low Income Families," *Lansing State Journal*, 18 August 1967, D1; Norm Sinclair, "New Guidelines Explained for Reo Housing Project," *Lansing State Journal*, 11 April 1968, F1; and Curt Hanes, "Housing Accepted by City," *Lansing State Journal*, 31 July 1968, D1.

46. Curt Hanes, "Council to Get 'Keep Reo' Plan," *Lansing State Journal*, 22 July 1968.

47. Lloyd Moles, "Lansing Renews Pledge to Aid in Reo Relocation," *Lansing State Journal*, 28 November 1969.

48. "White Motor Unit Plans Plant at Lansing, Michigan," *Wall Street Journal*, 21 October 1968, 28.

49. *Official Proceedings of the City Council of the City of Lansing*, 9 September 1968 and 30 September 1968, Lansing Local History Collection, Lansing Public Library, Lansing, Michigan; and Lloyd Moles, "Diamond Reo Area Figures in Third Renewal Project," *Lansing State Journal*, 26 June 1968.

50. See Lloyd Moles, "New Terms on Reo Appraisal Accepted," *Lansing State Journal*, 10 November 1969, 1; Moles, "Lansing Renews Pledge to Aid in Reo Relocation"; Lloyd Moles, "Diamond Reo Appraisal Funding Allocated," *Lansing State Journal*, 2 December 1969.

51. *Official Proceedings of the City Council of the City of Lansing*, 24 March 1968, 1 April 1969, and 2 February 1970, Lansing Local History Collection, Lansing Public Library, Lansing, Michigan; "Diamond Reo Plant Important to City," editorial, *Lansing State Journal*, 24 July 1968, A8; "White Motors Get Welcome by Clinton," *Lansing State Journal*, 2 February 1970.

52. Lloyd Moles, "Reo Rejects HUD's Offer," *Lansing State Journal*, 30 September 1970, 1. The Romney Papers at the Bentley Library, Ann Arbor, Michigan, and the HUD papers in the National Archives, Washington, D.C., have not shed any additional light on these events.

53. See Hays, *The Federal Government*.

54. Fred Parks, "White Motors," *Lansing Labor News*, 4 November 1965, 8.

55. See, for example, Rick Kibbey, "Urban Renewal," East Lansing *Paper*, 1 May 1969, 6, 7. "And the little man gets lost somewhere in the middle. He knows he's paying lots of taxes and he thinks that the cause of the problems is the Black man or the hillbilly on welfare. He doesn't see that they are just as trapped and messed over by the hot-shot politicos and businessmen as he is. He just sees his money go into urban renewal and forgets that urban renewal money is buying the land for the new Diamond Reo plant in Lansing."

56. Alvin A. Butkus, "The Silent Tycoon: Who Is Francis L. Cappaert? One of the Richest Men in America," *Dun's*, January 1972, 38–40. It was also reported in the *Lansing Labor News* that Cappaert had contributed to Richard Nixon's presidential campaigns in 1968 and 1972. See Lorraine Baldwin, "P and M: Diamond Reo," *Lansing Labor News*, 18 May 1973, 10.

57. See *Joint Issue*, early February 1973, 3; and "No Jobs—No Pension—No Reo," *Lansing Star*, 8–21 January 3.

58. Doris Dow, interview, Lansing, Michigan, 19 February 1992, 41. Unless otherwise noted, all interviews were conducted by the author on audiocassette, and remain in her possession.

59. Calvin Chamberlin, interview, Lansing, Michigan, 11 June 1992, 20 and 34.

60. Raymond Fuller, interview, Mulliken, Michigan, 19 March 1992, 35.

61. Lee Magielski, *Lansing Labor News*, 10 October 1975, 2.

62. "Ohio Liquidator Buys Diamond Reo," *Lansing Labor News*, 7 November 1975, 1.

63. Seventeen out of thirty informants in the Reo Oral History Project worked until the 1970s.

64. Arthur Frahm, interview, Lansing, Michigan, 10 February 1992, 35; Herbert Heinz, interview, Dansville, Michigan, 16 March 1993, 12, 26; Wayne Nunheimer, interview, Lansing, Michigan, 18 June 1992, 45; Louis Garcia, interview, Lansing, Michigan, 28 January 1992, 15–17. Louis Garcia was one of the few Mexican Americans in the plant. He had worked his way up from the pressroom to a superintendent position and had a closer relationship with Cappaert, even once flying down to Mississippi with him on business.

65. These had to do with the race, gender, and sexual orientation of the workers.

66. There is a great deal of work on memory and oral history. Works that have informed my thinking include: Kathleen M. Blee, "Evidence, Empathy, and Ethics: Lessons from Oral Histories of the Klan," *Journal of American History* (September 1993): 596; John Bodnar, "Power and Memory in Oral History: Workers and Managers at Studebaker," *Journal of American History* (March 1989): 1201; Jane Sherron De Hart, "Oral Sources and Contemporary History: Dispelling Old Assumptions," *Journal of American History* (September 1993): 582; and Alessandro Portelli, *The Death of Luigi Trastulli and Other Stories: Form and Meaning in Oral History* (Albany: State University of New York Press, 1991).

67. Edward O. Welles, "The Shape of Things to Come," *Inc.*, February 1992, 66.

68. Ibid.

69. Ibid.

70. "A Maker of Chassis for Motor Homes Fires 100 Workers," *New York Times*, 4 October 2000, C4.

71. "Spartan Motors Executive Plans to Step Down," *Lansing State Journal*, 25 March 2001, business section, pp. 1, 2.

72. See Daniel Kruger, "Labor Had Big Influence on GM," *Lansing State Journal*, 11 August 1999, 5A; Kruger is a professor of industrial and labor relations at Michigan State University and this is a viewpoint editorial he wrote for the local paper.

3. Segregated Fantasies

1. Bill Kent, "Fighting Off the Final Curtain," "Casino Addition to Preserve Historic Theater's Façade," *New York Times*, 21 January and 11 February 1996; and "Boardwalk Landmark Saved as Entrance to Hotel," *Philadelphia Inquirer*, 4 February 1996.

2. For descriptions of the Wild, Wild West, see www.atlantic-city.net/casino/information/wildwest.htm; and Bill Kent, "In a Cavern, in a Canyon," *New York Times*, 20 July 1997.

3. See this phrase in Hal Rothman, *Neon Metropolis: How Las Vegas Started the Twenty-first Century* (New York: Routledge, 2002), xiii.

4. McMurtry, *The Last Picture Show* (New York: Simon and Schuster, 1966). See also, for a similar way of using this book and the movie by the same name, Karal Ann Marling, "Fantasies in Dark Places: The Cultural Geography of the American Movie Palace," in *Textures of Place: Exploring Humanist Geographics*, ed. Paul C. Adams, Steven Hoelscher, and Karen E. Till (Minneapolis: University of Minnesota Press, 2001), 8–23.

5. On movie going, see Robert Butsch, "American Movie Audiences in the 1930s," *International Labor and Working-Class History* 59 (spring 2001): 107.

6. On the fantasies of the movie house, see Marling, "Fantasies in Dark Places," 8–23.

7. Josef Israels II, "The Movie Usher and How He Got That Way," *Liberty*, 28 April 1929, 75–79; Douglas Gormery, "The Movies Become Big Business: Public Theaters and the Chain Store Strategy," *Cinema Journal* 1 (fall 1978): 28; and David Nasaw, *Going Out: The Rise and Fall of Public Amusements* (New York: Basic Books, 1993), 235–36. On the balance between security and thrills, see John Hannigan, *Fantasy City: Pleasure and Profit in the Postmodern Metropolis* (London: Routledge, 1998).

8. *Atlantic City*, Republic Films, Los Angeles, 1944.

9. "Recreation," folder 33, box 3, "Works Projects Administration" record group, "New Jersey Writers' Project" subgroup, New Jersey State Archives, Trenton, New Jersey.

10. Lois Wallen, e-mail to author, 11 April 2002; and Butsch, "American Movie Audiences," 117.

11. *Atlantic City Host*, 25 August 1956, "Collection Various Organizational Events' Books" folder, Bunny Josephson Collection, Heston Room, Atlantic City Free Public Library (hereafter cited as ACFPL).

12. Mary "Kate" Dunwoody, "Atlantic City Movie Theaters," 14 May 1991, unpublished paper, "Art and Cultural Events, Theaters," vertical files, Heston Room, ACFPL.

13. Butsch, "American Movie Audiences"; and Lary May with the assistance of Stephen Lassonde, "Making the American Way: Moderne Theatres, Audiences, and the Film Industry, 1929–1945," *Prospects* 12 (1987): 89–124.

14. Buddy and Stanley Grossman, interview, Northfield, N.J., 8 April 1999; and Mary Wood of Wood's Pawn Shop, interview, 11 February 1999, Atlantic City, N.J. Unless otherwise noted, all interviews were conducted by the author on audiocassette, or notes were taken, and remain in his possession.

15. *Atlantic City Host*, 25 August 1956, ACFPL.

16. On Steel Pier, see the 1954 "Steel Pier Souvenir and Guide Book," Allen "Boo" Pergament Atlantic City Collection (private library), Margate, New Jersey.

17. "Rebirth on Interest in City Swings Sale," *Atlantic City Press*, 28 February 1955.

18. *Atlantic City Press*, 20 November 1956.

19. *New York Times*, 27 March 1958; and Kent, "Fighting Off the Final Curtain."

20. "The Warner is Coming Down," paper unknown, 8 November 1960, "Atlantic City, Warner" folder, Irving Glazer Files, Athenaeum Library, Philadelphia, Penn.

21. For more, see Mark E. Heisler, "Warren May Be Victim of Changing Era," *Atlantic City Press*, 20 November 1960; Irvin R. Glazer, "The Atlantic City Story," *Marquee*, 1st and 2d quarter, 1980, 6; David Naylor, *American Picture Palaces: The Architecture of Fantasy* (New York: Van Nostrand Reinhold, 1981), 207–8; and Kent, "Fighting Off the Final Curtain."

22. Gary Morris, "Beyond the Beach: AIP's Beach Party Movies," n.d., www.brightlightsfilms.com.

23. See a picture of the Boardwalk Bowl's opening in Vicki Gold Levi and Lee Eisenberg, *Atlantic City: 125 Years of Ocean Madness* (Berkeley, Calif.: Ten Speed, 1994), 146.

24. E-mail from local historian Anthony Kutschera to author, 16 October 2000; and Parker, "Theaters of Atlantic City."

25. Wade Greene, "On the Boardwalk: What a Difference a Century Makes!" *New York Times*, 12 July 1970; and Henry Spier, "Money Back Plan for Boardwalk Stores," *Philadelphia Bulletin*, 20 December 1964.

26. Typescript on Movies, "Art and Cultural Events, Theaters" vertical files, Heston Room, ACFPL; and Charles Librizzi, "Few Theaters Are Left for Atlantic City Vacationers," *Philadelphia Bulletin*, 25 June 1974.

27. On the Embassy, see Librizzi, "Few Theaters Are Left."

28. "Children Win Fight in Atlantic City," *Philadelphia Bulletin*, 23 November 1969.

29. Mark E. Heisler, "Family Movies Due," *Atlantic City Press*, 22 November 1969, "Art and Cultural Events, Theaters" vertical files, Heston Room, ACFPL. On the types of films shown and middle-class perceptions, see Jon C. Teaford, *The Rough Road to Renaissance: Urban Revitalization in America, 1940–1985* (Baltimore: Johns Hopkins University Press, 1990), 208–9, and Andrew Hurley, *Diners, Bowling Alleys, and Trailer Parks: Chasing the American Dream in the Postwar Culture* (New York: Basic Books, 2001), 314.

30. Eliot Michael Friedland, "Death of the 'World's Playground': An Examination of the Decline and Fall of Atlantic City, New Jersey" (M.A. thesis, Glassboro State University, 1972), 95–97; "Plan to Fill Empty Stores Outlined," *Atlantic City Press*, 19 March 1963; Woods, interview; and Larry Miller, interview, Atlantic City, N.J., 11 February 1999.

31. Jane Jacobs first developed the idea of the "eyes of the street" in her classic, *The Death and Life of Great American Cities* (New York: Random House, 1961). In his book on cities and decline, Ray Suarez makes a similar point about stores closing early and emptiness, *The Old Neighborhood: What We Lost in the Great Suburban Migration, 1966–1999* (New York: Free Press, 1999), 20, 82–83, 87. On the problem of high vacancy rates in downtown areas, see Witold Rybcynski and Peter D. Lineman, "How to Save Our Shrinking Cities," *Public Interest* 135 (spring 1999): 30–44.

32. In terms of numbers of conventioneers, the figures remained pretty steady over the 1960s and early 1970s. For this data, see Atlantic City Housing Authority and Urban Redevelopment Agency, "Market Research for Specialty Shopping Center, Uptown Renewal Site, Atlantic City, New Jersey," April 1974, 10–11, Heston Room, ACFPL.

33. "A Dowager's Decline," *Newsweek*, 8 June 1970, 86; Michael Pollack, "The City in Shock," *Atlantic City Press*, 28 March 1982; and G. G. LaBelle, "Veneer Wears Thin in Atlantic City," Trenton *Times Advertiser*, 16 April 1972.

34. John Roak, "Inspector Calls 'Walk Upgrading Everybody's Job," *Atlantic City Press*, 1 August 1972.

35. "Cross Incident Brings Warning," *Atlantic City Press*, 30 April 1955; Minutes of Commissioners, 21 July 1955, 491, City Clerk's Office, Atlantic City, New Jersey. On the shifts in the neighborhood, see the City Directory of Atlantic City, 1955, 1956, 1957, Heston Room, ACFPL.

36. Dunwoody, "Atlantic City Movie Theaters." On drive-ins, see Hurley, *Diners*, 298–99.

37. Buddy and Stanley Grossman, interview; "Newsletter of the Greater Atlantic City Chamber of Commerce," May 1970, Heston Room, ACFPL. For more on the relocation of businesses and institutions, see Friedland, "Death of the 'World's Playground,'" 95–96.

38. Atlantic City Housing Authority and Urban Redevelopment Agency, "Market Support for Specialty Shopping Center Uptown Renewal Site, Atlantic City, New Jersey," April 1974, 10–11, Heston Room, ACFPL.

39. See, for example, Jordan Sayles, interview by Cythnia Ridge, Atlantic City, N.J., 24 April 1978, Atlantic City Living History, Oral History Project, Heston Room, ACFPL; and James Howard Kuntsler, *The Geography of Nowhere: The Rise and Decline of America's Man-Made Landscape* (New York: Simon and Schuster, 1993), 228–29; and Daniel Heneghan, "Casinos' Beginning Rooted in AC Decay," *Atlantic City Press*, 12 November 1986.

40. On the importance of air conditioning to Atlantic City's decline see William Mandel, "Shore Lures Stars," *Philadelphia Bulletin*, 13 June 1971; Peter B. Brophy, "A People Which No Longer Remembers Has Lost Its History and Soul," *Atlantic City Press*, 25 June 1978. On air-conditioning and the retreat to the private, see Alan Ehrenhalt, *The Lost City: The Forgotten Virtues of Community in America* (New York: Basic Books, 1995), 94–95.

41. Brophy, " A People Which No Longer"; Allen M. Pergament, interview, Morgate, N.J., 3 March 1999; and Hannigan, *Fantasy City*, 189–92.

42. Among others making this argument are Michael Pollack, "The City in Shock," *Atlantic City Press*, 28 March 1982; and Charles E. Funnell, *By the Beautiful Sea: The Rise and High Times of That Great American Resort, Atlantic City* (New York: Knopf, 1975), 153–53, 156.

43. Pierre Hollingsworth, interview, Absecon, N.J., 19 August 1999; Wade Green, "On the Boardwalk: What a Difference a Century Makes!" *New York Times*, 12 July 1970; and Funnell, *By the Beautiful Sea*, 157–58.

44. On desegregation efforts, see Pierre Hollingsworth, interview; Louis Emanuel, "CORE Breaks Off Hotel Job Talks," *Atlantic City Press*, 11 March 1966; "NAACP Newsletter," signed by Mr. Lloyd Holland, vice president, [3 March 1966], "Printed Matter, NAACP by State, New Jersey, 1966–1970" folder, box J7, record group 5, NAACP Papers, Library of Congress; and Brad Bennett, "Civil Rights Movement Has Long History in A.C.," *Atlantic City Press*, 21 February 1993.

45. Hollingsworth, interview; and Lois Wallen, interview, Margate, N.J., 11 October 1999.

46. On people leaving Atlantic City for more space, see Ducktown Revitalization Association, "Atlantic City's Italian Village," "Ducktown" file, vertical files, Heston Room, ACFPL.

47. On white perceptions of African Americans and how they treat their property, T. K., interview, Atlantic City, N.J., 13 August 1999; Leslie Kammerman, interview by Cynthia Ridge, Atlantic City, N.J., n.d. [circa 1978], Atlantic City Living History, Oral History Project, Heston Room, ACFPL; and "Civil Rights Body Urged," *Atlantic City Press*, 23 June 1951. For examples from other places, see Arnold Hirsch, *Making the Second Ghetto: Race and Housing in Chicago, 1940–1960* (Cambridge: Cambridge University Press, 1983); Thomas J. Sugrue, "Crab-grass Politics: Race, Rights, and Reaction against Liberalism in the Urban North," *Journal of American History* 82 (September 1995): 551–78; Jonathan Rieder, *Canarsie: The Jews and Italians of Brooklyn against Liberalism* (Cambridge: Harvard University Press, 1985), 85; Stephen Grant Meyer, *As Long As They Don't Move Next Door: Segregation and Racial Conflict in American Neighborhoods* (Lanham, Md.: Rowman and Littlefield, 2000), 7.

48. Martin Sherman, *Rose* (London: Metheun, 1999), 22–33, quote on 32.

49. Bruce Boyle, "Of the Inlet Irish: It Was Summertime and the Card Fell Right,"

Philadelphia Bulletin, 22 December 1980, and "Technology, Racism, and Rolling Chairs May Revive Us Yet," *Philadelphia Bulletin,* 23 September 1981.

50. James N. Riggio, "Boardwalk a Symbol of Black Frustration," *Philadelphia Inquirer,* 2 June 1970.

51. On race and flight, see Gaeton Fonzi and Bernard McCormick, "Bust-Out Town," *Philadelphia Magazine,* August 1970, 58; and Boyle, "Technology, Racism, and Rolling Chairs." See in addition the thoughts of the fictional characters to Atlantic City in Sherman, *Rose,* 32; and Warren B. Murphy and Frank Stevens, *Atlantic City* (Los Angeles: Pinnacle Books, 1979), 126.

52. U.S. Bureau of Census, *1970 Census of Population,* vol. 1, part 32 (Washington, D.C.: U.S. Government Printing Office, 1973), 14–15.

53. Robert Goodman, *The Luck Business: The Devastating Consequences and Broken Promises of America's Gambling Explosion* (New York: Free Press, 1995), 21–23; and Laura Mansnerus, "Great Expectations: Money Has Poured into Atlantic City. But a Second Wave, Ever Poised, Still Hasn't Broken," *New York Times,* 2 April 2000.

54. Frank J. Prendergast, "Investor to Raze 2 Resort Theaters," *Atlantic City Press,* 3 May 1978.

55. *Atlantic City Press,* 29 May 1978; and undated typescript, "Art and Cultural Events, Theaters," vertical files, Heston Room, ACFPL. See a picture of the Strand's marquee on the night Resorts opened in Daniel Heneghan, "Still Rolling the Dice," *Atlantic City Press,* 23 May 1993.

56. *New York Times,* 14 November 1983; and "Arson Suspected in Atlantic City Fire," *Philadelphia Inquirer,* 14 November 1983.

57. For figures on Atlantic City visitors, see John Contarino, "The Times of Our Life: A Special Look at 15 Years of Casino Gaming," *Atlantic City,* May 1993, 26.

58. Michael Pollock, *Hostage to Fortune: Atlantic City and Casino Gambling* (Princeton: Center Analysis of Public Issues, 1987), 17.

59. Donald Janson, "In the Mayor's Race Atlantic City Focuses on Blight," *New York Times,* 11 May 1986.

60. Steven P. Perskie and Robert Goodman quoted in Mansnerus, "Great Expectations."

61. On the design of casinos, see David Margolick, "Under LV's Neon Beats a Heart of Denim," *New York Times,* 16 February 1984; and Hannigan, *Fantasy City,* 161.

62. The polls were reported as part of "Big Gamble in Atlantic City," *Bill Moyers Reports,* CBS Television, 28 July 1986.

63. "Atlantic City Retread," *New York Times,* 1 August 1989.

64. Paul E. Wiseman, "Money Talks; AC Talks Back," *Courier Post,* 26 July 1988.

65. Bill Kent, "The Bus Stops Here: Where Do You Have to Go to Get the Story on Gambling," *New York Times,* 18 January 1998.

66. On suburban growth, see Donald Janson, "Casinos Transform AC's Suburbs," *New York Times,* 11 July 1986; "Big Gamble in Atlantic City"; David Vis, "Growth—Atlantic City Explodes and Even More Is on the Way," *Atlantic City Press,* 22 August 1988; and Ted G. Goertzel and John W. Cosby, "Gambling on Jobs and Welfare in Atlantic City," *Society* 34 (May/June 1997): 62–66.

67. On current movies, see *Atlantic City Press,* 27 August 2000. On plans to build a theater in Atlantic City, see *Atlantic City Press,* 13 August 1993. On video poker, see Goodman, *The Luck Business,* 121–22.

68. For a critique of this form of growth, see Jane Holtz Kay, "Tales of the City," *Na-*

tion 267 (6 July 1998): 135–38; Marc V. Levine, "Downtown Development as an Urban Growth Strategy: A Critical Appraisal of the Baltimore Renaissance," *Journal of Urban Affairs* 9 (1987), 103–23; M. Christine Boyer, "Cities for Sale: Merchandising History and at South Street Seaport," in *Variations on a Theme Park: The New American City and the End of Public Space*, ed. Michael Sorkin (New York: Hill and Wang, 1992), 181–204; and Hannigan, *Fantasy City*, 129–48.

69. Michael Sorkin, introduction to *Variations on a Theme Park*, xv.

70. For two recent looks at deindustrialization, see Jefferson Cowie, *Capital Moves: RCA's Seventy-Year Quest for Cheap Labor* (Ithaca: Cornell University Press, 1999; reprint, New York: New Press, 2001) and William M. Adler, *Mollie's Job: The Story of Life and Work on the Global Assembly Line* (New York: Scribner, 2000).

4. Greening Anaconda

1. Several well-known historical studies tell the story of change in turn-of-the-century Anaconda. See, for example, Thomas A. Rickard, *A History of American Mining* (New York: Macmillan, 1932), 347–62; or Michael P. Malone, *The Battle for Butte: Mining and Politics on the Northern Frontier, 1864–1906* (1981; reprint, Helena: Montana Historical Society Press, 1995), 30–31. Jerry Hansen, interview, Anaconda, Montana, 12 July 1996. Unless otherwise noted, all interviews were conducted by the author and recorded on audiocassette; tapes remain in his possession.

2. Cheryl Beatty, interview, 12 July 1996.

3. Ray Ring, "Turning the Old West into the New West," *High Country News*, 19 January 1998; ARCO, "Old Work News: The First Report in a Series" (Anaconda: Atlantic Richfield Company, 1993), 5; "The Old Works Is a Great Bit of Work," *Billings Gazette*, 20 June 1997.

4. For a detailed description of the dispersion of pollutants within this enormous Superfund complex, see Howard E. Johnson and Carole L. Schmidt, *Clark Fork Basin Project: Status Report and Action Plan* (Helena: Office of the Governor, 1988). See also "Old Works Golf Course: Course Construction," www.oldworks.org/coursecon.html. On the golf course design and the U.S. statute, see U.S. Environmental Protection Agency, Region 8, and the Montana Department of Health and Environmental Sciences, Solid and Hazardous Waste Bureau, "Record of Decision: Old Works/East Anaconda Development Area Operable Unit, Anaconda Smelter NPL Site," document control number 7760-037-DD-CZVB, 8 March 1994 (hereafter cited as ROD 1994), DS-51–DS-62.

5. These are the provisions of ROD 1994.

6. Jim Robbins, "Town Pins Hopes on Superfund Site," *New York Times*, 6 April 1997.

7. Beatty, interview; Jim Davison, interview, Anaconda, Montana, 13 July 1996.

8. Useful discussions of the contours, methodology, and direction of environmental history include: Donald Worster et al., "Environmental History: A Roundtable," *Journal of American History* 76 (1990): 1087–147; William Cronon, introduction to *Uncommon Ground*, ed. William Cronon (New York: Norton, 1996), 23–56; *Journal of Historical Geography* 20 (1994): 1–43.

9. While the history of technology is almost as broad as environmental history, this chapter is most influenced by Langdon Winner, *The Whale and the Reactor: A Search for Limits in an Age of High Technology* (Chicago: University of Chicago Press, 1986). Also see: Jeffrey K. Stine and Joel A. Tarr, "At the Intersections of Histories: Technology and the Environment," *Technology and Culture* 39 (1998): 601–40; Aida Davison, *Technology and the Contested Meanings of Sustainability* (Albany: State University of New York Press, 2000).

10. Kent C. Ryden, *Mapping the Invisible Landscape: Folklore, Writing, and the Sense of Place* (Iowa City: University of Iowa Press, 1993).

11. Barry Bluestone and Bennett Harrison, *The Deindustrialization of America: Plant Closings, Community Abandonment, and the Dismantling of Basic Industry* (New York: Basic Books, 1982), 15; Paul D. Staudohar and Holly E. Brown, eds., *Deindustrialization and Plant Closure* (Lexington, Mass.: Lexington Books, 1987); Peter B. Doeringer et al., *Turbulence in the American Workplace* (New York: Oxford University Press, 1991). The figure on job loss was taken from Gilda Haas, *Plant Closures: Myths, Realities, and Responses* (Boston: South End, 1985), 12.

12. For an excellent discussion of this pattern of change, see Michael P. Malone, "The Collapse of Western Metal Mining: An Historical Epitaph," *Pacific Historical Review* 55 (1986): 455–64.

13. David M. Emmos, *The Butte Irish: Class and Ethnicity in an American Mining Town, 1875–1925* (Chicago: University of Illinois Press, 1989); Mary Murphy, *Mining Cultures: Men, Women, and Leisure in Butte, 1914–41* (Chicago: University of Illinois Press, 1997).

14. Malone, *Battle for Butte*, 215–17; George Wyant, interview, Anaconda, Montana, 11 July 1996.

15. Malone, *Battle for Butte*, 216–17; Wyant, Hansen, Beatty, and Davison, interviews. Eban Goodstein's study, *The Trade-Off Myth: Fact and Fiction About Jobs and the Environment* (Covelo: Island Press, 2000), has shown that there is no definitive link between environmental legislation and plant closure in any U.S. industry.

16. Beatty and Davison, interviews. For a description of the "ripple effect" of plant closures, see Bluestone and Harrison, *Deindustrialization of America*, 67.

17. See John A. Hird, *Superfund: The Political Economy of Environmental Risk* (Baltimore: Johns Hopkins University Press, 1994), 9–20.

18. Ibid.

19. Kevin Miller, "Arsenic Found in Milltown Water Supplies," *The Missoulian*, 15 December 1981; Miller, "Arsenic Probe is Stepped Up; Warning Issued," *The Missoulian*, 16 December 1981; Miller, "Quantity and Toxicity of Arsenic in Milltown Top Previous Levels," *The Missoulian*, 22 December 1981. David Roach, "Contamination Leaves Residents Perplexed," *The Missoulian*, 16 December 1981.

20. Beatty and Davison, interviews.

21. ROD 1994, DS-4–DS-5. Charlie Coleman, interview, Helena, Montana, 22 July 1996.

22. Davison, interview.

23. Staudohar and Brown, eds., *Deindustrialization and Plant Closure*; Haas, *Plant Closures*.

24. Hird, *Superfund*. Harold C. Barnett, *Toxic Debts and the Superfund Dilemma* (Chapel Hill: University of North Carolina Press, 1994).

25. Beatty, interview.

26. Davison, interview.

27. Sandy Stash, interview, Anaconda, Montana, 14 July 1996.

28. ROD 1994, DS-4–DS-5.

29. Colemen, interview. Peter Nielsen, interview, Missoula, Montana, 24 July 1996.

30. Coleman and Beatty, interviews.

31. "Governor's 'Getting Things Done'—MSU Visioning Grants Vision Our Future!!" prepared by the Montana State University Extension Service and the Montana State University School of Architecture, Anaconda, 1995. While this planning document

appears on its face to have been generated by the governor's office, Coleman, Beatty, and Stash all admitted it was fully funded by an ARCO grant. Beatty, interview.

32. Beatty, interview.

33. Stash, Coleman, Beatty, and Davison, interviews.

34. Stash and Beatty, interviews.

35. Ryden, *Mapping the Invisible Landscape.*

36. Wyant, interview; Joe Marusich, interview, Anaconda, Montana, 11 July 1996; Charlie Swihart, interview, Anaconda, Montana, 11 July 1996.

37. Wyant, interview; Joe Marusich, interview, Anaconda, Montana, 11 July 1996; Charlie Swihart, interview, Anaconda, Montana, 11 July 1996.

38. Beatty, interview.

39. Hansen, interview.

40. Nielsen, interview.

41. Andrew Young, interview, Helena, Montana, 24 July 1996.

42. Ibid.

43. Coleman and Nielsen, interviews.

44. Beatty, interview. For an interesting discussion of both the phenomenon of and the practical questions surrounding historical preservation in many deindustrialized places in the United States, see "Junk It, or Junket: Tourism and Historic Preservation in the Postindustrial World," *The Public Historian* 23 (2001).

45. For an excellent study of Flint, Michigan, and its inability to generate economic recovery, see David Perry, *A Town Abandoned: Flint, Michigan, Confronts Deindustrializaton* (Albany: State University of New York Press, 1996).

46. A study by Fredric L. Quivik—"Integrating the Preservation of Cultural Resources with Remediation of Hazardous Materials: An Assessment of Superfund's Record" (*The Public Historian* 23 [2001])—explains how, despite all the acknowledgements made by ARCO and city planners of the historical value of the smelter remains, historically significant remains were excavated and removed in order to accommodate the fairways for the sixth hole.

47. www.anacondamt.org.

5. From Love's Canal to Love Canal

1. For full coverage of Hickory Woods, see *Buffalo Beat*, 1 April 2000. See also the *Buffalo News*, 24 September 2000.

2. See William Cronon, *Nature's Metropolis: Chicago and the Great West* (New York: Oxford University Press, 1991), xv; Philip Shabecoff, *A Fierce Green Fire: The American Environmental Movement* (New York: Hill and Wang, 1993), 233. See the following works for new views of environmentalism, environmental justice, and deindustrialization: Mark Dowie, *Losing Ground: American Environmentalism at the Close of the Twentieth Century* (Cambridge: MIT Press, 2000); William Shutkin, *The Land That Could Be: Environmentalism and Democracy in the Twentieth Century* (Cambridge: MIT Press, 2000); Daniel J. Faber, ed., *The Struggle for Ecological Democracy* (New York: Guilford Press, 1998); Robert Gottlieb, *Forcing the Spring: The Transformation of the American Environmental Movement* (Washington, D.C.: Island Press, 1993); K. A. Gourlay, *World of Waste: Dilemmas of Industrial Development* (London: Zed Books, 1992); Joe Thornton, *Pandora's Poison: Chlorine, Health, and a New Environmental Strategy* (Cambridge: MIT Press, 2000).

3. Michael Brown, *Laying Waste: The Poisoning of America by Toxic Chemicals* (New York: Harper & Row, 1981); Adeline Gordon Levine, *Love Canal: Science, Politics, and Peo-*

ple (Lexington, Mass.: D.C. Heath, 1982); Milton Rogovin and Michael Frisch, *Portraits in Steel* (Ithaca: Cornell University Press, 1993).

4. James Schwab, *Deeper Shades of Green: The Rise of Blue-Collar and Minority Environmentalism in America* (San Francisco: Sierra Club, 1994).

5. Schwab, *Deeper Shades of Green*, introduction.

6. *Buffalo News*, 12 October 2000.

7. Ann Hillis, "Love Canal's Contamination," Love Canal Collection, State University of New York (SUNY) Buffalo Archives; Joe Dunmire, interview with author, 21 August 2000. Unless otherwise noted, all interviews were conducted by the author in Buffalo, N.Y., on audiocassette, and the tapes remain in his possession.

8. William Irwin, *The New Niagara: Tourism, Technology, and the Landscape of Niagara Falls, 1776–1917* (University Park: Pennsylvania State University Press, 1996), 144–46.

9. Edward T. Williams, *Niagara: Queen of Wonders* (Boston: Chapple Publishing Co., 1916), 166, 171.

10. See H. William Feder, "The Evolution of an Ethnic Neighborhood That Became United in Diversity: The East Side of Niagara Falls, N.Y., 1880–1930" (Ph.D. diss., State University of New York, Buffalo, 1999), 13. See also Pierre Berton, *Niagara: A History of the Falls* (Toronto: McClelland and Stewart, 1992).

11. See John Horton, Edward Williams et al., *History of Northwestern New York*, 2 vols. (New York: Lewis Historical Publishers, 1944), 2:3.

12. Love published two major pamphlets and his company printed its own newspaper for several years during the 1890s. See the following pamphlets: "Model City: Niagara Power and Development" (Lewiston, N.Y., 1893) and "Model City: Niagara Power and Development Company" (Lewiston, N.Y., c. 1894–1895). Love's company newspapers included the following between 1894 and 1897: *Model City Search Light*, *Model City Standard*, and *Model City Power.*

13. Ibid.

14. Ibid.

15. Ibid.

16. Ibid.

17. As the following issues of the *Buffalo Courier* illustrate, Love's Canal received positive press coverage: 24 May 1894, 1 August 1894, 27 October 1894, and 19 December 1894, 1 May 1896.

18. See the *Buffalo Courier*, "Western New York" section, on the following dates for reports on the growth and final failure of Love's Canal: 16 and 19 January 1896, 16 March 1896, 30 March 1896, 25 April 1896, 1 May 1896. See also Edward Williams's 1916 commentary on Love's failure, printed in his book *Niagara: Queen of Wonders*, 166–71.

19. J. Howard Pratt, *Memories of Life on the Ridge* (Albion, N.Y.: Orleans County Historical Association, 1978), 204, 208.

20. For national and international coverage of Niagara Falls, see, for example, the following: "The Harnessing of Niagara," *Cassier's Magazine, 1895; Illustrated London News*, 3 March 1906. For coverage of the tunnel dig, see the *Niagara Falls Journal* and the *Buffalo Daily Courier*, 1890–1895. For a recent survey of its social meanings, see Feder, "Evolution of an Ethnic Neighborhood," 52, 110–113.

21. Tesla quoted in Feder, "Evolution of an Ethnic Neighborhood," 179. Tesla's sentiment was hardly new.

22. See the circulating letter of J. B. Harrison, Corresponding Secretary of the Niagara Falls Association, 19 December 1882, vertical file, Buffalo and Erie County Histor-

ical Society, Buffalo, N.Y.; see also *London Illustrated News*, 3 June 1906, and Irwin, *New Niagara*, 63–96.

23. Ibid.

24. Irwin, *New Niagara*, 213–14.

25. John Muir reprinted in *Major Problems in American Environmental History*, ed. Carolyn Merchant (Lexington, Mass.: D.C. Heath, 1993), 391–94.

26. Anthony N. Penna, *Nature's Bounty* (New York: M. E. Sharpe, 1999), 184–85, Whipple quote, 210–11.

27. See Gordon Morris Bakken, "An Inversion Layer in Western Legal History: Air Pollution in Butte, Montana," in *Law as Culture and Culture as Law: Essays in Honor of John Phillip Reid*, ed. Hendrick Hartog et al. (Madison: Madison House Press, 2000), 264–91; John T. Cumbler, "Conflict, Accommodation, and Compromise: Connecticut's Attempt to Control Industrial Wastes in the Progressive Era," *Environmental History* 5, no. 3 (July 2000): 314–35; Robert Dale Grinder, "The Battle for Clean Air: The Smoke Problem in Post-Civil War America," in *Pollution and Reform in American Cities*, ed. Martin Melosi (Austin: University of Texas Press, 1980); Christine M. Rulen, "Businessmen against Pollution in Late Nineteenth Century Chicago," *Business History Review* 69 (autumn 1995): 351–97; Joel Tarr, *The Search for the Ultimate Sink: Urban Pollution in Historic Perspective* (Akron, Ohio: University of Akron Press, 1996).

28. Irwin, *New Niagara*, 214–16; Martin Melosi, *Effluent America* (Pittsburgh: University of Pittsburgh Press, 2001), 261–62.

29. In recent decades, a hazardous waste company has managed a disposal plant in Love's old Model City. In September 2000, the Army Corps of Engineers began a public review process for remediation of the site—a process that began with local citizens' complaints about environmental hazards. For coverage of the LOOW remediation initiative, see the U.S. Army Corps of Engineers public notification in the *Buffalo News*, 10 September 2000; and *USA Today*, 6 September 2000.

30. Albert Hooker, *Chloride of Lime in Sanitation* (New York, 1913). The book contains an impressive assortment of footnotes summarizing then current health studies on municipalities that used chloride of lime, or bleaching powder, to disinfect bacterial and disease-laden waters.

31. Robert E. Thomas, *Salt and Water, Power and People: A Short History of Hooker Electrochemical Company* (New York, 1955).

32. J. R. McNeil, *Something New under the Sun* (New York: Norton, 2000).

33. See District Judge John J. Curtin's "Decision and Order," 1994, in case *United States of America, the State of New York, and UCD-Love Canal, Inc. v. Hooker Chemicals and Plastics Corporation et al.*, 79-CV-990C, United States District Court, Western District of New York, a copy of which is located in the Love Canal Collection, SUNY Buffalo Archives.

34. Dunmire, interview.

35. According to a remediation expert's report, Hooker analysts had mistakenly assumed that all of the clay surrounding the canal was of the same porosity. There were in fact different grades of clay, the less absorbent of which allowed chemicals to leach into groundwater systems. The school board's disregard of Hooker's initial warnings about breaching canal soil also caused the tragedy, as streets, sewer lines, and housing foundations cut through the dump and became virtual expressways for leaching chemicals. See *United States of America et al. v. Hooker Chemicals*, 118–19.

36. Ibid.

37. See the report of the Hooker Process Study Department, quoted in *United States of America et al. v. Hooker Chemicals*, 47–49.

38. See Gibbs, "Learning from Love Canal: A Twentieth-Anniversary Retrospective," originally published in *Orion Afield* (spring 1998), and republished in *A Forest of Voices*, ed. Chris Anderson and Lex Runciman (Mountain View, Calif.: Mayfield Publishing Company, 2000), 550–54.

39. See Lois Marie Gibbs, *Love Canal: The Story Continues* (Gabriola Island, B.C., Canada: New Society Publishers, 1998), 19–55; "ETF Report and Proposal," March 1979, box 8, Love Canal Collection, SUNY Buffalo Archives.

40. See the following works on the rise of modern environmentalism in general: Samuel P. Hays, *Conservation and the Gospel of Efficiency: The Progressive Conservation Movement, 1890–1920* (Cambridge: Harvard University Press, 1959); Daniel G. Payne, *Voices in the Wilderness: American Nature Writing and Environmental Politics* (Hanover, N.H.: University Press of New England, 1996); Shabecoff, *Fierce Green Fire;* Zachary A. Smith, *The Environmental Policy Paradox* (Englewood Cliffs, N.J.: Prentice Hall, 1992).

41. See John G. Mitchell with Constance L. Stallings, *Ecotactics: The Sierra Club Handbook for Environmental Activists* (New York: Pocket Paperbacks, 1970), 1–19; also Garrett De Bell, *The Environmental Handbook: Prepared for the First National Environmental Teach-In* (New York: Ballantine Books, 1970).

42. See "Ten Years of Triumph," a pamphlet celebrating the tenth anniversary of the Citizen's Clearinghouse for Hazardous Waste (Falls Church, Va., 1993), 2–3; Robert D. Bullard, ed., *Unequal Protection: Environmental Justice and Communities of Color* (San Francisco: Sierra Club, 1994).

43. I am indebted to Pat Virgil of the Buffalo and Erie County Historical Society for information on deindustrialization on the Niagara Frontier. Virgil traced the Niagara region's deindustrial trends, using company records and newspaper clippings to compile a master file on corporations that have left the Buffalo/Niagara Falls area since World War II.

44. Luelly Kenny, interview, 21 March 2000; Dunmire, interview; Brown, *Laying Waste*, 29–65.

45. Bob Mullen, interview, 24 May 2000.

46. Gibbs, *Love Canal*, 1–12; ETF founding report, box 8, Love Canal Collection, SUNY Buffalo Archives.

47. "Patricia Brown and the Ecumenical Task Force," handbill, SUNY Buffalo Archives.

48. Lois Gibbs, interview, 5 February 1999.

49. The SUNY Buffalo Archives contain the largest collection of Love Canal material currently available to scholars, and many of these documents are available on-line through the Love Canal Collection at ublib.buffalo.edu/libraries/projects/lovecanal/. The university also recently came into possession of the papers of Love Canal activist Patricia Brown. I am indebted to archivist Christopher Densmore and his staff for their aid in mining the archives.

50. Lois Gibbs to David Axelrod, 24 May 24 and 12 July 1979, in Lois Gibbs Papers, Tisch Library, Tufts University.

51. Ann Hillis, "Love Canal's Contamination: The Poisoning of an American Family," Love Canal Collection, SUNY Buffalo Archives.

52. Ibid.

53. Ibid.

54. Grace M. McCoulf, "Senate Subcommittee of Toxic Substances and Chemical Wastes," 5 April 1979, reprinted in Love Canal Collection, SUNY Buffalo Archives.

55. Cynthia Hamilton, "Women, Home, and Community: The Struggle in an Urban Environment," in *Forest of Voices*, 542–48.

56. Gibbs, *Love Canal*, 160.

57. McCoulf, "Senate Subcommittee."

58. Dunmire, interview.

59. Rogovin and Frisch, *Portraits in Steel*, 6–7.

60. For Muskie quote before the American Society of Engineers, 2 April 1979, see ETF papers, folder 74, box 11, Love Canal Collection, SUNY Buffalo Archives; see also quote of a Union Carbide official in the *New York Times*, 8 June 1980.

61. Alice Stark, "The Continuing Impact of Love Canal" (panel discussion at the twelfth conference of the International Society for Environmental Epidemiology, Buffalo, 21 August 2000).

62. Nancy Kim and Edward Fitzgerald, ibid.

6. The Wages of Disinvestment

1. Thomas J. Sugrue, *The Origins of the Urban Crisis: Race and Inequality in Postwar Detroit* (Princeton: Princeton University Press, 1996).

2. The oft-cited phrase from Mumford is: "The city, as one finds it in history, is the point of maximum concentration for the power and culture of a community. . . . [H]ere is where human experience is transformed into viable signs, symbols, patterns of conduct, systems of order. Here is where the issues of civilization are focused." Lewis Mumford, *The Culture of Cities* (New York: Harcourt Brace Jonanovitch, 1938).

3. Camden *Courier*, Greater Camden edition, 1909, and 35th anniversary issue, June 1917, Camden County Historical Society, Camden.

4. David L. Kirp, John P. Dwyer, and Larry A. Rosenthal, *Our Town: Race, Housing, and the Soul of Suburbia* (New Brunswick: Rutgers University Press, 1995), 29; Jefferson Cowie, *Capital Moves: RCA's Seventy-Year Quest for Cheap Labor* (Ithaca: Cornell University Press, 1999; reprint, New York: New Press, 2001), 38–39.

5. See Norman I. Fainstein and Susan S. Fainstein, "New Haven: The Limits of the Local State," in *Restructuring the City: The Political Economy of Urban Redevelopment*, rev. ed., ed. Susan S. Fainstein et al. (New York: Longman, 1986), 27–79.

6. William Jenkins, interview, Camden, 18 September 1998; Joseph Balzano, interview, Camden, 21 November 1997. Both men were active in Camden during the Pierce era. All interviews were conducted by the author.

7. For a retrospective account of the redevelopment plan and its results, see Kevin Riordan's feature, "Dreams Unrealized in Camden," *Courier Post*, 14 March 2000.

8. "Introduction to the Comprehensive Plan for the City of Camden," brochure, 1962, 3, on file, Rutgers University Library, Camden. *Comprehensive Plan* (Camden, 1962), 77, 116, 196; transcript of the hearings on the plan 28 May 1962, case 103A, Office of the Municipal Clerk, City of Camden.

9. Popularly referred to by scholars as the result of progrowth coalitions, such efforts cropped up with the support of federal funds for urban renewal in older industrial cities across the Northeast and Midwest. See John H. Mollenkopf, *The Contested City* (Princeton: Princeton University Press, 1983), esp. 12–46.

10. *Courier Post*, 5 February 1959, 18 January 1962, 21 January 1966.

11. *Courier Post*, 24 January 1967, 14 January 1970; John Odorisio, interview, Haddorfield, N. J., 25 March 1998.

12. *Courier Post*, 23 January 1970, 24 January 1970.

13. Details of the unsuccessful efforts to charge Charles "Poppy" Sharp, founder and leader of the Black People's Unity Movement, and the Reverend Sam Appel, chaplain at Rutgers University's Camden campus can be found in Appel's papers at the Presbyterian Historical Society, Philadelphia, and in contemporary news accounts in the *Courier Post*.

14. This pattern was not unique to Camden. See Gerald Gamm, *Urban Exodus: Why the Jews Left Boston and the Catholics Stayed* (Cambridge: Harvard University Press, 1999).

15. Quoted in a retrospective account of Camden's industrial decline, *Courier Post*, 7 February 1986.

16. Dennis Culnan, "Focus on Camden," *New Jersey Business* 25 (December 1979): 55.

17. *Courier Post*, 14 March 1975, 24 December 1975.

18. *Courier Post*, 24 May 1981, 28 June 1981.

19. *Philadelphia Inquirer*, 20 April 2000.

20. *New York Times*, 14 November 1982.

21. *Courier Post*, 7 September 1989. A report in the same paper on 20 May 1990 indicated that the city had received the $3.2 million in state funds necessary to balance its budget in 1981 in return for providing the land for Riverfront Prison. Tom Knoche, first director of Camden Land Trust, interview, Camden, 16 September 1997.

22. See, for instance, reports in the *Courier Post*, 25 July 1993, 8 April 1995, 13 December 1996, 19 February 1998, 20 February 1998.

23. *Courier Post*, 14 May 1997. By contrast, Pierce's 1959 election had drawn 37,000 voters to the polls.

24. *Courier Post*, 30 April 2000.

25. *Courier Post*, 12 February 1998.

26. "Statement of Imminent Peril," released as part of the hearings to create the state financial review board, Trenton, 12 August 1998, possession of the author. Two years later, for example, Commissioner of Community Affairs Jane Kenny used the same rationale in defense of special legislation for a complete state takeover of Camden. *Courier Post*, 22 August 2000.

27. *Philadelphia Inquirer*, 20 August 1999.

28. *Courier Post*, 14, 15, 20–23 July 1999; *New York Times*, 21 July 1999, N.J. sec., and 1 August 1999.

29. This connection was drawn in a news report in the *Washington Post*, 11 April 2000.

30. *Courier Post*, 14 June 2001, report of Milan's sentencing.

31. *Philadelphia Inquirer*, 31 March 2000, 1 April 2000; *Courier Post*, 31 March 2000, 1 April 2000.

32. *Philadelphia Inquirer*, 1 May 2000.

33. *Courier Post*, 6 May 2000.

34. *Courier Post*, 24 May 2000.

35. *New York Times*, 1 April 2000; *Philadelphia Inquirer*, 25 May and 14 June 2000. Kenny subsequently made the case for state intervention in essays in the *Courier Post*, 22 August 2000; and the *Philadelphia Inquirer*, 5 September 2000.

36. *Philadelphia Inquirer*, 13, 23, September, 16 October, 3 November 2000.

37. *Philadelphia Inquirer*, 22 November 2000; *Courier Post*, 22 November 2000. The

full text of the "Multi-Year Recovery Plan," as it was called, appeared on the New Jersey Department of Community Affairs website, at www.state.nj.us/dca/camdensummary.htm.

38. *Philadelphia Inquirer,* 22 September 2000.

39. Bryant's 24 June 2000 op. ed. piece in the *Inquirer* had ridiculed the state's offer of $12.5 million in additional funds for redevelopment as "almost laughable," charging the effort was a ploy to disenfranchise minorities in urban areas.

40. *Philadelphia Inquirer,* 24, 25 May 2001; *Courier Post,* 25 May 2001.

41. *New York Times,* 25 May 2001.

42. Her proposed compromise, immediately rejected by the state, was to confine the powers of the appointed COO to those already exercised by the chairman of the Local Finance Board, who had statutory control of all Camden city expenditures in excess of forty-five hundred dollars. Fax, 31 May 2001, in the files of Rutgers, Camden, Provost Roger Dennis, a central figure in trying to negotiate an agreement among the interested parties.

43. Jeffrey L. Nash to Wayne R. Bryant, 12 June 2001, copy in the files of Rutgers, Camden, Provost Roger Dennis.

44. *Philadelphia Inquirer,* 30 August, 6 September 2001; *Courier Post,* 8 September 2001; *Philadelphia Inquirer,* 2 October 2001.

45. *Philadelphia Inquirer,* 20 November 2001. A small rally in opposition to the bill formed under the leadership of Camden council member Ali Sloan El, the sole member independent of Camden County Democratic control. The open letter to the legislature he circulated that day raised the specter of racial discrimination, but neither the rally nor his remarks before the committee were reported.

46. *Courier Post,* 7 December 2001; *Philadelphia Inquirer,* 7 December 2001.

7. California's Industrial Garden

The author thanks Richard White, James Gregory, Thomas Sugrue, George Sánchez, Phil Ethington, the History Department at Stanford University, and the Department of History and the Michigan Society of Fellows at the University of Michigan.

1. AnnaLee Saxenian, *Regional Advantage: Culture and Competition in Silicon Valley and Route 128* (Cambridge: Harvard University Press, 1994); Sharon Zukin, *Landscapes of Power: From Detroit to Disney World* (Berkeley: University of California Press, 1991).

2. Barry Bluestone and Bennett Harrison, *The Deindustrialization of America: Plant Closings, Community Abandonment, and the Dismantling of Basic Industry* (New York: Basic Books, 1982); Richard M. Bernard and Bradley R. Rice, eds., *Sunbelt Cities: Politics and Growth Since World War II* (Austin: University of Texas Press, 1983); Carl Abbott, *The Metropolitan Frontier: Cities in the Modern American West* (Tucson: University of Arizona Press, 1993); Jefferson Cowie, *Capital Moves: RCA's Seventy-Year Quest for Cheap Labor* (Ithaca: Cornell University Press, 1999; reprint, New York: New Press, 2001).

3. For an excellent study of Oakland during World War II, see Marilyn Johnson, *The Second Gold Rush: Oakland and the East Bay in World War II* (Berkeley: University of California Press, 1993). On the sunbelt, see Bruce Schulman, *From Cotton Belt to Sunbelt: Federal Policy, Economic Development and the Transformation of the South, 1938–1980* (New York: Oxford University Press, 1990); and Ann Markusen, Peter Hall, Scott Campbell, and Sabina Deitrick, *The Rise of the Gunbelt: The Military Remapping of Industrial America* (New York: Oxford University Press, 1991). On the position of cities within the capitalist marketplace, see Paul E. Peterson, *City Limits* (Chicago: University of Chicago Press, 1981); and John H. Mollenkopf, *The Contested City* (Princeton: Princeton University Press, 1983).

4. Richard A. Walker, "Industry Builds the City: The Suburbanization of Manufac-

turing in the San Francisco Bay Area, 1850–1940" (photocopy); Edgard J. Hinkel and William E. McCann, eds., *Oakland, California, 1852–1938: Some Phases of the Social, Political, and Economic History* (Oakland: U.S. Works Progress Administration and the Oakland Public Library, 1939); Beth Bagwell, *Oakland: The Story of a City* (Novato: Presidio Press, 1982); Shirley Ann Wilson Moore, *To Place Our Deeds: The African American Community in Richmond, California, 1910–1963* (Berkeley: University of California Press, 2001).

5. "Industrial Empire," in *Oakland Tribune 1946 Year Book* (Oakland: Oakland Tribune, 1947); "Industry Has Growing Pains," in *Oakland Tribune 1945 Year Book* (Oakland: Oakland Tribune, 1946); Postwar Development Department, Oakland Chamber of Commerce, "Help Us Build a Bigger, Better Oakland," pamphlet, 1944; Oakland Chamber of Commerce, "It's an Amazing New West" (1946), "How to Win the Markets of the New West" (1948), "Why They Chose the Metropolitan Oakland Area of California: Facts that Led National Industries to Locate Branch Plants in Alameda County, California" (1951), pamphlets, Institute of Governmental Studies, University of California, Berkeley (hereafter cited as IGS). On the deep nineteenth-century legacy of American boosterism, see William Cronon, *Nature's Metropolis: Chicago and the Making of the Great West* (New York: Norton, 1991).

6. "Industrial Empire"; "Industry Has Growing Pains"; "Help Us Build"; Oakland Chamber of Commerce, "It's an Amazing New West," "How to Win," "Why They Chose." For an account of the ways in which prewar suburbanization was led by industrial, not residential, dispersal, see Richard A. Walker, "A Theory of Suburbanization: Capitalism and the Construction of Urban Space in the United States," in *Urbanization and Urban Planning in Capitalist Society*, ed. Michael Dear and Allen Scott (New York: Methuen, 1981), 383–429. For an account of postwar suburbanization that emphasizes the close linkages between neighborhoods and large factories, see Greg Hise, *Magnetic Los Angeles: Planning the Twentieth-Century Metropolis* (Baltimore: Johns Hopkins University Press, 1997).

7. Hise, *Magnetic Los Angeles*, 31–50; Kenneth T. Jackson, "The Spatial Dimensions of Social Control: Race, Ethnicity, and Government Housing Policy in the United States, 1918–1968," in *Modern Industrial Cities: History, Policy, and Survival*, ed. Bruce M. Stave (Beverly Hills, Calif.: Sage, 1981), 94; Gwendolyn Wright, *Building the Dream: A Social History of Housing in America* (Cambridge: MIT Press, 1981); Kenneth T. Jackson, *Crabgrass Frontier: The Suburbanization of the United States* (New York: Oxford University Press, 1985); Gail Radford, *Modern Housing for America: Policy Struggles in the New Deal Era* (Chicago: University of Chicago Press, 1996); George Lipsitz, *The Possessive Investment in Whiteness: How White People Profit From Identity Politics* (Philadelphia: Temple University Press, 1998); David Freund, "Making It Home: Race, Development, and the Politics of Place in Suburban Detroit, 1940–1967" (Ph.D. diss., University of Michigan, 1999).

8. David L. Kirp, John P. Dwyer, and Larry A. Rosenthal, *Our Town: Race, Housing, and the Soul of Suburbia* (New Brunswick, N.J.: Rutgers University Press, 1997); John E. Ullmann, *The Suburban Economic Network: Economic Activity, Resource Use, and the Great Sprawl* (New York: Praeger, 1977); Richard Harris, "Chicago's Other Suburbs," *Geographical Review* 84, no. 4 (1994): 394–410; Jon C. Teaford, *The Rough Road to Renaissance: Urban Revitalization in America* (Baltimore: Johns Hopkins University Press, 1990).

9. Andrew E. G. Jonas and David Wilson, "The City as Growth Machine: Critical Reflections Two Decades Later," in *The Urban Growth Machine: Critical Perspectives Two Decades Later*, ed. Jonas and Wilson (Albany: State University of New York Press, 1999), 7. The classic formulation of the growth machine thesis can be found in Harvey Molotch,

"The City as Growth Machine: Toward a Political Economy of Place," *American Journal of Sociology* 82 (1976): 309–30.

10. Fred Cox quoted in *Hayward Daily Review*, 3 January 1950.

11. Michael Kazin, *The Populist Persuasion: An American History* (New York: Basic Books, 1995), 1–6; Freund, "Making It Home," 3–57; Becky Nicolaides, *My Blue Heaven: Life and Politics in the Working-Class Suburbs of Los Angeles, 1920–1965* (Chicago: University of Chicago Press, 2002).

12. *San Leandro News-Observer,* 27 August 1948; *Wall Street Journal,* 4 March 1966; "San Leandro, California: Land of Sunshine and Flowers," pamphlet in "Historical Scrapbook of San Leandro," vol. 1, Local History Room, San Leandro Public Library; San Leandro Chamber of Commerce, "Your Success Story—Annual Report 1951," San Leandro Public Library; Alameda County Taxpayers Association, "News and Facts" (1955–1970), IGS.

13. On the California tax revolt, see David O. Sears and Jack Sitrin, *Tax Revolt: Something for Nothing in California* (Cambridge: Harvard University Press, 1982); and Clarence Y. H. Lo, *Small Property Versus Big Government: Social Origins of the Property Tax Revolt* (Berkeley: University of California Press, 1990). On taxes as one cornerstone of a broader New Right politics in California, see Lisa McGirr, *Suburban Warriors: The Origins of the New American Right* (Princeton: Princeton University Press, 2001).

14. East Shore Park Civic League representative quoted in the *San Leandro Reporter,* 13 February 1948. See also *San Leandro News-Observer,* 27 June, 4 and 18 July, 28 November, 1947; Jack Maltester, interview, San Leandro, Calif., 1 March 1999; Wes McClure, interview, San Leandro, Calif., 16 February 1999. Unless otherwise noted, all interviews were conducted by the author on audiocassette, and the tapes remain in his possession.

15. *San Leandro Reporter,* 5 and 12 March 1948; *San Leandro News-Observer,* 26 March, 2, 9, and 16 April 1948; Maltester, interview, McClure, interview.

16. On San Leandro's industrial strategy and its program to recruit industry to the city, see "Industrial Locations of the West: San Leandro," *Pacific Factory,* January 1957, and the collection of pamphlets and flyers in "Historical Scrapbook of San Leandro," vols. 1 and 3, Local History Room, San Leandro Public Library.

17. *San Leandro News-Observer,* 17 December 1948. For pamphlets and other materials related to the program to sell industry to San Leandro residents, see "Historical Scrapbook of San Leandro," vols. 1–7, Local History Room, San Leandro Public Library. For the larger, nationwide campaign, see Elizabeth Fones-Wolf, *Selling Free Enterprise: The Business Assault on Labor and Liberalism, 1945–60* (Urbana: University of Illinois Press, 1994).

18. *San Leandro News-Observer,* 12 September 1947, 9 January 1948. On the historical shifts in the inclusiveness of "Caucasian" and in the broader development of whiteness, see Matthew Frye Jacobson, *Whiteness of a Different Color: European Immigrants and the Alchemy of Race* (Cambridge: Harvard University Press, 1998). On blockbusting as a tactic of the real estate industry, see Amanda Seligman, "'Apologies to Dracula, Werewolf, and Frankenstein': White Homeowners and Blockbusters in Postwar Chicago," *Journal of the Illinois Historical Society* 94, no. 1 (spring 2001): 70–95.

19. *San Leandro News-Observer,* 12 September 1947, 9 January 1948, 21 May 1948; *San Francisco Chronicle,* 4 January 1948; letter from C. L. Dellums to Baptist Ministers Union, "1950 NAACP Outgoing" folder, box 9, C. L. Dellums Collection, Bancroft Library, University of California, Berkeley.

20. On housing statistics, see Jackson, "Spatial Dimensions of Social Control"; Aaron, *Shelter and Subsidies*; Freund, "Making It Home." On the complexity of California's postwar military- and educational-industrial complexes, see Roger Lotchin, *Fortress California: From Warfare to Welfare* (New York: Oxford University Press, 1992); and Rob Kling, Spencer Olin, and Mark Poster, eds., *Postsuburban California: The Transformation of Orange County Since World War II* (Berkeley: University of California Press, 1991).

21. "Standard Market Data for San Leandro, California," "Historical Scrapbook of San Leandro," vol. 3, Local History Room, San Leandro Public Library; *Official Statement of the City of San Leandro, Alameda County, California: City of San Leandro 1958 Library Bond, Series A* (San Leandro: City of San Leandro, 1958); *Wall Street Journal*, 4 March 1966.

22. *Fremont News-Register*, 18 February 1966, 3 April 1967, 22 and 23 February 1971.

23. Eden Writers, *Hayward: The First One Hundred Years* (Hayward: Hayward Centennials Committee, 1975); *Information Directory of the Hayward Area, California* (Hayward: Hayward Chamber of Commerce, 1950); *A Master Plan for Future Development* (Hayward: City of Hayward Planning Commission, 1953); Stanley Weir, *Separate Efforts, Similar Goals and Results: A Study of the New Public City of Fremont, California, for Comparison with Private New Communities* (Berkeley: Center for Planning and Development Research, July 1965), 10–15; Oral History Associates, *City of Fremont: The First Thirty Years, A History of Growth* (Sausalito, Calif.: Mission Peak Heritage Foundation, 1989), 33; Jack Parry, interview, Fremont, Calif., 5 May 1999.

24. Ronald Bartels, "The Incorporation of the City of Fremont, an Experiment in Municipal Government" (M.A. thesis, University of California at Berkeley, 1959), 12–14, 20, 31–38; Weir, *Separate Efforts*; Oral History Associates, *City of Fremont*; Parry, interview.

25. *Fremont News-Register*, 2 June 1955, 10 November 1955, 3 May 1956; Weir, *Separate Efforts*, 10–12; Oral History Associates, *City of Fremont*, 34–37; Parry, interview. For an account of zoning as a dimension of urban planning, see Marc Weiss, *The Rise of the Community Builders: The American Real Estate Industry and Land Planning* (New York: Columbia University Press, 1987); and Nigel Taylor, *Urban Planning Theory Since 1945* (Thousand Oaks, Calif.: Sage Publications, 1998). For a wonderful analysis of suburban protoenvironmentalism, see Andrew Rome, *The Bulldozer in the Countryside: Suburban Sprawl and the Rise of American Environmentalism* (New York: Cambridge University Press, 2001).

26. Weir, *Separate Efforts*, 13–14; Bartels, "Incorporation," 98–106; Parry, interview; Fremont Planning Department, *Fremont: The Planned City* (Fremont: City of Fremont, December 1963); Harold F. Wise Associates, "Preliminary General Plan for Fremont" (photocopy, Fremont Public Library, 1956).

27. Oral History Associates, *City of Fremont*, 52; Weir, *Separate Efforts*, 13–14.

28. *Fremont News Register*, 14 June 1956, 31 October 1957, 27 March 1958, 21 December 1960, 19 March 1964; "General Motors" file, Fremont Public Library. On the decentralization of American industry, including automobile manufacturing, see Larry Sawers and William K. Tabb, eds., *Sunbelt, Snowbelt: Urban Development and Regional Restructuring* (New York: Oxford University Press, 1994).

29. Catherine Bauer Wurster, *Housing and the Future of the San Francisco Bay Area* (Berkeley: Institute of Governmental Studies, 1963), 32; Weir, *Separate Efforts*, 45–48; *Fremont News Register*, 3 April 1967; U.S. Bureau of the Census, *1970 Census of Population and Housing, San Francisco-Oakland, California* (Washington, D.C.: U.S. Government Printing Office, 1973).

30. *Fremont News Register,* 3 October 1957, 5 March 1964, 8 April 1967.

31. *Fremont News Register,* 18 and 28 February, 1, 2, 9, and 21 March, 1, 3, 7, 12 April, 6 and 14 June 1966.

32. U.S. Bureau of the Census, *U.S. Census of Housing and Population: 1960, San Francisco-Oakland, California* (Washington, D.C.: U.S. Government Printing Office, 1961); U.S. Bureau of the Census, *1970 Census;* "News/Facts: Property Tax Rates," published by the Alameda County Taxpayers Association, 1962–1973 IGS; Auditor of Alameda County, "Alameda County Tax Rates, Fiscal Year," n.d., Bancroft Library, University of California, Berkeley; Auditor-Controller of Alameda County, "Tax Rates, County of Alameda, Fiscal Year," n.d., Bancroft Library, University of California, Berkeley.

33. Donald McCullum and John Reading quoted in *Hearing Before the U.S. Commission on Civil Rights,* Oakland, California, May 4–6, 1967, 443, 451, 455–56. On discourses of race, power, and decline in 1960s urban America, see Robert A. Beauregard, *Voices of Decline: The Postwar Fate of U.S. Cities* (Cambridge, Mass.: Blackwell, 1993); Robin D. G. Kelley, *Yo Mama's Disfunktional: Fighting the Culture Wars in Urban America* (Boston: Beacon Press, 1997); John Hartigan Jr., *Racial Situations: Class Predicaments of Whiteness in Detroit* (Princeton: Princeton University Press, 1999); Michael, B. Katz, *The Price of Citizenship: Redefining the American Welfare State* (New York: Metropolitan Books, 2001).

34. William L. Nicholls and Earl R. Babbie, *Oakland in Transition: A Summary of the 701 Household Survey* (Berkeley: Survey Research Center, June 1969), 5, 129; *Oakland's Economy: Background and Projections* (Oakland: Oakland City Planning Department, 1976), 29; U.S. Bureau of the Census, *United States Census of Manufactures, Area Statistics: California* (Washington, D.C.: U.S. Government Printing Office, 1958, 1963, 1967, 1972).

35. On San Francisco–led regionalization efforts, see Association of Bay Area Governments, *Emergence of a Regional Concept* (Berkeley: Association of Bay Area Governments, 1976).

8. Deindustrialization, Poverty, and Federal Area Redevelopment

The author thanks William R. Childs, Jeff Cowie, Susan M. Hartmann, Joseph Heathcott, and Laura J. Hilton for their thoughtful comments and suggestions.

1. The issue of exploring the intersection of politics, economics, and social change in historical analysis draws on the work of Theda Skocpol and Brian Balogh. See Theda Skocpol, *Protecting Soldiers and Mothers: The Political Origins of Social Policy in the United States* (Cambridge: Harvard University Press, 1992); and Balogh's introduction to *Integrating the 1960s: The Origins, Structures, and Legitimacy of Public Policy in a Turbulent Decade* (University Park: Pennsylvania State University Press, 1996).

2. For a general history of the ARA see Sar Levitan, *Federal Aid to Depressed Areas: An Evaluation of the Area Redevelopment Administration* (Baltimore: Johns Hopkins Press, 1964); and Gregory Wilson, "Before the Great Society: Liberalism, Deindustrialization, and Area Redevelopment in the United States, 1933–1965" (Ph.D. diss., Ohio State University, 2001).

3. Memo, no author, 10 October 1935, "Memo to Mr. Ross on Resume of S.E.R. Work" folder, box 1, record group 69, Records of the Works Projects Administration, Records of the Federal Emergency Relief Administration, Records of the Sectional Economic Research Project, 1933–1937, National Archives, College Park, Maryland; memo, Alfred C. Wolf to J. Donald Kingsley, 8 January 1947, "Previous Programs" folder, John R. Steelman Files, Papers of Harry S. Truman, Harry S. Truman Library, Independence, Missouri (hereafter cited as Steelman Files-HSTL).

4. Memo, "Procedure Used by OPM for Handling Priority Unemployment in Distress Areas," "Previous Programs" folder, Steelman Files-HSTL.

5. See *U.S. Statues at Large*, 60 (Washington, D.C.: U.S. Government Printing Office, 1946), pt. 1, 23.

6. The advent of the CEA and the Joint Economic Committee signaled the institutionalization of economists as policy makers, and reflected the growing cooperation of intellectuals, or "experts," and the state. On the nature of the relationship between economists and the state, see Edward S. Flash Jr., *Economic Advice and Presidential Leadership: The Council of Economic Advisers* (New York: Columbia University Press, 1965); Mary O. Furner and Barry Supple, eds., *The State and Economic Knowledge: The American and British Experiences* (Cambridge: Cambridge University Press, 1990); as well as Michael A. Bernstein, "American Economics and the American Economy in the American Century: Doctrinal Legacies and Contemporary Policy Problems," in *Understanding American Economic Decline*, ed. Michael A. Bernstein and David E. Adler (New York: Cambridge University Press, 1994), 361–93.

7. Conley Dillon, "Channeling Government Contracts into Depressed Areas," *Western Political Quarterly* 16 (June 1963): 279–93.

8. For a summary of the contradictions within federal community development policy, see Alice O'Connor, "Swimming against the Tide: A Brief History of Federal Policy in Poor Communities," in *Urban Problems and Community Development*, ed. Ronald F. Ferguson and William T. Dickens (Washington, D.C.: Brookings Institution Press, 1999), 77–138. On industrial policy and planning in the United States, see Otis L. Graham Jr., *Toward a Planned Society: From Roosevelt to Nixon* (New York: Oxford University Press, 1976); Claude E. Barfield and William A. Schambra, eds., *The Politics of Industrial Policy* (Washington, D.C.: American Enterprise Institute, 1986); Otis L. Graham Jr., *Losing Time: The Industrial Policy Debate* (Cambridge: Harvard University Press, 1992); and Patrick D. Reagan, *Designing a New America: The Origins of New Deal Planning, 1890–1943* (Amherst: University of Massachusetts Press, 1999).

9. John Kenneth Galbraith, *The Affluent Society* (New York: Houghton Mifflin, 1958).

10. Jacob J. Kaufman and Helmut J. Golatz, *Chronic Unemployment in Pennsylvania* (University Park: Pennsylvania State University Press, 1960), 1.

11. On this trend see Donald R. Gilmore, *Developing the "Little" Economies* (New York: Committee for Economic Development, 1960).

12. Unemployment figures from Senate Committee on Banking and Currency, *Area Redevelopment—1961, Hearings*, 87th Cong., 1st sess., 18, 19, 26 January and 20 February 1961.

13. For developments in the South see Bruce Schulman, *From Cotton Belt to Sunbelt: Federal Policy, Economic Development, and the Transformation of the South, 1938–1980* (New York: Oxford University Press, 1991); and James C. Cobb, *The Selling of the South: The Southern Crusade for Industrial Development, 1936–1990*, 2d ed. (Urbana: University of Illinois Press, 1993).

14. Peter K. Eisinger, *The Rise of the Entrepreneurial State: State and Local Economic Development Policy in the United States* (Madison: University of Wisconsin Press, 1988), quote on 3.

15. Press release, 7 February 1956, "Industrial Development Plan: Releases, 1955–58" folder, box 19, George M. Leader Papers, Pennsylvania State Archives, Harrisburg; "New State Industry-Aid Plan Offered," *Pittsburgh Post-Gazette*, 8 February 1956, 4.

16. PIDA statistics in Commonwealth of Pennsylvania, *Pennsylvania Industrial Development Authority: Thirty-five Years of Job-Creating Loans* (Harrisburg: Pennsylvania Department of Commerce, 1991). See also Glenn H. Petry's "The Impact of the Pennsylvania Industrial Development Authority on Employment in Depressed Areas" (honors thesis, Pennsylvania State University, 1967).

17. The study (Washington, D.C.: U.S. Department of Commerce, 1965) is a testament to the growing connection of experts and policy makers across political boundaries and of the exchange of ideas between the United States and Europe. On a related note see Daniel Rogers, *Atlantic Crossings: Social Politics in a Progressive Age* (Cambridge: Harvard University Press, 1998).

18. See William F. Hartford, *Where Is Our Responsibility? Unions and Economic Change in the New England Textile Industry, 1870–1960* (Amherst: University of Massachusetts Press, 1996), 183–95; and Roger H. Davidson, *Coalition Building for Depressed Areas Bills: 1955–1965* (Indianapolis: Bobbs-Merrill, 1966), 6–11.

19. *Congressional Record*, 84th Cong., 1st sess., 1955, 101, pt. 9:11754–56.

20. Davidson, *Coalition Building*, 6.

21. See U.S. Congress, Joint Committee on the Economic Report, Subcommittee on Low-Income Families, *Hearings: Low-Income Families*, 84th Cong., 2d sess., 18, 19, 21, 22, 23 November 1955. On the South see Schulman, *From Cotton Belt to Sunbelt*, and Cobb, *Selling of the South*.

22. *Congressional Record*, 85th Cong., 2d sess., 104, pt. 7: 8526.

23. Ibid., 8532.

24. *Congressional Record*, 84th Cong., 2d sess., 102, pt. 11:14445.

25. On the legislation see Paul Douglas, *In the Fullness of Time: The Memoirs of Paul H. Douglas* (New York: Harcourt, Brace, Jovanovich, 1972), 517; and Senate Committee on Labor and Public Welfare, *Area Redevelopment: Hearings before the Subcommittee on Labor on S. 2663*, 84th Cong., 2d. sess., 4, 6, 9, 23, 26 January and 3, 9, 10, 24 February 1956, 790 (hereafter cited as *ARA Hearings, 1956*). For an overview of development policies related to Native Americans see Larry Burt, "Western Tribes and Balance Sheets: Business Development Programs in the 1960s and 1970s," *The Western Historical Quarterly* 23 (November 1992): 475–95; and Thomas Francis Clarkin, "The New Trail and the Great Society: Federal Indian Policy During the Kennedy-Johnson Administrations" (Ph.D. diss., University of Texas, 1998).

26. On developments within the Eisenhower administration in 1954 see "Minutes, Advisory Board on Economic Growth and Stability," 24 February 1954, "Advisory" folder, box 318, official files, Papers of Dwight D. Eisenhower, Dwight D. Eisenhower Library (hereafter cited as DDEL), Abilene, Kansas; and letter, Batt to George Brown, special assistant to the secretary of labor, 16 February 1953, "Batt" folder, box 89, Papers of James P. Mitchell, DDEL. See also Davidson, *Coalition Building*, 6.

27. On gender roles in the anthracite region see John Bodnar, *Anthracite People: Families, Unions, and Work, 1900–1940* (Harrisburg: Pennsylvania Historical and Museum Commission, 1983); Michael Kozura, "We Stood Our Ground: Anthracite Miners and the Expropriation of Corporate Property, 1930–1941," in *"We Are All Leaders": The Alternative Unionism of the Early 1930s*, ed. Staughton Lynd (Urbana: University of Illinois Press, 1996), 199–237; and Thomas Dublin, *When the Mines Closed: Stories of Struggles in Hard Times* (Ithaca: Cornell University Press, 1998).

28. Matheson and shop steward quotes in *ARA Hearings, 1956*, 71.

29. Ibid., 450.

30. On gender, the family, and juvenile delinquency in 1950s America, see, among others, James Gilbert, *A Cycle of Outrage: America's Reaction to the Juvenile Delinquent of the 1950s* (New York: Oxford University Press, 1986); Elaine Tyler May, *Homeward Bound: American Families in the Cold War Era* (New York: Basic Books, 1988); Joanne Meyerowitz, ed., *Not June Cleaver: Women and Gender in Postwar America, 1945–1960* (Philadelphia: Temple University Press, 1994); and Michael Kimmel, *Manhood in America: A Cultural History* (New York: Free Press, 1996).

31. See Senate Banking and Currency Committee, *Area Redevelopment Legislation*, 86th Cong., 2d. sess., 18 August 1960, 99–100.

32. Davidson, *Coalition Building*, 22–7; and Levitan, *Federal Aid*, 18–20.

33. For a summary of this see David Steigerwald, *The Sixties and the End of Modern America* (New York: St. Martin's Press, 1995).

34. Press release, 5 March 1964, "Pennsylvania, 1965" folder, box 16, record group 378, Records of the Economic Development Administration, Records of the Office of the Administrator, William L. Batt Jr., Area Redevelopment Administration, subject files, 1961–1965, National Archives, College Park, Maryland (hereafter cited as ARA-NARA); U.S. Department of Commerce, Area Redevelopment Administration, *Directory of Approved Projects as of June 30, 1965* (Washington, D.C.: U.S. Department of Commerce, 1965).

35. U.S. Department of Commerce, Area Redevelopment Administration, *Directory of Approved Projects*.

36. Transcript of Harold Williams speech, 21 January 1964, "Speeches, Lectures, Statements ARA" folder, box 1, William L. Batt Jr. reading files, 1961–1965, ARA-NARA; press release, 5 March 1964, box 16, William L. Batt Jr. subject files, 1961–1965, ARA-NARA; U.S. Department of Commerce, Area Redevelopment Administration, *Directory of Approved Projects*.

37. Statistics from U.S. Bureau of the Census and various labor market reports in record group 16, Papers of the Department of Labor and Industry, Pennsylvania State Archives, Harrisburg.

38. Daniel L. Goldy to William L. Batt Jr., 13 February 1962, "Interior" folder, box 2, Records of H. W. Williams, general subject and signature files, 1962–1965, ARA-NARA; Clarkin, "The New Trail," 136, 383–89.

39. Press release, "ARA Aids Industrial Development on U.S. Indian Reservations to Generate New Job Opportunities," 11 October 1964, "Bureau of Indian Affairs" folder, box 9, Records of Gordon E. Reckord, mixed administration and program files, ARA-NARA.

40. See Burt, "Western Tribes," 480–94.

41. See correspondence in "Civil Rights" folder, box 5, William L. Batt Jr. subject files, 1961–1965, ARA-NARA.

42. William L. Batt, Jr., oral history interview, transcript, 1966, 1967, John F. Kennedy Library, Boston, Mass., 109.

43. See various monthly division reports in box 14, William L. Batt Jr. subject files, 1961–1965, ARA-NARA.

44. Memo, George Robinson to Batt, 21 April 1965, "Office of Economic Opportunity" folder, box 6, Records of the Office of the Deputy Administrator, H. W. Williams, general subject and signature files, 1962–1965, ARA-NARA.

45. Memo, "Administration of Title IV," box 7, Records of Gordon E. Reckord, ARA-NARA.

46. Memo, "Federal Aid to Depressed Areas," 11 October 1964; R. S. Adkins to Charles Schultze, 19 January 1965; press release, "Message on Area and Regional Development," 25 March 1965; all in "Background Budget Papers E" folder, box 1, Legislative Background, Appalachia Regional Development and Public Works Collection, Lyndon Baines Johnson Library, Austin, Texas.

47. Memo, "Facts About EDA," "Pubic Works and Economic Development Act of 1965" folder, box 3, Records of Benjamin Chinitz, ARA-NARA.

48. Both quotes in Walter I. Trattner, *From Poor Law to Welfare State: A History of Social Welfare in America*, 6th ed. (New York: Free Press, 1999), 322. See also Michael B. Katz, *In the Shadow of the Poorhouse: A Social History of Welfare in America*, 10th anniversary ed. (New York: Basic Books, 1996); and James Patterson, *America's Struggle against Poverty in the Twentieth Century* (Cambridge: Harvard University Press, 2000).

49. On community development and industrial policy see Ferguson and Dickens, *Urban Problems and Community Development*; and Eisinger, *Rise of the Entrepreneurial State*; as well as R. Scott Fosler and Renee A. Berger, eds., *Public-Private Partnership in American Cities* (Lexington, Mass.: D.C. Heath, 1982); and R. Scott Fosler, ed., *Local Economic Development: Strategies for a Changing Economy* (Washington, D.C.: International City Management Association, 1991).

9. Collateral Damage

This chapter was presented at the conference "Winning and Losing in the New Economy: Work, Employment, and Society" held in Notthingham, England, on 12 September 2001.

1. Barry Bluestone and Bennett Harrison, *The Deindustrialization of America: Plant Closings, Community Abandonment, and the Dismantling of Basic Industry* (New York: Basic Books, 1982).

2. For a detailed discussion of the local efforts to buy one of the mills, see Staughton Lynd, *The Fight against Shutdowns* (San Pedro: Singlejack Books, 1982).

3. In 1919, the U.S. bishops' *Pastoral Letter on Social Reconstruction* provided a foundation in Catholic social teaching for the obligation of the state in economic affairs in appealing for economic justice. Within the religious community, the *Pastoral* became the basis for lobbying for New Deal reforms over the next two decades. With the dismantling of the welfare state by the Reagan administration in the 1980s, U.S. bishops in their *Pastoral Letter of the Economy* (1984) felt compelled to reiterate the themes from the earlier pastoral letter in light of changes in contemporary capitalism, deindustrialization, and the plight of American workers and their unions. In so doing, it provided a moral and ethical challenge to current U.S. economic policy.

4. Sharon Turco, "History Defines Campbell's New Look," *Vindicator,* 4 July 1999, A1.

5. Youngstown State University Center for Urban Studies, *Youngstown: State of the City* (Youngstown: Center for Urban Studies, 1995), 1–2. Also see David Rusk, *Cities Without Suburbs* (Washington, D.C.: Woodrow Wilson Center Press, 1993).

6. Thomas Petzinger Jr., *Wall Street Journal*, 18 October 1978, 48.

7. Eileen Keerdoja, "Youngstown's Woes," *Newsweek*, 20 March 1978, 14.

8. "A Huge Pink Slip for an Ohio City," *Business Week*, 3 October 1977, 39.

9. John Russo was periodically called by publications such as *Time* magazine to check on Youngstown's situation.

10. Mark Shields, "The Pain of Youngstown," *Washington Post*, 26 October 1984, A23.

11. "Youngstown's Uneasy Future As the Mills Close Their Doors," *U.S. News and World Report*, 11 February 1980, 70.

12. David Moberg, *Shutdown* (Chicago: In These Times, n.d.), 2–11. This book is a reprint of a four-part series first appearing in *In These Times*, 27 June, 4 July, 11 July, and 18 July 1979.

13. Bluestone and Harrison, *Deindustrialization of America*.

14. Larry Adelman, *The Business of America* (San Francisco: California Newsreel, 1984).

15. Dale Maharidge and Michael Williamson, *Journey to Nowhere: The Saga of the New Underclass* (1985; reprint, New York: Hyperion, 1996).

16. James M. Perry, "Down and Out: Idle Mills, a Dearth of Hope Are Features of Ohio's Steel Towns," *Wall Street Journal*, 20 January 1983, 1, 14.

17. Peter Kilborn, "The Twilight of Smokestack America," *New York Times*, 8 May 1983, sec. 3, p. 1.

18. "The Talk of the Town," *New Yorker*, 29 April 1985, 28.

19. Quoted in "Songs on Bruce Springsteen's New Album Inspired by 'Journey to Nowhere,'" *CBS This Morning*, CBS News, 22 January 1996.

20. "Songs on Bruce Springsteen's New Album."

21. *Nightly Business Report*, Community Television Foundation of South Florida, 10 July 1998.

22. Roger Smith, "Lockups Lead Way to New Economy," *Vindicator*, 27 June 1999, A1–A4.

23. Vincent Duffy and Linda Wertheimer, "Youngstown Escape," *All Things Considered*, National Public Radio, 30 July 1998, transcript 98073011–212.

24. Jane Pauley, "House of Correction? Community Outrage over Profit-Driven Prison in Youngstown, Ohio," *Dateline NBC*, NBC News Transcripts, 11 October 1998.

25. Ed Bradley, "Medium Security, Maximum Problems," *60 Minutes*, CBS News, 2 May 1999.

26. Pauley, "House of Correction?"

27. Bradley, "Medium Security, Maximum Problems."

28. Barry Yoeman, "Steel Town Lockdown," *Mother Jones*, May/June 2000, 40.

29. Ibid.

30. Kevin Dressor, cover illustration, "Welcome to Youngstown: A Story of the Mafia, the FBI, a Congressman, and the Most Crooked City in America," *New Republic*, 10 and 17 July 2000.

31. Chris Whitley, "Homocide Rate Remains High," *Vindicator*, 28 November 1999, A1–A3.

32. Elizabeth Marchak, "Youngstown Black Women Suffer Reign of Violence," *Plain Dealer*, 14 March 2000, A1.

33. C. Allen Pierce Jr., interview by authors, Youngstown, Ohio, 11 July 2000. See also Latisha Bunkley, "Youth Who Kill: A Case Study Approach" (M.A. thesis, Youngstown State University, 1999); C. Allen Pierce, "Epidemic Theory as Applied to Incidence of Homicides" (paper presented at the 34th annual meeting of the Academy of Criminal Justice Sciences, Louisville, Kentucky, 14 March 1997); Christopher T. Lowenkamp and C. Allen Pierce, "Comparative Analysis between High and Low Homicide Rate Cities" (paper presented at the 35th annual meeting of the Academy of Criminal Justice Sciences, Albuquerque, New Mexico, 13 March 1998).

34. Richard Bee and Yih-wu Liu, "An Analysis of Crime and Economic Conditions

in a Declining Area," *Akron Business and Economic Review* 15, no. 4 (winter 1984): 25–29. Also see Richard Bee and Yih-wu Liu, "Modeling Criminal Activity in an Area of Economic Decline," *The American Journal of Economics and Sociology* 42, no. 4 (October 1983): 385–92.

35. Jolie Solomon with Bruce Shenitz and Daniel McMinn, "Mickey's Secret Life," *Newsweek*, 31 August 1992, 70.

36. Ibid.

37. Jim Gilmore, Paul Judge, and Paul Solman, "How to Steal $500 Million," *Frontline*, Public Broadcasting Service, 8 November 1994.

38. Marcus Gleisser, "Ex-Football Player Pleads Guilty to Jury Tampering," *Plain Dealer*, 6 August 1996, 4C.

39. Gilmore, Judge, and Solman, "How to Steal $500 Million."

40. Solomon et al., "Mickey's Secret Life."

41. Ibid.

42. John Kobler, "Crime Town USA," *Saturday Evening Post* 236 (9 March 1963): 71–76.

43. "Sheriff in an Ohio Town Faces Bribery and Extortion Charges," *New York Times*, 7 February 1999, 19.

44. Mark Niquette, "Mob's Pull in Valley is an Investment in Microsoft," *Vindicator*, 7 March 1999, A1–A3.

45. Jack Hunter, "A Closer Look at Youngstown's History with Former Mayors Jack Hunter and Pat Ungaro" (panel discussion in Universal Café series, First Unitarian Church, Youngstown, Ohio, 17 July 2000); Pierce, "Epidemic Theory."

46. "The Ten Most Corrupt Cities," *George* 3, no. 2 (March 1998).

47. Jeff Glaser, "The Sopranos Come to Youngstown, Ohio: The Feds Target a Local Hero in a Shady Town," *U.S. News and World Report*, 6 March 2000.

48. James F. McCarty, "Traficant Plays Familiar Role," *Cleveland Plain Dealer*, 6 February 2000, 1B.

49. Ibid.

50. William Claiborne, "A Rust Belt Democrat Will Not Go Gently," *Washington Post*, 26 February 2000, A3.

51. Ibid.

52. Mark Rollenhagen, "Trial Shows Mob Still a Concern in Youngstown: Strollo Racketeering Case Starts Tuesday," *Cleveland Plain Dealer*, 14 February 1999, 1B.

53. Rick Porello, *To Kill an Irishman: The War That Crippled the Mafia* (Cleveland: Next Hat, 1998), 184.

54. Ibid.

55. *Creating a Culture of Lawfulness: The Palermo, Sicily, Renaissance*, conference booklet (Palermo: United Nations and Sicilian Renaissance Institute, 2000).

56. Allesandra Siracusa, "Educating for Citizenship: Reconstructing the Identity of Our City" (paper presented at the conference, "Creating a Culture of Lawfulness: The Palermo, Sicily, Renaissance," 14 December 2000).

10. Envisioning the Steel City

1. Warren Cohen, "Gary's New Beauties: Hoping for a Makeover," *U.S. News and World Report*, 13 March 2000, 27.

2. *CNN World Today*, Cable News Network, 10 March 2000, transcript.

3. Ibid.

4. On the term "deindustrialization," see Barry Bluestone and Bennett Harrison, *The Deindustrialization of America: Plant Closings, Community Abandonment, and the Dismantling of Basic Industry* (New York: Basic Books, 1982), 6–7.

5. *Chicago Tribune*, 6 March 1988; Gary *Post-Tribune*, 1 January 1985.

6. For studies that challenge the timing of "deindustrialization," see Jefferson Cowie, *Capital Moves: RCA's Seventy-Year Quest for Cheap Labor* (Ithaca: Cornell University Press, 1999; reprint, New York: New Press, 2001); and Thomas J. Sugrue, *Origins of the Urban Crisis: Race and Inequality in Postwar Detroit* (Princeton: Princeton University Press, 1996).

7. Robert Bruno shows the way that steel-production labor created a sense of class identity that united the residents of Youngstown, Ohio. Robert Bruno, *Steelworker Alley: How Class Works in Youngstown* (Ithaca: ILR Press, 1999).

8. "A Tired Town's Beauty Queen Solution," *ABC News*, American Broadcasting Companies, 28 February 2001.

9. On Gary, see Raymond Mohl and Neil Betten, *Steel City: Urban and Ethnic Patterns in Gary, Indiana, 1906–1950* (New York: Holmes and Meyer, 1986); Ronald Cohen and Raymond Mohl, *The Paradox of Progressive Education: The Gary Plan and Urban Schooling* (Port Washington, N.Y.: Kennikat Press, 1979); James B. Lane, *City of the Century: A History of Gary, Indiana* (Bloomington: Indiana University Press, 1978); and Andrew Hurley, *Environmental Inequalities: Class, Race, and Industrial Pollution in Gary, Indiana, 1945–1980* (Chapel Hill: University of North Carolina Press, 1995).

10. David Harvey, *The Urbanization of Capital* (Baltimore: Johns Hopkins University Press, 1985), 25.

11. "Gary: The Largest and Most Modern Steel Works in Existence," *Scientific American*, 11 December 1909; "Gary—Pittsburg[h]'s Future Rival," *American Review of Reviews* 39 (February 1909).

12. Daniel Vincent Casey, "The Sum of a Thousand Short Cuts," *System* 15 (January 1909). On the steel industry, see John P. Hoerr, *And the Wolf Finally Came: The Decline of the American Steel Industry* (Pittsburgh: University of Pittsburgh Press, 1988).

13. Gary *Post-Tribune*, 5 June 1986; Paul Glastris, "Steel's Hollow Comeback," *U.S. News and World Report*, 8 May 1986, 49–51.

14. William E. Schmidt, "A Steel City Still Needs Help Despite Big Steel's Comeback," *New York Times*, 4 September 1989.

15. Matt O'Connor, "U.S. Steel, Now USX, Regroups," *Chicago Tribune*, 9 July 1986.

16. Hurley, *Environmental Inequalities*.

17. Graham Romeyn Taylor, "Creating the Newest Steel City," *Survey* 22 (April 1909).

18. *Scientific American*, 11 December 1909.

19. Henry Fuller, "An Industrial Utopia: Building Gary, Indiana, to Order," *Harper's Weekly* 51 (12 October 1907).

20. John Kimberly Mumford, "This Land of Opportunity: Gary, the City That Rose from a Sandy Waste," *Harper's Weekly* 52 (4 July 1908); Charles Pierce Burton, "Gary—A Creation," *Independent* 70 (16 February 1911); Eugene J. Buffington, "Making Cities for Workmen," *Harper's Weekly* 53 (8 May 1909).

21. *Chicago Tribune*, October 5–9, 1919. Throughout the strike, the mills at Gary Works remained, as advertised, untouched by protesting workers. On the strike, see David Brody, *Labor in Crisis: The Steel Strike of 1919* (Philadelphia: Lippincott, 1965).

22. Indianapolis *Indiana Daily Times*, 5, 6 October 1919.

23. One of the most common references to Gary dates from this period. In *The Mu-*

sic Man, a con man tells the people of River City, Iowa, that he is a graduate of a Gary musical academy, class of 1903. The town librarian catches him when she learns that the city did not exist until 1909. There is also an absurdity to the hustler's comparisons of Gary to the cultural centers of Paris, Rome, and New York. Clearly the townspeople know little of Gary's true purpose as a city; however, the audience certainly would.

24. *Chicago Examiner,* 27 January 1922; "Gary's Bootlegging Administration," *Literary Digest,* 21 April 1923; "The Gary Liquor Scandal," *Outlook,* 18 April 1923; "Sin in Gary? Yes," *Newsweek,* 8 August 1944; "Steel and Sex," *Quick,* May 1955.

25. Robert H. Zieger, *The CIO: 1935–1955* (Chapel Hill: University of North Carolina Press, 1995), 54–60.

26. Federal Writers Project, Indiana, *Calumet Region Historical Guide* (Gary: German Printing, 1939); A. B. Hendry, "The Angry Housewives of Gary," *Coronet,* June 1951; Bernard Spong, "How We Cleaned Up Gary," *Male,* February 1953; Joan Younger, "Time for Another Murder," *Ladies Home Journal,* December 1953.

27. "Gary Turns Her Back on Bias," *Ebony* 11, no. 9 (July 1956).

28. On Richard Hatcher and Gary politics, see Edward Greer, *Big Steel: Black Politics and Corporate Power in Gary, Indiana* (New York: Monthly Review Press, 1979); and Alex Poinsett, *Black Power, Gary Style: The Making of Mayor Richard Gordon Hatcher* (Chicago: Johnson Publishing, 1970).

29. Richard Mercer Dorson, *Land of the Millrats* (Cambridge: Harvard University Press, 1981), 18.

30. Ibid., 24.

31. Ibid., 11. On white flight and urban segregation see Arnold Richard Hirsch, *Making the Second Ghetto: Race and Housing in Chicago, 1940–1960* (New York: Cambridge University Press, 1983); and Sugrue, *Origins of the Urban Crisis.*

32. Dorson, *Land of the Millrats,* 166.

33. Ibid, 198.

34. Ibid., 199–200.

35. Ibid., 195.

36. Ibid., 212; "Work Experiences in the Calumet Region," *Steel Shavings* 7 (1981).

37. Glastris, "Steel's Hollow Comeback"; Hoerr, *And the Wolf Finally Came,* 39–48.

38. Hoerr, *And the Wolf Finally Came,* 427–46. On the steel industry and labor negotiations see Judith Stein, *Running Steel, Running America: Race, Economic Policy, and the Decline of Liberalism* (Chapel Hill: University of North Carolina Press, 1998).

39. Gary *Post-Tribune,* 20, 21 September 1987.

40. Ibid.

41. Ibid.

42. Godfrey Hodgson and George Crile, "Gary: Epitaph for a Model City," *Washington Post,* 4 March 1973.

43. Schmidt, "Steel City."

44. Gary *Post-Tribune,* 30 September 1985.

45. Gary *Post-Tribune,* 21 September 1987.

46. *Chicago Tribune,* 4 August 1985.

47. Hurley, *Environmental Inequalities,* 1–2.

48. Ibid.; *Chicago Tribune,* 17 April 1988.

49. Gary *Post-Tribune,* 2 January 1994.

50. Gary *Post-Tribune,* 8, 9 January 1994.

51. Gary *Post-Tribune,* 21–27 October 1994.

52. Gary *Post-Tribune*, 3, 8 January 1995.

53. *Chicago Tribune*, 17 April 1988.

54. Karen Springen, "The Donald Goes West," *Newsweek*, 15 March 1999; remarks by Secretary Andrew Cuomo, 28 April 1999, National Press Club, Washington, D.C., transcript, Housing and Urban Development.

55. Housing and Urban Development, press releases, "Cuomo Awards $1.1 Million in Grants to Fight Drugs and Crime in Public Housing in East Chicago, Gary, and Hammond, Indiana," 20 October 1998, and "Cuomo Announces $19.8 Million Hope VI Grant to Gary, Indiana, to Transform Public Housing and Help Residents," 1 September 1999; Robert A. Catlin, *Racial Politics and Urban Planning: Gary, Indiana, 1980–1989* (Lexington: University Press of Kentucky, 1993), 147–91; Chicago Department of Aviation, press release, "A Proposal for the Future of O'Hare," 29 June 2001.

56. "Gary Gambles on a New Image," Gary *Post-Tribune*, 24 October 1993.

57. Michael Moore, "Flint and Me," *Money*, July 1996, 86.

58. "Lawmaker in Huff over Buffaloans in the Buff," CNN website, 23 June 2000.

59. Moore, "Flint and Me," 86.

60. See, for example, Steven Dandaneau, *A Town Abandoned: Flint, Michigan, Confronts Deindustrialization* (Albany: State University of New York Press, 1996); and Kathryn Marie Dudley, *End of the Line: Lost Jobs, New Lives in Postindustrial America* (Chicago: University of Chicago Press, 1994); and Bruno, *Steelworker Alley*.

61. Dorson, *Land of the Millrats*; Hodgson and Crile, "Gary"; Fuller, "Industrial Utopia." On deindustrialization and inner cities, see Sugrue, *Origins of the Urban Crisis*.

11. Monuments of a Lost Cause

1. The quote is from the official Allegheny County website at www.county.allegheny.pa.us/economic/advances/sum2000/monconn.asp, accessed in November 2000. For a recent study of the redevelopment process, see Roy Lubove, *Twentieth-Century Pittsburgh* (Pittsburgh: University of Pittsburgh Press, 1996).

2. *Pittsburgh Post-Gazette*, 12 November 2000, D1.

3. See Lubove, *Twentieth-Century Pittsburgh* for the quote about eliminating blue-collar tinge. The vexed relationship between the old steel image and the new high-tech image produces gnashing of teeth in the local media, for example in Linda Dickerson, "Perspectives: Bayer's Leader Says to Tear Down the City's Old Image," *Pittsburgh Post-Gazette*, 2 April 2000.

4. For the industry's impact on labor, see, among others, John Bodnar, *Immigration and Industrialization: Ethnicity in an American Mill Town, 1870–1940* (Pittsburgh: University of Pittsburgh Press, 1977); John P. Hoerr, *And the Wolf Finally Came: The Decline of the American Steel Industry* (Pittsburgh: University of Pittsburgh Press, 1988). Hoerr points out, for example, that wages were extremely low in the industry until World War II, but even when wages improved, strikes or threats of strikes were omnipresent in the steelworkers' lives. For a recent study of technological innovation, see Mark M. Brown, "The Architecture of Steel: Site Planning and Building Type in the Nineteenth-Century American Bessemer Steel Industry" (Ph.D. diss., University of Pittsburgh, 1995).

5. Kirk Savage, "The Past in the Present: The Life of Memorials," *Harvard Design Magazine* (fall 1999): 14–19. For a similar argument, see James E. Young, "Memory and Counter-Memory: The End of the Monument in Germany," *Harvard Design Magazine* (fall 1999): 6. The study of commemoration is a growth industry. Some of the more influential studies from the past fifteen years include David Lowenthal, *The Past Is a Foreign*

Country (Cambridge: Cambridge University Press, 1985); Pierre Nora, "Between Memory and History: *Les Lieux de Mémoire*," *Representations*, no. 26 (spring 1989): 7–25; John Bodnar, *Remaking America: Public Memory, Commemoration, and Patriotism in the Twentieth Century* (Princeton: Princeton University Press, 1992); James E. Young, *The Texture of Memory: Holocaust Memorials and Meaning* (New Haven: Yale University Press, 1993); John R. Gillis, ed., *Commemorations: The Politics of National Identity* (Princeton: Princeton University Press, 1994); and the special issue *Constructions of Memory: On Monuments Old and New* of *Harvard Design Magazine* (fall 1999). Usually overlooked but equally valuable are theoretical studies from the social sciences, such as Paul Connerton, *How Societies Remember* (Cambridge: Cambridge University Press, 1989); and David Middleton and Derek Edwards, eds., *Collective Remembering* (New York: Sage, 1990).

6. Bopaya Bidanda, "The 'Old Economy' Still Works in Pittsburgh," *Pittsburgh Post-Gazette*, 18 October 2000.

7. The term is credited to Indian art historian A. K. Coomaraswamy, and appeared in a book he coedited entitled *Essays in Post-Industrialism: A Symposium of Prophecy Concerning the Future of Society* (London, 1914). For more on this see Roger Lipsey, *Coomaraswamy: His Life and Work* (Princeton: Princeton University Press, 1977), 110–15; and Howard Brick, "Optimism of the Mind: Imagining Postindustrial Society in the 1960s and 1970s," *American Quarterly* 44 (September 1992): 350–51.

8. *Memorial of the Celebration of the Carnegie Institute* (Pittsburgh, 1907), 66–67.

9. James D. Van Trump, *An American Palace of Culture: The Carnegie Institute and Carnegie Library of Pittsburgh* (Pittsburgh: Carnegie Institute and Pittsburgh History and Landmarks Foundation, 1970).

10. The fountain-monument was designed by Augustus Saint-Gaudens, the leading American sculptor of the time, and Henry Bacon, later to become the architect of the Lincoln Memorial in Washington, D.C.; Vernon Gay, *Discovering Pittsburgh's Sculpture* (Pittsburgh: University of Pittsburgh Press, 1983).

11. Bailey Van Hook, *Angels of Art: Women and Art in American Society, 1876–1914* (University Park: Pennsylvania State University Press, 1996).

12. Caroline A. Jones, *The Machine in the Studio: Constructing The Postwar American Artist* (Chicago: University of Chicago Press, 1996). The evocation of the majestic scale and sublimity of the steel mill is commonplace in writing about the steel industry; see, for example, Laurie Graham, *Singing the City: The Bonds of Home in an Industrial Landscape* (Pittsburgh: University of Pittsburgh Press, 1998).

13. In a press release dated 29 July 1985, the director of the art museum, John Lane, is quoted as saying, "One could hardly imagine a more appropriate conjunction of artist, material, and location than Serra, steel, and Pittsburgh"; object file, Carnegie Museum of Art, Pittsburgh. This was a recurring theme in almost everything written about the piece in 1985. The contemporary curator for the museum wrote in *Carnegie Magazine*, "Although Serra specifically disclaims any intention of creating a monument, it is difficult to imagine how this massive steel presence can fail to bring forth strong and varied responses from its viewers based on the vital importance of steel to the life and history of this city"; John Caldwell, "Collecting and the International: Seven New Acquisitions," *Carnegie Magazine*, November/December 1985, 10.

14. This works because the steel slabs are cut in slightly irregular trapezoid shapes that allow them to tilt outward even as their weight leans inward. For an excellent formal analysis of the work see Vicky A. Clark, "Richard Serra in Pittsburgh," *Carnegie Magazine*, July/August 1986, 24–29.

15. Serra himself uses the word "uplifting" to describe *Carnegie*, as quoted in Clark, "Richard Serra in Pittsburgh," 27.

16. Richard Serra, interview by Vicky Clark, transcript, 7 November 1985, 8, object file, Carnegie Museum of Art, Pittsburgh.

17. Ibid., 9.

18. Quoted in Clark, "Richard Serra in Pittsburgh," 28.

19. Indeed this application of an industrial model of design to high art is part of a larger shift in the notion of the artist's studio, away from the isolated space of the romantic genius toward a new ideal of industrial technician/manager. See Jones, *Machine in the Studio*. This is not to deny Serra's genuine respect for mill workers or his intimate understanding of the work they did.

20. Serra had this to say about the donor: "I was talking to Mrs. Roesch. Sometimes you feel like the concept of something isn't really made by you. It's made by other movements. I mean, she and I got together and the piece got made." Serra, interview, 42.

21. Vicky Clark et al., *International Encounters: The Carnegie International and Contemporary Art, 1896–1996* (Pittsburgh: Carnegie Museum of Art, 1996), 29.

22. The museum director and the building's architect considered several high-profile sculptors and eventually narrowed the field to Serra and Claes Oldenberg; Oldenburg was not able to make a proposal. See Patricia Lowry, "Controversy Swirls around Scaife Gallery Sculptor," *Pittsburgh Press*, 30 July 1985.

23. Carnegie Museum of Art, Pittsburgh, "Collection Handbook."

24. Kenneth Warren, *Big Steel: The First Century of the United States Steel Corporation* (Pittsburgh: University of Pittsburgh Press, 2001), 313. Warren's study, based on extensive research in U.S. Steel archives, is more sympathetic to the corporation than most accounts of this period. A different picture of Roesch emerges in Hoerr, *And the Wolf Finally Came*, 423. Hoerr claims, based on interviews with steel executives, that Roesch was trying to prevent plant closures by improving productivity, which brought him into conflict with company chairman David Roderick, who was more inclined toward closures.

25. Warren, *Big Steel*, 333–36; Hoerr, *And the Wolf Finally Came*, 11.

26. Ronald Lee Fleming and Renata von Tscharner, *PlaceMakers: Public Art That Tells You Where You Are* (Cambridge, Mass.: Townscape Institute, 1981), 49–51. More on the civic boosterism surrounding the work can be found in a video cassette, "Interview with George Segal," archived at the Youngstown Historical Center of Industry and Labor. The piece has since been moved from its original location downtown to the grounds of the Youngstown Historical Center of Industry and Labor.

27. On the Youngstown plant closings, see Staughton Lynd, *The Fight Against Shutdowns: Youngstown's Steel Mill Closings* (San Pedro, Calif.: Singlejack, 1982); Thomas Fuechtman, *Steeples and Stacks: Religion and Steel Crisis in Youngstown, Ohio* (Cambridge: Cambridge University Press, 1989); and Robert Bruno, *Steelworker Alley: How Class Works in Youngstown* (Ithaca, N.Y.: ILR Press, 1999). None of these studies mentions the Segal sculpture.

28. Interestingly, U.S. Steel at the same time sold its office tower in Pittsburgh to another corporation; see Dale A. Hathaway, *Can Workers Have a Voice? The Politics of Deindustrialization in Pittsburgh* (University Park: Pennsylvania State University Press, 1993), 172.

29. Press release, 29 July 1985. The deletion occurred in a draft press release dated 30 October 1985. Both are in the object file, Carnegie Museum of Art, Pittsburgh.

30. Hathaway, *Can Workers Have a Voice?* 61–65.

31. "Oakland's New 'Carnegie,'" *Pittsburgh Press*, 31 July 1985.

32. "Sculpture Misnamed," *Pittsburgh Press*, 6 August 1985.

33. David Carrier, "Accessibility: A Realistic Dream," *Pittsburgh Tribune-Review*, 7 November 1999.

34. Anna C. Chave has argued that minimalist sculptures like Serra's are assertions of power; see "Minimalism and the Rhetoric of Power," *Art Magazine* 64 (January 1990): 44–63.

35. See Lubove, *Twentieth-Century Pittsburgh*. A more detailed examination of preservation efforts for the Pump House can be found in Kristen Louise Bauersfeld, "The Challenges and Complexities of Landscape Planning and Exhibition Design at a Commemorative Site: The Homestead Pumphouse" (M.A. thesis, University of Pittsburgh, 1998).

36. "South Side Works: A Celebration in Art," invitation mailed in April 1998 by the City of Pittsburgh Department of City Planning. On the origins of the project see Patricia Lowry, "Five Art Proposals to Vie for South Side Mill Site," *Pittsburgh Post-Gazette*, 1 June 1998.

37. Tom Barnes, "UPMC's Sport Medicine Facility Leads Renewal at South Side Steel Site," *Pittsburgh Post-Gazette*, 4 June 2000.

38. Patricia Lowry, "South Side Steelworker Monument Draws Variety of Sculpture Ideas," *Pittsburgh Post-Gazette*, 9 June 1998, G-2; "Two Steel Sculptures Chosen for S. Side Works Display," 11 July 1998. For an account from the city's official website, see: www.city.pittsburgh.pa.us/artcomm/artcom5b.html.

39. Patricia Lowry, "Five Art Proposals to Vie for South Side Mill Site," *Pittsburgh Post-Gazette*, 1 June 1998; Lowry, "Two Steel Sculptures Chosen for South Side Works Display," *Pittsburgh Post-Gazette*, 11 July 1998; James O'Toole, interview by author, Pittsburgh, 22 February 2001.

40. Robert Bruno, *Steelworker Alley*, 164–67. The whole question of vernacular working-class memory needs much more attention in scholarly literature. On suburbanization and the demise of steelworker communities see Hathaway, *Can Workers Have a Voice?*, 189; Bodnar, *Immigration and Industrialization*; Judith Modell, *A Town Without Steel: Envisioning Homestead* (Pittsburgh: University of Pittsburgh Press, 1998).

41. O'Toole, interview.

42. O'Toole's design had strong support from the local architecture critic Patricia Lowry (see her commentary "South Side Steelworker Monument") and from the city planning department, Patricia Lowry, "Two Steel Sculptures Chosen for South Side Works Display," *Pittsburgh Post-Gazette*, 11 July 1998. While the literature on the public sphere is immense and intricate, of special use to me here is Bruce Robbins, ed., *The Phantom Public Sphere* (Minneapolis: University of Minnesota Press, 1993).

43. "South Side Works: Public Art Project," n.d., collection of the author.

44. A good overview of war memorials in the United States can be found in Kurt Piehler, *Remembering War the American Way* (Washington, D.C.: Smithsonian Institution Press, 1995). The invention of the modern soldier monument is discussed in Kirk Savage, *Standing Soldiers, Kneeling Slaves: Race, War, and Monument in Nineteenth-Century America* (Princeton: Princeton University Press, 1997). Perhaps the most theoretically sophisticated study of war memorials is Daniel J. Sherman, *The Construction of Memory in Interwar France* (Chicago: University of Chicago Press, 1999).

45. Author's notes, dedication ceremony for Steelworkers' Monument, 20 April 2001. For a brief account of the ceremony see Patricia Lowry, "A Stream of Tears Where Molten Metal Flowed," *Pittsburgh Post-Gazette*, 21 April 2001.

46. Author's notes, dedication ceremony.

47. The most recent example comes from a visit by President George W. Bush: "Bush drew one of his loudest rounds of applause with an appeal to civic vanity. 'You know, I've come to realize, having spent some time in Pittsburgh—particularly after hearing the briefings today—that while Pittsburgh used to be called "Steel Town," they need to call it "Knowledge Town."'" "Bush Delivers Pitch for Bioterror Budget," *Pittsburgh Post-Gazette*, 6 February 2002, A-7.

48. The most comprehensive history of Nine Mile Run is Andrew S. McElwaine's essay, "Slag in the Park: A History of Nine Mile Run," 1998, at slaggarden.cfa.cmu. edu/history. Further insights can be gained from the discussion by several historians published in Nine Mile Run Greenway Project, *Ample Opportunity: A Community Dialogue* (Pittsburgh: Carnegie Mellon University, 1998), 34–38. McElwaine's history makes clear that the efforts to save Nine Mile Run in the beginning of the twentieth century failed in part because the elites who espoused the park plan did not seek the cooperation or the input of the working-class and middle-class neighborhoods that surrounded the site.

49. Tom Baines, "Group Favors Rezoning Slag Site in East End for New Homes," *Pittsburgh Post-Gazette*, 2 April 1998; Joyce Gannon, "Developers Putting Housing on a City Slag Heap Hope for Mountain of Success," *Pittsburgh Post-Gazette*, 22 September 2000; Chris Swaney, "Houses Are to Replace a Pittsburgh Slag Heap," *New York Times*, 28 January 2001. The original master plan for the development is illustrated and discussed in Tim Collins and Kirk Savage, "Brownfields as Places: A Case Study in Learning to See Assets as Well as Liabilities, Opportunities as Well as Constraints," *Public Works Management and Policy 2* (January 1998): 210–19. On efforts to clean up riverfronts to appeal to "knowledge workers," see, for example, Eve Modzelewski, "Rivers and Shores Are Being Rediscovered as a New Playland for the Masses—And as a Key Cog in the Region's New Economy," *Pittsburgh Post-Gazette*, 5 August 2001; Patricia Lowry, "Places: Riverlife's Digital Vision for the North Shore Needs Some Revision," *Pittsburgh Post-Gazette*, 30 October 2001.

50. Historian Joel Tarr tells the story of how the CMU artists initiated the Nine Mile Run project in Nine Mile Run Greenway Project, *Ample Opportunity*, 63. The artists also give an account of the genesis of the project in Tim Collins and Reiko Goto, "Urban Reclamation: Place, Value, Use: The Nine Mile Run Project," in the on-line journal *Leonardo: Words on Works* (1997). *Ample Opportunity* includes transcripts of a series of community dialogues that took place in 1997. The most comprehensive and up-to-date account of the CMU team's activities can be found on their website: slaggarden.cfa.cmu.edu.

51. Collins and Goto, "Urban Reclamation." For more on the Harrisons' project, see *Zeitwenden, Rückblick: Eine Ausstellung der Stiftung für Kunst und Kultur* (Köln: DuMont, 1999).

52. This story has yet to be fully explained publicly. Historian Joel Tarr gives a brief account of the process in "Nine Mile Run Greenway Project," *Ample Opportunity*, 63, and a bit more detail can be found in Collins and Goto, "Urban Reclamation."

53. Ray Reaves, Stephanie Flom, John Stephen, and Tim Collins, "Final Recommendations: The Nine Mile Run Greenway Project" (Studio for Creative Inquiry, Carnegie Mellon University, 1999); see "Node 4: Slag Corridor."

54. See for example, Tom Barnes, "Parks Key To Attracting Young Tech Workers, Study Says," *Pittsburgh Post-Gazette*, 3 October 2000; Modzelewski, "Rivers And Shores."

55. Hathaway, *Can Workers Have a Voice?* 45–46. Hathaway here verges on an

antitechnology position, which is problematic given that the history of industrial development is a history of technological innovation. Automation is not intrinsically immoral; the moral questions involve the social policy needed to address the consequences of automation.

56. Marylynne Pitz, "Restoring Frick Park Stream Gets Under Way Next Month," *Pittsburgh Post-Gazette*, 27 September 2001; Brian O'Neill, "City Reclamation, Development Spark Hope," *Pittsburgh Post-Gazette*, 13 January 2002.

12. Making Sense of Restructuring

1. Jeremy Rifkin, *The End of Work* (New York: Putnam, 1997).

2. Barry Bluestone and Bennett Harrison, *The Deindustrialization of America: Plant Closings, Community Abandonment, and the Dismantling of Basic Industry* (New York: Basic Books, 1982), 6.

3. George Cheney and Lars Thoger Christensen, "Organizational Identity: Linkages between Internal and External Communication," in *The New Handbook of Organizational Communication*, ed. L. Putnam and F. Jablin (Thousand Oaks, Calif.: Sage, 2001), 231–69.

4. Stanley Aronowitz and William DiFazio, *The Jobless Future: Sci-Tech and the Dogma of Work* (Minneapolis: University of Minnesota Press, 1994).

5. Steve May, "Health Care and the Medicalization of Work: Policy Implications," *Eccles Yearbook* (1998): 5–36.

6. Pseudonyms have been used for workers quoted in this chapter in order to maintain their confidentiality.

7. Nikolas Rose, *Governing the Soul: The Shaping of the Private Self* (London: Free Association Books, 1989), xxiv.

8. Al Gini, *My Job, My Self: Work and the Creation of the Modern Individual* (New York: Routledge, 2000), ix.

9. Peter Drucker, *Organization of the Future* (San Francisco: Jossey Bass, 1997).

10. Steve May, "Therapy at Work," *At Work* (May/June 1999): 12–13.

11. To clarify the specific focus of this chapter, we define downsizing as an active, strategic, decision-making process that intentionally eliminates a substantial number of workers' jobs—regardless of the stated rationale or the process by which the elimination occurs.

12. Michael Hammer, *The Reengineering Revolution* (New York: HarperBusiness, 1995).

13. Alan Pham, "Layoff Consultants Help Ease Trauma," *Raleigh News and Observer*, 12 May 1996, F1.

14. William F. Cascio, "Downsizing: What Do We Know? What Have We Learned?" *Academy of Management Executive*, 7 (1993): 95–104.

15. Brian Montague, "Restructuring and Layoffs Here to Stay," *USA Today*, 19 February 1996, A1.

16. Lawrence Uchitelle and Norm Kleinfield, "Job Fears Gnaw at Nation," *Raleigh News and Observer*, 4 March 1996, A4.

17. "KEMET Electronics—Our Company," www.kemet.com, 1998.

18. Ibid.

19. "KEMET Announces Restructuring Plans for U.S. and Mexican Operations," *Inside KEMET* 12 (November 1997): 1.

20. Ibid, 1.

21. Within months, another company downsizing occurred and, in 2001, another. According to the company, these downsizings were due to the "inventory correction currently being experienced in the electronics industry." These actions, according to company documents, allowed "KEMET to bring employment levels more in line with current and projected business levels."

22. David Maguire, "What's Happening?" *Inside KEMET* 13 (March 1998): 2–4.

23. "KEMET Announces Restructuring Plans for U.S. and Mexican Operations, *Inside KEMET* 12 (November 1997): 1.

24. "KEMET Corporation Announces Reduction in Labor Force," *Inside KEMET* 16 (June 2001): 1.

25. Michael M. Phillips, "Globalization Comes to a Southern Town; Shelby, NC Residents Worry Despite Robust Economy," *The Wall Street Journal*, 6 February 1998, sec. 1A, p. 2.

26. Shelby Daily Star, *Our Heritage: A History of Cleveland County* (Shelby, N.C.: Shelby Daily Star, 1976).

27. Ibid, 163.

28. Barbara Myerhoff, *Number Our Days* (New York: Simon and Schuster, 1978).

29. Joanne Martin, *Cultures in Organizations: Three Perspectives* (New York: Oxford University Press, 1992).

30. Victor Turner, *Dramas, Fields, and Metaphors: Symbolic Action in Human Society* (Ithaca: Cornell University Press, 1974).

31. James Scott, *Domination and the Arts of Resistance* (New Haven: Yale University Press, 1990), xii.

32. Norman K. Denzin, "Interpretive Interactionism," in *Beyond Method: Strategies for Social Research*, ed. G. Morgan (Beverly Hills, Calif.: Sage, 1983), 129–46.

33. The narrative themes in this chapter are based on twenty-one interviews conducted by the second author during January and February of 1999, several months after the KEMET downsizing. The interviews were based on a semistructured interview schedule. Interviews lasted between 45 and 120 minutes and were conducted either in the interviewees' homes or at a local community college. After the interviews were completed, they were transcribed and summarized according to themes. The second author has retained the interview cassette tapes and both authors retain copies of the interview transcripts, with identifying information excluded for anonymity. The interviewees represent a cross-section of employees downsized at KEMET. On average, the downsized workers interviewed had eleven years of work experience at KEMET. Ages ranged from twenty-three to sixty-eight, with a mean age of forty-seven and a median of forty-six. Nineteen of the twenty-one interviewees were women and five were African American. Eighteen of the interviewees were married, with children, and nearly all were born in Cleveland County, North Carolina. Almost all interviewees had a high school education (or a GED), and seven had some college, usually a few courses at a community college. In addition to these interviews, the first author has conducted eighty-five interviews with downsized workers in the telecommunication, pharmaceutical, financial services, and consulting industries. Although these interviews are not directly quoted in this chapter, they were used to supplement our overall understanding of the experience of downsizing for various workers.

34. Kenneth Burke, *A Rhetoric of Motives* (Berkeley: University of California Press, 1969), 22.

13. Worker Memory and Narrative

1. The interviews that form the basis of this chapter were conducted by Drs. Joy L. Hart and Tracy E. K'Meyer between August and December 1997. A total of twenty-four people were interviewed. Each person was interviewed twice, first by Hart and then by K'Meyer. Each interviewee had experienced a plant closing in the Louisville, Kentucky, metropolitan area. For the purposes of this chapter we used interviews with those who experienced the closing of International Harvester in 1985 or Johnson Controls in 1995. We chose these plants because of their relative size and because their closings were exactly a decade apart. The interviews, audio cassettes, and transcripts are on deposit in the Oral History Collection of the University Archives, University of Louisville, Louisville, Kentucky.

2. Barry Bluestone and Bennett Harrison, *The Deindustrialization of America: Plant Closings, Community Abandonment, and the Dismantling of Basic Industry* (New York: Basic Books, 1982).

3. Michael Wallace and Joyce Rothschild, "Plant Closings, Capital Flight, and Worker Dislocation: The Long Shadow of Deindustrialization," in *Deindustrialization and the Restructuring of American Industry*, ed. Michael Wallace and Joyce Rothschild (Greenwich, Conn.: JAI Press, 1988), 1–35; Kenneth Root, "Job Loss: Whose Fault, What Remedies?" in *Deindustrialization and the Restructuring of American Industry*, 65–84; Terry F. Buss and C. Richard Hofstetter, "Powerlessness, Anomie, and Cynicism: The Personal Consequences of Mass Unemployment in a Steel Town," *Micropolitics* 2 (1983): 349–77; Terry F. Buss and R. Stevens Redburn, *Shutdown at Youngstown* (Albany: State University of New York Press, 1983); Clifford L. Broman, V. Lee Hamilton, and William S. Hoffman, "Unemployment and Its Effects on Families: Evidence from a Plant Closing Study," *American Journal of Community Psychology* 18 (1990): 643–59.

4. Michael Frisch, "Oral History and the Presentation of Class Consciousness: The *New York Times* v. The Buffalo Unemployed," in *A Shared Authority: Essays on the Craft and Meaning of Oral and Public History* (Albany: State University of New York Press, 1990), 59–80.

5. Kathryn Marie Dudley, *The End of the Line: Lost Jobs, New Lives in Postindustrial America* (Chicago: University of Chicago Press, 1994); Gregory Pappas, *The Magic City: Unemployment in a Working-Class Community* (Ithaca: Cornell University Press, 1989).

6. Thomas Dublin, *When the Mines Closed: Stories of Struggles in Hard Times*, with photographs by George Harvan (Ithaca: Cornell University Press, 1998); Michael Frisch, *Portraits in Steel*, with photographs by Milton Rogovin (Ithaca: Cornell University Press, 1993); Cedric N. Chatterley and Alicia J. Rouverol, *"I Was Content and Not Content": The Story of Linda Lord and the Closing of Penobscot Poultry* (Carbondale: Southern Illinois University Press, 2000).

7. Barbara Allen, "Story in Oral History: Clues to Historical Consciousness," *Journal of American History* 79 (1992): 606–11; Samuel Schrager, "What is Social in Oral History," *International Journal of Oral History* 4 (1983): 76–98; Alicia J. Rouverol, "Retelling the Story of Linda Lord," in *"I Was Content,"* 117–31.

8. Certain factors shaped the stories we collected. The narrators could be easily identified and located. A few were chosen because of personal contact with the authors. But most of the twenty-four subjects were identified through union contacts. Both companies had been closed shops and both union presidents were in town, in touch with former workers, and willing to help. We worked with union officials, attended meetings, and followed

up on suggestions from other workers. Third, since participation was completely voluntary, the people interviewed shared a willingness, albeit with varied enthusiasm, to tell their story to an acquaintance or, in most cases, a complete stranger. These workers saw themselves as articulate and having a good story to tell. Some saw the interview as an opportunity to help others by sharing their advice. A few—the retirees or those on medical leave—may have just looked forward to visitors. It is possible that these people are some of those doing best since the closings. They all had phones or home addresses, allowing them to be reached to request an interview. Most interviewees chose to be interviewed in their own homes, showing comfort and even pride in their living arrangements. It is possible that other people declined to be interviewed or could not be reached because of their living conditions. Also, the people who agreed to be interviewed had enough leisure time to fit this project into their schedules. Such factors may distinguish them from individuals declining to be interviewed, who did not respond to our telephone calls or letters of inquiry, or who could not be located. Finally, as in all projects relying on interview data collection, the findings are influenced by the questions employed.

9. International Harvester workers in the plant were members of UAW Local 1336, which was organized 15 June 1955. Workers in the foundry were members of Local 817, which was organized 10 October 1949. This and other information on union local organization was furnished by the Circulation Office of the UAW, Detroit, Michigan.

10. "International Harvester to Lay Off 400 Workers," Louisville *Courier-Journal*, 17 February 1981; "Harvester Blames Slow Sales in Plan to Lay Off Hundreds," *Courier-Journal*, 6 August 1981; "Harvester Slowdown Will Result in Layoffs of 1,600 in Louisville," *Courier-Journal*, 6 February 1982; "International Harvester Will Close Plant: Plan to Fight Bankruptcy Would Cost 800 More Jobs," *Courier-Journal*, 30 July 1982; "Harvester to Begin Shutting Down Plant By End of Month," *Courier-Journal*, 3 September 1982; "Going Back to Harvester Was Answer to Worker's Prayers," *Courier-Journal*, 4 January 1983; "Harvester to Close Louisville Foundry, Idling 710 Workers," *Courier-Journal*, 19 November 1983; "Harvester, 2 Locals Agree on Closing Plan," *Courier-Journal*, 8 December 1983; "Farm Business Infertile for Harvester: Huge Furrow Cut in Truck Profits," *Courier-Journal*, 5 August 1984; "Foundry: Though Working Conditions Could Be a Problem, Wages and Benefits Were Always Good at the International Harvester Facility and Many Found Their Life's Work There," *Courier-Journal*, 5 August 1984; "Harvester to Sell Plant to 2 Local Businessmen," *Courier-Journal*, 12 December 1984; "Harvester Shuts Down Last of Local Operations," *Courier-Journal*, 10 April 1985.

11. Johnson Controls workers were members of UAW Local 1283, which was organized March 17, 1954.

12. "Johnson Controls Will Stop Making DieHards When Sears Pact Runs Out," *Courier-Journal*, 22 April 1994; "Johnson Controls Inc.: Shares Slip $1.50 with Loss of Sears Roebuck Contract," *Wall Street Journal*, 22 April 1994; "Life After DieHard," *Barron's*, 13 June 1994; "Johnson Controls Inc.: Tentative Closing Planned at Two Auto Battery Plants," *Wall Street Journal*, 5 August 1994; "Speaking of Dividends: Johnson Controls Makes it 20 in a Row," *Barron's*, 21 November 1994; "Battery Firm Plans to Close Louisville Plant; 245 Jobs to End," *Courier-Journal*, 25 April 1995; "Business Brief—Johnson Controls Inc.: Net Income Increases 20% Beating Analyst Estimates," *Wall Street Journal*, 25 October 1995.

13. Several narrators told stories about production being moved to other U.S. cities, including Toledo, Ohio; Winston-Salem, North Carolina; and "St. Joe," Missouri.

14. For another example of this see Dudley, *End of the Line*. Autoworkers in Kenosha, Wisconsin, lobbied for management to keep their plant open in return for their extra hard work.

15. On the relationship between plant closings and union power see David Jaffee, "The Political-Economic Environment and the Geographic Restructuring of Manufacturing: Theoretical Perspectives and a State-Level Analysis," in *Deindustrialization and the Restructuring of American Industry*, 85–108.

16. A search of articles in the *Wall Street Journal* from 1980 to 1981 did not identify an article with this or a similar quote from Archie McCardell. Thus the interviewee may have misstated or misremembered the quotation, the years, or the publication title. Nevertheless, his memory of having read such an article reinforces the point that the workers believed the management had nefarious motives for closing the plant, including punishing the union.

17. We did not uncover in the interview the extent of Phillips's knowledge about specific provisions of NAFTA or other agreements or laws that would have allowed the workers to sue. Yet, his invocation of a rumored set of provisions demonstrates his belief that there is or should be protection for downsized workers, while emphasizing his conviction that the company's management was cheating the workers.

18. For another example of government readiness to move cities away from heavy industry see Dudley, *End of the Line*, 154–77.

19. For a discussion of shop floor cultures that privilege hard work in adverse conditions see Melissa K. Gibson and Michael J. Papa, "The Mud, the Blood, and the Beer Guys: Organizational Osmosis in Blue-Collar Work Groups," *Journal of Applied Communication Research* 28 (2000): 68–88.

20. This finding is similar to that in Ruth Milkman, *Farewell to the Factory: Autoworkers in the Late Twentieth Century* (Berkeley: University of California Press, 1997). Milkman argues that workers who took a buyout option from General Motors reported being happier in the aftermath. One main reason given by workers in that case was their happiness in being away from the arbitrary authority in the plant. The similarity between our study and Milkman's is that in both cases workers expressed satisfaction with new jobs that allow autonomy and the use of diverse skills. One difference is that in our study workers cited health concerns more often. This could be due to differences in health conditions in the respective plants.

21. Bluestone and Harrison, "The Impact of Private Disinvestment on Workers and Their Communities," in *Deindustrialization of America*, 49–81; Dudley, "Broken Promises," in *End of the Line*, 135–53; Wallace and Rothschild, "Plant Closings"; Brenda Cochrane, "Union Maids No More: Long-Term Impact of Loss of a Union Job on Women Workers," *Labor Studies Journal* 13 (1988): 19–34.

22. During most of these workers' careers in heavy industry, many manufacturing companies had a policy of twenty-five, thirty, or thirty-five years and out, allowing retirement as early as fifty-five years old for dangerous work.

23. This is consistent with a wide body of research in social psychology that has identified the beneficial consequences of maintaining "positive illusions" about oneself. See Shelley E. Taylor and Jonathan D. Brown, "Positive Illusions and Well-Being Revisited: Separating Fact from Fiction," *Psychological Bulletin* 116 (1994): 21–27.

24. Dudley, "Mapping the Moral Terrain," in *End of the Line*, 154–71; Rouverol, "Retelling the Story"; Michael Burawoy, *Manufacturing Consent: Changes in the Labor Process Under Monopoly Capitalism* (Chicago: University of Chicago Press, 1979).

25. For a useful discussion on this point see Michael Frisch, foreword to *"I Was Content"*; and Alicia J. Rouverol, introduction to *"I Was Content."*

26. For examples of how personal circumstances shape the reaction to a plant closing see the interviews in Dublin, *When the Mines Closed*; and Chatterley and Rouverol, *"I Was Content."*

CONTRIBUTORS

BARRY BLUESTONE is the Russell B. and Andrèe B. Stearns Trustee professor of political economy and director of the Center for Urban and Regional Policy at Northeastern University. Bluestone was a member of the senior policy staff of Congressman Richard Gephardt and continues to serve as a policy adviser to the Democratic leadership in both the House and the Senate. His books include, with Bennett Harrison, *The Deindustrialization of America* (Basic Books 1982), *The Great U-Turn: Corporate Restructuring and the Polarizing of America* (Basic Books, 1988), *Growing Prosperity: The Battle for Growth with Equity in the Twenty-First Century* (University of California Press, 2001), and with Irving Bluestone, *Negotiating the Future: A Labor Perspective on American Business* (Basic Books, 1992).

JEFFERSON COWIE is assistant professor of history at Cornell University's School of Industrial and Labor Relations. He is the author of the prize-winning book *Capital Moves: RCA's Seventy-Year Quest for Cheap Labor* (Cornell University Press, 1999; reprint, The New Press, 2001), which examines one company's relocations through four cities and two countries. His other writings have focused on labor history, popular culture, and globalization issues in publications such as *Dissent, The American Prospect, International Labor and Working-Class History*, and *Labor History*. He is currently working on a book titled *Stayin' Alive* that examines changes in national understandings of workers and social class in civic and popular culture during the pivotal decade of the 1970s.

KENT CURTIS is an independent scholar working in the boundary between higher education and environmental activism. A graduate of the New School for Social Research and the University of Kansas, he is currently developing a new public education program for the Gulf of Maine Council, teaching United States history classes at the University of Massachusetts, Boston, and revising his dissertation, "An Ecology of Industry: Mining and Nature in Western Montana, 1865–1907." In 2002, he published three environmental issue series (coastal environment, drinking water, and development and conservation) for regional publications in Massachusetts. He has also begun research on a larger study of the term "ecosystem."

Lisa M. Fine is an associate professor of history at Michigan State University. She received her B.S. from the School of Industrial and Labor Relations at Cornell University, and her M.A. and Ph.D. from the University of Wisconsin, Madison. Her first book was *The Souls of the Skyscraper: Female Clerical Workers in Chicago, 1870–1930* (Temple University Press, 1990). She is presently working on a book on the Reo Motor Car Company of Lansing from 1904 to 1975, to be published by Temple University Press. Earlier parts of this work in progress have appeared in *Labor History* (1993) and *Journal of Social History* (2000).

Tami J. Friedman is a senior associate at the University of Wisconsin–based Center on Wisconsin Strategy, a research and policy institute committed to improving living standards and economic performance. She received a Ph.D. in U.S. history from Columbia University in May 2001. Her dissertation examines the migration of the U.S. carpet industry from the North to the South after World War II; its impact on local, state, and regional economic development; and its effect on organized labor and civil rights. She is a former editor of *Dollars and Sense*, the popular economics magazine.

Howard Gillette Jr. is professor of history at Rutgers University in Camden, where he is completing a book on the impact of disinvestment on the city of Camden. Professor Gillette is the author, most recently, of *Between Justice and Beauty: Race, Planning, and the Failure of Urban Policy in Washington, D.C.* (Johns Hopkins University Press, 1995). His essays have appeared in a wide range of journals. Professor Gillette is past president (1999–2001) of the Society for American City and Regional Planning History and codirector of the Mid-Atlantic Regional Center for the Humanities, a joint project of Rutgers, Camden, and Temple University. He was a founder and the first director of George Washington University's Center for Washington Area Studies.

Joy L. Hart is an associate professor of communication at the University of Louisville. Her work focuses primarily on organizational communication. In particular, her research examines narrative, identity, and communication skill. She has published articles in several international and national journals, including *American Communication Journal, International Journal of Personal Construct Psychology, Journal of Business Communication, Sociological Analysis,* and *Women's Studies in Communication.*

Joseph Heathcott grew up in Evansville, Indiana, in a family that experienced the strikes, layoffs, and plant closings of the 1970s and 1980s. Today, he is an assistant professor in the Department of American Studies at Saint Louis University. He did his graduate work at Indiana University, where he was a research associate in the Division of Labor Studies, and he taught for two years as a visiting professor at Washington University. His research focuses on the changing landscape of cities and metropolitan regions after World War II. Currently he is completing a book manuscript on the infamous Pruitt-Igoe public housing project, and is working on a social history of urban renewal in the United States.

TRACY E. K'MEYER is an associate professor of U.S. history at the University of Louisville, where she is also the codirector of the Oral History Center. She is the author of *Interracialism and Christian Community in the Postwar South: The Story of Koinonia Farm* and is currently working on a book on the civil rights movement in Louisville, Kentucky. In the field of oral history she has published articles on the study of community and memory, the teaching of oral history methodology, and the use of personal narratives in the study of religion.

SHERRY LEE LINKON is a professor of English, coordinator of American Studies, and codirector of the Center for Working-Class Studies at Youngstown State University. She is a Carnegie Scholar and YSU campus coordinator for the Visible Knowledge Project, a national research project investigating teaching and learning with technology in humanities courses. Her research and teaching focus on working-class pedagogy, representations of class and work, American literature, and critical explorations of students' learning in interdisciplinary courses. She is the editor of three books, including *Teaching Working Class* (University of Massachusetts Press, 1999), which was selected by the readers of *Lingua Franca* as one of the ten best academic books of the 1990s. She is also coauthor with John Russo of *Steeltown U.S.A.: Work and Memory in Youngstown* (University Press of Kansas, 2002).

STEVE MAY is associate professor of communication studies at the University of North Carolina, Chapel Hill. His work focuses on organizational communication, with particular attention to the blurring of boundaries between public and private, labor and leisure, and work and home. He also studies organizational ethics and corporate social responsibility. He is the coeditor of *Management Communication Quarterly* and his research has appeared in *The Journal of Applied Communication Research, Communication Education, Policy Yearbook,* and *Management Communication Quarterly,* among others. He is currently completing a book on work and identity in the new century.

LAURA MORRISON received her M.A. from the University of North Carolina, Chapel Hill. She is currently a lecturer at the College of the Albemarle. Her most recent research explored the impact of downsizing on employees, family, and community in rural North Carolina. She has also studied organizational discourse, workplace trends, and worker identity.

RICHARD NEWMAN received a Ph.D. in history from the State University of New York, Buffalo, in 1998 and currently teaches African American and environmental history at Rochester Institute of Technology. He is working on a broad environmental and land-use history of Love Canal, and has published an essay on the subject in *Women's Studies Quarterly* (spring/summer 2001). In addition, he is the author of *The Transformation of American Abolitionism: Fighting Slavery in the Early Republic* (University of North Carolina Press, 2002), and coeditor of *Pamphlets of Protest: An Anthology of African American Protest Literature, 1790–1860* (Routledge, 2000). He is an educational consultant for Strong Museum in Rochester, and he has held Mellon Fellowships at the Massachusetts Historical Society and the Library Company of Philadelphia.

S. PAUL O'HARA is a Ph.D. candidate in U.S. history at Indiana University, Bloomington. He is currently a dissertation fellow with the Indiana Historical Society. His dissertation examines the debate over the meaning and use of urban spaces that occurred with the rise of industrial Chicago; the rearrangement of the city that created an industrial periphery of communities such as Gary, Indiana; and the relationship between Chicago and its outskirts.

JOHN RUSSO is the coordinator of labor studies and codirector of the Center for Working-Class Studies at Youngstown State University. He has written widely on labor and social issues and is recognized as a national expert on labor unions. His current research interests involve an edited volume on *New Working-Class Studies* and a book on the history of the GM assembly complex in Lordstown. He recently coauthored with Sherry Lee Linkon *Steeltown U.S.A: Work and Memory in Youngstown* (University Press of Kansas, 2002). For his research and community activities, Dr. Russo has been awarded Distinguished Professorship Awards in both scholarship and public service by Youngstown State University.

KIRK SAVAGE is associate professor in the history of art at the University of Pittsburgh. He has lectured and published widely on public monuments in the United States. He is the author of *Standing Soldiers, Kneeling Slaves:*

Race, War, and Monument in Nineteenth-Century America (Princeton University Press, 1997).

ROBERT O. SELF is assistant professor of history and urban studies at the University of Wisconsin, Milwaukee. He was a fellow in the Michigan Society of Fellows from 1999 to 2002, and his first book, *American Babylon: Race and the Struggle for Postwar Oakland*, will be published by Princeton University Press in 2003.

BRYANT SIMON, a graduate of the University of North Carolina, has taught history at the University of Georgia since 1995. His first book was *A Fabric of Defeat: The Politics of South Carolina Textile Workers, 1910–1948* (University of North Carolina Press, 1998). He is the coeditor of *Jumpin' Jim Crow: The New Political History of the New South* (Princeton University Press, 2001). He is currently writing a book about Atlantic City, New Jersey.

GREGORY S. WILSON is assistant professor of history at the University of Akron. His dissertation explores the creation of area redevelopment policy at the local, state, and federal levels between 1933 and 1965, examining the intersection of politics, culture, economics, and the environment. In addition, he serves as cofounder of the *Northeast Ohio Journal of History*, an online publication, and in 2001–2002 was selected as a Carnegie Teaching Scholar by the Institute for Teaching and Learning at the University of Akron.

INDEX